JAMES J GASKIN

Varieties of Irish History

JAMES J GASKIN

Varieties of Irish History

ISBN/EAN: 9783744717328

Printed in Europe, USA, Canada, Australia, Japan

Cover: Foto ©ninafisch / pixelio.de

More available books at **www.hansebooks.com**

VIEW OF DALKEY ISLAND AND SORRENTO FROM THE VICO ROAD

VARIETIES

OF

IRISH HISTORY;

FROM

ANCIENT AND MODERN SOURCES AND ORIGINAL
DOCUMENTS.

BY

JAMES J. GASKIN,

AUTHOR OF "GEOGRAPHY AND HISTORY MADE INTERESTING," "THE SPEECHES,
LECTURES, WRITINGS, POEMS, AND MEMOIR OF THE
LATE EARL OF CARLISLE."

DUBLIN:
WILLIAM B. KELLY, 8, GRAFTON-STREET.
1869.

DUBLIN:
Printed by J. F. O'Toole & Son
6 & 7, Great Brunswick-street.

DIRECTIONS

FOR PLACING THE CHROMO-LITHOGRAPHS.

1. DALKEY ISLAND AND SORRENTO, . *to face Title.*
2. KINGSTOWN, ... ,, p. 106
3. KILLINEY BAY AND HILL, . . ,, ,, 150
4. BRAY HEAD AND ESPLANADE, . . ,, ,, 313

The Map to be placed on a Guard at the end of the Volume.

strength of his youth and the premature decline of his manhood), he made Dalkey what it is to-day,—even though obstructed at every step in every movement which he originated—in a spirit of honour, courage, and honesty of purpose—for its advancement. Your father fortunately lived to witness some portion of his boyhood's prophecy relative to this place fulfilled; then he "passed away" in peace and hope to the silent tomb, leaving—

> "That which should accompany old age;
> Honour, love, obedience, troops of friends."

Walk in his footsteps—imitate his example, always wearing the honest garment of his rectitude and independence, the robe of his self-respect, and, above all, be possessed, like him, of a feeling heart; continue as you have done in your official capacity of Chairman, in conjunction with your spirited and energetic Fellow-Commissioners, to devote your zealous exertions to the onerous and manifold duties which naturally devolve upon you, and thus succeed in realizing, to the fullest extent, his prophecy and ardent aspirations of seeing Dalkey,—with all its natural capabilities, fully developed—including the completion of the new harbour and landing-pier (the foundation-stone of which you so auspiciously laid),—one of the most desirable and fashionable watering-places in Ireland or elsewhere.

Hoping sincerely for such result, and ardently desirous that you may be spared for the accomplishment,

I am, dear Sir,
Yours faithfully,
JAMES J. GASKIN.

GASKIN'S IRISH VARIETIES.
MADE INTERESTING.

INTRODUCTION.

THE present work is in great part based on a lecture delivered by the Author before a highly influential, intelligent, and fashionable audience in the Concert Room of the Queen's Royal Hotel, Dalkey. The lecture had its origin from a conversation on Dalkey, its ancient port, holy wells, and its seven castles, with Mr. Henry Parkinson, T.C., and Mr. J. Burke. By these gentlemen, the idea of delivering the lecture on the antiquarian and historical associations of the place, in connexion with the beauties of the Bay of Dublin, was first suggested.

The welcome with which the lecture was received, the warm approval elicited throughout its delivery (manifesting the intensity of the interest felt on the subject), and the express desire of many resident ladies and gentlemen of influence, that matters of so much local concern should assume a more permanent form than that of a mere lecture, have induced the Author to compile and publish the following pages containing the substance of the lecture, and very many additions, which he hopes will render the work more acceptable and entertaining, and more worthy as an historic record of the just celebrity of this and other localities on the shores of our charming Bay.

The Author has used every exertion, and spared himself no labour of research to attain these objects.

The Concert Hall of the Queen's Royal Hotel, Dalkey, formed a portion of the celebrated "Castle House"—the hospitable mansion erected by Sir John Hasler,* who with his friend Sir Harcourt Lees, came over to Ireland in the Court of Viceroys, the former with the Duke of Rutland, and Sir Harcourt with the Marquis of Townshend.† The history of this house is replete

---

* The present Mr. John Hasler, Poor-law Guardian of the Rathdown Union, and the active and intelligent Commissioner of the Kingstown Township, and Surgeon Hasler of Killiney, are grandsons of the hospitable Sir John Hasler, who did so much in the last century to beautify Dalkey and preserve its ancient castles, one of which stood at the entrance to his gardens, which reached the sea, on part of which Mr. Edward Harrison's (the worthy Town Commissioner), establishment is built. It was here the *find* of Saxon coins of the time of Edgar took place (referred to in this work), while removing the old castellated pillars of Sir John Hasler's gateway. Portions of the walls and extensive stabling of this mansion are yet standing. Sir John Hasler entertained, on many occasions, the humorous and facetious, though somewhat eccentric, Sir Boyle Roche of Dublin Castle. See *Appendix*, "The Castle of Dublin in the Olden Time."

† The Marquis of Townshend, Lord Lieutenant of Ireland, was the patron of the elder Sheridan. The following anecdote and witticism is related of this great actor :—During Lord Townshend's viceroyalty Mr. Grenville and his brother left Bath for Dublin, on a visit to his Excellency. Sheridan was then acting in Dublin, with powerful effect and immense success; drawing full houses. Soon after their arrival, the Marquis of Townshend, wishing that

with interesting associations of the past and present centuries—replete with vivid memories of scenes of festive gaiety, genial wit, good humour, and genuine enjoyment. Irish hospitality was dispensed as freely and cordially at the Castle House as it was at Ulick Burke's "Open House" near the "Valley of Diamonds," in the county Wicklow, or in the early part of the last century, at the hospitable mansion of the celebrated Thomas Mathew, Thomastown, county Tipperary, where Swift resided as a guest for many months at a time..*

This volume of IRISH VARIETIES would be incomplete without special notice of the classical village of Glasnevin and Delville House, where the celebrated and learned Doctor Delany† "assembled his coterie of wits in the

---

they should see Sheridan in "King John," ordered the performance of that play. On the morning of the day fixed for the performance, however, he wrote them a note, informing them that he had just received a letter from Sheridan, stating that he had been thrown out of his carriage, and had strained his shoulder so violently that it was impossible for him to act "King John;" but, rather than that the young gentlemen should be disappointed, he would appear in a *Comedy*, and play, as well as he could, "Sir Charles *EASY*."

* Irish hospitality in the last century. See page 296.

† "Dr. Delany, preaching at our parish church immediately after our marriage, was so kind as to join us coming out, and accompany us home, to wish the young couple joy, a favour we were all extremely proud of. At parting, he gave us all an invitation to dine at his beautiful Villa at Glasnevin, about a mile distant from Dublin. What opinion I conceived of him and his improvements, may be seen in the following lines, composed in one of his lovely arbours:—

Augustan age of Queen Anne; where the patriot Dean Swift, and the enduring Stella have charmed the feast; and in whose immediate vicinity, Addison, Sheridan, Parnell, Southern, and Tickell, have resided."

"DELVILLE, THE SEAT OF THE REV. DR. DELANY.

"Hail happy Delville! blissful seat!
The muses' best belov'd retreat!
With prospects large and unconfin'd;
Blest emblem of their master's mind!
Where fragrant gardens, painted meads,
Wide op'ning walks, and twilight shades,
Inspiring scenes! elate the heart!
Nature improv'd and rais'd by art!
So Paradise delightful smil'd,
Blooming, and beautifully wild.
Thrice happy Sage, who safe retir'd,
By heav'n and by the muse inspir'd;
In polish'd arts, or lays sublime,
Or god-like acts employ your time,
Here nature's beauties you explore,
And searching her mysterious store;
Thro' all her operations find
The image of the sov'reign mind,
And in each insect, plant, and flow'r,
Contemplate the creating pow'r,
Nor is thy love of him alone,
In fruitless speculation shown;
Thro' life you happily exert
The Christian virtues of your heart;
To give new schemes of culture birth,
And bless and beautify the earth;
To raise th' afflicted from despair,
And make the friendless wretch thy care;
To thee highest bliss is given,
A soul to praise, and copy heaven."[a]

* * * *

---

[a] "The Memoirs of Mrs. Lætitia Pilkington," wife to the Rev. Mr. Matt Pilkington, written by herself. Wherein are occasionally interspersed all her poems, with anecdotes of several eminent persons, living and dead. The first edition of Mrs. Pilkington's Memoirs was published at Dublin in 1741—with the life of the inimitable DEAN SWIFT.—See *Appendix*.

THE DALKEY REVELS.

The sayings and doings of those humorous and facetious "wits" who flourished during the memorable reign of the *last* and *noblest* of the "Kings of Dalkey," his coronation speeches, court, and adherents, are published in this Work in a complete form, for the first time, taken from the *Dalkey Gazette*, printed in connection with *Faulkner's Journal*, from 1791 to 1798—copies of which are preserved in the Chief Secretary's Library, Dublin Castle.

The *revels* of the past merry monarchs of the "Kingdom of Dalkey" form a peculiar feature of the local festivities of that picturesque island towards the close of the last century, and are scarcely paralleled for wit and humour in the annals of local pastimes.

During these gay revels (in the Castle House, afterwards occupied by Sir George Massey, gentleman Usher, in Dublin Castle), our national poet, Moore (the Béranger of Ireland), the memorable T. O'Meara, (the "migh T.— O'Meara,") a popular and witty attorney, Stephen Armitage, a king of infinite jest, of most excellent fancy, and a host of celebrities, spent many convivial and jovial hours.

Many illustrious and bright particular stars of the musical firmament shed the brilliant light of their welcome presence on the sportive scene, and contributed to the pleasure and exquisite enjoyment of all. On several occasions, that prince of ballad singers, the unrivalled Incledon, appeared at the annual elections of the king of Dalkey. He was created, and with due ceremony and grave solemnity, installed as knight of the monarchy by the style and title of "Sir Charles Melody," (the last created knight under that happy kingdom), and sang his grand and favourite air, "Black Ey'ed Susan," and Stevens's celebrated song, "The Storm," to the infinite delight of the king's right merrie court.* On one of these occasions, he was accompanied by that great vocalist, Madame Mara,† who graced the scene of revelry with her fascinating presence, and whom Incledon introduced to King Stephen, to his courtiers and "Lords of Misrule." These scenes belong to the past; burlesque and frolic have given place to

* The vessel in which Charles Incledon sailed from the Pigeon House, after having fulfilled his engagement at the Theatre Royal, Dublin, was wrecked near Dalkey Island.
† Madame Mara was the most impressive singer that ever lived; her exquisite beauty and fascination was only exceeded by her surpassing accomplishments. She is justly placed at the summit of the musical profession; because, in majesty and simplicity, in grace, tenderness, and pathos, in the loftiest attributes of art, in the elements of the great style, she far transcended all her competitors in the list of fame. She was the first *artiste* who gave to Handel's compositions their natural grandeur and effect. Historians say that her singing of

"I know that my Redeemer liveth,"

was something marvellous.

more refined and chastened amusements. However the Author may justly affirm that the social réunions and festivities of the present day among the fashionable circles of Kingstown, Dalkey, Killiney, Clontarf, Shanganagh, Howth, and Bray, may fairly challenge comparison for good taste, elegance, and refinement.

Social life at Dalkey, Killiney, and Dunleary, in times past, was enlivened by many illustrious and distinguished men of various professions who left the impress of their genius upon science and literature, and adorned social life by the bright corruscations of their wit, the fascinating elegance of their converse, and the lustre of their lives.

In Dalkey, John Philpot Curran (the greatest wit of the age), "full many a time and oft," set the table in a roar with his meteor flashes.*

---

* Curran also flashed the dazzling emanations of his genius and brilliant humour over the convivial board at the hospitable villa (Marino) of the late Earl of Charlemont, where he met the "consistent Lucas;" Flood, in "all the verdure of his leafy honours, that tree of the forest that was too great to be transplanted;" Grattan, who astounded the Irish senate with the splendour and power and majesty of his eloquence. It was here that Curran first read his popular song, "The Deserter's Meditation," which he had written in the West of Ireland, under the following circumstances : As Mr. Curran was travelling upon an unfrequented road, he perceived a man in a soldier's dress sitting by the road-side, and apparently much exhausted by fatigue and agitation. He invited him to take a seat in his chaise, and soon discovered that he was a deserter. Having stopped at a small inn for refreshment, Mr. Curran observed to the soldier that he had committed an offence of which the penalty was death, and that his chance of escaping it was but small : "Tell me, then," continued he, "whether you feel disposed to pass the little remnant of life that is left you in

Here (in one of the ancient castles), that great and enlightened antiquarian, accomplished artist, and distinguished musician, the late Dr. Petrie (the author of an essay on the Round Towers of Ireland, and for many years President of the Royal Irish Academy), resided upwards of sixty years ago, where he became inspired with an indelible love of Ireland and her past history, in all its ever-varying lights and shades.*

Here sojourned Curwen and Arthur Young, the celebrated agricultural tourists. Here penitence and fasting, or whether you would prefer to drown your sorrow in a merry glass?" The following is the deserter's answer, which Mr. Curran, in composing it, adapted to a plaintive Irish air :—

"If sadly thinking, with spirits sinking,
   Could more than drinking my cares compose,
A cure for sorrow from sighs I'd borrow,
   And hope to-morrow would end my woes.
But as in wailing there's nought availing,
   And death unfailing will strike the blow,
Then for that reason, and for a season,
   Let us be merry before we go.

"To joy a stranger, a way-worn ranger,
   In every danger my course I've run ;
Now hope all ending, and death befriending,
   His last aid lending, my cares are done :
No more a rover, or hapless lover,
   My griefs are over—my glass runs low ;
Then for that reason, and for a season,
   Let us be merry before we go."

---

* A highly important work has just issued from the press, entitled "The Life and Labours in Art and Archæology of George Petrie, M.R.I.A.," &c., by William Stokes, M.D., D.C.L., &c., in which will be found at large a most valuable repertoire and history of the useful labours of this illustrious Irishman and eminent antiquarian. See page 160.

Introduction. xiii

tarried Macklin (the inimitable actor), on his way to Tinnahinch, where, at the hotel—afterwards the seat of the Grattans*—he wrote his "Man of the World," of "Sir Pertinax Macsycophant" fame.

Here the celebrated Sir John Stevenson, Mus. Doc.,† who was knighted by Earl Hardwicke,

---

* Tinnahinch House is situated in a rich and verdant valley, with the Dargle River winding silently along immediately in front of it, and finally disappearing at the entrance of the narrow glen, as completely as Virgil's Velino at its sudden fall. This beautifully situated mansion, which was originally the principal inn at Powerscourt, was purchased in 1782, together with the adjacent estate, for £50,000, by a vote of the Irish Parliament for that great orator, statesman, and illustrious Irish patriot, Henry Grattan, after the celebrated "Declaration" of both houses of the Irish Parliament—"*That no power on earth had a right to make laws for this country, but the King, Lords, and Commons of Ireland.*" Arthur Young, the great agricultural tourist, stopped here for a considerable time in 1776. "But as neither splendour of wealth, nor beauty and grandeur of habitation, nor any earthly acquirement, save integrity, magnificent and intellectual greatness, can bestow universal and enviable notoriety, so Tinnahinch was unnoticed and unknown, until it became the residence of that proud, unsullied, and inflexible statesman, Henry Grattan, who died as he lived, in the service of his country." Grattan's statue by Chantry, erected by the members of the Irish House of Commons, in testimony of their admiration of his talents and their gratitude for his exertions in obtaining for Ireland a free trade with Great Britain and the colonies, now graces the City Hall, Dublin. *See Appendix*,—The Right Honorable Thomas O'Hagan's, (Lord Chancellor of Ireland), letter to the Earl of Charlemont, on the proposed statue in Dublin to Grattan.

† Among the many remarkable men who distinguished themselves in Ireland during the last century, Sir John Stevenson's name deserves to be recorded. His life presents an instructive as well as interesting page in our history. Raising himself from obscurity by his own exertions and industry, he acquired celebrity as a musician, and equalled, both in his professional and social character, the best and most honoured of his cotemporaries. There are many with us still who recollect him in that festive intercourse which his genius adorned, and but few unacquainted with the part which he took in the adaptation of our National Melodies to the most brilliant gems of Moore's lyric

xiv   *Introduction.*

Viceroy of Ireland, engaged himself for many seasons in the early part of the present century, adorning the social and festive board of the genial and kind-hearted "Terry M'Grath, whose harmonizing of the beautiful song, "Faithless Emma" can never be exceeded—a vocal gem of purest ray serene.*

The list of illustrious Irishmen and others who here resided and honoured and adorned the social réunions of the place might be extended indefinitely; sufficient, however, has

fancy; while his sacred compositions hold a place among the best choral services, and are still to be heard in the swelling notes of the organs of our ancient cathedrals, with which his earlier career and subsequent fame are so intimately associated.

Our great national bard and Stevenson were spirits of a kindred nature. Their ardent love of literature, music, and the muses; their social and congenial dispositions and mutual sympathies, produced a cordial intimacy and firm bond of union between these sons of genius which ripened into an abiding friendship. To their charming intellectual and friendly intercourse Moore pays the following graceful tribute in an eloquent, felicitous, and sublime vein of poetry peculiarly his own.

"He who, if aught of grace there be
In the wild notes I write or sing,
First smooth'd their links of harmony,
And lent them charms they did not bring:
He, of the gentlest, simplest heart,
With whom, employ'd in his sweet art,
(That art which gives this world of ours
A notion how they speak in heav'n;)
I've pass'd more bright and charmed hours,
Than all earth's wisdom could have giv'n."

* The genial and kind-hearted "Terry M'Grath," vicar-choral of Christ Church and St. Patrick's Cathedrals, teacher of singing to the family of Sir Walter Scott, and the amiable, much respected, and highly-prized artist and composer, Francis Robinson, Esq., Mus. Doctor, were junior members of the glorious coterie of talent which beamed with bright effulgence during this brilliant era of social and intellectual supremacy in our loved and lovely land of music and song.

Introduction. xv

been done to attest the former social status of this highly favoured locality.*

The Varieties also include a chapter of the political history of Ireland during the "infamous" administration of Lord Townshend in 1768.† The satirical songs, squibs, and ad-

---

* Social *réunions* of men of distinguished abilities were more common in the last century than in the present. The convivial society, called the "Monks of the Screw," of which Curran was the life and soul, met repeatedly at a charming country seat of his near Rathfarnham, which he appropriately called the "Priory." What an array of talent, from time to time, graced this festive board. Lord Mornington, one of the original members of the celebrated Beefsteak Club, composer of the beautiful glee, "Here in Cool Grot," Professor of Music to Trinity College, Dublin, and also his favourite, J. Parkinson, Mus. Doc., and Vicar-Choral of Christ Church and St. Patrick's Cathedrals (grandfather of the present Dr. Parkinson, of Tudor House, Dalkey); the Marquis of Townshend, when Viceroy; Yelverton, afterwards Lord Avonmore; Dr. O'Leary, Grattan, Flood, George Ogle, Judge Johnson, Hussy Burgh, with many other notables, were "Monks of the Screw." This society met, for several years, every Saturday during the law-terms, at a house in Kevin-street. Curran was elected Prior, and "never did an election of the kind fall upon a more sociable, a better natured, or more witty and heart-enlivening a man."

† The following papers ("Baratariana") will reach you, my Lord, in another country. They will contribute to amuse those leisure moments when you reflect on transactions that must once have agitated your bosom. They will recall those motley times of embarrassed indolence—of broken councils—of sordid society—when business waited, while Dennis jested and Cunningham advised. You will look back to the sea on which you once were tossed, and feel a cry to be on shore, though naked *and without a friend.* In those moments of reflection and of *safety*, you will recollect that you have introduced into this country a long train of mischiefs; that you have left a name, as little to be forgotten, as it can be beloved; that the men who opposed you were not your enemies, nor the men who supported you your friends; that your largesses were rejected by the spirit of indignant poverty;* that your favours, when they were received, were written in the sandy memory of disgusted hirelings, but your injuries engraven on the marble of the Constitution. Softened and stung by these considerations, you will lament the time when you were called *from the ranks to which you belong,* and, from the ludicrous singularity

dresses from the celebrated "Baratariana" collection, which are not (like the letters of Junius, the great modern *Juvenal* of satire* and galling irony) written by one person, but are the combined productions of Flood, Grattan, and several other eminent Irishmen of the day. The notice of illuminated works and arts in ancient Ireland before the irruption of the Northmen and wild Scandinavian hordes, from the learned and valuable notes on ornamentation, from S. Ferguson's ode "The Cromlech of Howth," which is beautifully illustrated by Miss Stokes, must prove highly interesting and instructive to every Irishman, while the history of the introduction of English gardening into this country, which supplanted the bad Dutch taste, after the *Huguenots* had established the *first* florist club in Dublin, will, it is to be hoped, afford satisfaction to the members of the various horticultural societies of Ireland. The author refers with pleasure to the list of eminent and distinguished Irishmen and women who have shed lustre on their country by their

of your genius, transplanted to a station where honours did not grow around you, and where, of all whom you have served, and of all whom you have injured, your adversaries are those alone of whom you cannot complain."—*Dedication to Lord Townshend, ex-Viceroy of Ireland*, 1771.—"*Baratariana.*"
* Satire is sure to find a willing ear,
And they who blame the sneerer love the sneer ;
But righteous tributes no emotion raise,
And those that love the virtues hate the praise.

celebrity in poetry, history, painting, music, and the drama, during the last two centuries, and the early part of the present century.

It now only remains to conclude this brief introduction to the author's VARIETIES OF IRISH HISTORY, by the expression of his sincere thanks for the many courtesies and kindnesses he has received from the resident gentry and inhabitants generally of Dalkey, Kingstown, Bray, Killiney, Shanganagh, and other places of interest in the vicinity of the City of Dublin; and the author anxiously hopes that he has discharged the duty of local historian to their satisfaction, and he avails himself of this opportunity of returning thanks to those ladies, noblemen, and gentlemen who honoured him with their names as subscribers to the special edition of this Work.

GASKIN'S IRISH VARIETIES,
ETC.

DALKEY.

SECTION I.
FORMER TRADE, COMMERCE—THE LEARNED AND FACETIOUS "KNIGHT OF INNISHOWEN,"* ETC.

DALKEY, a beautifully picturesque spot—a fashionable watering-place, the *junior Scarborough* of the Irish Sea—Dalkey, a rising and prosperous township, where peace and harmony prevail in its municipal councils—health-abiding Dalkey,† that woos the sigh

---

* The Knight of Innishowen, the *nom de plume* of Mr. J. Sheehan, the talented editor of the celebrated *Comet* newspaper.

† "They tell me nobody insures their lives about Dalkey, for fear they should pay the amount of the policy three times over in premiums; in fact, they say that very few people die about this part, at least, of Dalkey at all." "Most assuredly," said Sir Lucius, "the people about this favoured spot along the shore, and on the rocks, and on the hills that encircle the sea, live to a patriarchal age. When they go off at last, nobody seems to know what they die of. At all events, they go off gently, and easily." "Like the old people of Scyros in the 'Odyssey,'" suggested Friar John.

"'No want, no famine, the glad natives know,
Nor sink by sickness to the shades below ;
But when a length of years unnerves the strong,
Apollo comes, and Cynthia comes along.
They bend the silver bow with tender skill,
And void of pain, the silent arrows kill.'"

"Beautiful thought!" said the knight; "it must have been running in Moore's head when he wished for that 'bright little

of the southern gale with so much effect—Dalkey, with its pure and salubrious atmosphere, limpid springs, holy wells, religious educational institutes, and gorse-crowned hills, on one of which is perched a Danish ruin—Dalkey, within half an hour's drive of the Irish capital, with its "Coolamore Harbour," of historic associations, granite quarries, lead mines,* and well-arranged baths—Dalkey, whose marine terraces and villas of rural beauty, with their appropriate *Irish* names, are securely

"Moored in the rifted rock"—

Dalkey, a fitting home for *convalescents*—

"Where smiling spring its earliest visit pays,
And parting summer's ling'ring bloom delays"—

Dalkey, the "Port of the Seven Castles,"—was a place of great importance, and emporium of the trade of Ireland with France, Spain, and Holland.

In an enrolment of the 33rd of Edward III., dated February 8th, 1358, it is stated: "The Provost and Bailiffs of the town of Dalkey were commanded to allow the master of a Spanish ship arrested by them to depart."

It is stated in Hollinshed's Chronicles of the early part of the 15th century: that "Dalkee and Wickinlowe were amongst the chief haven towns of Ireland."

isle,' where we were to live without bother, and die at our ease, enjoying the glow of the sunshine, the balm of the air, the neverdying verdure of the meads and bowers, and the eternal summer of the place ; where

"' Our life should resemble a long day of light,
And our death come on holy and calm as the night !' "
—"The Knight of Inniahowen," in *Temple Bar Magazine*.

* "Near Dalkey is a lead mine, where it is said some hundred tons of ore have been raised. I got 42 grains of lead from 90 grains of it, fluxed with equal parts of salt of tartar."—Rutty's "Natural History of the County Dublin," 1772.

Up to 1610, no part of the river Liffey to the eastward of the present site of Essex-bridge, was embanked. Its waters often approached within a few yards of Trinity College. The Liffey, the Dodder, and Ballybough rivers (the present Tolka), were often altered in their course by land floods and storms, which exceedingly embarrassed the navigation of the channel. Up to this period (1610), when the quay embankments were commenced, all foreign vessels discharged their cargoes at the Port of Dalkey,* which at the time was also a well-frequented resort of shipping engaged in the international commerce between this country and Great Britain. The trade of Dalkey gradually declined after the Liffey embankment had been completed.

Dalkey Sound or Port was proposed as a proper site for an asylum harbour, and a plan prepared by the Committee of Inland Navigation.

PROPOSED HARBOUR.

The following extracts are taken from the Parliamentary Reports which were compiled (1803) to show the disadvantages that arise from the present harbour (Dublin Bay), the impossibility of improving it, and pointing out the Sound of Dalkey as an eligible one for the Port of Dublin.

"When I consider the abundance of sand that is constantly increasing the dimensions of the North and South Bulls, I cannot help expressing my fears, that human skill will be defeated in any attempt to improve the harbour, for the removal of the Bar, to admit large vessels into safety, is the great object to be effected. But when I look upon the chart of the Bay and Harbour of Dublin, and keep in view the

* The "Port of the Archbishop of Dublin."

unbounded resources of the increasing sands, it appears to me, that stubborn nature has but little left to do to defeat every attempt at improvement, by stopping up that narrow pass between the point of the Bar and the Lighthouse.

"This was so much apprehended, that the necessity of forming one at Dalkey Sound, with a canal from thence, took up much attention of our late Parliament* for many sessions, as appears from the various reports on the several plans laid before the House of Commons for that purpose.

"How far that object is capable of being converted to such a great national purpose, shall be the subject of a few succeeding pages.

"The situation of Dalkey Sound is on the southeast extremity of the Bay; it is a strait formed by that island, and rocks extending to the northward and eastward, and the lands of Dalkey on the west. The entrance into this strait from the open sea is about 1,000 feet broad; the other entrance, which is from the Bay, is about 700 feet broad—the former something more than a cable's length, the latter something less. The whole of it 3,650 feet, which is about five cables' length; with a sunk rock in the centre, and a rugged rocky shore on each side.

"In the Sound is good anchorage, from seven to ten fathom at low water. The stream of flood and ebb is more rapid in it than in any other part in or about the Bay, being at the rate of four miles an hour, when at the strongest. When it blows from the north, the water is disturbed during the continuation of the flood: there is protection from the other points any where within the shelter of the island, or the opposite shore, both being high and steep.

"Such is this harbour as nature has formed it; and the improvements proposed, agreeable to the

* The Irish Parliament.

fourth report from the Committee of Inland Navigation, are precisely those in the plans by Sir Thomas Page :—' To run out a rampart at the south end of the island (Dalkey), about 100 yards long, to break off *the heavy sea* coming from the S.E., building a good pier from the centre of the island into the Sound, about 100 yards on each side of which vessels may lie, according to the winds.' The pier proposed would divide the length of the Sound into two parts, with a passage of 700 feet at the end of it."*

The project was, however, abandoned in favour of Howth ; but this proving an utter failure, Dunleary was finally selected. Immense masses of granite, from the quarries of Dalkey, were swallowed up in the stupendous works and huge piers ; a million of money was expended ; and, after all, how insignificant, how insecure is the result, compared with the splendid and safe harbour that could have been constructed at the Port of Dalkey for a comparatively inconsiderable outlay, and which would have been more imposing and magnificent than that at Kingstown.†

I have on many occasions seen the destructive effects of a violent storm in Kingstown Harbour on

---

* The first stone of the new harbour at Dalkey was laid September 9th, 1868, by Mr. James Milo Burke, J.P., the courteous and talented Chairman of the Dalkey Town Commissioners. See Appendix.

† "There was a harbour for you, friar !" said the knight ; "such a one as you advocate running up into the mainland from a sound, and opposite an island—('The port of Eleusis, opposite the island of Salamis').—Protected by the surrounding heights on three sides, and on the fourth by the island coast—landlocked, you may call it. We could do the same at Dalkey. We could utilize this beautiful and convenient station, and restore it to its former fame, by cutting a harbour of refuge up into the land, half-a-dozen of acres or so, about Cullamore or Queenstown."

Friar John thought it was all a question of cost, and where was the money to come from ?

"A hundred thousand pounds at the utmost," was the knight's estimate ; and he was fortified in his opinion by an enterprising

the shipping, and the insecurity of the anchorage; on the contrary, at Dalkey, vessels lay secure in ten fathoms water, protected from the N.E. wind, which sweeps every part of Dublin Bay, by those natural breakwaters—Dalkey Island, the Muglins, and Maiden Rocks. The Channel or Sound of Dalkey is 1,200 yards long, 338 wide, and 308 at south entrance.

> "O night,
> And storm, and darkness, ye are wondrous strong,
> Yet lovely in your strength!"—*Byron.*

On Friday evening, September 25th, 1868, the Bay of Dublin presented a magnificent appearance. A terrific gale was blowing from the north-east, lashing the shore from Dalkey Sound, Bullock, and Sandycove to Scotchman's Bay, in "a peal of strong harmonies." 'Twas grand in the extreme!—the white-crested waves hugged the granite-bound coast with fury. This glorious tempest was accompanied with fierce rain. It forcibly recalled to my mind the fearful day on which the gallant Captain Boyd and

---

young engineer residing at Bray, who would not refuse the job. "Kingstown harbour, began fifty years ago, and only finished thoroughly the other day, cost little short of a million of money. What a paltry little water hole it is after all, and what little value the nation has for its money!"

"Howth was another of those jobs," observed Friar John. "Precisely so," replied Sir Lucius, "a real ould Irish job! badly constructed; at the mouth of an estuary, which is for ever and ever throwing up its sand-banks; abandoned for Kingstown; patronized now by fishermen only.—*Voila tout!*"

"Melancholy," cried the friar. "So many hospitals, so many schools, so many refuges for the wanderer and the stranger, so many life-boats might have been built for all those sums squandered on jobbery, in order that hereditary swells might get into parliament, and the fellows who got them in might become swells, and cut a dash with the people's money! And there's the railway system in every direction, and the joint-stock companies for exploiting every industrial system under the sun. Corruption! corruption! corruption!"—"The Knight of Innishowen."

others lost their lives at Kingstown, while heroically striving to save a number of shipwrecked sailors from a watery grave. I visited the "land-locked Coolamore" in the midst of the storm (at high tide), to ascertain if the security of Dalkey Sound in a N.E. gale, alleged by the Inland Navigation Committee, in 1797, was a fact. The rushing winds and dark clouds, with the savage sounds of the tempest's mirth, as it lashed, hissed, and rebounded, on the northern portion of these natural breakwaters, the Muglins, Maiden Rocks, and Dalkey Island, presented a sublime spectacle; while the "strait of St. Benedict," between the island and the mainland, in which a hundred vessels could securely ride at anchor, was, comparatively-speaking, as smooth as the pier-encircled harbour of Kingstown—so much so, that the concrete foundation of the new pier, then being built by the eminent contractor, Mr. Cunningham, which was completely covered by the tide, was uninjured. Had the tidal wave rolled in from the N.E., without being impeded by the island and Maiden Rocks, not a vestige of the foundations would have been left. Feeling interested in this historic "Port of the Archbishop of Dublin," I was much gratified on witnessing its natural capabilities and surroundings, in resisting the fury of a fearful N.E. gale, that blew a ship ashore on the same evening at Ballybrack; on which occasion, the lives of several persons were saved by the heroic and intrepid conduct of Mr. Edmond D. Gray, son of Sir John Gray, M.P.*

> "Then is its triumph hour,
> It springs to sudden power,
> As mounts the billow o'er the quivering mast."

I afterwards visited the "oldest inhabitant" of Dalkey, Bullock, and Dunleary—Mr. John Byrne— a respectable pilot of the olden time—a native of

* See Appendix.

8 *"Dentist M'Clean," and the Dalkey Sea Rover.*

Dunleary—born within a "stone's throw" of "Juggy's Well"—a well-informed man, who, for upwards of forty-five years, braved many a storm in the Channel and Dublin Bay, while guiding merchant vessels, and sailing packets through the eccentric courses and strange tidal currents of the treacherous "Kish," Burford,* Bennet's,† and Rosbeg banks—and in the yachting and regatta seasons, during the first half of the present century, assisted by the celebrated pilot, "Bill Harwood," brother to the witty Counsellor Harwood, he steered the Armitts, Alexanders, Plunkets, Burrowes, Blakeneys, Scots, Latouches, Baron George's family, and the hospitable and kind-hearted "Dentist M'Clean,"‡ on marine excursions, pleasure

* Burford Bank, in Dublin Bay, lies on a direct line drawn from the Kish to Howth lighthouse. It is so-called from a ship of war of that name, which struck on it in the year 1780.
† In 1798, a large brig, with all her crew, was lost on Bennet's Bank. A Mr. E. Hamerton, a public notary, stated that from the end of January, 1797, to January, 1803, 124 vessels were wrecked and damaged in Dublin Bay.
‡ "Dentist M'Clean," as he was called by the good people of this charming place, held a first-class position in the city: he was one of the most eminent of his profession. He lived for a considerable time in Dalkey House, which is situated close to the ruined abbey; he also lived in Bullock Castle, where Irish hospitality in its most legitimate sense was dispensed. It appears that Mr. M'Clean was the life and soul of the neighbourhood. On one occasion, in a memorable storm, he and Bill Harwood, the Methuselah of Dalkey pilots, were blown away in an open boat from the "Sound" into Holyhead. All the celebrities of the period afterwards sailed in this boat. There were no pleasure parties on the "Island," Lambay, or St. Nessan's Isle, without "Dentist M'Clean's Sea-rover." When he was leaving Dalkey House, he gave the boat to "Rod Bill." It was afterwards purchased (upwards of thirty-six years ago) by Mr. Pat Byrne, the respectable vintner of Castle-street, Dalkey. He had the boat encased in canvas, then turned it over, to form the roof of a summer-house, *al fresco*, in his gardens—the Tivoli of Dalkey, in days long vanished, when thousands of cars were plying on the "Rock Road," to this interesting locality. Hundreds of puncheons of John Jameson's "5 years old," *unadulterated* (a fact), were drunk under the timbers of the Sea-rover—which is now fast hastening to decay. Mr. M'Clean allowed Bill Harwood a pension, which was regularly paid to him through

parties, and pic-nics. This patriarch of the Dalkey pilots, who erected the tents on the "common" for the memorable Blakeney sod-party, alluded to in another portion of this work, has retained his memory and faculties as green and fresh as the day King George departed from "Dunleary." His recollections are truthful, and of the common-sense order. He does not " hold" with a certain old land-marine who haunts the "Coolamore"—an insipid, selfish old boatman and squatter, who thoroughly understands the *economy of truth*, and spins as many yarns (having no regard to chronology) as the guides of Glendalough, who manufacture legends to suit the "quality."

Our ancestors highly valued the Port of Dalkey for its safety and convenience; and hence it was that used on state occasions for the landing and sailing of Lord Deputies, Viceroys, and armies commanded by eminent generals.

LANDING OF VICEROYS, LORDS DEPUTY, ETC., AT THE PORT OF DALKEY.

1386. Philip De Courtney was the first Lord Deputy who landed here.

Shortly after the landing of Sir John Stanley, Lord Deputy in the following year, De Courtney was charged by some of the colonists with viceregal

---

Pat Byrne. He died in 1855, at the age of 101 years. A short time previous to the death of this veteran pilot, he requested Mr. Byrne and others to accompany him to the old graveyard which encircles the ruined church of Dalkey. He there pointed to a certain patch of ground, in which he requested them to have him buried after death. On digging his grave, some short time afterwards, according to his request, the workman struck on a large flag, on which three ancient crosses were cut. This was removed, and it now forms the headstone of the last resting-place of honest Bill Harwood, the Pilot of Dalkey.

exactions and oppressions; and though it was formally declared that no grounds existed for such charges, yet Stanley seized, under the royal writ, all poor Courtney's goods, horses, &c., and the ex-viceroy narrowly escaped from arrest and imprisonment, and with difficulty and danger reached England with his wife and children. Subsequently, Courtney obtained from the king and council in England one thousand marks as compensation.

1387. Sir John De Stanley, as Marquis of Dublin, with full power under the King's authority, given at his manor of "Kenygton."

In the year 1399, the Earl of Rutland (*Duke of Aumarle*), High Constable of England, "with a hundreth sails of Ships of Warr arrived here, who was more belovid of the Kyng (Richard II., then in Dublin), than any of his Blood, and by his advice he was most directed. Of his Coming, the Kyng was exceeding glad, and Joy appeared in his Face when he saw him, accusing him of his long Absence; which he humbly excused to the Kyng's Contentment."

During six weeks they remained in Dublin, where, the historian* says, "They lived in joy and delight; but in all that time, by Reason of foul Weather, and Contrary Winds, wee nevir heard out of *England;* which, undoubtedly, was a Presage, that God was displeased with the Kyng."

"At last a small Barque (the messenger of ill News) arrived at Dalkey, the Port of *Dublyn;* wherein

---

* "Story of King Richard II., his last being in *Ireland*. Written by a French Gentleman, who accompanied the King in that Voyage, to his leaving Ireland in 1399; and translated into English by Sir George Carew, Lord President of Munster under Queen Elizabeth." Charles the First conferred the title of Earl of Totness, in Devonshire, on a descendant of Sir George Carew. Camden mentions this nobleman with high respect, "on account " of his great love for antiquities," and for the light he gave him " into some of the affairs of Ireland."

Advertisement was brought to the Kyng, that *Henry*, Duke of *Lancaster*, was arrived in *England*; that he had a strong Army in the Field; that he had beheaded the Lord *Thresorer*; that at his Arrival the Archbishop of *Canterbury* preached to the People to persuade them to assist the Duke, telling them, how King *Richard* had wrongfully banished *Henry*, whom the Pope, our holy Father, hath now confirmed Kyng of the Realme.

"The Kyng sent to the Erle of *Salisbury*, saying unto him, Fair Cousin, you must presently embarque yourself for *England*, land in Wales, gathir unto you such Forces, as you can raise to resist *Lancaster* in his foolish Enterprise. The Erle protested upon his Faith, that he would either effect his commands, or die in the Performaunce of them. The Kyng on his Parte assured *Salisbury*, that he woud loose no time in securing him with all his Forces, Swearing by Great Othes, that if *Lancaster* did fall into His hands, he woud cause hym to dye such a Death, as the Fame thereof shoud sound as far as *Turky*."

Previous to King Richard the Second's arrival in Dublin, in 1399, the historian says, he encamped in a rugged and almost inaccessible tract of country, under the shadow of the "Three Rock Mountain," which can be seen from Dalkey Hill—a sort of neutral ground for the O'Byrnes, O'Tooles, and the *Palesmen*. "The Kyng's Standard, wherin he had three Leopards, was advaunced, undir the which he Knighted the Duke of *Lancaster's* Son,* who was a

---

* This was the son of him who soon after dethroned King Richard, and assumed the title of King Henry IV.; and this puny young bachelor, now knighted, was afterwards the victorious King Henry V.—Ware's "Antiquities."

"How few in Dublin are aware that their forefathers of the Pale—

'Have seen young Harry with his beaver on,
His cuisses on his thighs—gallantly armed,'

careering through these valleys; that amidst these mountains (the

fair and puny Batchelor, and to honour him the
more, he made at the same time eight or ten other
Knights. *   *   *   *   *   *
Herupon the nexte day the Kyng dislodgid, and
marched towards *Dublin.* The enemy attended us
with fierce and fearful outcries, and skirmished often
with us. Aftir the Kyng's departur, McMorough, con-
templating his Power, and his own Weakness, being
diffident of the Success of this Warr, sent after the
Kyng, beseeching him to permit him to come in
Safety unto him, being desirous, as he said, to submit
himself to his mercy, or, if he wuld not be so pleasid,
to send some of his Lordes unto hym to intreate of
Peace and Accord. This news brought much Joy
into the *English* Camp, every Man being weary of
Toile, and desirous of Rest. The Kyng, by the
advice of his Councill, sent the Erle of *Gloucester*
unto *McMorough,* to charge him with his Crymes,
and with the Damages which he had done unto the
Kyng's Liege People, and to treat farther with him
as he was instructed.

"The Erle, with a part of the rere Guard of the
Army (which he commanded), departid from the
Kyng, attended with a Guard of two Hundrith Lances,
and a thousande good Archers. Among othir Gentil-
men I was one that went with him to see *McMorough,*
his Behaivour, Estate and Forces, and to what issue
the Treaty would grow unto. Between two Woodes,
not far from the Sea, McMorough (attendid by mul-
titudes of the *Irish*) descended from a Mountain,
mounted upon a Horse without a saddle, which cost
him (as it was reported) four Hundrith Cows. For
in that Country they barter by Exchange, Horses
for Beasts, and one commodity for anothir, and not

Dublin), the hero of Agincourt achieved his earliest exploits of
arms; and here, beneath the royal standard, received his *first*
order of knighthood from the unfortunate Richard."—Dalton's
"History of the County Dublin."

for reddy money. His Horse was fair, and in his
descent from the Hill to us, he ran as swift as any
Stagg, Hare, or the swiftest Beast that I have seen.
In his right Hand he bear a great long Dart, which
he cast from him with much dexterity. At a Wood's
side his Men stayed behynd him, and he met the Erle
at a little Ford. He was tall of stature, well composed, strong and active. His Countenance fierce
and cruel. Much speech passed between the Erle
and him, of the breach of his Faith to the Kyng, of
the murdering of the Erle of *March*, and othir of the
Kyng's subjects. To be short, this Parly produced
little effect. McMorough departid to his Men, and
the Erle of *Gloucester* to Kyng Richard, unto whom
he recounted all the Passages betwene them, the
sum whereof was, that oonly he would submit
himself without further conditions, and that othir
Composition he wuld not make during Lyfe. The
Kyng at this report was much enraged, swearing
by Saint *Edward* that he would nevir depart out
of *Ireland* untill he had *McMorough* in his Hands
living or dead. But the good Kyng did not dream
of the misfortune, which shortly after fell upon
hym.*

" Immediately upon the Erle's return of the Answer
aforsaid, the Kyng dislodged and marched the next
day to the city of *Dublyn;* which is a good Town,
the best in that Realme, seated upon the Sea, and
rich in Merchandise, wher wee found such plenty of
Victuals to relieve our Army, Horse and Foot, consisting of Thirty Thousande or therabouts, that the
prices of the same did not much increase."

1399. The Earl of Salisbury embarked his small
train and baggage at the Port of the Archbishop of

---

* This meeting of Gloucester, Henry of Lancaster, afterwards
the celebrated Henry V., and M'Murough, in 1399, is the subject
of a highly interesting illuminated picture, in a very curious MS.
on vellum, preserved in the British Museum.

Dublin (Dalkey). King Richard assured him, that within six days after his departure, no matter what should happen, he would put out to sea.
"With this brave Erle (*Salisbury*), myself, and companion, shipped ourselves, and we landed at *Conway*, which, upon my credit, is a fair and strong Town."*

1414. Sir John Talbot (Lord Furnival), afterwards the *celebrated Earl of Shrewsbury.*
Camden's "History of Queen Elizabeth," translated into English, fol. ed. Lon. 1675.—" Whereas, page 37, the translator says that Francis Abbott was the first Earl of Shrewsbury, it must be a mistake for the fifth Earl, and so (to do Mr. Camden justice) it is in the original, for the Talbots have been successively Earls of Shrewsbury ever since John Talbot, Marshal of France, was created Earl of Shrewsbury by King Henry VI., A.D. 1442, in which name the honour has continued to this present time (1718). For though the honour of dukedom is extinct upon the death of Charles Talbot, Duke of Shrewsbury, this year, 1718, yet he is succeeded in the earldom and estate by —— Talbot, Esq., a Roman Catholic. The same mistake is made in the History of England, in two vols., 8vo, printed in 1701, in the 14th page of the 2nd vol."—" Emendatio Authorum, or a Collection of Several Palpable Mistakes made by some of our English Historians."

1534. Sir Wm. Skeffington.
1548. Sir Edward Bellingham.
"Sir Edward Bellingham routed the O'Mores of Leix and Ossory,† wounding their chief, who died in captivity, a pensioner, and in London."

---

* "The Story of King Richard the *Second* his last being in Ireland." Translated from the French by George, Earl of Totness.
† The Prince of Ossory, in the eleventh century, behaved in a wretched way to the sons of Brian Boru, as they returned with their Dalgais, or chosen troops, from the field of Clontarf. He

1553. Sir Anthony St. Leger (for the fifth time).

1565. Sir Henry Sydney, having landed as Lord Deputy at Dalkey, proceeded to the house of Thomas Fitzwilliam at Merrion, from whence he made his solemn entry into Dublin.

1584. Sir John Perrot.*

" It may be remarked that even the most hostile of the ' meere Irish' were generous to appreciate high and noble qualities in an English Lord Deputy. When Sir John Perrot, whose government had been marked by zeal for his Queen, mingled with judicious and kindly management of the natives, was embarking for England, he stepped into the boat amidst the cheers and acclamations, mingled with weeping (how like the departure of the good Earl of Carlisle !) of all classes, who had been happy under his administration ; ' and old Tirlough, the chief of Tyrone, followed him to the water side, all bathed in tears.' It was a singular thing that he should be

opposed their passage through his territories, when the wounded men of Brian's army asked permission that their comrades might tie them to stakes fixed in the ground, and thus they might combat. It is thus beautifully alluded to by Moore :—

" Forget not our wounded companions, who stood
   In the day of distress, by our side :
While the moss of the valley grew red with their blood,
   They stirred not, but conquered and died :
The sun that now blesses our arms with his light,
   Saw them fall upon Ossory's plain,
Oh ! let him not blush when he leaves us to-night,
   To find that they fell there in vain."

* Sir John Perrot appears to have been a pious man. A short picture of all he did when Deputy, is in the following lines by Nicholas White :—

"Pacificavit Conaciam, relaxavit Mediam,
   Ligavit Monomiam ;
Extirpavit Scotos,
   Refrenavit Anglos.
Et his omnibus peræque vectigal acquisibat Reginæ."
He told Queen Elizabeth " he could please and pacify her Irish subjects better than her English."

succeeded by one who, on the testimony of the English historians, was corrupt and impolitic, self-aggrandizing, a cruel tyrant, violent, avaricious, hateful and hating; such was Sir Wm. Fitzwilliam—the worst governor ever inflicted by England upon her unhappy sister, Ireland."—*Dublin University Magazine.*

1599. Robert Devereux, Earl of Essex, landed here with a strong force, against Hugh O'Neil, Earl of Tyrone.*

* Robert Devereux, Earl of Essex (Queen Elizabeth's particular favourite), a distinguished soldier, and passionately fond of military glory, was created Lord Deputy of Ireland in 1599, and sent over with a larger force, and invested with more extensive powers than had ever been committed to a Viceroy, to extricate the affairs of the government from the pressure which threatened them with destruction.

He had a commission for disposing of the lands of the insurgents, for proclaiming and executing martial law, and for placing and displacing all officers at pleasure. He had an army of 20,000 foot and 13,000 horse, and a military chest well provided with money to pay them.

Essex found even this force to be unequal to that of the enemy, whose troops were better disciplined and more patient of fatigue. He first led his troops into Munster, by the advice of certain privy counsellors, whose property lay in the south, which they wished should be protected. Here, he could do nothing effectual against the enemy, who, avoiding an open action, in which only he could have a superiority, attacked him from their retreats, hung for days together upon the rear of his army, which was considerably diminished and exposed to pressing difficulties. Meanwhile, Sir Henry Harrington, whom he had left in the Wicklow Glens with 600 men, was attacked by the O'Byrnes, and defeated.

Hugh O'Neil, Earl of Tyrone, had not been inattentive to his interest; and having received ammunition from Spain, seized particular passes necessary to his security, and received into pay a number of Scottish forces. He took possession of an advantageous situation in the neighbourhood of Newry, which he fortified by strong entrenchments, and there determined to await the approach of Essex. The Earl had now returned to Dublin from Munster. By this time he was acquainted with the number, with the strength, and with the military skill of the insurgents, and foresaw the difficulty of reducing them to obedience by open force. Impressed by this conviction, he had written to the Queen, and given it as his advice, that to guard the Irish coast, to prevent the enemy from receiving foreign aid, to waste their country, to destroy their provisions, and thus gradually consume their strength, was,

"In 1560, the troops, ammunition, and ordnance sent from England to be employed against Shane O'Neill, were landed at the crane on Merchants'-quay, Dublin."*

though more tedious, the sure and effectual method of compelling them to return to their allegiance.

Elizabeth was annoyed, rejected the advice, and enjoined him to march directly against Tyrone. Even now, instead of obeying, he marched into Leinster against the O'Moores and O'Connors.

In this expedition, equally unfortunate with that into Munster, he so diminished his army, that he was obliged to write to England for a supply of 1,000 men.

He was equally unsuccessful in an attempt which he made to call the attention of Tyrone towards Baleek. There, 1,500 men, detached under the command of Sir Couyers Clifford, being attacked at disadvantage by the chieftain O'Rourke, were defeated; and, had they not been relieved by a body of horse, which fortunately came up to their assistance, would have been entirely destroyed. At last, Essex resolved upon an expedition to the north; but, on reviewing his troops, he found that he could not lead there more than 1,300 foot and 300 horse. With this inconsiderable force he set forward, and reached the borders of Ulster about the middle of September. To engage the enemy with such inferior numbers might have been fatal; he therefore parleyed with Tyrone, and concluded a truce of six weeks, to be renewed for a like space until the 1st of May, neither party to commence hostilities without fourteen days' notice. By this step, Essex still more highly provoked Elizabeth, who expressed her resentment in a letter to him on the occasion, in very warm terms. In confidence that by a personal interview he would be able to revive that affection with which the Queen had formerly treated him, he set off from Dalkey immediately for London, not only without permission, but in express contradiction to her order. To guard against the advantage which his enemies, of whom he had many, would take of this rash step, by making an impression unfavourable to him on the mind of her Majesty, immediately on his arrival he hastened to her apartment, cast himself on his knees, and endeavoured to disarm her resentment. Surprised by the unexpected appearance of her favourite, which prevented reflection, and excited a sudden emotion of that regard which he had long experienced, she received him graciously. The comfortable hopes with which this reception inspired him were transient. With recollection, the displeasure of Elizabeth returned. She confined Essex to his apartments, and then committed him to the Tower. Having regained his liberty, he was hurried, by the impetuosity of his temper, into an act of open rebellion, for which he was executed.

* "History of Dublin," by J. T. Gilbert, the learned Librarian of the Royal Irish Academy, a work of great historical research, which every lover of Irish history should be acquainted with.

1675. Arthur Capel, Earl of Essex, landed at Dalkey as Lord Deputy, at which time its port was declining. He wrote the following interesting letter during his year of viceroyalty :—

"*Dublin Castle, June* 1*st,* 1675.
" *To Mr. Secretary Coventry.*

" SIR,—In my last I promised you a further account of the Spanish ship which was taken in this bay. The particulars whereof, and the several circumstances relating thereunto, you will find in the examination herewith enclosed; and that it may be the more intelligible, happening to have a map by me of this port, I have caused the places to be marked in it where the thing was done. Here was another French ship lately in the port, which brought some goods from France, and owned herself to have a commission to take any of the French king's enemies. She went about three or four days, and is reported to lie at Lambay, being an island two leagues northward from Howth. It is believed she attends the coming out of some Dutch ships who are now in Dalkey Sound, lading goods to return home. I perceive the merchants of this city are much disturbed with these proceedings; but we have none here skilled in that sort of learning to inform me whether these French are by the marine laws justified in what they have done. I am, I confess, a little apprehensive of some affront from these privateers, it being easy for them to come into the harbour at their pleasure, and there plunder and fire what ships they think fit. Nothing can remedy this but his Majesty sending a small frigate hither (one of 20 or 25 guns will be best) to secure us.

"In former times, this port was seldom without one or two such; and, indeed, considering the customs his Majesty receives here, which is commonly £30,000 per annum, I think it may well deserve to be a little better looked after. Having thus represented the whole, I shall humbly submit it to his Majesty's consideration, and remain

"Your most faithful, humble servant,

"ESSEX."*

"The examination of James Tanner, Gent., Surveyor of the Port of Dublin, who being duly sworn and examined, saith—That, on the 22nd of this inst., May, a small sloop of about twenty tons, belonging to Brest, one Monsieur Le Gravell commander, of about twenty years of age, with thirty-six men and four guns, came to an anchor within musketshot of land, under Bullock, and continued there till the 26th inst., and then pursued a Dutch ship (from Norway) coming into the harbour, and lost her; then came to an anchor under the Hill of Howth, as near as she could be.

"That, on the 29th, a ship coming into the bay from the southward, Spanish bottom, with ten men aboard, from Bilboa, laden with fruits and irons, the sloop weighed, and, with the help of her oars, sixteen in number, came up with her, boarded her, and clapped fifteen men of his aboard, about seven o'clock that evening.

"Seven of the Spaniards escaped before in the boat, at which three guns were fired.

"The Spaniard was about forty tons, and was taken about two miles from the bar southward, about seven fathoms water, above a league within the two headlands of Howth and Dalkey.

"About nine that evening, the Spanish merchant, pilot, and one private seaman, were brought on board the sloop, the last of which seemed to have his hands tortured with matches.

"She stood off to sea with the Spanish ship about ten that night, with an intention to go to her post.

* Capel's Letters, A.D. 1675.

"This examinant's cause of knowledge is, that he came on board the said shallop at the very time the Spaniard was taken.
"JAMES TANNER.
" Cap. et jurat coram me,
" 29th May, 1675.
" John Topham."

HISTORICAL REMINISCENCES OF DALKEY.

In the year 1171, Murtough, Petty Prince of Hy-Kinselagh, when confederating with Roger O'Connor to besiege Dublin, encamped with his forces at Dalkey. In five years afterwards, Hugh de Lacy granted this place, with Dalkey Island, to the See of Dublin, a gift which was confirmed by Prince John, and subsequently by Pope Clement the Third. In 1178, the celebrated Archbishop O'Toole* (*Lorcan*

* This truly illustrious Irishman, and venerable and excellent prelate, who succeeded to the high preferment of Archbishop of Dublin in 1162, was the youngest son of the hereditary Lord or Petty Prince of the territory of Imaile, county Wicklow, the head of one of the septs eligible to the kingdom of Leinster, and which maintained the privilege of electing the bishops and abbots of Glendalough, even for centuries after that see was united to Dublin. His father's principality was situated in the district of Wicklow, to which he was also attached in the maternal line; his mother having been one of the O'Byrnes, a family equally revered in the memory of their countrymen. In the depth of the romantic "valley of the two lakes," which gave name to the See of Glendalough, and where the ruins of its little city and cathedral are still traceable, there was at this period one of those schools for which Ireland was justly celebrated; and within its walls the pious Laurence O'Toole imbibed the rudiments of his education. He was consecrated Archbishop of Dublin in 1162, at Christ Church, by Gelasius, Archbishop of Armagh, assisted by many bishops, the people offering up the thanksgiving of their hearts; and from that period the custom of sending the bishops of the Irish cities which the Danes had occupied to Canterbury for consecration, was utterly discontinued. This excellent prelate devoted himself at an early age to a monastic life, the duties of which he discharged in a very exemplary manner. This laid the foundation for his future dignities. He was remarkable for his benevolence, for the

O'Tuathal) assigned to Christ Church (amongst several) the church of St. Begnet of Dalkey, with all its tithes, and his grant was further assured by letters-patent from Prince John. The manorial rights and strictest chastity, for piety, temperance, hospitality, and, above all, for the love of his native country. Contrasted with the servility of his interested cotemporaries of the sacred order in this respect, his patriotic and noble conduct appears in shining colours. In 1167 was held the general council of the archbishops and chieftains of Ireland at Athboy, to acknowledge the sovereignty of Roderic, and to consider the means of resisting the expected invasion of Dermod M'Murough's Welsh auxiliaries under Strongbow. He assisted at the council, and firmly adhered to the independence of his country. Strongbow arrives—Dublin is besieged—the citizens, through the mediation of the Archbishop, treat for a surrender. During the negotiation the walls are scaled, and tho city treacherously taken, with fearful carnage.

In 1171, Hasculph, the late Danish governor of Dublin, arrived with thirty ships, and a strong and well-appointed force from the Isle of Man and the islands of the north. Archbishop O'Toole, on this occasion, considering that much national good might result from opposing the power of the new invaders by that of the old, became the most zealous in his appeals to the native princes to promote Hasculph's project; and his devoted patriotism, and the sanctity of his character, gave great weight to his exhortations. The people rose in arms to his call, collected all their strength, surrounded Dublin by land; while the Dane occupied the harbour, and threatened the hitherto victorious Strongbow with total annihilation. From the height of the citadel he beheld with alarm the allied natives at last united in the defence of their country, and extending their lines from sea to sea around him. Roderic was encamped at Castleknock, whence his army extended to the ancient town of Finglas; O'Rourke and the petty princes of Ulster mingled their forces along the strand of Clontarf; the Lord of Hy-Kinselagh occupied the opposite shores of Dalkey; while the Chief of Thomond advanced so near as Kilmainham to the walls of the metropolis; and even Archbishop Laurence communicated the inspiration of his character to this cause, and, gliding amidst the ranks of war, animated the several septs of his countrymen to the assertion of their common liberties.—Cambrensis Eversus, 1662.

Within the city were Earl Strongbow, Maurice FitzGerald, Raymond le Gros (the Achilles of the invasion), Milo de Cogan, and some other chosen chieftains; but their scanty soldiery bore a fearful comparison with the host that were to oppose them, and Strongbow, in the prudence of necessity, withheld them from an encounter that might but reveal their weakness. It was the crisis of Ireland's destinies, but her monarch was not equal to the emergency.

For two months the closest blockade was maintained. The garrison, reduced to extremities by famine, implored their commanders

royalties remained, however, annexed to the see. In 1200, the then Archbishop of Dublin had a grant of a Wednesday market here, and an annual fair, to be held

to lead them against the enemy. The fearful state of FitzStephen in Wexford aggravated the despair of those within the city. Negotiations with the Irish failed; a council was held, and it was resolved to sally forth on the besiegers. They sallied forth the following morning, and completely surprised the wing of Roderic's army—a merciless and miserable slaughter of the natives ensued. The victorious garrison returned, enriched with spoils and an ample store of provisions. Roderic himself narrowly escaped from the field; the native princes fled; the Danish allies retired. Hasculph, however, was taken prisoner and executed. Strongbow marched to the relief of FitzStephen.(a)

Thus, through fatal negligence and misconduct in the leaders, the powerful combination against the English invasion was crushed, and the relative situation of the contending forces, by the result of an almost hopeless but successful sally, entirely reversed.

Nevertheless, the patriotic Archbishop O'Toole exerted himself to revive the hopes of his countrymen, to animate them to continue the struggle, and to inspire them with hope and resolution in asserting the sacred cause of national independence.

Meanwhile, Henry II. procured the Bull of Pope Adrian. In obedience to the papal injunction, the principal archbishops, bishops, abbots, and native chieftains, ever influenced by religion and devotion to the Holy See, tendered their allegiance to Henry. Thus was secured the annexation of Ireland to the crown of England, not by the right of actual conquest, but by voluntary submission to the will of the head of the Roman Catholic Church.

Crawford, in his "History of Ireland" (1773), in speaking of the death of this prelate, says :—

"To remove unfavourable impressions received of him by Henry,

---

(a) "The History of Ireland, by Maurice Regan, servant and interpreter to Dermod M'Murough, King of Leinster. Translated from the Irish into French, and from thence into English by Sir George Carew, Lord President of Munster, in the reign of Queen Elizabeth [a copy of this piece is in the College Library]; to which are added Notes to illustrate some dark passages therein."—See Appendix.

"Whoever writes the history of Ireland during the English period, must make this piece the main basis of his account ; and the defects of your author must be supplied from Cambrensis, who, though he was not in Ireland during the first actions of the conquest, yet came soon enough after to be informed of the truth, arriving there in the quality of secretary to John, Earl of Moreton, in the year 1185."—Harris's "Hibernica."

on St. Begnet's Day, with such tolls and customs as the Mayor and Bailiffs of Dublin had, same to be applied and spent upon the murage and purage of the town.

In 1218, Reginald Talbot was seised of Dalkey, rendering therefor a goshawk annually; and his rights therein were confirmed to his family by various subsequent instruments. In 1273, his descendant, another Reginald, was summoned to attend a great council in Dublin, in right of this feod.

In 1306, it appearing by the King's letters that the wines sent to him out of Ireland were bad, mixed, and for the greater part sour, an inquiry was instituted, on the oaths of merchants, as to the cause; whereon they found that the wines in question were shipped about Michaelmas at Bordeaux, and were, after All Saints' Day, landed at Dalkey, whence they were re-shipped to "Skynburness," but on the latter occasion were tossed about by tempests until the Epiphany, and then delivered in the state of deterioration complained of, but not arising from any adulteration or default of the mariners or merchants.

1323. The Mayor, &c., of Dover received the royal command to have sufficient shipping on a given day at Dalkey, to convey thence men, arms, and provisions to his Majesty, for the service of the expedition against Scotland.

1337. King Edward confirmed Dalkey, with its church and tithes, to the See of Dublin.

1395. King Richard, do.

1360. The Provost and Bailiffs of this borough

and to intercede with him in behalf of his countrymen, oppressed by the lawless depredations of the British soldiers, he passed over to England. From thence he went to Normandy, to be present at the Council of Lateran. Worn out by the infirmities of age, he was taken ill upon his journey. Perceiving his last moments to approach, his country recurred to his thoughts; he lamented its sufferings, he expressed the anxiety of his heart for its deliverance in pathetic terms. Death closed his eyes for ever, but left the remembrance of his virtues to warm with gratitude the breasts of Irishmen, and to be admired by posterity."

received the royal command to permit the departure of a Spanish ship, which had been stopped to convey the Prior of St. John of Jerusalem, then also Chancellor of Ireland, inasmuch as he was not prepared to travel at that time.

1369. Reginald Talbot was sued in the Court of Exchequer, for delivering therein, as the rent of his estate at Dalkey, one goshawk, which, on inspection and examination, there proved unsound, unfit, and of no value; and insomuch as the same was a fraud on the court, and a grievous damage to the King, the said Reginald was fined.

1376. The King appointed inspectors to prevent the unlicensed exportation of corn from this harbour.

1396. King Richard granted to Archbishop Northalis, and his successors in the See of Dublin, that his and their bailiffs for the time being should exercise the office of Admiral or Water-Bailiff of the King within the manor, lordship, and port of Dalkey, and receive all fees thereunto belonging; and that no admiral or water-bailiff of the King should intermeddle with their authority. The importance of this grant appears from a cotemporaneous instrument, wherein it is stated that "there is no safe anchorage or good lying for great ships coming into the port of Dublin with wines, salt, corn, and other merchandises, freighted for Dublin from foreign parts, only at the port of the Archbishop of Dublin, in the town of Dalkey, which is six level miles from Dublin, and out of the port and liberties of the city, at which place they are bound to unload ; *and there is no other port in the neighbourhood where they can ride so safe from storm ;* and the merchants were wont to buy their goods at said port of Dalkey, and as well as in the ports of Dublin and other ports to land same, and to bring it up on cars or in boats to the city, and there land and pay the customs."

1451. The King appointed James Prendergast Bailiff of Dalkey.

1482. It appears by a record that this town could then raise 200 men-at-arms; that seven fairs were annually held here, by grant from King Edward the Fourth, as also weekly markets; and that the Bailiff had power to receive, out of all manner of wares and merchandise coming and resorting for sale to the said fairs and markets, such customs as were levied by the Mayor and Bailiffs of the city of Dublin; same to be employed in walling and paving the town.

1488. Sir Richard Edgecombe embarked for England. He had been appointed commissioner from Henry the Seventh to the disaffected Anglo-Irish nobles, in reference to the movement in favour of the Earl of Warwick, personated by the pretender Lambert Simnel, who was crowned in Dublin, in the Cathedral of the Holy Trinity (now Christ Church).* Sir Richard Edgecombe, after the successful issue of his commission, accompanied by the Archbishop and other distinguished individuals, proceeded to Dalkey, where his ships lay, accompanied by a force of 500 men, and embarked there.

The following interesting extracts, relating to the proceedings of Sir Richard Edgecombe in Dublin, are taken from his " Voyage into Ireland":—†

" The Mayor and Substance of Dublin of the Citty of Dublyn, receaved him at the Black Fryers Gate, 1488, at which he was lodged.‡

* * * *

" *Item.* On *Sonday*, the said Sir Richard went to

---

* The crown used on this occasion was borrowed from a statue of the Blessed Virgin, which stood in the church of St. Mary-les-Dames, near Cork-hill, Dublin.

† " The Voyage of Sir Richard Edgecombe into Ireland, in the year 1488. Collated, with a MS. of Dr. Sterne, late Bishop of Clogher, in the College Library." First published in 1774.

‡ This was the Dominican Abbey, near the old bridge, which now is the King's Inns, in Henrietta-street, Dublin, where the Rolls Office was kept.

the high Church of *Dublyn*, callid *Christ's Church*, and caused the Bushopp of *Meath* ther to declare as well the Pope's Bull of Accursing, and the Absolution for the same, as the Grace which the Kyng had sent by hym, to Pardon evry man that wuld do his Duty, unto the Kyng's Hyghness. And that day the Archbushopp of *Dublyn*, the Bushopp of *Meath*, and dyverse other Gret Men, dined with the seyd Sir Richard in his Lodging.

" *Item.* Monday, Sir *Richard Edgecomb*, at the especiale intreaty of the *Erle of Kildare*, came to *Maynoth*, where the seyd Erle lay, and there had right good cheer. At which place the seyd Erle made promise, that he wuld conform him in all things to the Kyng's Pleasure in such wise, that the Mynd of the seyd Sir Richard shuld be contentid; and that was the especiale cause, that the seyd Sir Richard went thither.   *   *   *

" *Item.* Wednesday, the Erle of *Kildare* and othir Lordes of *Irelaund* kept gret Councill at *St. Thomas Court* without the Citty of *Dublyn;* at which Council the seyd Erle and Lords agreed well to become the Kyng's true subjects as they seyd; and for their good abearing hereafter offered to be bound, and make as good Suretys as culd be devised by the Kyng's Laws. But in no wise they wuld agree and assent to the bond of *Nisi;* and for this bond certon of the seyd Councill came three or four Tymes that Day to the seyd Sir Richard Edgecomb in his Lodging at Black Fryers, and required hym to leave off calling for the seyd Bond, whych he wuld in no wise do, but gave short Answers, with right fell and angry Words; and that day no Conclusion was takin. Also the same Day the Lord of *Gormanstown* dined with the seyd Sir Richard at his Lodging.   *   *   *

" *Item.* Sunday, the seyd Erle and Councill agreed to be Sworne upon the holy Sacrament, to be the

Kyng's true liege Men from thence forth, after the Tenour of souch Ooth as was agreed betwenc the seyd Sir *Richard* and the seyd Erle and Lordes; whych Ooth the same Erle and Lordes graunted to certifie unto the Kyng's Grace under ther Seals, and offered then to have been sworn that Day at Aftirnoon; wherunto the seyd Sir *Richard* wuld in no wise agree for many causes, but wuld have them to be Sworne on the Forenoon; and that a Chaplan of his own shuld Consecrate the Same Host, on whych the seyd Erle and Lordes shuld be Sworn.

" *Item.* The seyd Sir Richard, at the Desire of the seyd Erle, went to the Monastry of St. *Thomas* the Martyr, where the Lordes and Councill were assemblide, and ther in a gret Chambir, callid the Kyng's Chambir, the seyd Sir *Richard* took Homage, first of the seyd Erle, and aftir that of othir Lordes, whose Name be written herafter in the Boke; and this done, the seyd Erle went into a Chambir wher the seyd Sir Richard's Chaplain was at Mass, and in the Mass Time the seyd Erle was shriven and assoiled from the Curse that he stood in by the Virtue of the Pope's Bull; and before the Agnus of the seyd Mass, the Host divided into thre Parts, the Priest turned him from the Altar, holding the seyd thre Parts of the Host upon the Patten, and ther, in the Presence of many persons, the seyd Erle, holding his right Hand over the Holy Host, made his solemn Ooth of Ligeance unto our Soverain Lord Kyng *Henry* the 7th, in souch form as was afor Devised; and in the Bushopps and Lordes, as appearith herafter, made like Ooth; and that done, and the Mass endid, the seyd Erle, with the seyd Sir Richard, Bushopps, and Lordes, went into the Church of the seyd Monastry, and in Choir therof the Archbushopp of *Dublyn*, began *Te Deum,* and the Choir with the organs sung it up solempnly; and that tyme all the Bells in the Church rung. This done, the Erle and most part of the seyd Lordes went home wyth the seyd Sir *Richard* into his Lodging, and dined with hym, and had right gret cheer; and the seyd Sir *Richard*, at the making of the seyd Erle's Homage, put a collar of the Kyng's Livery about the seyd Erle's neek, whych he wore throughout the seyd Citty of *Dublyn*.

"*Item.* The seyd Sir *Richard* went about nine of the Bell in the morning to the Guild Hall within the Citty of *Dublyn*, wher the Mayor, Baylifs, and Comminality of the same wer assemblid; and ther the seyd Sir *Richard* made them to be sworn unto the Kyng's Grace upon the Holy Evangelist, according to souch form as they have certified unto the Kyng's seyd Grace, undir ther Common Seal.

"*Item.* Both the Erle of *Kildare* and the seyd Sir *Richard*, and the Lordes Spiritual an Temporal, met at a Church callid Our Lady of the Dames in *Dublyn*; and ther gret instuance was made agen to the seyd Sir *Richard* to accept and take Justice *Plunket* and the Prior of *Kilmainham* to the Kyng's Grace, and that they mought have their Pardons in likewise as othir had, forasmooch as the Kyng had grantid Pardon generally to every Man. The seyd Sir *Richard* answerid unto theme with right sharp words, and seyd, that he knew better what the Kyng's Grace had commaunded him to do, and what his instructions were, than any of theme did, and gave with a Manful Spirit unto the seyd Justice *Plunket*, and Prior, fearful and Terrible words, insoemuch that both the seyd Erle and Lordes wuld give no answer therunto, but kept their Peace; and aftir great ire passed, the Erle and Lordes laboured with souch fair means, and made souch profers, that Sir *Richard* was agreed to take Justice *Plunket* to the Kyng's grace, and soe he did, and took his Homage and Fealty upon the Sacrament;

but in no wise he wuld axcept or take the Prior of *Kilmainham* to the Kyng's grace, and ere that he departed unto his Lodging, he took with hym divers Judges and othir Noblemen, and went into the Castle of *Dublyn*, and there put in Possession *Richard Archiboll*, the Kyng's Servaunt, into the office of the Constable of the seyd Castle, which the Kyng's Grace had givin unto him by his Lettres Patent; from the whych office the Prior of *Kilmainham* had wrongfully kept the seyd Richard by the space of two yeres and more, and ere then he departid out of the seyd church of Dames, the Erle of *Kildare* delivered unto Sir *Richard* both his certificate upon his Ooth undir the Seal of his Arms, as the obligation of his surities; and ther Sir *Richard*, in the presence of all the Lordes, deliverid unto hym the Kyng's Pardon undir his Gret Seal in the presence of all the Lordes, and ther took his leave of the seyd Erle of *Kildare* and Lordes Spiritual and Temporal; and that Day after Dinner Sir *Richard* departid out of *Dublyn* to a Place called DALCAY, six miles from *Dublyn*, where his ships lay; and the Archbishop of *Dublyn*, Justice *Bermingham*, and the Recorder of *Dublyn*, with many othir nobles brought him thither; and that night he took his skip, and ther lay at Road all Night."*

1488. In this year Dalkey was included in one of "*the four obedient shires* of the Pale."

"From Merrion, inclusive, to the water of the Dodder, by the new ditch to Saggard, Rathcoole, Kilbell, Rathmore, and Ballymore, &c.; thence to the county of Kildare, into Ballycultan, Harristown, and Naas; and so thence to Clane, Kilboyne, and Kilcok, in such manner that the towns of Dalkey, Carrickbrenan, Newtown, Rochestown, Clonken, Smethistown, *Ballyboteer* (Booterstown), with Thorncastle and Bullock, were in Dublin shire."†

---

* The above language is in the style of the reigns of Henry VII., Henry VIII., and Queen Elizabeth, before the English tongue came to be refined. † Liber Niger.

30 Earl of Sussex Embarks his Army at Dalkey.

It appears that the Irish who dwelt within the Pale, and acknowledged English authority, were considered as subjects, and had to a certain extent the protection of English laws; but all the Irish outside the Pale were styled "Irish enemies," not being recognized as subjects; while the Anglo-Irish, or Irish of English descent, who resisted the Government, "were termed English rebels." Various penal laws against the native Irish were passed in the Parliaments of the Pale, particularly the Statute of Kilkenny (A.D. 1367), in the reign of Edward III., which prohibited, under the penalty of high treason, any intermarriage, fosterage, or similiar connexion between the families of English descent and the native Irish; and imprisonment, fines, and forfeiture of lands and goods were inflicted on such English as permitted the Irish to graze cattle on their lands. In the reigns of the Henrys and Edwards other penal laws were passed against the native Irish without the Pale, to compel them to change their names, and take English surnames.

1538. Walter Cowley landed at Dalkey, with treasure for the King's service in Ireland.

1558. The Earl of Sussex embarked a large detachment of his forces at the port of Dalkey, on the 13th of September, to oppose the Scottish invaders at the isle of Rathlin, where, after sustaining much loss at sea, he effected a landing, slew many of the Scots, took the island, and placed a colony and garrison upon it. He then passed over to Cantyre and the islands of Arran and Comber: he spread desolation over them. He was eventually driven by a storm into Carrickfergus. At the end of nine weeks the Earl of Sussex returned to Dalkey.*

* In a MS. in the Library of Trinity College, Dublin, it is related, "that in an expedition against M'Connell, by the Lord Deputy Sussex, in 1557, he was attended by John Usher, captain, and Patrick Bulkely, petty captain, with sixty of the city trained

Grana Uile Arrives in the Bay.

1575. The celebrated Grana Uile's vessel arrived in the roads of Dalkey, after an interview with Queen Elizabeth, at a time when Dublin was wasted by a remarkable plague, thousands of the citizens having taken refuge in this "health-abiding" place. She afterwards landed in a small creek in Howth.*

bands; and, upon their return to Dublin, THE SIX WORTHIES was played by the city, and the mayor gave the public a goodly entertainment upon the occasion, fonnd four trumpeter's horses for the solemnity, and gave them twenty shillings in money."

"I will now proceed to that period in which Irish history first introduces the dramatic muse, mingling the waters of Jordan and Helicon.

"That the Irish clergy, as well as their brethren in England, occasionally exhibited mysteries and moralities previous to the reign of Henry VIII., may be safely inferred from the following record preserved amongst the MSS. of Robert Ware:—

"Thomas FitzGerald, Earl of Kildare, and Lord Lieutenant of Ireland, in the year 1528, was invited to a new play every day in Christmas, Arland Usher being then mayor, and Francis Herbert and John Squire, bailiffs; wherein the tailors acted the part of Adam and Eve; the shoemakers represented the story of Crispin and Crispianus; the vintners acted Bacchus and his story; the carpenters that of Joseph and Mary; Vulcan and what was related to him was acted by the smiths; and the comedy of Ceres, the goddess of corn, by the bakers. Their stage was erected on Hoggin-green (now called College-green), and on it the priors of St. John of Jerusalem, of the Blessed Trinity, and of All-Hallows, caused two plays to be acted; the one representing the Passion of our Saviour, and the other the several deaths which the Apostles suffered. From this record (which is the first express mention that has occurred to me of the representations of mysteries and moralities in Ireland), it should seem that it was customary with the chief magistrates of Dublin to invite the Lord Lieutenant to a new play every day in Christmas; and therefore, as I have already observed, it may inferred, that dramatic entertainments were exhibited in Ireland before this period. I have been informed that it was also formerly customary with the several corporations in Dublin, to invite the Chief Governor to a play at St. George's Chapel, on the anniversaries of their patron saints."—"An Historical Essay on the Irish Stage," by Joseph C. Walker, M.R.I.A. 1793.

* Grace O'Mally was the daughter of Owen O'Mally, and widow of O'Flaherty, two Irish chiefs in the county Mayo. Her castle, Carrick-a-Uile, was a strong square tower, fifty feet in height, divided into four stories, in each of which were loopholes for musketry. Lord Deputy Sidney wrote to the Council in London, in 1576, that Grace O'Mally "was powerful in galleys and sea-

32 Grana Uile—Bardic and Political Songs.

1602. "In consideration of a certain sum of money, paid at the King's instance, to a certain old and well-deserving servant in Ireland," John Wakeman had a grant of the possessions of the Monastery

men." Her fame attracted many desperate and hardy mariners from distant parts. Her larger vessels were in Clare Island, where she had a strong castle, and her smaller craft she kept at *Carrick-a-Owly*. Her piracies became so notorious, and her power so dangerous, that she was proclaimed, and £500 offered as a reward for apprehending her. This she disregarded for some time. She afterwards had an interview with Queen Elizabeth, and made her peace with her. On her return to Ireland, her vessel lay for some time in the roads of Dalkey Port. She afterwards landed in a little creek in Howth. She walked up to the castle, and found the gates shut (the family being at dinner). She soon discovered that the heir to the title was nursing not far off. She carried him on board ship, and immediately set sail, and arrived safe at Carrick-a-Owly; nor did she return him until paid a large ransom as a punishment for Lord Howth's inhospitality. For many years afterwards, whenever the St. Lawrence family went to dinner, the gates and doors were thrown open. This celebrated woman (Grana Uile) had been a prime topic of bardic song for many years, particularly during the last century. In 1753, during the political contests of the Duke of Dorset's administration in Ireland, the following popular song was written and sung throughout the country to an old and favourite air :—

GRANUWEAL.
"*An Old Song.*"

I.

A courtier, call'd Dorset, from Parkgate did sail,
In her Majesty's yacht, for to court Granuweal ;
With great entertainment he thought to prevail,
And rifle the charms of Granuweal.

CHORUS.

Sing Bulderoo, Didderoo, Granuweal,
The fox in the trap we have caught by the tail ;
Come fill up your bowls, and to drink never fail,
Sing success to the sons of brave Granuweal.

II.

Says the courtier to Granu, if you will be true,
I will bring you to London, and do for you too ;
Where you shall have pleasure that never will fail—
I'll laurel your shamrock, sweet Granuweal.

Chorus.

of the Blessed Virgin Mary, in Clondalkin, Dalkey, Howth, and Clonsillagh.

1649. The sea about Dalkey and the whole bay of Dublin was filled with the Parliament ships.

On the 14th of August 1649, Oliver Cromwell, who had contrived, by his intrigues, to be chosen Lord Lieutenant of Ireland, by an unanimous vote of

III.

Says Granu to Dorset, if that I would do,
Bring my fortune to London, my children would rue;
We would be like Highlanders eating of keal,
And cursing the union, says Granuweal.
Chorus.

IV.

Says Granu, I always was true to my King;
When in war, I supply'd him in money and men.
Our love to King George, with our blood we did seal,
At *Dettingen* battle, says Granuweal.
Chorus.

V.

Says Granu, I always still lov'd to be free;
No foe shall invade me in my liberty.
While I've Limerick, Derry, and the fort of Kinsale,
I'll love and not marry, says Granuweal.
Chorus.

VI.

Says Granu, you see there's a large stone put in
To the heart of the Church, by the leave of the King,
The works of this stone shall be weigh'd in a scale,
With balance of justice, says Granuweal.
Chorus.

VII.

I hope our brave Hartington, likewise Kildare,
Our trade and our commerce once more will repair,
Our lives we will venture with greatest assail,
Against French and Spaniard, says Granuweal.
Chorus.

VIII.

Now, my dear boys, we've got shut of these bugs,
I charge you, my children, lie close in your rugs;
They'll hide like a snake, but will bite I'll be bail,
I'll give them *Shillelagh*, says Granuweal.
Chorus—Sing Bulderoo, &c.

Parliament, landed at Ringsend, with 8,000 foot, 4,000 horse, an immense train of artillery, and other necessaries of war. Sir Jonah Barrington, in referring to his career of bloodshed, confiscation, and persecution, in this country, and the death of Charles the First, writes :—

"The English rebels subdued him [Charles], the Scots betrayed him, conjointly they beheaded him, but Ireland upheld him. She combatted his murderers ; and, as the reward of loyalty, she met the fate of rebels. The wrecks of Cromwell's desolation still appear scattered over every part of Ireland. Blood that escaped the massacres of Elizabeth, was only reserved to flow under the sword of usurpation ; and Cromwell has the credit of having done his business more effectually than any of his predecessors. He cooped up the surviving Irish in a contracted district, confined the clergy nearly to one county, confiscated two-thirds of Irish territory, and stained his sanguinary career by indiscriminate massacres in every fortress that resisted him.*

* The great mind of this successful usurper was perpetually intent on spreading the renown of his country ; and while he struck mankind with astonishment at his extraordinary fortunes, he seemed to ennoble, instead of debasing, the people whom he had enslaved. It was his boast that he would render the name of an Englishman as much dreaded and revered as that of a Roman was. It must also be acknowledged that in his civil and domestic administration he displayed as much regard to justice and clemency as his usurped authority, founded on no law, and depending only on the sword, could possibly admit. The seats of judicature were filled with men of integrity ; the decrees of the judges, amid all the virulence of faction, were upright and impartial, and to every man but to himself, the law was the great rule of conduct. And, what is more extraordinary, considering his birth, and the obscurity of his early life, his personal deportment corresponded with his elevation, and was not unworthy the greatest monarch. He maintained dignity without affectation, and supported before strangers the high idea which his great exploits and prodigious fortune had impressed them with. He was generous, without profusion, to those who served him ; and he knew how to find out, and engage in his interests, every man possessed of those talents which any particular employment demanded. His generals, his

"Never was any rebel so triumphant as he was in
Ireland; yet it is impossible to deny that perhaps a
less decisive or less cruel general than that splendid
usurper, might, by lenity, have increased the misery
in prolonging the warfare, and have lengthened out
the sanguinary scenes of an unavailing resistance.
But it is remarkable that Charles, the graceless son
of the decapitated monarch, on his restoration, confirmed under his seal the confiscation against the
Irish *royalists*, and actually *re-granted* their estates
and territories to the heirs and descendants of his
father's murderers."*

1725. A survey of 1725 states that Dalkey proper
consisted of 289 acres, 3 roods, and 22 perches, out of
which total, a Mr. Bull was then proprietor of 67a.
3r. 26p.; the Dean and Chapter of Christ Church,
Dublin, 7a. 0r. 31p.; Lord Newhaven, 28a. 0r. 4p.;
glebe, 14a. 1r. 14p.; the See of Dublin, 49a. 0r. 31p.;
while the "commons of Dalkey" comprised 123a.
0r. 36p.

1726. When Dean Swift returned to Ireland, 1726,
the ship in which he sailed anchored close to Dalkey
Island. As soon as it was known, several heads of the
different corporations and principal citizens of Dublin
went out to meet him in vessels and wherries,
adorned with flags of all colours and emblematical
devices. He was received with loud cheers and all
the honours which the celebrated " Drapier's Letters"
had so justly earned for him. In the evening he
was conducted through the city to his residence,
where joy-bells and bonfires "manifested the universal
gratitude of the people."

admirals, his judges, his ambassadors, were persons who contributed, all of them in their several spheres, to the security of
the Protector, and to the honour and interest of the nation. In
religion only he continued to act with the same hypocrisy to
which he owed his elevation. With the pretended saints he laid
aside the state of a sovereign; with them he sighed, he wept, he
canted, he prayed.

* Barrington's "Rise and Fall of the Irish Nation."

Ancient Survey of Dalkey,

According to a survey of Dalkey which took place in 1763, the entire parish consisted of 275a. 3r. 31p., the owners in fee at that time being:

	A.	R.	P.
Mr. Bull,	67	3	36
See of Dublin and } Glebe of Dublin, }	49	0	3
Sir William Mayne,	28	2	5
Mr. Baldwin, under } Christ Church, }	7	0	31
Commons of Dalkey,	123	0	36
Total,	275	3	31

The largest holders and residents under these gentlemen were, Messrs. Watson, Wilson, Archibold, and Sheppard. The old castles then standing were:

1. The "Goats' Castle" and garden, recently purchased by the Dalkey Commissioners for a town hall, which they purpose restoring without alteration of external appearance; 4a. 3r. 14p., Sir William Mayne owner. This includes Parkmore, on which the houses on the east side of Ulverton Road stand, held now by lease by William Porter, Esq.
2. The "House Castle" and garden, afterwards the property of Sir John Hasler, was situated at the rere of Mr. Edward Harrison, T.C.'s establishment; 2a. 7r. 0p.
3. The "Black Castle," which Sir John Hasler repaired, and in which he afterwards erected a billiard table. It was situated at the rere of Mr. P. Kavanagh's house, Castle-street, 1a. 2r. 12p.
4. "Wolverton's Castle" and garden, opposite Mr. J. I. Connolly's house; 5a. 2r. 35p. It

was on Mr. Bull's property, but in possession of a Mr. Archibold. This castle was taken down by the late Mr. Porter.*
5. " Dungan's Castle " and meadow, opposite Kent Terrace, 3a. 1r. 21p.
6. " Archibold's Castle," garden, and house, facing Tudor House, the residence of Dr. Parkinson.
7. " Old Dalkey House" stood on the avenue leading to Tudor House, and its extensive out-offices on the ground now occupied by the chapel. It belonged to a Mr. James Devitte. This house, according to an article in the *Gentleman's Magazine* before referred to, was the largest house in Dalkey. The late Mr. Conolly took it down, and built the present Bay View House with the materials.
8. " Howth View House" and garden, the present "Dalkey House," the property of Mr. Hugh O'Rourke, T.C., adjoining the ruined church; 1r. 12p.
9. "Farransheball" belonged to Mr. Wilson; 5a. 2r. 0p. It adjoined the present Dalkey Lodge, which was then (1763) occupied by a Captain Maunsel.
10. The sign of the ship " Mark Allen," an hostelry, on the site of which Mr. Lambe's house is built. At the rere of this hostelry stood a large cotton factory, afterwards burned, a portion of the walls of which are still standing. It was erected by Mr. Watson of Bullock Castle. Sir John Hasler used a part of it for a conservatory.

* The Bull property is now held in fee by the Vavasour family, and that of the Mayus has now passed into the possession of the Earls of Carysfort.

11. The opposite side of Castle-street, Dalkey, consisted chiefly of glebe land.
12. The commons commenced at Mr. D. Beggs, T.C.'s, extensive establishment.

DUBLIN BAY.

Dublin Bay at sunrise, and the graceful Killiney Bay at sunset, are Claudes, treasured in the cabinet of the memory, which neither accident can injure, nor beggary deprive one of.

Nature has done much for this far-famed "Beautiful Bay." She has disposed of some of the numerous objects of her creation in the most picturesque and artistic style, in decorating its gently sweeping and undulating shores. Edwin Hayes, R.A., the greatest *marine* painter that Ireland. has ever produced, whose numerous art productions, sketched in calm, sunshine, and storm, in the Bay of Dublin, have been highly prized by the Royal Academy of London, believes that, for the artist and lover of nature, it possesses more real and *ideal* beauty, caused by the happy grouping of its charming accessories, than any other bay he ever sketched, either on the coasts of England, Scotland, France, Spain, or Holland. To him, in the days of his youth, it was a never-failing source of interest and beauty. Creswick, another marine painter, of European reputation, said that Dublin Bay, in an autumnal sunrise, was one of the finest prospects of nature that he had ever seen. For miles round the Bay of Dublin we have grand succession of scenic effects, abounding in bold and striking contrasts—in picturesque foregrounds for the painter, and in dazzling bird's-eye views for the lover of nature.*

Nature, then, has been most lavish in dispensing her various charms on this horse-shoe enclosure of the Irish sea—

" All *nature* is but *art*, unknown to thee,
All *chance*, direction which thou canst not see,
All *discord*, harmony not understood,
All *partial evil*, universal good,"—POPE.

The amphitheatre of mountains which extends from Bray Head in the south, and terminates in the Dublin chain, where " Young Harry, with his beaver on," was knighted by the unfortunate Richard II., presents a strange contrast with the well-wooded, historic, and pastoral shores of Fingal, Clontarf (the Marathon of Ireland), and Sutton, on the north-east; while the caves of *Ben-Edair* (the Hill of Howth), in which it is known that seals have taken refuge in storms;† the " Needles," rearing their craggy heads most majestically above the waves ; the Bailey light, with its associations of sadness, in the north, present a *coup d'œil* of surpassing beauty; while the white-robed Poolbeg light (the Eddystone of Dublin Bay), which

---

* Kendrick's celebrated picture, "The Departure of her Majesty Queen Victoria and her attendant fleet from Dublin Bay in 1849," is engraved and published by Cranfield, Dublin.

Another artist, of whom Ireland may feel justly proud, J. Marquess, R.H.A., has produced some *first-class* pictures in connexion with Dublin Bay and Ireland's Eye. His recent work, "The Home of the Sea Gull," has been much admired.

† "On Friday and Saturday some of the Clontarf fishermen went in pursuit of seals to Howth. They swam into the caves with lights, where the dams bring forth their young. After a severe conflict, wherein the men were much torn, they were so fortunate as to take three large ones, and would have got four cubs, but were so fatigued and assaulted by a number of large seals, that they were obliged to make a precipitate retreat. The monsters are so extraordinary a sight, that numbers of people have resorted to examine them at Clontarf, where they are, near the wharf."— *Anthologia Hibernica*, Oct. 4th, 1793.

is approached by a wall 17,754 feet long, running through the sea, warns mariners of the dangers of the North and South Bulls or banks on either side of it.

> "Oh, Bay of Dublin ! my heart you're troublin',
> Your beauty haunts me like a fever dream
> Like frozen fountains that the sun sets bubbling,
> My heart's blood warms when I hear your name."
> — *Lady Dufferin.*

Dublin Bay, in a storm blowing from the north-east, is an extremely sublime sight. The expanse of water, which but yesterday seemed stretched in boundless repose, is to-day agitated by white-crested waves, and clouds of foam thundering on its rocky shore.

BEAUTIFUL BAY.

> "Bright is thy placid sea,
> Beautiful Bay;
> Dear is thy shore to me,
> Beautiful Bay;
> Cheek may be furrow'd deep,
> Hair may be grey,
> But I'll forget thee not,
> Beautiful Bay.
>
> "List to the merry group
> Spread o'er thy strand;
> Mark, too, the infant troop
> Spade in each hand:
> See how they delve and pant,
> Toiling away:*
> Are life's richer ones,
> Beautiful Bay?
>
> "Note how that urchin there,
> Tracing his plan,
> Builds up a mansion fair,
> Mimicking man;
> Sudden thy faithless shore,
> Sinking in spray,
> Leaves not a trace of it,
> Beautiful Bay.

* Children making a sandhouse on Killiney strand, and having it swept away by the next tide.

" So find our loves a grave,
           So sinks our joy ;
  Fate's but thy ocean wave,
            Man but thy boy.
  Hoping, we see our hopes
             Swept still away ;
  Emblem of life art thou,
             Beautiful Bay."*

HISTORICAL ASSOCIATIONS.

Hasculph, the Danish governor of Dublin, who had been vanquished by Strongbow and M'Murough, arrived in the Bay of Dublin in 1171. He had sixty ships in his fleet. Dr. Hanmer says that "they were mighty men-of-war, and well appointed after the Danish manner." The expedition was unsuccessful. Hasculph was defeated, and afterwards executed.

The celebrated Grace O'Mally (Granu Uile), arrived in the Bay of Dublin, in 1575, the year of the plague, after her interview with Queen Elizabeth, accompanied by some of her best ships.

The Earl of Sussex sailed from the Bay of Dublin in 1558, with a large force, to oppose the Scottish invaders at the Isle of Rathlin.

The Earl of Essex arrived in the Bay of Dublin, 1599, with 20,000 foot and 5,000 horse, sent by Queen Elizabeth to oppose Hugh O'Neil, Earl of Tyrone, in Ulster.

In 1644, the whole of the sea in the Bay of Dublin was filled by the "Parliament ships."

* This song is published by Addison, Hollier, and Lucas, Regent-street, London.

Oliver Cromwell, as Lord Lieutenant of Ireland, arrived in the Bay of Dublin during a storm in 1649, with an army of 8,000 foot, 4,000 horse, and a formidable train of artillery, and all other necessaries of war.

A remarkable scene took place in the Bay of Dublin in 1726, on the return of Dean Swift to Ireland. He was received with the greatest honours the citizens' of Dublin could bestow on him, his "Drapier's Letters" having raised him to the acme of popularity. The various corporations of the country, accompanied by thousands of the principal citizens, went out in boats and wherries to meet him, and escorted him in triumph to his residence.

When her gracious Majesty Queen Victoria visited Ireland, August 5th, 1849, the royal squadron, consisting of ten war steamers, lay in Dublin Bay. They were brilliantly illuminated in the evening. This sight was one of unsurpassed grandeur.

THE BAY OF DUBLIN.

My native Bay, for many a year
I've loved thee with a trembling fear,
Lest thou, though dear and very dear,
 And beauteous as a vision,
Shouldst have some rival far away—
Some matchless wonder of a bay,
Whose sparkling waters ever play
 'Neath azure skies elysian.

'Tis Love, methought, blind Love that pours
The rippling magic round these shores,
For whatsoever Love adores
 Becomes what love desireth ;
'Tis ignorance of aught beside
That throws enchantment o'er the tide,
And makes my heart respond with pride
 To what mine eye admireth.

And thus, unto our mutual loss,
Whene'er I paced the sloping moss
Of green Killiney, or across
 The intervening waters ;
Up Howth's brown sides my feet would wend,
To see thy sinuous bosom bend,
Or view thine outstretch'd arms extend
 To clasp thine islet daughters.

Then would this spectre of my fear
Beside me stand—how calm and clear
Slept, underneath, the green waves near
 The tide-worn rocks' recesses ;
Or when they woke, and leapt from land,
Like startled sea-nymphs, hand in hand,
Seeking a southern silver strand
 With floating emerald tresses.

It lay o'er all, a moral mist,
Even on the hills, when evening kissed
The granite peaks to amethyst,
 I felt its fatal shadow ;
It darkened o'er the brightest rills,
It lowered upon the sunniest hills,
And hid the wingéd song that fills
 The moorland and the meadow.

But now that I have been to view,
All even Nature's self can do,
And from Gaeta's arch of blue,
 Borne many a fond memento ;
And from each fair and famous scene,
Where Beauty is, and Power hath been,
Along the golden shores between
 Misenum and Sorrento ;

I can look proudly in thy face,
Fair daughter of a hardier race,
And feel thy winning, well-known grace,
 Without my old misgiving ;
And as I kneel upon thy strand,
And kiss thy once unvalued hand,
Proclaim earth holds no lovelier land,
 Where life is worth the living.*

* From " Underglimpses and other Poems," by Denis Florence M'Carthy, with the permission of the author, Ireland's greatest living poet, whose verses flow on like a shining river.

SECTION II.

DALKEY—THE PURITY AND SALUBRITY OF ITS ATMOSPHERE—OPEN AIR FETES.

The purity of the Dalkey air has, from the most remote times, been esteemed by the citizens of Dublin. When this city was visited and wasted by a most remarkable plague in 1575, the terrified inhabitants, with one accord, rushed to Dalkey as to a sanctuary, a sure refuge against the awful visitation. An immense camp was formed on the hills, on the shore, on the common, and also on Dalkey Island. On this occasion the grass grew in the streets of the deserted city.

In the years 1704, 1705, and 1706, a virulent plague raged within the city, and again the citizens repaired to Dalkey, which preserved its ancient reputation undiminished.

The canvas tents extended in every direction, music and amusement was the order of the day, and the fearful idea of the prevailing distemper was effectually dispelled.*

* For years Dalkey has been the favourite summer resort of all the leading medical men of Dublin, many of them having built handsome villas, foremost amongst whom stands Sir Dominic Corrigan, Bart., the eminent physician, author, and naturalist, who has expended thousands in the formation of a small boat harbour and fish ponds at his charming residence, Inniscorrig. Surgeon Tuffnell has also done much for Sorrento, by the improvement he has of late effected at his house in that portion of Dalkey. It is also worthy of note, that not a single case of cholera occurred during the last visitation, save and except one, and that was a young man improperly sent in the last stage, it may be said, by his friends, out of Kingstown to die in Dalkey. Many people have lived to a great age in Dalkey. Dr. Parkinson had a few years ago under his charge three persons whose united ages amounted to 320 years. One was a superannuated pilot, named Pat, aged 105; he used to walk, up to a few weeks of his death, from Bullock to Dalkey every morning, to attend his devotions. The second was also an old pilot, well known as Red Bill; he was over 100 when he died.

Modern Dalkey.

And now, at this day, what is the proud position of Dalkey ? Let the value of land for building purposes attest. The "common" covered with magnificent villas and stately mansions; the rocks themselves bear witness to the march of improvement and the advancing tide of civilization, supporting the noble and numerous structures wherein reside the wealthy citizens of our metropolis seeking health and relaxation in the pure air, amid the romantic and unrivalled scenery of the surrounding country.

Nor was it in the fatal and disastrous event of pestilence alone that the citizens of Dublin availed themselves of this healthy and invigorating retreat. In the happy and merry days of the "good old times," the rocks and dells of Dalkey common were, on festivals, and even ordinary week-days, crowded with numerous pic-nics and sod parties. The fashionable world of Dublin assembled there, and had their rural *fetes* (al fresco) on a magnificent scale.*

The last, and perhaps the grandest, of these great

The third was a woman called "Mud Macklin;" she lived on Dalkey Hill, supported in her old age by an attached and grateful servant, who had served her mistress in better days. Mrs. Macklin reached the age of 114 before she died, and often told Dr. Parkinson strange stories of 1782, when she entertained a large party of the Volunteers at her house, before they marched into Dublin.

* The Knight of Innishowen, writing of Modern Dalkey in "*the season*," says—" There was music, too, in all directions, music afloat—fiddles, and flutes, and cornopeans, and the voices of the merry boys and girls, rivalling each other in snatches, not from Tommy Moore, who is laid on the shelf, but from the Christy Minstrels, or the last opera; music on the heights, where the ancient piper was enthroned, "æriâ sub rupe," on a druidical dais of granite or gorse, in front of the coast-guard flagstaff, maintaining Ireland's pristine fame by giving, in his best style, the planxty that was played before Moses; music on the shore from Cliff Castle to Cullamore, and thence to Milo Burke's well, the Khyber Pass, and Sorrento—from every villa and cottage around, where the sea-bathing daughters of Eblana, coming hither with the swallows, and departing with the fall of the leaf, resort to play in the hygienic waters half the day, and on their Broadwoods half the night.

open air *fetes*, was given by the Alexanders and the Armitts, and by the late highly esteemed and popular Commander of the Forces in Ireland, Sir Edward Blakeney, then Lieutenant-Colonel of the 18th Royal Irish Fusileers (at that time quartered in Dublin).

On the morning of as beautiful a day in June as ever beamed, the inhabitants of the leading thoroughfares of the city, and those along the road sides from Dublin to Dunleary, were surprised at the unusual crowds, continual and constant stream of open carriages of all kinds, conveying the youth and beauty of the aristocracy of the city to the chosen scene; and when the fine band of the Fusileers, in their magnificent full-dress uniforms of blue and gold, were seen to pass along on the same route, innumerable bodies of the middle classes of the city and eastern suburbs were hastily formed, and followed in their wake. At noon, not only the majority of the original and principal party were assembled in a beautiful and extensive green amphitheatre, surrounded by rocky and lofty cliffs, but these rocky eminences themselves were covered by a crowd of smaller parties,—tributary stars around the more splendid galaxy that occupied the centre of the brilliant scene.

Two splendid marquees had been erected, one for the accommodation of the ladies, the other for the dinner party; beautiful pleasure yachts, which conveyed a portion of the invited guests to the scene, lay at anchor in Dalkey Sound, and, with their white sails and coloured streamers, contributed their share of life and beauty to the attractive scene.

Imagine what a fair and bright spectacle was presented, when the groups of quadrille dancers, the beauty and gallantry of the city and its vicinity, commenced their graceful movements on the green sward, to the exquisite music of one of the finest of military bands. What a delight to the happy multitude of spectators who beheld and admired the grace and tempered gaiety of high life!

The pencil of that accomplished painter, Watteau, in his finest pictures of the *fetes champetre* of the French, never pourtrayed a scene so exquisitely beautiful and romantic.

Ere the sun had gone down on this charming *tableau* many of the company (including some first-class amateur vocalists and performers) went aboard the gaily-dressed yachts lying at anchor in Dalkey Sound. The gentlemen sang with grand effect "Anacreontic Moore's" fine song—

"'Tis when the cup is smiling before us,
  And we pledge round to hearts that are true, boys, true,
That the sky of this life opens o'er us,
  And heaven gives a glimpse of its blue.
Talk of Adam in Eden reclining,
  We are better, far better off thus, boys, thus
For him but two bright eyes were shining,
  See what numbers are sparkling for us.

"When on one side the grape juice is dancing,
  And t'other a blue eye beams, boys, beams;
'Tis enough, 'twixt the wine and the glancing,
  To disturb e'en a saint from his dreams.
Tho' this life like a river is flowing,
  I care not how far it goes on, boys, on;
While the grape on the bank is still growing,
  And such eyes light the waves as they run."

And afterwards the entire company (ladies and gentlemen) sang the pure, the beautiful, and the unequalled

"Hark the vesper hymn is stealing,"

by Moore, his songs and sacred melodies then being fashionable in every class of society. Alas! superseded, in these days of *modern refinement*, by comic, serio-comic songs, and puerile love ditties!*

* If the majority of those productions which now convulse theatres, and find their way, with great applause, into drawing-rooms, were shown to us as the favourites of the people of two centuries back, we should be astonished to think how, even unenlightened as they were, they could have tolerated such unredeemed trash.

Oh! that such scenes of rational and healthful pleasure, of innocent enjoyment, in which the higher, the middle, and the poorer classes mingled together, gaily and merily, are no more; they belong to the memory of the past.

The mild temperature of the climate of Dalkey is shown by the arbutus, which loves a soft marine exposure, thriving here with astonishing luxuriance. In the garden of Mr. J. J. Wilson, Eastmount, Dalkey, are growing as fine arbutus trees as any in Killarney. Every gentleman in Dalkey should encourage its growth, which would form a relief to its numerous granite walls.

> "Beneath thy granite heights and towers,
> There the rich arbutus' coral berries glow."

SECTION III.

"A TOPOGRAPHICAL DESCRIPTION OF DALKEY AND THE ENVIRONS, IN A LETTER TO JOHN LODGE, ESQ., DEPUTY-KEEPER OF THE ROLLS."

[WRITEN UPWARDS OF ONE HUNDRED YEAR AGO.]

"*Dalkey Lodge, March 28th,* 1768.

"DEAR Sir,—Being alone and confined to the house on a day of incessant rain, by way of amusement, to attempt the following account of this romantic place, if it affords you the least entertainment, I shall consider my time well spent, and my labour well employed.

"Dalkey is a small town or village in the half-barony of Rathdown, county of Dublin, distant six miles and a half S.E. from the metropolis. It is numbered among the ancient manors belonging to the

Archbishopric of Dublin, was a place of considerable strength, but, at present, consists of the venerable remains of some old castles, the ruins of an ancient church, some good dwelling-houses, and about twenty cabins, for the most part occupied by poor labouring people, and serving indiscriminately for themselves, their cattle, and their swine.

"By the ruins, it appears the town was formerly defended by seven castles, and on the south by a moat or ditch, which is still open. The entrance to the west was through a gateway, secured by two castles, of which few or no traces remain. From various circumstances, I am inclined to believe that the east end was walled in, but it is now open on that side. The present road to the common leads directly through the town; but the old one ran on the south, across some grounds long since converted into meadow; but so tenacious are the inhabitants of the right of passing this way, that they usually carry their dead through the old road, although it is both an indirect and inconvenient passage to the church-yard. Upon these occasions, I am told, the meadow gates are thrown open, or, in case of obstruction, levelled with the ground. In my recollection, the street was so much incumbered with rocks, that it was absolutely impassable for carriages, and even a single horse must step from rock to rock, in continual danger of falling; but these obstructions have been in part removed by cutting a carriage-way through the rocks, and smoothing the surface of the ground between them. One of the castles has been repaired, and, by means of some additional buildings, converted into a commodious habitation. A second has been roofed, and affords room for a good billiard table. A third and fourth are inhabited by publicans; indeed, the most antique and complete of the whole is occupied as a stable. A sixth, or rather the small remains of it, may be found in the walls of an old cabin. And the seventh has been totally demolished a few years ago, merely for the sake of the stones. To illustrate this description, I have enclosed a sketch of one of the castles, from a view taken by my ingenious friend, Mr. Beranger, who, with great industry and correctness, hath drawn a curious collection of ruins, principally in the neighbourhood of Dublin, and means to have them engraven and made public, if suitable encouragement be not wanting. After diligent search and strict inquiry, no inscription can be found to show by whom or when these castles were erected. A few years since, I am credibly informed, that a piece of oak timber, with some characters thereon, was discovered in one of them; but as no one that saw it could decipher the meaning, I presume it was soon converted into fuel.

"I shall, therefore, forbear entering into a minute discussion of their antiquity, but barely mention the conjectures of others, and submit the rest to your better judgment. These castles, in the opinion of some, were built in the reign of Henry II., to favour the landing of the English, who might be safely and speedily transported hither from Wales, whence, it is certain, the first adventurers were embarked for Ireland. Others suppose they were erected by the Ostmen or Danes, who, about the ninth century, either built or fortified the city of Dublin, extended their conquests on this side as far as Bray and the Wicklow mountains, and, at length, like a deluge, overspread the kingdom.

"At these periods of time, it is supposed the harbour of Dublin was not navigable for ships of burden, who might lie in the Sound of Dalkey, land either men or merchandizes on the common, and send them to the castles (which, perhaps, were then made use of as storehouses), where they could remain in security from the depredations of the mountaineers until they were conveyed to Dublin, on the road to which are other castles built at proper distances, to insure their safety in the passage. What greatly strengthens this opinion is the remains of a very strong causeway, that runs across part of the common, and was evidently calculated to facilitate the carriage of goods between the coast and the town. Certain it is, however, that Dalkey has been a considerable landing-place between England and Ireland; and even some of our chief governors, from time to time, have landed here; particularly, Sir Edward Bellingham, in the reign of Edward VI.; Sir Anthony St. Leger, in the reign of Queen Mary; Sir John Perrot,* in the reign of Queen Elizabeth, and others.

"By an exemplification of some Acts of Parliament, passed in the 22nd year of Edward IV. (1482), and to be found in the *Black Book* of the Archbishop of Dublin, folio 242, it appears that, long before that time, the town of Dalkey could raise 200 men-in-arms; and seven fairs, besides weekly markets, were annually held here; and that the Bailiff had power to levy and receive, from all manner of wares and merchandize coming and resorting for sale to said fairs and markets, such customs as were levied by the Mayor and Bailiff of the customs of Dublin, to be employed in walling and paving the town.

"Besides these castles, the ruins of the old church are not unworthy of notice. The belfry is Gothic and picturesque, the inside arch dividing the church from the chancel well executed, the east window in the antique style, and the baptismal font still there. By some old church records, it is learned that a clergyman was once presented for the cure of souls in this parish (now united to Monkstown and Killiney) at the yearly stipend of five pounds; also, that, in

* The counties of Ulster were laid out by Sir John Perrot, A.D. 1584.

the year 1641, John Wilson was vicar of Dalkey and Killiney, and lost his life by means of the rebellion.

"At the east end of the town, adjoining the common, is a summer lodge, belonging to Robert Barry, Esq. This house, being partly ancient and partly modern, makes but an indifferent appearance in front, where, having little or no prospect, the owner, perhaps not injudiciously, hath closed up most of the windows on that side. In the rear, indeed, it hath a pleasing and romantic view open to the sea, and a garden laid out with skill and taste, planted with a variety of fruit-trees, flowering shrubs, and evergreens, and decorated with busts, statues, and other ornaments. This house is united to one of the old castles, and contains, besides lesser apartments, a spacious parlour and dining-room, with circular bow windows, that open into the garden. In a neighbouring castle, Mr. Barry hath erected the billiard-table, already noticed. Opposite the church, and near the centre of the town, is DALKEY HOUSE, of interesting associations, the occasional retreat of Crosdaile Malony, Esq., who hath lately improved it with some additional offices; but the house itself is so unluckily situated, that it looks directly into the churchyard—a termination which, however disagreeable it may be to some, it must be confessed, we cannot too often or too seriously contemplate. The garden is well-furnished with fruit-trees, &c.

"On the west side of the town stands DALKEY LODGE,* a neat house belonging to a citizen. This lodge is well-situated, and commands a variety of beautiful, extensive, and romantic prospects, particularly in front, to the north—the castle and surrounding rocks of Bullock; the bay of Dublin, with all the ships

* Dalkey Lodge is at present occupied by Mr. Thomas E. Henry, who evidently pays much attention to preserve the beauties of this venerable mansion.

in their passage to and from the harbour, the new lighthouse* and adjacent works, the Hill of Howth, skirted in summer with a mixture of delightful spots of corn and other grounds; the opposite coast of Fingal (Clontarf), enlivened with numberless white villas, and, at particular times, even the mountains of Mourne and Carlingford; in the rear, the Hill of Dalkey, Killiney, and Rochestown, terminated with an obelisk, and the house and noble improvements of Lord Viscount Loftus, with the intervening gardens, meadow, corn, and pasture fields, all together affording a charming contrast to the scene last mentioned ; and, from the east window, may be seen the ruins of Dalkey, with part of St. George's Channel and the vessels sailing along the coast. But however enchanting these several prospects may be, they are nothing comparable to the rising sun, which, viewed through the opening between the castles, beggars all description. To this house commodious offices are annexed, with flower-garden before and kitchen-garden behind, at the upper end of which a rustic hermitage is erected, and a small shrubbery planted in the modern taste. Add to this, that the whole garden is on a hanging level, from whence it derives great advantage in point of prospect and utility.

"Adjoining to the town, on the east side, is a large common, containing, by actual survey, 123 acres. Although this common is remarkably rocky, it, nevertheless, affords most excellent pasture for sheep. Some veins of lead ore have been discovered thereon, and assays made towards working the mines, but hitherto without success; and yet many circumstances induce me to think, that a rich vein of ore may, one

---

* This curious edifice (the Poolbeg lighthouse), was designed and executed by a Mr. John Smith, under the directions of the Ballast Office Committee. It is built in the midst of the sea, where the ingenious artist was obliged first to create a kind of rock, and then to erect a tower upon it, which tower has hitherto resisted the power of the contending elements.

day or other, be found. Here the poorer inhabitants of the town graze their cattle; and from the rocks several kinds of fish are killed, besides large quantities of better sorts, taken on the coast, which also abounds with crabs and superior lobsters. The neighbourhood affords some wild fowls, hares, rabbits, and foxes, and of late eagles have made their appearance in these parts. About a quarter of a mile distant from the common, the island of Dalkey, or, as it called in some old sea charts, the island of St. Benedict, presents itself to view; it contains, by estimation, twenty-one acres, and is esteemed a very good marsh for cattle. In the summer season it is grazed; and in the winter, frequented by plenty of duck, teal, widgeon, and other fowls. This island is destitute of inhabitants and buildings, excepting the remains of an old church, dedicated, I suppose, to the beforementioned St. Benedict. Here it may not be unentertaining to mention, the reveries of some speculative persons respecting this church and island. One supposes that the island was formerly united with the neighbouring coast, by an isthmus or neck of land, long since destroyed; a second, that it was the residence of some hermit, who caused the church to be built for the exercise of his private devotion; a third, that it was erected for the accommodation of the principal inhabitants of Dublin, who retired hither when the city was visited by an extraordinary plague or pestilence; and a fourth, that the clergy, by building this and other churches in places remote and difficult of access, thereby meant to inflame the devotion of their followers, and possibly to impose a penance, when they obliged them to frequent such obscure places of worship. Be that as it may, the island is now frequented only by parties who go out for fishing and pleasure, and sometimes land here for the purpose of dining and refreshment.

"Eastward of the island is a cluster of barren rocks,

well known by the name of the Muglins, among whose immense cavities large quantities of fish are taken. Here the two noted pirates, M'Kinley and Zeckerman, are hung in chains, for the horrid murder of Captain Glass, &c., the particulars of which are circumstantially and pathetically related in the *Gentleman's Magazine* for 1766.* On the summit of Dalkey Hill may be seen *Clogh-hobber—gilline-stone*—which, at a distance, has more the appearance of a small house or cabin than a rock. Notwithstanding the immense size and weight of this stone, it seems to have been raised from its former bed, and turned over on the contrary side, where it is supported by a few lesser ones. To what end or by what means it was placed in this elevated situation, is to me unknown; but it is not improbable that it was raised in the times of paganism, by way of altar to offer sacrifices to the unknown deity.

"About half a mile north of Dalkey, stands Bullock, or rather Bloyke—*i.e.*, the little bank—the former being only a corruption of its proper name; and very likely it is, that the two great banks in the bay of Dublin, well known by the name of the North and South Bulls, were so called from a like corruption of their real one. This is a small seaport, situated near the southern entrance of the bay, and capable of being made a safe harbour for larger vessels than at present frequent it. On the land side the town is enclosed with a stone wall, and defended by an old Gothic castle, which is kept in good repair, and one of the most perfect that I have seen.

"Near the gateway, and under shelter of the castle, is a comfortable dwelling-house, built and occupied by John Watson, Esq. This house stands so near the verge of the sea, that, when a strong N.E. wind sets in, the waves breaks over the adjacent rocks, and fall

* See Appendix.

down in the most awful and beautiful cascades that can be imagined; while the spray falls iu large quantities over the house. But what renders it still more remarkable, is the hospitality and politeness that reign within, and cause it to be frequented by all the well-bred gentry of the neighbourhood. A new quay, faced with hewn stone, hath been lately built for the convenience of conveying stones to the lighthouse works. The rest of the town consists of the very small remains of an old church, and a number of cabins, mostly inhabited by fishermen, who, in the season, supply the Dublin markets with cod, haddock, herrings, and other fish, as also with crabs and lobsters, which are taken on the coast, or brought from the Saltees. The whole town is held under the last-mentioned gentleman, who, upon all occasions, manifests an uncommon degree of benevolence and humanity, not only to his immediate tenants and neighbours, but also to such unfortunate strangers as, by adverse winds or storms, have been wrecked upon the coast.

"A little to the southward of Dalkey is a spacious house, belonging to the Right Honorable Henry, Lord Viscount Loftus, of Ely. This house is situated on the west side of Killiney, or, as it is now called, Loftus Hill, and, for prospect, cannot be surpassed, having in front the city, bay, and harbour of Dublin, with an immense number of villas and improvements along the coast, and an inland prospect equally rich. Although the house is large and roomy, yet, it must be confessed, the offices are mean and small, of which his lordship is so sensible, that he intends to build a new range, agreeable to a plan provided for that purpose. As for the gardens, they are inclosed with high stone walls, stocked with the best fruit-trees, and such a collection of flowers as must captivate the most insensible eye. Possessed of an unbounded passion for improvement, and a skill equal to that passion, this nobleman hath converted the most barren hills and rocks into good meadow and pasture fields, and laid them down remarkably neat and level, in the execution of which he hath been frequently obliged, first, to blast the rocks that spread themselves over the surface of the ground, and then draw mould to cover them. Besides this laborious, and, indeed, expensive undertaking, he has cut a carriage-road round the hill, and planted the west side with various kinds of trees and shrubbery. This road is walled in; and, viewed in passing it, resembles the Welsh mountains, especially on the sea side, where the pending rocks hang frightful overhead, and appear ready to tumble down on the trembling passenger. The obelisk, erected on the top of this hill, may be seen at many miles' distance, but hath little either in the design or execution to recommend it, being in both respects vastly inferior to that of Stillorgan; but, as a good landmark, and an ornament to the house and neighbourhood, I wish to see it repaired, and not suffered to fall to decay. By an inscription thereon, it appears to have been built in 1741, the year after the great frost, by John Mapas, Esq., with the benevolent intention of providing employment for the industrious poor. It is with peculiar satisfaction I learn that his lordship intends still further improvements, and, among others, to build an elegant banqueting-room somewhere about the back of the hill.

"At a distance of a little more than a mile southwest of Dalkey, stands Rochestown, the seat of John Mapas, Esq., grandson to the gentleman above-mentioned. From a slight view taken of this house in passing by, it appears to be large and well furnished with offices; but the situation rather too low and confined in prospect. The demesne, indeed, is enriched with beautiful plantations of timber trees, and even common ditches are well stocked with them. By judiciously cutting down part of the trees, he hath made some opening to the house, which, till then, must have wanted air as well as prospect. As for the surrounding parks, they are well enclosed, and in general highly improved; and some very rocky coarse grounds have been lately cleared and encompassed with stone walls. Here I saw grazing a large number of sheep, and round the neck of each was hung a bell, the tinkling of which produced a kind of rural music not at all unpleasing. New roads have been recently opened through this gentleman's estate, and various improvements made, whereby it hath risen considerably in value, to which its vicinity to the capital and to the sea not a little contributed.

"Before I conclude, it may not be improper to subjoin a few general observations on this part of the country, which, besides an agreeable diversity of hill, dale, meadow, pasture, and corn ground, hath something uncommonly wild and romantic along the coast, where it remains almost in a state of nature, partly covered with rocks, and partly with a common, but, to me, beautiful evergreen—I mean furze—the blossoms whereof have a richness and fragrance particularly pleasing to many persons as well as myself.

"The air, I find, is remarkably healthy, with this singular property, that in summer it is less warm, and in winter less cold, than will be found in more inland parts.

"Here frost seldom becomes intense, or snow remains on the ground forty-eight hours. The physical cause of this property, Dr. Smollett ascribes to the saline particles with which the atmosphere is impregnated, and which resist the operation of freezing; for a very great degree of cold is required to freeze salt water, nor will it freeze at all until it has deposited its salt. As for fresh water, the neighbourhood is amply supplied by means of excellent springs, which may be found in almost every field; but so careless are the inhabitants of this necessary element, that they seldom or ever clean their wells, much less cover them; and, therefore, rarely drink the waters in perfection.* The fuel chiefly consumed here is sea coal; this is imported from Whitehaven, and in the summer season may be purchased at Dunleary for fifteen shillings a ton.

"Goats-whey may be had in perfection from the adjacent hills, and convenient places for bathing in sea water are to be found on the coast, especially near Bullock, where boats at all times can be had for the accommodation of such as choose to re-create themselves on the water, or take the diversion of fishing.

"Having now finished the task I proposed, and, by this time, I believe, sufficiently tired you, I must, at least for the present, take leave, and assure you that I am,

"Dear Sir, &c.,

"*Dalkey Lodge*, 1768." "PETER WILSON."

"DALKEY HOUSE."

William Macartney, Esq., who was for many years representative of the borough of Belfast in the Irish Parliament, died at Dalkey House, in 1793. The wits of the day and many eminent scholars of Trinity College enjoyed his hospitality at Dalkey. The following is an extract of a poem, the

* There were at one time several famous wells in Dalkey. Amongst others, mentioned in early history, those of "St. Begnet" and our "Lady's Well," which has been enclosed and carefully preserved by Mr. Charles Leslie, owner of that beautiful marine residence, Corruic-na-Greina.

"Fount near the sea! thou art sought no more
By the pilgrim's foot, as in time of yore,
When he came from afar, his beads to tell,
And to chant his hymn at our Lady's Well."

"Prophecy of Hermes," which was first read at the festive board of William Macartney, and afterwards published in the *Anthologia Hibernica* :—

* * * * * * * *

"Genius, give o'er," he said, "thy murmurs cease,
I come to soothe thee with the voice of peace:
Hermes I am : I come from sceptred Jove,
Who heard thee from the starry realms above.
Though Rome is under fierce barbarians' sway,
Nor science, nor the arts, shall e'er decay ;
Two northern isles in future days shall rise,
Whose fame shall flourish to the fulgid skies—
Albion, which now is destitute of fame,
In future times shall aggrandize her name ;
O'er her, and o'er her beauteous sister-isle,
Thou sole shalt rule, with heart-delighted smile ;
Science shall there a settled empire raise,
And inborn merit, there acquire the bays :
Nor shall your Roman pupil's praise decay,
But flourish in true judgment's genial ray ;
Virgil, in Dryden's softened lines shall flow,
And, every beauty heighten'd, doubly glow ;
A second Homer shall in Pope appear—
Pope ! who so sweetly charms th' enraptur'd ear.
Hail, magic bard ! thy bright approach I see—
Hail, mighty Shakspeare ! critics, bend the knee ;
Yield, Terence, Plautus, all ye comic band,
For Shakspeare, King of Fancy, is at hand !
But see, in all the pride of epic lore,
Milton uprises from the rocky shore !
He rises, chief of the poetic choir,
Whom none dare emulate, but all admire :
He rises, monarch of the tuneful train,
And by his name ennobles Anglia's plain.
Hail, Anglia ! hail, thou blest poetic land !
Unrival'd and supreme, I see thee stand ;
In statesman, poets, and in warriors, great ;
Thou rul'st in poetry, in war, and state.

"And thou IERNE ! Saint-protected isle !
Shall bask in Learning's vivifying smile :
On thee the Muses shall their influence shed,
And crown with honour each deserving head.
Thine own sweet Goldsmith, gently-pensive bard
Shall claim the laurel as his just reward ;
The laurel and the never-fading bays—
An offering suited to his deathless lays :
As long as gratitude remains imprest
On every candid or congenial breast,
As long as memory can a thought retain,

So long shall live 'SWEET AUBURN'S GOLDEN PLAIN.'
Thou seat of classic lore, Eblana, hail !
Where modesty and science shall prevail ;
Where all the liberal arts their throne shall raise,
And candid judgment shall dispense the bays.
And thou, Eliza, Albion's potent Queen,
Of mind exalted, and of noble mien,
All hail!—To thee the liberal arts shall raise
A trophy, lasting as thy deathless praise ;
Thou, first, Ierne shalt with learning grace,
Nor aught thy pious efforts will efface :
In morals virtuous and in manners free,
Her sons shall, with affection, think on thee.
Hail, sacred walls ! hail, academic grove !
Where generous youth shall oft, relaxing, rove :
Shall rove—or, panting, wait the sage decree,
As fate impartial, and as candour free.
In judgment nice, in eloquence refin'd,
Thy sages shall improve, instruct the mind.
Thy youth, with emulative spark inspir'd,
And every breast with thrilling ardour fir'd,
A fair posterity shall quickly rise,
Virtuous, brave, ingenious, and wise.
There Genius ! there thy power shall be supreme,
Thou, their protector ! thou, their constant theme !
Ierne's youth with Romans then shall vie,
And merit soar above the vaulted sky :
Albion, conjoin'd with fair Ierne's Isle,
In learning, peace, and plenty, then shall smile."

DALKEY WAS ONE OF THE PORTS FROM WHICH ABSENTEES WERE FORBIDDEN TO TRAVEL WITHOUT OBTAINING A LICENSE FOR THAT PURPOSE.

ABSENTEEISM.

25 Henry VI., A.D. 1448.

Chap. I. An act that the king's officers may travel by sea from one place to another within the land of Ireland.

There are many ordinances in the reign of Edward III. which forbid the nobility and public ministers from leaving Ireland without obtaining licence for that purpose. "Hence," says our act, "there is doubt and diversity of opinion, whether if any ministers or officers of the king did pass by the coasts of the sea from the ports of Dyvelin (Dublin), Drogheda, Molagh-hide, or Dalkey, or elsewhere, to Weysford, Waterford, Cork, or other places, by the whole seacoast within the land of Ireland, that their offices were void, as if they had passed into England."

Chap. II. An act that the king's subjects or officers in Ireland may be absent by the commandment of the king, the governor, or the council, without seizure of their lands, rents, benefices, or offices, &c.

The absentees of Ireland have in every age been its greatest enemies. An ordinance of the 42 Edward III. states, that by their dereliction the country was spoiled: that, "pluseures seigneuries et terres illocques par noz ditz progcintours feurent donez et grantez a divers seigneurs et auters persones noz-foialt Dengleterre, qi tieur guerdons avoient par leur continuele demoeure fur leur dites seigneuries purreit sauvement estre defenduz a touz jours: et coment de longtemps out pris les issues et profitz sans defens on garde covenable y mettre sique par leur defaute et noun chaler sont les ditz mals avenuz en perdition de la dite terre," &c. This was A.D. 1368; let any one at this day (1790), examine the drainage from this isle by absentees, he will wonder that it is not "avenuz en perdition" to use the words of King Edward.

IRISH ABSENTEES, &c.
From the Anthologia Hibernica, 1793.

One serious ill, indeed, arrests my view—
Would it were lighter, would it were less true!
The richest nobles of Ierne's Isle
Leave their domains, where health and beauty smile—
Where a "bold peasantry" might sing their praise,
And wish them peace, and health, and length of days—
Where every prospect that enchants the sight,

Each heartfelt pleasure, and each true delight,
Might crown their wishes—where the splendid board,
And all that grandeur, all that wealth afford,
Attend their call—yet these, and more than these, they slight
For noon-day beds, and revelry at night—
They slight them, and at fashion's due command
Squander their riches in a foreign land.
Shame! when the storm-toss'd Swiss, and Highland boor,
Adore their countries, tho' despised, tho' poor,
Love their low huts—and think their native soil
The spot where heaven's most cheering blessings smile.

Alas! review the Irish peasant cot!
Want is his portion, misery his lot—
Nor these the worst; for whilst his thoughtless lord
Tastes all the pleasures foreign courts afford,
A rack-rent minion stints his stripe of ground,
And all the horrors of a gaol confound!—
So when the shepherd leaves his fleecy care,
To strive with tempests and inclement air,
The storm descends, the timorous victims fly,
The wolf appears—they bleat their last—and die!
But, is there none with patriot ardour fired,
Fraught with humanity, by love inspired?
Is there, who feels with all a parent's zeal
The labourer's grievance, and the poor man's weal?
Is there, whom even the lowliest never fear'd,
By all beloved, respected, and revered?
Is there, who proves by his exalted plan
The greatest noble, and the most generous man?—
Yes—one at least—one darling son remains
To grace Ierne, and protect her swains,
One who, with noble pride, and honest scorn,
Disdains to quit his fields of waving corn,
Disdains to roam abroad in exil'd pride,
And swell proud Fashion's overflowing tide—
The muse, exulting, boasts she can proclaim
A LEINSTER'S VIRTUES, and a LEINSTER'S NAME;*
Proudly she boasts—and may each noble son
Of fair Ierne the contagion shun,
Fashion's contagion gallantly withstand,
And dwell securely in his native land,
Cherish his peasantry, deserve their praise,
And pass in calm contentment all his days!
TRINITY COLLEGE,
August, 1793.

* Father to Ireland's present beloved Duke, whom Her Most Gracious Majesty the Queen and the late Prince Albert honoured with a visit at his princely residence, Carton, Maynooth, on the 10th August, 1848.

"And castles infinite have been erected long before the advent of the English, standing up like grey warders, and reproaching the devastating hand of Time, but now
"All tenantless, save to the crannying wind."

DALKEY—THE "PORT OF THE SEVEN CASTLES."

Their erection ascribed by some to the Saxons, by others to the Danes and soldiers of the " Pale."

Historians say that Dalkey was a fortified town, enclosed with walls, defended by seven castles. At no remote period a portion of the wall was still standing. The erection of the castles has been assigned by some historians to the Danes, to maintain their Irish acquisitions; others say they were built by the early English settlers for the security of the " Pale " against the incursions of the celebrated Irish septs, the O'Byrnes and O'Tooles. It has been alleged by others that these castles were built in the reign of Queen Elizabeth, for the purpose of protecting the troops employed in opposing the incursions of pirates, who then frequented the coast in great numbers.*

THOUGHTS WHILE PONDERING ON THE RUINS OF DALKEY CASTLES AND ABBEY.

 While sad I gazed, and drew the pensive sigh,
 The hoary sage, old TIME, came tottering by ;
 As though decrepid grown, he forward bent ;
 And him I questioned—*What* the monument?

* The origin of these castellated ruins is still a matter of great uncertainty.
"One of those castles, I may observe, *en passant*, is not in such a dilapidated state that it might not be restored and beautified, after the style carried out by the Marquis of Kildare at the old castle of Maynooth. The ruins of the old abbey and its poetic graveyard, would, with a few kind and judicious touches of restoration here and there, form an historic *enciente* or enclosure, where the pilgrims of the soul might enter for half an hour's good and wholesome contemplation, not the less to be indulged in from the material comforts which awaited them at that excellent hostelry, the Queen's Hotel, hard by."—*Temple Bar.*

The builder *whom ?*—for his insatiate rage
Had both o'erwhelm'd beneath the ruin of age—
Right stern he looked at me, nor answer made,
But in the yielding air his vigorous wings display'd !

To FAME I next applied—who walk'd before—
A shatter'd trumpet in her hand she bore—
'O thou th' inspirer art of all that lives !'—
I just began—and, lo ! her *bosom* heaves
With vast despair—her *eyes*, all swoll'n, confess
More pungent woe than words could e'er express. . .

Amaz'd and wond'ring much at what I'd seen,
Aside I turn'd, to muse what all might mean—
When, by the friendly gleam of twilight shown,
I saw OBLIVION step from stone to stone.
His ancient vest the twisting ivy bound,
And oblong chin the wild-moss crept around :
Jealous and sour his looks ; I could descry
Disdain and anger flash from either eye :
In beaten paths he trod, yet could not find
He left so much as one faint track behind—
"O thou," exclaimed I—"Yes, thou sure MUST know !—
Ah ! show me, reverend sire ! before you go "—
No more permitted me, and scarce I'd spoke,
Till from his chest these hollow murmurs broke—
"Small boots inquiry, or to thee or thine,
I care not what it was—IT NOW IS MINE.
TIME crumbles into dust, and feebly FAME descends ;
OBLIVION swallows all :—thus human grandeur ends." . .

The great probability is that the construction of the seven castles of Dalkey was anterior to the English or even the Danish invasion. The following very interesting letters, relative to the discovery of Saxon coins, in connexion with the ruined castle near the Queen's Hotel, were written by George Smith, Esq., Abbeylands, and E. Clibborn, Esq., the courteous and talented Secretary of the Royal Irish Academy. Both of these gentlemen were intimate friends of that great Irish antiquarian, musician, and archæologist, the late Dr. Petrie.

"*Royal Irish Academy, 30th June*, 1868.

"DEAR SIR,—In reply to your question, I have to say that I have a distinct recollection of a conversation I had with the late Dr. Petrie on the subject of the great number of Saxon coins found from time to time at and near Dalkey, and he tried to account for it on the supposition that Dalkey may have been a Saxon settlement or town, and a trading port of very considerable antiquity, though we have no distinct notice of its existence as such. There was one find of Saxon coins discovered in a building which resembled the pier of a gate, which, when partially pulled down, exhibited a cavity, in which many hundred coins were safely deposited; and as they were all Saxon, he inferred that the building itself must have been older than the Danish or English periods. Indeed, Dr. Petrie was disposed to consider some of the Dalkey castles to be as old as the coins; but whether he specified any one or more of them as Saxon, my memory will not enable me to say.

"His remarks on the castles of Dalkey grew out of the fact, that I was a pupil of his, and, as such, copied a picture of his of Dalkey castle, and had at the time some explanation as to the architectural details of that and the other buildings called the Dalkey castles. Hoping these crude remarks may be of some service to you in your inquiries, I am yours most truly,

"E. CLIBBORN.

"P.S.—I recollect a Mr. John Hilton having resided at Dalkey. He was an intelligent person, and he told me of the discovery of a vellum MS., which had been built up in the wall of the castle next or near his house. I never could get any information whether it was Saxon or Irish, or into whose hands it passed.

"J. J. Gaskin, Esq."

"*Abbeylands, Ballybrack, 29th June,* 1868.

"SIR,—I beg to acknowledge the receipt of your note of the 26th inst., relative to some Saxon coins found several years since at Dalkey. I regret I can give you but slight information relative to them. I recollect the coins were of Edgar, I think sixty-five in number, thirty-one of which were of different numbers. I gave them to my esteemed friend Dr. Petrie; what he did with them I know not.—Faithfully yours,

"GEORGE SMITH."

DALKEY CASTLES—SAXON COINS.

FROM THE IRISH TIMES.

"*Dublin, 22nd July,* 1868.

"SIR,—In reference to your letter in yesterday's *Irish Times*, I beg to mention that, about the year 1840, at the sale of the widow Petrie's executors in Dame-street, amongst many other articles of *vertu*, I purchased a small cabinet of Saxon coins (found at Dalkey), about two hundred in number, placed in holes, drilled for each in six or seven solid deal shelves. As I valued them very highly, I presented them to my late uncle, George Meyler, of Dundrum; and as they were not sold at the recent clearing out of family chattels by the executors of my late brother, Captain George Meyler, at Strahan and Brothers' (the celebrated auctioneers) sale in Leinster-street, perhaps Miss Anna Meyler, of Dundrum, can give some information about them. The widow Petrie alluded to was mother to the late Dr. Petrie. There were engraved plates accompanying the coins.—I remain, dear sir, faithfully yours,

"WALTER THOS. MEYLER."

The conclusion to be derived from the discovery is, that the castles of Dalkey are very ancient, and that there was considerable trade between the Saxons and Dalkey at the period of their construction, without at all supposing a settlement of the Saxons in Ireland, of the existence of which there is otherwise no evidence.

The assertion that the Danes built these castles is supported by several high authorities.

In the "Annals of the Four Masters," it is stated that "they possessed places of strength along the coast south of the Liffey, in the county of Dublin, with some parts of Wicklow."

Again, Crawford, in his "History of Ireland," p. 74, 1753, says: "The Danes built castles and strong places for the security of their power."

Warner, the Irish historian, also says: "The Danes, from being pirates, in the year 883, became masters of the country; and being animated with their great success, began to build castles and fortifications; and these, with the raths, are some of the oldest monuments of human industry that are now to be seen in Ireland."*

---

* "During the two centuries and a-half of tyranny and military despotism, in which the Danes and Norwegians were permitted to crush Ireland, the vicinity of Dublin suffered in a particular degree by their harassing incursions; and even when their general authority as a dominant nation was broken down at the memorable battle of Clontarf, this county was especially exposed to their predatory and revengeful assaults."—*Dalton.*

"Virkar, o'er the wintry ocean,
From Hyrinda wanders far;
To the hostile shore of Erin,
He has borne the storm of war."
  *   *   *   *
"I have seen the bird of carnage
Wing its way from Erin's land;
Gorged, it seeks its native region,
Blood has stained the hostile strand."
—*Scandinavian Poetry.*

Ledwich, another high authority, observes, in the *Anthologia Hibernica*, that " the Danes had several methods of fortifications, some of which were unknown to the more ancient inhabitants. They secured their towns by stone and earthen walls, and erected, in convenient places on the seashore, strong castles of lime and stone."

Another eminent writer says " that the wealth of the Wicklow and Dublin hills attracted the attention of the Danes."

When Chateaubriand visited the East, he suddenly came upon the supposed site of an ancient city. He exclaimed to his cicerone—a goatherd—" ' Where, then, is Sparta? Have I come so far without being able to discover it ? Must I return without beholding its ruins?' I was heartily vexed. As I was going down from the castle, the Greek exclaimed, ' Your lordship, perhaps, means Palæochori?' At the mention of this name, I recollected the passage of D'Anville, and cried out in my turn, ' Yes; Palæochori! the old city—where is that ? Where is Palæochori ?' ' Yonder, at Magdula,' said the cicerone, pointing to a white cottage with some trees about it, at a considerable distance in the valley. Tears came into my eyes when I fixed them on this miserable hut, erected on the forsaken site of one of the most renowned cities of the universe, now the only object that marks the spot where Sparta flourished, the solitary habitation of a goatherd, whose whole wealth consists in the grass that grows upon the graves of Agis and of Leonidas."

If the castles of Dalkey are really attributable to the era of "royal Danes," imagine a native of that kingdom, an enthusiastic antiquarian and archæologist, after eight or ten centuries had passed, visiting Dalkey—the great military station of his ancestors. No longer does the standard of the Raven float from its castles. He approaches these memorials of Denmark with glowing eye and kindling excitement. He questions an ebony-visaged personage, standing at its outer gate, if he may enter, when he is politely handed *this card*—

DENNY MORAN,
CHIMNEY SWEEPER
TO HIS EXCELLENCY THE LORD LIEUTENANT AND THE COMMANDER OF THE FORCES.
RESIDENCE, DALKEY CASTLE.
[Established 1840.]

INTERESTING DESCRIPTION BY WAKEMAN[*] OF DALKEY AND BULLOCK CASTLES.

"DEAR SIR,—The following remarks upon the age and character of the Dalkey and Bullock castles, as coming from one who has carefully drawn, measured, and critically examined those most interesting remains, may probably be acceptable to you at the present moment. You are quite at liberty to make any use you may think proper of my communication :—

" When no documentary evidence of the age of a structure can be obtained, it is generally possible, by a careful examination of the building, to determine the period to which the work should be assigned. In Ireland, our earliest structures, whether churches, towers, or castles, are almost invariably very plain in character; but there is scarcely an ancient edifice in the country in which some attempt

---

[*] Author of *The Archæologia Hibernica*.

at ornament—a moulding or sculptured corbel, for instance—does not occur. Now, from the eleventh century, down to the period of the Revolution of 1688, there was no century which did not possess a style of ornamentation more or less peculiar to itself. In the castles or tower houses of Dalkey, Bullock, Monkstown, Kilgobbin, Puck's Castle, and Shanganagh, all structures of the same, or nearly the same age, and exhibiting the same form of windows, mouldings, &c., we find in the arches and apertures a struggle between the semicircular and the earliest form of pointed arch head, for predominance. It is a fact well known to the architectural antiquary, that, towards the close of the twelfth century, the semicircular form of arch was very generally superseded by the first pointed or 'Gothic.' True it is, that the older form of arch is found in buildings of almost any age of the Christian period in Ireland; but it is equally true that the pointed arch head, formed of *curved* lines, does not, in one instance, occur as an original feature in any structure in Ireland older than the twelfth century.

"In the castles of Dalkey and Bullock, and more particularly in the latter, first pointed doorways, evidently original, are found side by side with others which have round or semicircular headings. This circumstance alone would indicate that the buildings cannot be older than about the middle of the twelfth century—a period to which the plain depressed moulding, which runs round the external angles of the small semicircular windows, would seem to point. The simple barrel-arch, which forms the vault at Bullock, Dalkey, and elsewhere, is also highly characteristic of the same age. A similar remark applies to the continuous row of pointed arches which projected from the interior of the wall of the upper chamber of the Dalkey castle, now destroyed, and of which my sketch, taken more than twenty years ago, is a faithful representation. But of all the architectural evidences of the age of the buildings under notice remaining, a warrior's head, which stands out from the south-western angle of the western tower of Bullock castle, at a considerable distance from the ground, is the most important. This head is represented as protected by a conical helmet, without vizor, but furnished with a *nasal* or straight bar, which defended the front of the face, and particularly covered the nose of the wearer. There are numerous sculptural and pictorial authorities for assigning this curious carving to a period not later than A.D. 1200. Taken by itself, it might possibly be considered older; but as the building to which it is an original appendage contains features, such as first pointed and other arches of the so-called 'Gothic' style, we cannot suppose that it can date much earlier than about the year 1160. One other little attempt at ornamentation worthy of notice, may be observed in the larger castle of Dalkey; it is the arrangement in chevron fashion (on a line with the base of the tower parapet) of the stones of the chimney. This has a most decidedly twelfth-century look.

"The larger remaining structure at Dalkey is a strong quadrangular tower, measuring internally 29 feet 3 inches, by 19 feet. The thickness of the walls, which rest upon a solid rock, varies from about 8 feet to 5 feet 6 inches. There were originally three stories, to which access was gained by a rude stone stair, passing diagonally along the internal side of the wall from floor to floor. The first floor, which was of wood, has disappeared; but provision for its supports remains. Off this is a little chamber, and passage which seems to have conducted to a *garderobe*. The second floor rests upon a strong barrel or semicircular arch of stone. The third floor is of wood, and contains a staircase leading to the parapet, which is now quite plain, though indications of the old battlements or 'corbie steps' may still be traced. The original entrance, now stopped up, was on the ground floor, facing the sea. It is pointed, and was defended by a bartazan or projecting turret, commonly called, now and of old, a *murthering-hole*, projecting from the top of the tower. The windows are small splayed openings with flat or semicircular heads. It is an interesting fact, that about sixty years ago this castle was, for one summer, the residence of the late lamented Dr. Petrie.

"The smaller remaining castle at Dalkey measures internally 22 feet 10 inches, by 13 feet. It was divided into two stories, of which the lower was timber, as the holes for rafters show. The second story forms a strong vault of stone. The wall of the tower which faces the road is seven feet in thickness, and contains straight flights of steps, which lead from floor to floor, and to the battlemented parapet, from which a number of steps ascend to a watch-tower; all the doorways and windows in this tower are either pointed, square-headed, or semicircular. The doorway is commanded by a *murthering-hole* of the kind usually found in towers of the twelfth century.

"Bullock castle is an oblong building, originally two stories high, with towers of unequal height, and rising above the body of the structure at either end. The seaward tower, upon the ground-floor, contains the original doorway and inner porch. From the right hand side of the latter feature rises a spiral stair, communicating to the upper apartments, and to a series of small rooms in the same tower, which appear to have been bedrooms. Beneath, or through the opposite tower, is a round-headed gateway, leading into the spacious courtyard or bawn of the castle. The upper portion of this tower was divided by floors into small closets, probably bedrooms. The apartments between the towers are large, measuring

23 feet 6 inches, by about 17 feet. The first and second stories were furnished each with an ample fireplace and spacious deeply-recessed windows, with round or rather semicircular-headed opes. The ground-floor is vaulted by a heavy barrel arch of stone. There is a *garderobe* to the first floor, and the whole of the upper walls are gracefully battlemented, in a style which is almost peculiar to Ireland. At an angle of the bawn or courtyard, may be seen a small watch-tower with similar finishings.

"Monkstown, Kilgobbin, Shanganagh, and Puck's castles scarcely come within the range of my observations, but I may say they display many features in common with the Dalkey structures. Monkstown and Puck's have suffered much from modern alterations, but enough of their original work remains to indicate their character. My sketch of the Dalkey castle, now destroyed, was made about 1841, at which time the vault was used as a forge. It stood nearly opposite Mr. Connolly's bakery, as many people still residing in Dalkey remember.

"Yours very truly,
"W. F. WAKEMAN."

FACTS AND FANCIES, BY THE KNIGHT OF INNISHOWEN, FROM "TEMPLE BAR" MAGAZINE.

Dalkey Castles—Ancient Temples—Wicklow Gold Mines—The O'Byrnes and O'Tooles—Linen, Woollen, and Tabinet Manufactures.

"I have been often thinking," said Lucius, "when looking into the merits of the speculation indulged in so sarcastically by Gibbon, but glanced at more earnestly by Hallam, and more ably developed by Creasy in one of the best of his 'Fifteen Decisive Battles of the World,' how it would have been with Dalkey and its Seven Castles, and its islands, as well as the Dublin Bay islands, and this part of our coast—indeed, with all Ireland herself—if the Saracens had won the battle of Tours, and overwhelmed France, Germany, and the entire north of Europe. They would have come to England, of course, and given as good an account of it as the Romans or the Normans, considering the poor sticks, with scarcely a bit of British oak amongst them, that supported the Heptarchy in those days. Then, in due course, they would have crossed St. George's Channel, and looked in upon us where the Norman-Welsh (not the Sassenach) invaders landed. Ireland was strong enough in monasteries and churches, the '*templa serena*' of the wisdom of the time, the highest type of the civilization of the middle ages, the *via conservatrix* of the sublime and the beautiful of the old world, and the pioneer of the intellectual wonders of the new."

"It was civilization worthy of the name," said the friar. "Those temples were indeed worthy of its worship, and in every respect appropriate to the noble line of the Roman poet to which you have so aptly alluded :

"'Edita doctrinâ sapientum templa serena.'

"'Those temples of learning, religion, and rest,
Were raised by the faith of the *Monks of the West.*'"

"Not a bad rendering, by-the-bye," observed the knight. "You ought to send it with the original Lucretian line to Archbishop Trench, who is a scholar and a gentleman. He would be sure to preach a sermon on it at St. Patrick's, on the anniversary of its magnificent restoration by Sir Benjamin Lee Guinness. Whether he would or not, however, his grace and all accurate and unprejudiced scholars are aware of the fact, and acknowledge it, that from the seventh century Ireland began to educate and send her missionaries to every part of Europe in furtherance of her great work of Christian civilization. She gave academic instruction and hospitality, moreover, to the poor wandering scholars of those days—the pilgrims after wisdom, who were attracted to her from every quarter of the known world. She had abundance of the precious metals worked into the ornaments and vessels of her religious worship, besides the gold bracelets and collars of the laity of both sexes; and the Wicklow gold-mines were then, if not in as full work as in the days of the Phœnicians, nor their shares at as high a premium as those of those modern Wicklow diggings, the *Connorree* copper mines, ! ! ! they did at least as good a stroke of business as the tin mines of Cornwall. The Danes, whose commercial enterprise equalled that of the Phœnicians, although they did not conduct their exchanges so regularly, and whose political economy was almost as hard-headed, and quite as hard hearted, as that of the Whigs, estimated the value of Ireland's resources, as we can easily understand, by the number of settlements which they formed around her coast; and amongst these the wealth of the Wicklow hills attracted their attention. The lords of the soil, however, those unfortunate O'Byrnes, O'Tooles, and Kavanaghs, who have been always giving trouble to their godfathers and godmothers, were just as uncivil to those highly enlightened and disinterested foreigners as they were afterwards to their Norman-Welsh visitors, although the former came under the auspices of the gods of Scandinavia, preaching the divine religion of the sword, and the latter under the openly proclaimed and sacred sanction of two consecutive popes of Rome. It has been ever and always the vernacular blot and misfortune to show the cold shoulder, and too often the red hand, to those who came over to us for our mental and material improvement, knowing what was for our good in either case much better than we knew it ourselves, and treating them like filibusters, instead of receiving them as apostles of progress."—*The Knight of Innishowen.*

"It is strange to say, that although the Danes and Ostmen held possession of Ireland for upwards of two centuries and a-half, it was never brought under the power of the Romans. Tacitus ('Vita Agricola') says:—'In his fifth voyage, taking his passage in the first ship, by many successful battles he vanquished nations till then unknown, and planted garrisons in that part of Britain which lay opposite to Ireland; and this he did rather from a motive of hope and fear, for Ireland being situated between Britain and Spain, and commodious also for the Gallick Sea, would unite the most powerful parts of the empire with a strong communication of interests. If it need be compared to Britain, it is less in compass, but larger than the islands in our seas. The soil and climate, nature and dispositions of the people, differ but little from those of Britain; but the ports and havens that give admission into it, are better known by means of a more extensive commerce, and a greater resort of merchants. Agricola had received several of the petty princes of that nation, who had been driven out of it by some domestic sedition, and under colour of friendship detained them with him till an opportunity should present. I have often heard him say that Ireland might be subdued and brought under by one legion and moderate succours, and that it would be a great advantage against Britain, which then would be surrounded by the Roman arms, and the prospect of liberty removed out of sight.' Thus far Tacitus, from whose words Camden draws this conclusion, that numbers of people from Spain, Gaul, and Britain, had retired into Ireland to withdraw their necks from the Roman yoke. I must observe, that in England, France, and other countries the Roman arms and inscriptions on marble, as so many miracles of antique workmanship, have been discovered, which were left there by the ancient Romans; but in Ireland none of these curiosities are to be seen, no, not so much as the Roman coin, unless such as has been brought into it from other parts, from whence one may conclude, with William of Nenburg, that Ireland has been inaccessible to the Roman arms, though they held the dominion of the Orcades."—Sir James Ware's "Antiquities of Ireland," p. 187.

" What tho' the Orcades have own'd our power ?
What tho' Juvernus tam'd, and Britain's shore,
That boasts the shortest night ?"—*Juvenal.*

THE COMMONS OF DALKEY—"THE KILRUDDERY HUNT."

The district formerly known as the " Commons of Dalkey," extended from the village to the eastern extremity of the Bay, the Sound and the rocky hill of Dalkey on its south. This, in particular, was a locality of singularly romantic beauty—a creation of nature in her most sportive mood, and wholly untouched, as it would appear, by the hands of man, until 1817, when Lord Wentworth, Viceroy of Ireland, laid the first stone of the pier at Dunleary; and then commenced a rude incursion on the natural and distinctive features of the landscape, by the government contractors, the Messrs. Henry, Mullen, and Mahon.

The " Commons of Dalkey" are mentioned in the following celebrated and favourite old song, called " *The Kilruddery Hunt*,"* now scarce attainable,

* The lands of Kilrothery, or Kilruddery, were formerly the property of the Abbey of St. Thomas, in "Thomas-court, Dublin," and granted to the Brabazon family on the 31st of March, 1545, together with other church lands. The first title. conferred upon this illustrious house was Barons of Ardee, 1616, to which the earldom of Meath was added, 16th April, 1627.

a copy of which was presented to George IV. by
the then Earl of Meath, which perpetuates the local
history of Kilruddery and its vicinity at the period
of its composition, 1744. It was written by a Rev. Mr.
Fleming,* of Adam and Eve Chapel, Dublin, formerly
an officer in the Austrian service. He was a relative
of the celebrated Roman Catholic preacher of that
name, who died (universally regretted) in 1793.
Before its publication, and only a few days subsequent to the event it commemorates, the song was
first sung at the house of one of the sportsmen, on
the Bachelor's-walk, Dublin.

THE KILRUDDERY HUNT.

A MOST REMARKABLY ADMIRED OLD SONG.

Songs commemorative of a good day's sport are common in
Ireland, and resemble the "Kilruddery Hunt" in enumerating the
sportsmen, the ground run over, and the finale; a jovial dinner,
with sometimes the description of a will made by the dying animal.
A specimen of one composed about the close of the seventeenth
century, although sadly messed by an ignorant transcriber, has
been preserved in the British Museum among the Sloane Manuscripts, No. 900 ; the "Fingallian Hunting of the Hare," where the
hospitality of St. Lawrence's Hall (Earl of Howth's) is commended,
and the sportsmanlike qualifications of Michael St. Lawrence and
his companions are duly set forth.†

> Hark ! hark ! jolly sportsmen, awhile to my tale,
> Which to pay your attention I'm sure cannot fail ;
> 'Tis of lads, and of horses, and dogs that ne'er tire,
> O'er stone walls and hedges, through dale, bog, and briar ;
> A pack of such hounds, and a set of such men,
> 'Tis a shrewd chance if ever you meet with again :
> Had Nimrod, the mightiest of hunters, been there,
> 'Fore God, he had shook like an aspen for fear.

---

* See Appendix.
† In this song, the dying hare is thus made to settle her worldly
affairs :

> "But in a fine mead, she being almost spent,
> She made her last will, aye, and testament.
> 'Cropt ear, with thee I will not stay ;
> Nor with true running Cutty, that show'd such fair play ;
> But to thee, brave Hector, I yield up my life,'—
> And so Hector bore her, and ended the strife."

Written in 1744.

In seventeen hundred and forty and four,
The fifth of December, I think 'twas no more,
At five in the morning by most of the clocks,
We rode from Kilruddery* in search of a fox.
The Loughlinstown landlord, the bold Owen Bray,†
And Squire Adair, sure, was with us that day,
Joe Debill, Hall Preston, that huntsman so stout,
Dick Holmes,‡ a few others, and so we set out.

We cast off our hounds for an hour or more,
When Wauton set up a most terrible roar ;
Hark to Wanton ! cried Joe, and the rest were not slack,
For Wanton's§ no trifler esteem'd in the pack.
Old Bonny and Collier came readily in,
And every hound join'd in the musical din ;
Had Diana been there she'd been pleas'd to the life,
And one of the lads got a goddess to wife.

Ten minutes past ten was the time of the day
When Reynard broke cover, and this was the way :
As strong from Killegar‖ as though he could fear none,
Away he brush'd round by the house of Kilternan ;¶
To Carrickmines** thence, and to Cherriwood,†† then
Steep Shankhill‡‡ he climb'd, and to Ballyman Glen,§§
Bray common he cross'd, leap'd Lord Anglesea's wall,‖‖
And seem'd to say, "Little I value you all."

---

* Kilruddery, about a mile and a-half from Bray, the seat of the Brabazons, created Earls of Meath in 1627.
† Mozeen, a celebrated comedian, advised all travellers landing from England "sick of the seas," to visit Owen Bray.

    "Without any delay,
For you'll never be right till you see Owen Bray,
With his *Ballin a mona ora*,
A glass of his claret for me."

‡ Married, in 1756, Elizabeth, daughter of the Hon. Captain Mowlesworth.
§ A favourite hound of Lord Meath's.
‖ A deserted farmhouse, Enniskerry side of the Scalp Mountain.
¶ On the Dublin side of the Scalp Mountain.
** Once the residence of Lord Castleconte.
†† A wood close to the village of Loughlinstown, co. Dublin.
‡‡ A high hill, the east side of the Scalp Mountain.
§§ A romantic glen, through which flows a stream, Farrily's Brook, separating the counties of Dublin and Wicklow.
‖‖ Has disappeared, and no tradition of its existence remains,

The Death of the Duke of Dorset.

He ran bushes and groves* up to Carbury Byrne's ;†
Joe Debill, Hall Preston, kept leading by turns;
The earth it was open, yet he was so stout,
Though he might have got in, he chose to keep out.
To Malpas'‡ high hill was the way then he flew,—
At Dalkey-stone common§ we had him in view;
He drave on by Bullock,∥ through shrub Glenagery,¶
And so on to Monkstown, where Laury grew weary.

Through Rochestown wood** like an arrow he pass'd,
And came to the steep hills of Dalkey at last;
There gallantly plung'd himself into the sea,
And said in his heart, "Sure none dare follow me."
But soon, to his cost, he perceiv'd that no hounds
Could stop the pursuit of the staunch-mottled hounds;
His policy here did not serve him a rush,
Five couple of Tartars were hard at his brush.

To recover the shore, then, again was his drift,
But ere he could reach to the top of the chft,
He found both of speed and of running a lack,
Being waylaid and killed by the rest of the pack.
At his death there were present the lads that I've sung,
Save Laury, who, riding a garron, was flung:
Thus ended, at length, a most delicate chase,
That held us five hours and ten minutes' space.

We return'd to Kilruddery's plentiful board,
Where dwell hospitality, truth, and my lord :††
We talk'd o'er the chase, and we toasted the health
Of the men that ne'er struggled for places or wealth.

---

* Ritson's reading, he ran Rush's Grove, now Cork Abbey.
† It is remarkable that a man named Carbury Byrne lately resided here : he was a respectable carpenter.
‡ The hill next to Killiney, on which an obelisk was erected by Colonel Malpas in 1741. On the Killiney range a small pyramid marks the spot where the young Duke of Dorset was killed, 14th Feb., 1815, by a fall from his horse, hunting in the very track of the hounds described in this song.
§ No longer a common.
∥ Once a small fishing village, now a fashionable resort for the gentry of Dublin.
¶ A mile and a-half from Kingstown. It is now simply Glenagery; the "Shrub" no longer remains. On it is built the seat of the highly popular Edward Fox, Esq., J.P.
** About half a mile from Glenagery.
†† Chaworth, the sixth Earl of Meath, born in 1686. He died at Calais, on his way to Aix-la-Chapelle, 14th of May, 1763, and was buried at Canterbury.

Owen Bray baulk'd a leap:—says Hall Preston, 'twas odd—
"'Twas shameful, cried Jack, by——
Said Preston, I halloo'd, "Get on though you fall,
Or I'll leap over you, your blind gelding and all."

Each glass was adapted to freedom and sport,
For party affairs we consign'd to the court;
Thus we finish'd the rest of the day and the night
In gay flowing bumpers and toasts of delight.
Then, till the next meeting, bid farewell each brother—
So some they went one way, and some went another;
And as Phœbus befriended our earlier roam,
So Luna took care in conducting us home.

The neighbourhood of Dalkey commons afforded (in 1750) plenty of wild fowl, hares, rabbits, foxes, and eagles.

Curwen, the naturalist, who spent a considerable time in Dalkey and the surrounding country, in the early part of the present century, speaks of the immense number of goldfinches, greenfinches, and bullfinches, to be found on Dalkey commons and Killiney hills: "here also," he says, "skylarks are found in abundance."

A rare species of lark has been found here, being that which Buffon describes as "le cochevis ou la grosse aloutte huppee."

"Far up in the Cathedral dome that arches over the Common, the lark and finch chant—

"GLORIA IN EXCELSIS."

INTERESTING ASSOCIATIONS OF THE "CASTLE HOUSE," SIR JOHN HAZLER'S MANSION AND MARINE VILLA AT DALKEY IN THE LAST CENTURY.

Sir John Hazler was Chamberlain in Dublin Castle at the same time that the celebrated Sir Boyle Roche (whose name and surprising "Bird of Ubiquity" has

M

done such good service, both in books and speeches) was Gentleman-Usher during Earl Camden's vice-royalty, 1796. Sir John Hazler was one of the most hospitable men of the last century. The wits, members of the Irish Parliament, and artists, who met at Daley's Coffee-house (the corner of Foster-place, Dublin), had the *entrée* at all times to his establishment in Dalkey, where, in addition, some of the greatest actors and singers of the day were entertained. Sir Boyle Roche was a constant visitor, as well as the facetious Kane O'Hara, who wrote "Midas."

Eustace Budgell, who, on the arrival of George the First from Hanover, was appointed Under-Secretary to the Lords-Justices of Ireland, and afterwards became a distinguished member of the Irish House of Commons, the personal friend of Addison, secretary to Lord Wharton, Lord Lieutenant of Ireland; a writer of great ability, and author of many important works,—dated many of his letters from the Castle House, Dalkey.*

Charlotte Brooke, an eminent Irish writer, daughter of Henry Brooke, a distinguished dramatist, a native of the county Cavan, resided in Dalkey for some time previous to 1790. Her first publication (a translation of a song from the Irish, a monody by Carolan) was written here, and afterwards appeared in Walker's "Historical Memoirs of the Irish Bards."

CAROLAN'S MONODY ON THE DEATH OF MARY M'GUIRE: TRANSLATED FROM THE IRISH BY MISS BROOKE.

"Were mine the choice of intellectual fame,
    Of spelful song, and eloquence divine—
Painting's sweet power, philosophy's pure flame,
    And Homer's lyre, and Ossian's harp, were mine;

---

* Pope, in the prologue to his "Satires," enumerating the libellers against his reputation, has the two following lines on Budgell:
"Let Budgell charge low Grub-street on my quill,
And write whate'er he please—except my will."

"Reliques of Irish Poetry." 83

The splendid arts of Erin, Greece, and Rome,
  In *Mary* lost, would lose their wonted grace ;
All would I give to snatch her from the tomb,
  Again to fold her in my fond embrace.

"Desponding, sick, exhausted with my grief,
  Awhile the founts of sorrow cease to flow.
In vain—I rest not—sleep brings no relief :—
  Cheerless, companionless, I wake to woe.
Nor birth, nor beauty, shall again allure,
  Nor fortune win me to another bride ;
Alone I'll wander, and alone endure,
  Till death restore me to my dear one's side.

"Once every thought and every scene was gay—
  Friends, mirth, and music, all my hours employ'd :
Now doom'd to mourn my last sad years away,
  My life a solitude—my heart a void !
Alas ! the change !—the change again no more !
  For every comfort is with Mary fled ;
And ceaseless anguish shall her loss deplore,
  Till age and sorrow join me with the dead.

"Adieu, each gift of nature and of art,
  That erst adorned me in life's early prime !
The cloudless temper, and the social heart,
  The soul ethereal, and the flights sublime !
Thy loss, my *Mary*, chas'd them from my breast :
  Thy sweetness cheers, thy judgment aids no more ;—
The muse deserts a heart with grief opprest—
  And lost is every joy that charm'd before."

In 1788, her "Reliques of Irish Poetry" appeared, a work universally and justly admired.

In "Mervyn's Letters" (1797), it is stated that Mr. *Payne*, a young man who successfully courted the Muses, "lived in a house which overlooked the old *graveyard* of Dalkey," where "philosophy and mirth, literature and sociability, continually dwelt."*
He wrote a number of ballads, and also parodies on scenes from Shakspeare.

* The present Dalkey House and grounds, as well as Bullock Castle and House, have lately been much improved by the owner, Mr. Hugh O'Rorke, Commissioner of the Dublin, Kingstown, and Dalkey Townships,—a gentleman who has built some first-class mansions, not alone in Dublin, but at Sandycove, Bullock, Dalkey,

ETTY SCOTT,

THE GOLD DREAMER OF DALKEY.

"Thou hast been call'd, O sleep! the friend of woe,
But 'tis the happy who have call'd thee so."—*Southey.*

"And dreams, in their development, have breath,
And tears and tortures, and the touch of joy;
They leave a weight upon our waking thoughts—
They make us what we *were not*—what they will—
And shake us with the vision that's gone by."—*Byron.*

Towards the close of the autumn of 1834, the inhabitants of Dalkey and the surrounding district, then rural in the extreme, became much interested and excited, on account of the rather singular dreams— a sort of emanation from mournful fancies—with which Etty Scott, of " Dalkey Stone Common," had long been troubled. Her father, a Scotchman, was one of the skilled workmen who were brought to this part of the country by the eminent contractor, Mr. Smith, whose two grandsons are still residing in

and parts of Wicklow, and thereby gave constant employment to numerous deserving tradesmen and others, instead of leaving his justly and honorably acquired capital in the coffers of a bank, under the shadow of the two-and-a-half per cents.

Mr. O'Rorke is one of those shrewd Irishmen, of quick perception and great natural intelligence, who, in 1848, after Ireland had passed through a political fever and heart-rending famine, saw the immediate necessity of reforming and enlarging certain commercial dealings through the country. He then laid the first stone of his future success, working with perseverance, unremitting industry, and self-reliance. While others were panic-stricken by the wail of sorrow and woe which went through the land, he grappled manfully with difficulties, and surmounted them with the most signal success. He saw the wants and necessities (commercially) which the country required. He created and fostered a home manufacture to supply those wants, successfully competing with England and Scotland in quality and price, thereby practically serving his native land. Mr. O'Rorke has become a deservedly rich man; while hundreds of families are reaping material benefits from the laudable exercise of his unwearied exertions in the cause of Irish industry. Such men confer real and lasting benefits on their country.

the neighbourhood. He, in conjunction with the Messrs. Henry, Mullen, and M'Mahon, were the gentlemen appointed by Government to construct the harbour at Kingstown. Etty Scott was an only daughter—a beautiful, kind-hearted girl; but, strange to say, at times, there was an unearthly light in her dark eyes. Her rich brown hair clustered down her neck, and lay in massive curls upon her sunburnt bosom. To strangers, who met her while wandering across the hills to Rochestown and Shanganagh, her manners were shy and reserved; to some of her companions, she was both affable and affectionate—yet, at times, she became silent and moodish. While the quarrymen colonists, with pipe and dance, were amusing themselves after their daily toil, Etty spent her evenings reading romances and stories of the "Scottish Borderers;" nevertheless, she was looked up to with respect by the "squatters" of the common and the good people of the village. In 1817, the first great powder-blast took place in the quarries of Dalkey, which now present the appearance of having been riven asunder by some earthquake or convulsion of nature. The granite stones taken from these immense chasms, have furnished the enormous amount of material for the construction of the Dunleary and Kingstown harbours—which occasioned the hills at the time to be somewhat abundantly peopled. By the aid of a simple combination of the mechanical powers—principally a series of three inclined planes and three large metal wheels, each with a strong endless chain passing through a groove—one man was enabled to set in motion and control six trucks or carriages, aggregately bearing twenty-five tons of granite—a task which, on common roads, in the ordinary mode of draught, could not be accomplished with fewer than thirty-five horses. 'Etty Scott's father, an intelligent, shrewd man for his position in life, had the charge of one of those *inclined planes.* Scott, amongst others, "pitched his tent,"— or rather constructed, for himself and Etty, a rude yet storm-proof cabin, consisting of three rooms, enclosed by a loose stone wall, totally unconscious of mortar, which encircled about a-third of an acre— on the commons, situated under " *Geraldine,*" the property of Mr. Patrick Byrne. Here, on a wet and stormy night, in the middle of October, 1834, the pastoral Joan of Arc of this wild district—then of as little value as the wide-spreading prairie of South America—the dreaming enthusiast, and indirect prophetess of its future value and prosperity— Etty Scott, the quarryman's daughter, who for months had been weaving wild fancies in dreamland, first communicated the particulars of her vision of the rock near the seashore, where vast treasures were hid, to her father, his fellow-labourers, and their families, and also to the " natives " of Dalkey, some of whom were fishermen, pilots, and humble traders. For weeks Etty's dream of there being immense quantities of gold concealed under the " Long Rock," became the topic of general conversation.

The granite-bound shore of the ancient strait of St. Benedict, where those beautiful mansions, "*Inniscorrig,*" " *Elsinore,*" " *Lota,*" &c., now stand, suddenly became crowded with anxious and wealth-seeking spectators. Etty's enthusiasm rose with public excitement. The fever of the anticipated gold *find* still increased. Her dreams were no longer looked upon as shadows ; they were daily becoming seeming realities, which would make an *El Dorado* of her adopted home—Dalkey, the " Port of the Seven Castles."

ETTY SCOTT,
THE BEAUTIFUL DREAMER OF SECRETED TREASURES.

" Thou art like the depths where the seas have birth,
Rich in the wealth that is lost from earth—
All the sere flowers of our days gone by,
And the buried gems in thy bosom lie.

" Yes, thou art like those dim sea caves—
A realm of treasures, a realm of graves !
And the shapes through thy mysteries that come and go,
Are of wealth and terror, of power and woe "

The gold-dreamer's manner to the villagers and people of the hills became importunate and demonstrative. Ballads were written and sung through the streets, in which the name of our heroine was freely introduced. In the meantime, Pat Byrne, an *honest* dairyman, and well-known opponent to the general union and partnership milk-and-water company, who owned the " Long Rock," not by lease—for leases were unknown in Dalkey in those days—became seized with the treasure epidemic, and believed himself the *Monte Christo* of the place—and *vale* " King of Dalkey." At the suggestion of Etty, a preliminary meeting was held on the " common," a council of goldfinders formed, money liberally subscribed to purchase tools, powder, torches, &c.,—she again, in the most solemn manner, repeating her dreams and vision. Riches, immense riches, promised —faithfully promised, to her followers, who strictly attended to her instructions, in accordance with the spirit of her dreams. Her commanding and well-proportioned figure, dark flashing eye, dishevelled hair, and earnest manner, surrounded by a set of believers in her prophetic power, each carrying a torch previous to their taking possession of the " Rock," over which ceremony she was to preside, formed an *ensemble* worthy of the pencil of a great artist. This youthful " Meg Merrilies " of Dalkey Common became awe-inspiring, while, with a deep-toned voice, she exhorted them—

" WATCH WELL—WORK WITH ENERGY ! BUT, ABOVE ALL, BELIEVE IN MY DREAM, AND BE SILENT AS THE GRAVE WHILE WORKING. WAIT WITH PATIENCE THE FITTING MOMENT ; FOR THE SECRETED TREASURE OF THE DANE WILL BE SURELY FOUND IF YOU TO HEARKEN TO MY VOICE."*

* The majority of the Irish peasantry are aware that the Danes plundered indiscriminately wherever they went, not sparing

Etty Scott succeeded in transmitting the odic force of her day-dream into thirty-six stalworth hard-wrought sons of toil. They became absolute slaves to her "golden councils"—they forsook their legitimate employment in the quarries, and blindly yoked themselves to the rude chariot of a peasant girl's romantic and excited enthusiasm. She was, for the time, queen of all she surveyed. Large sums of money were spent in blasting-powder and flambeaux. Never did men work with such energy for twelve hours a day, in strict accordance with Etty's mysterious injunctions. They were actuated in their labour by one thought alone—the speedy recovery of the immense treasures and bags of gold and silver, which she seriously and dramatically affirmed were concealed by the old rulers of the country under the "Long Rock," which is washed by the waters of Dalkey Sound—she stating that it was revealed to her in dreams, that the Danes who pillaged the whole country, and massacred the people, in the eleventh century, were obliged to fly from Dalkey without being able to take the enormous treasures, which they had hid near the "Long Rock," away with them.

During Etty's exhortations to the people, and while the miners were blasting the rocks by the ton weight, she was never known to smile. This solemn mien of hers gave additional zest and interest to the whole proceedings.

The group of workmen presented at times a most picturesque appearance. The ringing of the hammers on the boring irons; the blazing torches stuck

even churches or the shrines of the saints, which were then immensely rich, and abounded with costly ornaments of gold and silver. They almost invariably despatched their plunder to one of their seaports, where it was concealed until their ships were ready to carry it off to Denmark or Norway. Very little value fell into the hands of the Irish after they were successful in a battle against the Danes.

in the crevices of the rocks; the moaning wind and rolling waves; the occasional dislodgment and hurling of a mass of rock into the sea—while the " gold-dreamer," gazing intently on the group below, sat on a rock, with a game-cock in one hand, while with the other she held a " black-hafted knife," ready to spill the blood of chanticleer, when the fiend, gnome, ghoul, or spirit of good or ill omen (the expected harbinger of the gold of which she dreamt) should make its appearance. This novel scene was repeated night after night, and day after day, in the presence of thousands of people, many of whom, including my intelligent cicerone, Mr. Pat Byrne, are now alive to tell the tale. Facts are stubborn things, and

"Truth is stranger than fiction."

A month passed away, and still no treasure met the miners' anxious gaze, or the wistful look of the Dalkey gold-dreamer. She still entreated them to persevere—that their hour of triumph was at hand, when their efforts would be crowned with the most signal success.

"All went merry as a marriage bell,"

up to this period. Alas! a change shortly came o'er the spirit of poor Etty's dream. One dark evening, in the midst of the gold excitement, a number of persons met in Mr. P. Byrne's garden, Castle-street, Dalkey—then a great resort for the Dublin and Dunleary folk. A few medical students formed a conspiracy to ruin Etty's long-cherished hopes. Two black cats, brought from Dublin, were produced; long cords were attached to their tales, to which were fastened several sponges, saturated with spirits of wine and turpentine; while their bodies were rubbed with dry phosphorus, which occasioned no pain. They were conveyed in boats to the base of the Rock, where thirty-five men were working—their presiding genius being Etty. The cats were silently unbagged in a recess—the matches applied to the sponges. In a few minutes, strange spectral visions presented themselves in the surrounding darkness, springing and flying from rock to rock, in all directions. The miners stood aghast in groups, when the full diapason of feline screams and mewlings were echoed through the night. They felt as if they were invited to revel with the hideous ghoul of the place. Fear, intense fear, took possession of all present—save Etty. The workmen and spectators fled in all directions. The joke was soon discovered—loud laughter resounded from all quarters—Etty, the gold-dreamer of Dalkey's wild commons, went home to her rude cottage, and dreamed again :—

"On her parted lips there's a quivering thrill,
As on a lyre ere its chords are still ;
On the long black lashes that fringe her eye,
There's a large tear gathering heavily—
A rain from the clouds of her spirit press'd ;
Sorrowful Etty ! this is not rest !"

The broken-hearted gold-dreamer of Dalkey sickened and died ; but not before she saw her dream of the " Long Rock " partly fulfilled. In a few months after this remarkable and exciting scene, thousands of pounds (paid to the squatters in gold) were expended, by persons who had been brought by curiosity to Dalkey, in purchasing the little patches of land, some of it perched on beetling rocks, from those squatters and natives who subscribed to Etty's dream, and worked and lost their time on her vision of the Long Rock. One of the most indefatigable of Etty's miners was Pat Kavanagh, *alias Ali Baba*. Some believer in eastern romance told him to repeat these words when the spectre of the Dane would make its appearance, which would ensure him a large proportion of the gold. He did so on the first appearance of luminous pussy, and he was ever afterwards called Ali Baba. He died a few years ago, in the service of the talented and much-respected Dr. Parkinson, of Tudor Hall, whose private worth and benevolence is only exceeded by his innate desire to do good to all who may come within the circle of his professional duties.

A DALKEY LAND-ACQUIRING MANIA IMMEDIATELY SUCCEEDED THE GOLD FEVER.

The late Mr. Martin Burke was the first in the field. He not only purchased the most desirable sites facing the Coolamore, but actually rented Dalkey Island from the Government, which, it is to be hoped, will yet be the property of the Commissioners.

Pat Byrne, one of Etty's miners, sold the Long Rock for a very considerable sum. On it is built "Lota," "Elsinore," and "Inniscorrig."*

J. Molloy, another of Etty's miners, sold his place at a high figure. It contained part of Mr. Leslie's beautiful lawn, and the ground where Loretto Abbey stands, which was purchased by the late Judge Ball's sister, for £700.

The Briens (Etty's miners) sold their place, on which Knockallen stands.

The Denisses (Etty's miners) sold their place, on which Tempe-terrace stands.

Edward Neil, one of Etty's miners, and Michael Brien, sold their place, on which Prince Patrick's-terrace stands.

Etty Scott and father sold their place, since purchased by Pat Byrne, on which Geraldine and Ballymurphy is built.

* "He had seen nothing like it (the Dalkey Acropolis) this side of fair Parthenope herself; and there was one delightful retreat here (Inniscorrig), that which had been erected and beautified, to afford him relaxation from the labours of an arduous profession, by the Queen's chief Irish physician, Sir Dominic Corrigan, Bart., which reminded him, in some respects, of the poet Sanazar's beautiful Mergillina, the gem of the Bay of Naples, in the days when the Argonese dynasty ruled over South Italy, some interesting vestiges of which remain to this day."—*Knight of Innishowen, in "Temple Bar" Magazine.*

Pat M'Guire, James Smith, and Pat Leary, sold their portion of the Dalkey commons to Mr. Gerard Tyrrell, T.C., on which he has built some elegant mansions and marine villas.

Montpellier, the beautiful residence of Mr. Thomas Perrier Davies, is built on a portion of the commons of Dalkey, which also belonged to one of Etty's followers.

VICO ROAD, DALKEY—A LOVELY SCENE.

"Fair is the form that gently waves
The artist's scarf on yonder steep,*
Where the bold shore of Vico braves
The rolling of the restless deep."

"Sweet 'Fern Hill,'† gay, enchanting place,
Where nature looks with loveliest face;
Where roseate health has fixed her reign,
And pleasure's craft sails o'er the main."

One of the most lovely scenes around this delightful coast, is from the place known as the Vico-road, commanding the whole expanse of the exquisite bay of Killiney, unrivalled in its beauty, with only one exception (that of Naples), and singularly like it in all its features, except in the absence of Vesuvius—this formidable neighbour, being though "a thing of beauty," certainly *not* "a joy for ever," we can afford to dispense with. Some pretty villas stud the hillside; and the ever-changing aerial colouring which gives to this charming spot a fascination peculiarly its own, leaves only one thing to be desired, viz., the annihilation of the *invidious wall*, which, at the end

* Mrs. Gonne, an *artiste* whose sketches from nature are highly prized by connoisseurs.

† Fern Hill and Hanna Mount, the property of Mr. Henry Gonne, are built on a terrace overhanging the Naples-like bay of Killiney. These beautiful nestled marine villas in the side of the hill have a southern aspect. The view of Shanganagh, Bray Head, the "Golden Spears," and the Wicklow Mountains, from Fern Hill, is unsurpassed.

of the road, bars the progress of the lovers of nature's charms, along the curving shore of Killiney, Ballybrack, and Shanganagh. As the taste and civilization of the age makes this truly lovely shore more known, it is to be hoped this barrier will be sacrificed to the universal tribunal of public opinion.

The following picture of the exquisite scene that bursts upon the view as the train rushes through the tunnel at Dalkey, is given in a poem by Denis Florence M'Carthy, called "Spring Flowers from Ireland," which appeared in the *Dublin University Magazine* for May, 1865. Of this poem, one of the many uncollected pieces of the author, a distinguished living writer, himself an eminent poet, has written :—"The lore of our native land has never been expressed with finer feeling, or with a finer handling, than in this poem." We extract a few stanzas, which refer directly to our subject. The poet, writing from abroad, has a home-sick vision of the many beautiful scenes that adorn his native land. The Pass of Keimaneigh, the scene of his " Alice and Una," and the Arbutus Islands of Killarney, glide as in a panorama before his eyes; and he then proceeds to his favourite " Vale of Shanganagh " :—

> " I see the long and lone defiles
> Of Keimaneigh's bold rocks uphurled ;
> I see the golden-fruited isles
> That gem the queen-lakes of the world ;
> I see—a gladder sight to me—
> By soft Shanganagh's silver strand,
> The breaking of a sapphire sea
> Upon the golden-fretted sand.
>
> " Swiftly the tunnel's rock-hewn pass,
> Swiftly the fiery train runs through;
> Oh, what a glittering sheet of glass !
> Oh, what enchantment meets my view !
> With eyes insatiate I pursue,
> Till Bray's bright headland bounds the scene—
> 'Tis Baiæ by a softer blue !
> Gaeta by a gladder green !

" By tasseled groves, o'er meadows fair,
  I'm carried in my blissful dream,
To where—a monarch in the air—
  The pointed mountain* reigns supreme;
There, in a spot remote and wild,
  I see once more the rustic seat
Where Carrigoona, like a child,
  Sits at the mightier mountain's feet."

But we must quote no further from a poem, which we hope soon to see in a collected edition of the author's works.

PRIMITIVE CHRISTIAN CHURCHES AT DALKEY AND KILLINEY.†

"The cloud-capt towers, the gorgeous palaces,
The *solemn temples*, the great globe itself,
Yea, all which it inherits, shall dissolve,
And, like an unsubstantial pageant faded,
Leave not a wreck behind."

Dalkey and Killiney churches, now in ruins, present features of high antiquity. Portions of them have been rebuilt, and are, therefore, characteristic of later periods. Strange to say, neither of them are mentioned in Archdall's "Monasticon Hibernicum"— an ancient history of the abbeys, priories, and other religious houses in Ireland. Dalkey Church, the ruins of which are situated under the shadow of the most perfect of the old castles, has been known by the title of St. Bonett, St. Boneis, St. Begnet, St. Bennett, and St. Benedict. In the year 1178, the celebrated Archbishop O'Toole assigned the Church of St. Begnet of Dalkey, with all its tithes, and his grant was further confirmed by letters-patent from Prince John.

* The great Sugar Loaf, which rises sublimely over Carrigoona.
† The late Dr. Petrie observed, in his excellent work, that there now exists in this country some hundreds of churches, which, in point of antiquity (at least), may be classed among the most remarkable structures of Christian times now to be found in Europe.

The erection of the churches of Dalkey and Killiney (like the castles), has been ascribed to the Danes, who became Christians in the year 947.* They are of much older origin; they may have remodelled them. St. Jerome incontestably proves that there were Christian churches in Ireland in the fourth century; and in the "Annals of the Four Masters," in the year 650, we are told that "St. Beraid, Abbot of Dublin, died that year." From this it appears there was a monastery church established in Dublin at an early period, although, like Dalkey and Killiney churches, not mentioned in the "Monasticon Hibernicum." Dr. Petrie attributes the church at Killiney to the fifth century—a primitive Christian temple, at present in "ruinous perfection." This great Irish scholar often expressed a wish to be buried near this ruin, where the first beams of the morning sun would rest on his grave. He had a profound veneration for this place.

Here, in the winter months, the night-wind shakes with solemn effect the ivied tapestry which drapes this ancient church.

The following interesting details of Killiney Church

---

* In Dr. Hanmer's "Ancient Chronicles of Ireland," it is stated that "the Abbey of the Blessed Virgin Mary in Dublin (Mary's Abbey) was founded by the Danes, in the year 948."

"These people, on their first conversion to the Christian faith, most probably constructed their churches after the manner of the Irish; but their connexion with their countrymen in Britain brought them acquainted with the new method of building; and masons were brought over to construct their sacred edifices in the Norman or Gothic fashion: whence Christ Church, in 1038, and St. Patrick's, in 1190; the Cathedral of Waterford, about 1100; that of Limerick, in 1170; and Cork, about the same period, were the first Gothic buildings Ireland saw.—Ware's 'Bishops;' Harris' 'Dublin.' The native Irish also adopted this celebrated style of architecture soon after its first introduction; and the cathedral at Cashel, 1170, and the Abbey of Holy Cross, 1112, are no mean specimens of the taste and style of the times."—Archdall's "Monasticon."

are taken from Wakeman's "Archæologia Hibernica,"* an illustrated work of great merit:—"This ruin is situated near the village of the same name, at a distance of about nine miles from the metropolis, and of two from the terminus of the Kingstown and Dalkey Railway, and will be found particularly interesting to the student of Irish church architecture. Its extreme dimensions upon the interior are thirty-five feet, the nave measures but twelve feet and eight inches, and the chancel nine feet and six inches in breadth. The church originally consisted of a simple nave and choir, lighted in the usual manner, and connected by a semi-circular arch; but at a period long subsequent to its original foundation, an addition, the architecture of which it will be well to compare with that of the more ancient building, has been made on the northern side. The original doorway, which, as usual, is placed in the centre of the west gable, is remarkable for having a cross sculptured upon the under part of its lintel. It measures in height six feet and one inch, in breadth, at the top two feet, and at the bottom two feet four inches. The next feature to be noticed is the choir arch. This, which may be looked upon as a most characteristic example of its class, measures in breadth, where the arch begins to spring, four feet seven inches, and at the base four feet ten inches and a-half; its height is only six feet and a-half. The chancel windows display the inclined sides, so indicative of antiquity when found in Irish ecclesiastical remains; but, with the exception of that facing the east, they are in a state of great dilapidation. The eastern window is spear-headed both within and without, and exhibits the usual splay. The comparatively modern addition on the northern side of the nave, which appears to have been erected as a kind of aisle, is connected with the ancient church by several openings broken through the north side-wall. It will be well to compare its

* Published by M'Glashan and Gill, Dublin.

architectural features with those of the original structure. The door-way offers a striking contrast to that in the west gable, and its eastern window is equally different from that in the ancient chancel, being larger and chamfered upon the exterior. There is an extremely ancient font in this church.

Grose,* in his "Antiquities of Ireland," makes mention of our early Christian churches.

* Francis Grose, the celebrated antiquarian, died in 1791, and was buried in Drumcondra churchyard, near Dublin.
"The following address to the people of Scotland was written by Mr. Robert Burns, the Ayrshire Poet, when Captain Grose, the British antiquarian, was on his peregrination in Scotland, in the year 1791, collecting materials for his publication of the antiquities of that country. The ideas in this, like the rest of Mr. Burns' productions, are singular and eccentric, and exhibit a just picture of the sentiments of the peasantry of Scotland, respecting any gentleman who is professedly an antiquarian. He is deemed to be in colleague with Satan, and to be a dealer in magic and the black art,—a vulgar prejudice, which all the light and learning of the present day have not yet been able totally to eradicate."—*Belfast Northern Star*, April, 1792.

ADDRESS TO THE PEOPLE OF SCOTLAND, RESPECTING FRANCIS GROSE, ESQ., THE BRITISH ANTIQUARIAN. BY MR. ROBERT BURNS, THE AYRSHIRE POET.

> Hear, Land o'Cakes, and brither Scots,
> Frae Maiden Kirk, to Johnie Groat's,
> If there's a hole in a' your coats,
>   I red you tent it ;
> A chield's amang ye taking notes,
>   And faith he'll prent it.
>
> If in your bounds you chance to light
> Upon a fine, fat, fadgel wight,
> O' stature short hut genius bright ;
>   That's he—mark weel !
> And wow he has unco flight
>   O' cawk and keel.

THE "ANTHOLOGIA HIBERNICA,"

Ledwich has written interesting articles on the pagan, Roman, and "Ancient Churches of Ireland," in this celebrated Irish magazine. The poet Moore, in his "Diary," says :—

"This magazine—*The Anthologia Hibernica*—one of the most respectable attempts at periodical literature that has ever been ventured on in Ireland—was set on foot by Mercier, the College bookseller, in the year 1793, and carried on for two years, when it died, as all such things die in that country, for want of money and—of talent; for the Irish never either fight or write well on their own soil. My pride at seeing my name in the list of sub-

---

At some auld howlet-haunted biggin,
Or kirk deserted by its riggin,
Its ten to one ye'll fine him snug in
    Some eldritch part,
Wi deils, they say, Lord save's! colleaguing
    At some *black art*.

Ilk' ghaist that haunts the ha' or chamer,
Ye gipsy gang that deal in glamer,
And yon, deep read in hell's grammer;
    Warlocks and witches,
Ye'll quake at his conjuring hammer,
    Ye midnight ———

It's tauld he was a sodger bred,
And one wou'd rather fa' than fled;
But now he's quat the spurtle blade
    And dog-skin wallet,
And taen the antiquarian trade,
    I think they call it.

He has a south o' odd nick-nackets,
Auld airn caps, and gingling jackets,
Would had the Lothians three in tackets,
    A twa'month gued;
And pitcher pots, and auld san-backets,
    Afore the flood.

Of Eve's first fire he has a cinder;
Auld Tubal-Cain's fire shool and fender,
That which distinguished the gender
    Of Balaam's ass;
A broomstick o' the witch of Endor,
    Weel shod wi brass.

scribers to this publication—'Master Thomas Moore,' in full—was only surpassed by that of finding myself one of its 'esteemed contributors.' It was in the pages of this magazine, for the months of January and February, 1793. that I first read, being then a schoolboy, Rogers's 'Pleasures of Memory,' little dreaming that I should one day become the intimate friend of the author; and such an impression did it then make upon me, that the particular type in which it is there printed, and the very colour of the paper, are associated with every line of it in my memory (1833). It was in this year (1793) that for the first time I enjoyed the honour and glory (and such it truly was to me) of seeing verses of my own in print. I had now indeed become a determined rhymer; and there was an old maid—old in my eyes, at least, at that time—Miss Hannah Byrne, who used to be a good deal at our house, and who, being herself very much in the poetical line, not

> Besides he'll cut you aff fu' gleg,
> The shape of Adam's philebeg;
> The knife that cutted Abel's craig,
>   He'll prove you fully,
> It was a faulding jocteleg,
>   Or laug kail gully.
>
> But would you see him in his glee,
> (For meikle glee, and fun has he,)
> Then set him down and twa or three
>   Gude fallows wi' him;
> And Port! O Port! shine thou a wee,
>   And then ye'll see him!
>
> Now by the powers of verse and prose,
> Thou art a dainty chield, O Grose!*
> Whae'er of thee shall ill suppose,
>   They sair misca' thee;
> I'd tak the rascal by the nose,
>   Would say, "shame fa thee!"

* When Captain Grose first came to Ireland, his curiosity led him to see everything in the capital worth seeing; in the course of his perambulation, he one evening strolled into the principal meat market of Dublin, when the butchers, as usual, set up the constant outcry of "What do you buy? What do you buy, master?" Grose parried this for some time, by saying, "he wanted nothing." At last a butcher starts from his stall, and, eyeing Grose's figure from top to bottom, which was something like Dr. Slop's in "Tristram Shandy," exclaimed: "Well, sir, though you don't want anything at present, only *say* you buy your meat of me, and you'll make my fortune." A portrait of this celebrated antiquarian is published in the *Anthologia Hibernica*.

only encouraged, but wrote answers to my young effusions. The name of 'Romeo' (the Anagram of that of Moore), was the signature which I adopted in our correspondence, and 'Zelia' was the title under which the lady wrote. Poor Hannah Byrne! not even Sir Lucius O'Trigger's '*Dalia*' was a more uninspiring object than my 'Zelia' was. To this lady, however, was my *first* printed composition addressed in my own proper name, with the following introductory epistle to the editor:—

"Aungier-street, Sept. 11, 1793.

"SIR,—If the following attempts of a youthful muse seem worthy of a place in your magazine, by inserting them you will much oblige a constant reader,

"TH-M-S M—RE."

"TO ZELIA,

On her charging the author with writing too much on love. Then follows the verses, and concludes thus—

"When first she raised her simplest lays,
In Cupid's never-ceasing praise,
The god a faithful promise gave,
  That never should she feel Love's stings;
Never to burning passion be a slave,
  But feel the purer joy this friendship brings."

"The second copy of verses also appeared in the *Anthologia Hibernica*.

"TO ZELIA.

"My gardens are crowded with flowers,
  My vines are all loaded with grapes;
Nature sports in my fountains and bowers,
  And assumes her most beautiful shapes.

"The shepherds admire my lays,
  When I pipe they will flock to the song;
They deck me with laurels and bays,
  And list to me all the day long.

"But their laurels and praises are vain,
  They've no joy or delight for me now;
For Celia despises the strain,
  And that withers the wreath on my brow."

The following sketch of Moore's youth, &c., is from the pen of an artist (Herbert, the celebrated portrait painter) who was personally known to the poet's family. It was first published in 1830:—

THE POET MOORE, HIS EARLY EFFUSIONS OF GENIUS.

In reading over the lives of men distinguished in arts, arms, literature, &c., we feel great pleasure in a memoir where we can trace, during the progressive course from childhood to maturity, that development of talent which so strongly indicates future excellence. Reflecting on this subject, I have been induced to submit an account of a poet, one of the greatest his country has ever produced. If to have known him from his birth, and to have witnessed those early effusions of genius which surprised and delighted his friends, may qualify me for the task, why, then, I think, I may attempt it without incurring the imputation of vanity. I had the pleasure of knowing his parents from the time of their marriage; so that I had frequent opportunities of seeing my young friend after his probationary state of infancy, when introduced to visitors. At three years old he was an entertaining little fellow, with his childish prattle, which he commenced with in clambering up my knee. When seated there, we began to converse. I have often been astonished at his intellectual discourse; but at five years his mind expanded to a degree unparalleled by any child that ever came under my observation. So matured was he at that period, he threw aside all child's play, toys, &c., and clinging to me with earnest entreaty to recite passages from Shakspeare, which sometimes I indulged in, and which he attended to with all the patient endurance of a sage, and entered so fully into the subject, that I was induced, at his own request, to give him instructions in some speech for his recital. He chose Hamlet's soliloquy on his mother's marriage—he soon got perfect in the words, and (with such tuition only as I was capable of giving) he spoke that beautiful and difficult speech before a large party of friends at my house. The astonishment and pleasure enjoyed by the whole party were fully evinced by the most unqualified approbation. He was then under six years of age; and such discrimination, taste, and ability, as he exhibited, would have done credit to any young man. Had his parents, like Master Betty's, been induced to lead him on to that pursuit, we should not have pronounced that young Roscius such a wonder, for he was more than double the age of Master Moore at his *debut*.

I next recognized him at the celebrated English school, under Mr. Samuel Whyte, from whom the late R. B. Sheridan had received his lessons of elocution. Under Mr. Whyte's tuition, my little friend became a perfect prodigy—he bore off all the premiums at examinations, and was caressed by the auditors, amongst whom were persons of the first note. When Moore arrived at his twelfth year, he was a finished speaker. At that period I had a private performance—*Henry the Fourth*—at my house, to which I invited all my friends. Young Moore performed Prince John of Lancaster in a manner so easy and natural, we could have wished the part longer, to have enjoyed more of his interesting performance. After the play, he spoke the poem of the Old Man and his Ass with great point and humour; so that he shone conspicuously, and gave further proof that the stage would have been graced by his personal exertions, had he turned his thoughts to that profession. His genius, however, led him to poetry, and he commenced writing his *little* songs. I had the good fortune to witness the first efforts of his pen, and often saw those young ladies, his models, who presented that variety of character which he painted with such truth of nature in those matchless ballads. Every one was a faithful portrait. There was a young gentleman, *Wesley Doyle*, who frequented Mrs. Moore's evening parties at that period. He had a sweet voice, fine taste for singing and accompaniments, having been cultivated in music by his father, Dr. Doyle, a celebrated musical professor. This young Doyle sang our poet's labours in succession, as delivered from the muse in his peculiarly sweet manner. It was truly a delectable treat to witness the united efforts of those highly-talented young aspirants; no such entertainment could be had, even in the highest circles.

Our young hero's next display was in Trinity College, Dublin, where he entered as a pensioner. The Historical Debating Society was then in full health and vigour. Young Moore, in his first speech, made an impression on the auditors that engaged their attention, and struck deeper at every successive debate. He invited me to his rooms, in College, to hear him and his fellow-students at rehearsal; their compositions were exceedingly clever, but my friend had the best, and his delivery was easy and natural, much superior to any that competed with him— his speeches had all the effect of extemporary effusions.

Near the period of 1798, Trinity College was disturbed in its internal management by the insidious arts of spies and informers, who never stopped at any charge that promised reward; lies and calumny were more current than truth. They reported that several students had been sworn United Irishmen. To ascertain the credit that was to be given to this vile information, Lord Chancellor Clare held a scrutiny at the college, and examined the students himself, as patron or guardian. In the course of this inquiry young Moore was questioned: his answer was so prompt and ingenuous, that Lord Clare was satisfied he was clear of imputation; but there was strong reason to believe some of his fellow-students were guilty, and he desired to know from him what he knew of them as regarded the accusation against them. Moore hesitated to give an answer to that

peremptory demand of his lordship, upon which Lord Clare repeated the question: then our young friend made such an appeal as caused his lordship to relax, rigid and austere as he was. The words I cannot exactly remember; the substance was as follows:—that he entered college to receive the education of a scholar and a gentleman; that he knew not how to compromise these characters by blowing upon his college companions; that he had not a single associate that, so far as he knew, he could not acquit; and that he felt his own speeches in the debating society had been ill-construed, when the worst that could be said of them was, if truth had been spoken, that they were patriotic; that he had always been taught to believe patriotism a virtue, not a crime; then how could he venture to speak of the character of another, when he could not defend his own from the tongue of calumny; that he was aware of the high-minded nobleman he had the honour of appealing to, and if his lordship could for a moment condescend to step from his high station and place himself in his situation, then say how he would act under such circumstances, it should be his guidance. Lord Clare passed him, and proceeded with the inquiry; some were expelled; and, sad to say, the debating society was put down. Thus that monster, rebellion, destroyed the finest school of oratory that was then known in Europe, where some of the brightest ornaments in eloquence were matured and polished; the effect has been felt by parliament, the bar, the pulpit, and the stage; for such a dearth of talent have we to deplore as we never felt since the origin of that society until its suppression. It is to be hoped some liberal-minded man, of influential power, setting the value on education that it merits, will restore that establishment to its original use, and let us have the cultivation of our living language as well as those dead languages that require so much study, pains, penalties, and wealth, in the attainment. His "Anacreon," though written at an early age, was not published until he went to London; the admiration and approval it met with at the high bar of criticism are so well known and felt, as to render any panegyric from me frivolous.

Having now traced our friend from infancy to riper years, I leave him to the enjoyment of that fame which he has so deservedly acquired. I cannot, however, close this memoir without offering him my most grateful return for all the pleasure afforded me by his fascinating powers; but not to these alone am I indebted to him—to his patronage in my professional life, both as a portrait-painter and actor: his influential power was considerable with persons of the highest fashion, and he exerted that power for me with the zeal of an ardent friend; nay, he voluntarily wrote an article in one of the Dublin periodicals, defending my going on the stage, and eulogising my performance. Until the present opportunity, I had no public way of making my acknowledgment; and I could not get forward with my view of Irish times, characters, &c., if I had not selected, at an early part of my work, those nearest my heart. I am, therefore, proud to have it in my power to select Anacreon Moore as one of my country's brightest ornaments;—a splendid poet, a virtuous patriot, a sincere and indefatigable patron and friend.

The early Christian churches in Ireland had high stone pediment roofs, and, instead of under crofts, had upper crofts, situated between the stone pediment roof and the circular arch which covered the church, and, in this respect, bore a stricter resemblance to the Messarabic churches in Spain.* Their steeples, also, were, in general, round, and frequently detached from the building, as in the churches of Monaipchan, Cormac's Chapel, &c. There are, also, ancient stone-roofed churches of the same construction as Glendalough in the island of Zante, described by a French engineer in 1757.

Lord Barymore left a fine house at Castle Lyons, county of Cork, formerly called Castle Lehan, on the foundation of O'Lehan's castle. In throwing down some of the old walls of the castle, a chimney-piece was discovered with the following inscription, "Lehan O'Cullone hoc fecit, MCIIII.," which proves that stone buildings were much earlier in Ireland than some modern antiquarians allow them to have been.

Those holy men who built our early Christian churches, and preached the Gospel of Christ throughout the entire of the country, obtained the name of the "Island of Saints" for Ireland. Their actions, together with the times wherein they flourished, may be read in "The History of the Bishops, &c., of Ireland."

Our ancestors were deep in learning, pious in their religion, wise in their institutions, just in their laws, and continued for many ages the most generous and valiant people that ever lived upon the face of the earth.

Several of the early Christian churches in Ireland were built near raths, tumuli, and upright or pillar stones.†

---

* Swinbourne's Travels.
† "Thou shalt sail for the great south mountain, where there is wood, and on the south side, under the mountain, is a place free from wood, in which are erected three large stones" (a cromleach). *Icelandic MS.*, sixth century.

VIEW OF KINGSTOWN, FROM THE BOYD MEMORIAL EAST PIER

KINGSTOWN.

[FORMERLY DUNLEARY.]

SECTION IV.

HISTORICAL AND POLITICAL ASSOCIATIONS, ETC.

THIS highly favoured seaport, fashionable watering-place, and rendezvous for yachts, is considered the wealthiest and most populous township in Ireland. It is beautifully situated on an eminence over the sea, commanding a magnificent prospect of the lovely Bay of Dublin* and Hill of Howth. Its name, in by-gone days, ere the Royal Irish Mail was carried by coach to Howth, and from thence shipped to Wales, was DUNLEARY. Its ancient and euphonic appellation was changed to that of Kingstown, when the last of "The Four Georges"

* With respect to the view of the Bay of Dublin from Kingstown, and its beauties, they have been long the theme of the admirers of nature in her boundless domain, the subject often of the painter's pencil and of the poet's muse.

> "Beyond the wave, in giant clusters piled,
> Blue mountains swell magnificently wild ;
> Or, in continuous chain, ascending high,
> Seem azure tap'stry pendent from the sky.
> In one wide curve, reflecting back the day,
> A living mirror, shines the spacious Bay :
> Studded with barks—anon the view retires,
> Where Dublin rears her dim-discovered spires,
> Or marks where Howth, far frowning 'mid the waves,
> Yawns thro' a thousand billow-beaten caves—
> Where the loud surge its thund'ring volume throws,
> And tortur'd echo never finds repose ;
> Above the beacon-tow'r, which, through the night,
> Crowns the steep cone-rock with its orb of light ;
> Thence one vast void, as far as the eye can sweep,
> Till the horizon mingles with the deep."

quitted its rock-bound shore in 1821, waving "affectionate adieus," with an *au revoir* to the Irish shores, which was never realized (after having made professions of peace and conciliation to his enthusiastic, and warm-hearted subjects). Alas ! in this case,
"Hope told a flattering tale."
The Bard of Erin, in his "Memoirs," edited by Earl Russell, in noting "the king's visit to Ireland," in his Diary, September 9, 1821, says : " Breakfasted with Lord John, and afterwards went to look for Lord Lansdowne, who arrived last night. Found him *au troisième* in the Hôtel du Mont Blanc; starts again for the Pyrenees to-morrow. A good deal of talk about the royal visit to Ireland, the good sense with which the king has acted, and the servile style in which poor Paddy received him; Mr. O'Connell preeminent in blarney and inconsistency. Many good results, however, likely to arise from the whole affair, if the king but continues in the same state of temperature towards Ireland in which he is at present."
September 10, 1821 : " Find that Lord Powerscourt, with whom the king dined the day he embarked from Ireland (Dunleary), was courageous enough to have a song of mine, 'The Prince's Day,'* sung before him, immediately after 'God save the King,' and that his majesty was much delighted with it."

* AIR—*Saint Patrick's Day.*

Tho' dark are our sorrows, to-day we'll forget them,
  And smile through our tears, like a sunbeam in showers :
There never were hearts, if our rulers would let them,
  More formed to be grateful and blest than ours.
    But just when the chain
    Has ceas'd to pain,
And hope has enwreath'd it round with flowers,
    There comes a new link
    Our spirits to sink—
Oh ! the joy that we taste, like the light of the poles,
Is a flash amid darkness, too brilliant to stay ;
But, though 't were the last little spark in our souls,
  We must light it up now, on our Prince's Day.

"This song is laudatory, for I thought at the time he deserved such; but upon reading it rather anxiously over, I find nothing in it to be ashamed of. What will those cowardly scholars of Dublin College say, who took such pains, at their dinner the other day, to avoid mentioning my name; and who, after a speech of some Sir Noodle, boasting of the poetical talent of Ireland, drank, as the utmost they could venture,

"Maturin and the rising poets of Erin,"

what will these white-liveried slaves say to the exhibition at Lord Powerscourt's? The only excuse I can find for the worse than eastern prostration into which my countrymen have grovelled during these few last weeks is, that they have so long been slaves, they know no better, and that it is not their own fault if

> Contempt on the minion who calls you disloyal!
> Tho' fierce to your foe, to your friends you are true;
> And the tribute most high to a head that is royal,
> Is love from a heart that loves liberty too.
> While cowards, who blight
> Your fame, your right,
> Would shrink from the fame of the battle array,
> The standard of Green
> In front would be seen—
> Oh! my life on your faith I were you summon'd this minute,
> You'd cast every bitter remembrance away,
> And show what the arm of old Erin has in it,
> When roused by the foe, on her Prince's Day.
>
> He loves the Green Isle, and his love is recorded
> In hearts which have suffer'd too much to forget:
> And hope shall be crown'd, and attachment rewarded,
> And Eriu's gay jubilee shine out yet.
> The gem may be broke
> By many a stroke,
> But nothing can cloud its native ray,
> Each fragment will cast
> A light to the last,—
> And thus Erin, my country, tho' broken thou art,
> There's a lustre within thee that ne'er will decay;
> A spirit which beams through each suffering part,
> And now smiles at all pain on the Prince's Day.

110 *O'Connell presents a Laurel Crown to Geo. IV.*

they know no medium between brawling rebellion and foot-licking idolatory.

"Mr. O'Connell, accompanied by a deputation of ten other gentlemen, presented a laurel crown, on his knee, to his majesty. His name was announced by Lord Sidmouth. The sovereign was pleased to notice him in the most marked and condescending manner. He shook his hand, and accepted the appropriate tribute with dignity and affection."

FAREWELL ADDRESS OF HIS MAJESTY BEFORE HE ENTERED THE STATE BARGE AT DUNLEARY.

"My friends! when I arrived in this beautiful country, my heart overflowed with joy—it is now depressed with sincere sorrow; I never felt sensations of more delight than since I came to Ireland. I cannot expect to meet any superior, nor many equal, till I have the happiness to see you again. Whenever an opportunity offers, whenever I can serve Ireland, I shall seize on it with eagerness. I am a man of few words—short adieus are best—God bless you all, my friends—God bless you all."

"This song we (*Dublin Evening Post*, 1821), understood was selected by Lord Powerscourt. The beautiful strain of feeling and of poetry which runs through it, excited the admiration of all present. His Majesty appeared even more delighted than any other person who heard it; he evinced the pleasure which he felt by his countenance, and the constant motion of his hands. He marked the singing of the following words with the most emphatic action:

"He loves the Green Isle, and his love is recorded
  In hearts which have suffer'd too much to forget:
And hope shall be crown'd, and attachment rewarded,
  And Erin's gay jubilee shine out yet.
    The gem may be broke
    By many a stroke,
But nothing can cloud its native ray
    Each fragment will cast
    A light to the last,
And thus Erin, my country, tho' broken thou art,
There's lustre within thee that ne'er will decay,
A spirit which beams through each suffering part,
And now smiles at all pain on the Prince's Day."

The king said at the Curragh, "If I live two years, I purpose revisiting Ireland: if not, I shall recommend it to my successors to become *personally acquainted with my* Irish subjects, of whom I am proud—indeed, I am delighted with them."

The following—the most satirical poem Lord Byron ever wrote next to his
  "English Bards and Scotch Reviewers,"
and which has been suppressed in all the *recent pirated* editions of his works, was aimed at the servility of the king's reception by the Irish people.

THE IRISH AVATAR.*

Avatar, in the Hindoo mythology, signifies the incarnation or metamorphosis of of some deity.

Ere the daughter of Brunswick is cold in her grave,
  And her ashes still float to their home o'er the tide,
Lo! George the triumphant speeds over the wave,
  To the long-cherish'd isle which he loved like his—bride. †

True, the great of her bright and brief era are gone,
  The rainbow-like epoch where Freedom could pause
For the few little years, out of centuries won,
  Which betray'd not, or crush'd not, or wept not her cause.

True, the chains of the Catholic clank o'er his rags,
  The castle still stands, and the senate's no more,
And the famine which dwelt on her freedomless crags
  Is extending its steps to her desolate shore.

To her desolate shore—where the emigrant stands
  For a moment to gaze ere he flies from his hearth;
Tears fall on his chain, though it drops from his hands,
  For the dungeon he quits is the place of his birth.

* By the kind permission of John Murray, Esq., Albemarle-street, London.

† "August 8th, 1821, half-past 10 o'clock.

"The struggle is over! Hope, fear, anxiety, are now alike at an end. CAROLINE, Queen of England, is no more!

"His Majesty arrived in Dublin on his birth-day, 12th August, 1821."

But he comes ! the Messiah of royalty comes !
  Like a goodly Leviathan roll'd from the waves !
Then receive him as best such an advent becomes,
  With a legion of cooks, and an army of slaves !

He comes in the promise and bloom of threescore,
  To perform in the pageant the sovereign's part—
But long live the shamrock which shadows him o'er !
  Could the green in his *hat* be transferr'd to his *heart !*

Could that long-wither'd spot but be verdant again,
  And a new spring of noble affections arise—
Then might freedom forgive thee this dance in thy chain,
  And this shout of thy slavery which saddens the skies.

Is it madness or meanness which clings to thee now ?
  Were he God—as he is but the commonest clay,
With scarce fewer wrinkles than sins on his brow —
  Such servile devotion might shame him away.

Ay, roar in his train ! let thine orators lash
  Their fanciful spirits to pamper his pride—
Not thus did thy Grattan indignantly flash
  His soul o'er the freedom implored and denied.

Ever-glorious Grattan !* the best of the good !
  So simple in heart, so sublime in the rest !
With all which Demosthenes wanted endued,
  And his rival or victor in all he possess'd.

Ere Tully arose in the zenith of Rome,
  Though unequall'd, preceded, the task was begun—
But Grattan sprung up like a god from the tomb
  Of ages, the first, last, the saviour, the *one !*

With the skill of an Orpheus to soften the brute ;
  With the fire of Prometheus to kindle mankind ;
Even Tyranny listening sate melted or mute,
  And Corruption shrunk scorch'd from the glance of his mind.

But back to our theme ! Back to despots and slaves !
  Feasts furnish'd by Famine ! rejoicings by Pain !
True freedom but *welcomes,* while slavery still *raves,*
  When a week's saturnalia hath loosen'd her chain.

---

* A memorial statue is about being erected in College-green, Dublin, to this illustrious Irishman. A. M. Sullivan, Esq., T.C., initiated this patriotic movement, having caused £300 to be placed in the Royal Bank as a first offering to this national undertaking

Let the poor squalid splendour thy wreck can afford
 (As the bankrupt's profusion his ruin would hide)
Gild over the palace, Lo! Erin, thy lord!
 Kiss his foot with thy blessings denied!

Or *if* freedom past hope be extorted at last,
 If the idol of brass find his feet are of clay,
Must what terror or policy wring forth be class'd
 With what monarchs ne'er give, but as wolves yield their prey?

Each brute hath its nature, a king's is to *reign*,—
 To *reign!* in that word see, ye ages, comprised,
The cause of the curses all annals contain,
 From Cæsar the dreaded to George the despised!

Wear, Fingal, thy trapping! O'Connell, proclaim
 His accomplishments! *His!!!* and thy country convince
Half an age's contempt was an error of fame,
 And that "Hal is the rascaliest, sweetest *young* prince!"

Will thy yard of blue riband, poor Fingal, recall
 The fetters from millions of Catholic limbs?
Or, has it not bound thee the fastest of all
 The slaves, who now hail their betrayer with hymns?

Ay! "Build him a dwelling" let each give his mite!
 Till, like Babel, the new royal dome hath arisen!
Let thy beggars and helots their pittance unite—
 And a palace bestow for a poor-house and prison!

Spread—spread, for Vitellius, the royal repast,
 Till the gluttonous despot be stuff'd to the gorge!
And the roar of his drunkards proclaim him at last
 The Fourth of the fools and oppressors call'd "George!"[*]

---

[*] "Lines composed on the occasion of his royal highness the Prince Regent being seen standing between the coffins of Henry VIII. and Charles I., in the royal vault at Windsor.

"Famed for contemptuous breach of sacred ties,
 By headless Charles, see heartless Henry lies;

Let the tables be loaded with feasts till they groan!
Till they *groan* like thy people, through ages of woe!
Let the wine flow around the old Bacchanal's throne,
   Like their blood which has flow'd, and which yet has to
    flow.

But let not *his* name be thine idol alone—
On his right hand behold a Sejanus appears!
Thine own Castlereagh! let him still be thine own!
   A wretch, never named but with curses and jeers!

Till now, when the isle which should blush for his birth,
   Deep, deep as the gore which he shed on her soil
Seems proud of the reptile which crawl'd from her earth,
   And for murder repays him with shouts and a smile!

Without one single ray of her genius, without
   The fancy, the manhood, the fire of her race—
The miscreant who well might plunge Erin in doubt
   If *she* ever gave birth to a being so base.

If she did—let her long-boasted proverb be hush'd,
   Which proclaims that from Erin no reptile can spring—
See the cold-blooded serpent, with venom full flush'd,
   Still warming its folds in the breast of a king!

Shout, drink, feast, and flatter! Oh! Erin, how low
   Wert thou sunk by misfortune and tyranny, till
Thy welcome of tyrants hath plunged thee below
   The depth of thy deep in a deeper gulf still.

My voice, though but humble, was raised for thy right,
   My vote, as a freeman's, still voted thee free,
This hand, though but feeble, would arm, in thy fight,
   And this heart, though outworn, had a throb still for *thee!*

   Between them stands another sceptred thing—
   It moves, it reigns, in all but name, a king.

" Charles to his people, Henry to his wife,
In him the double tyrant starts to life;
Justice and death have mix'd their dust in vain,
Each royal vampire wakes to life again.
Ah, what can tombs avail! since these disgorge
The blood and dust of both—to mould a G—ge. —BYRON.

The Glory of Grattan and Genius of Moore. 115

> Yes, I loved thee and thine, though thou art not my land,
>   I have known noble hearts and great souls in thy sons,
> And I wept with the world o'er the patriot band
>   Who are gone, but I weep them no longer as once.
>
> For happy are they now reposing afar,—
>   Thy Grattan, thy Curran, thy Sheridan, all
> Who, for years, were the chiefs in the eloquent war,
>   And redeem'd, if they have not retarded, thy fall.
>
> Yes, happy are they in their cold English graves !
>   Their shades cannot start to thy shouts of to-day,—
> Nor the steps of enslavers and chain-kissing slaves
>   Be stamp'd in the turf o'er their fetterless clay.
>
> Till now I had envied thy sons and their shore,
>   Though their virtues were hunted, their liberties fled ;
> There was something so warm and sublime in the core
>   Of an Irishman's heart, that I envy—thy *dead*.
>
> Or, if aught in thy bosom can quench for an hour
>   My contempt for a nation so servile, though sore,
> Which though trod like the worm will not turn upon power,
>   'Tis the glory of Grattan,* and genius of Moore !
>
> *Sept.* 16*th*, 1821.

Moore, in his Diary, Nov. 3, 1821, in alluding to this satire, says:—" Received Lord Byron's tremendous verses against the King and the Irish, for their late exhibition in Dublin ; *richly deserved* by my servile countrymen, but not, on this occasion, by the King, who, as far as he was concerned, acted well.

Nov. 4, 1821.—" The Blessingtons drove me to Holland House, and waited for me. Read Byron's verses to Lord and Lady Holland, and Allen ; much struck by them, but advised me not to have any hand in printing them."

George IV., with that blandishment of manner of which he was such a professor, feasted on everything Irish, wore everything Irish, lauded everything Irish, and particularly eulogized our great Irish

---

* See Appendix.—Patriotic letter of the Right Hon. Thomas O'Hagan, Lord Chancellor of Ireland, to the Earl of Charlemont, relative to the proposed statue in College-green, Dublin, to Henry Grattan.

square, St. Stephen's Green, although ruinous absenteeism, consequent upon the extinction of the Irish Parliament, had then denuded "the faire citie" of Dublin of a resident nobility and gentry.

"OH WIRRA STHRU."

'Twas how *he* thought each scene so fair
'Twas how he praised each street and square,
'Tis a pity people *don't live there!*
    Oh wirra sthru."

A thousand associations rendered Ireland dear to George IV., and George IV. dear to Ireland. When he was not only far from power, but opposed to power, she clung to him with prodigal affection. The Address of eighty-nine was one of the first fruits of her infant independence, and his coronation *Gazette* proved that he did not forget it. Nine Irish names elevated to the peerage were proofs that prosperity is not always without a heart, and that even in palaces gratitude may be met with. Independent of any personal affection for the reigning king, his visit to Ireland presented a phenomenon; it presented the first instance in Irish history of an English monarch visiting Ireland as a friend. When other monarchs came over, it was not a visit, but a visitation. Blood heralded their approach; blood marked their progress; blood tracked their return! Even their Viceroys, till the accession of the Brunswick dynasty, but too truly justified the bitter witticism of the late Sir Hercules Langrishe: "In what history," said a modern viceroy (Earl Fitzwilliam)—" in what history, Sir Hercules, shall I find an account of all the Irish Lords Lieutenant." "Indeed, I do not know, my Lord," replied Langrishe, "unless it be in a continuation of *rapine* (Rapin)."*

* This want of a history of the Irish viceroys is now supplied by Gilbert's history. The author of this work has also written on the viceroyalty of the late Earl of Carlisle.

The *London Observer*, 1821, alluding to the King's visit, says :—
"The interested vileness which has hitherto poisoned the royal ear of England, with respect to that country, which represented its warmth as barbarism, its fidelity as treason, its poverty as affected, and its mournings over sufferings without end or parallel as causeless discontent, will now lose its vocation. He will see a hardy, generous, afflicted, but forgiving people—poor, but liberal—persecuted, but patient—hospitable of the little that has been left them, and when all is gone, ready to give their blood for him. He will see in their country a reproachful loveliness—fertile, but uncultivated—wild, but magnificent—beauteous, but neglected—presenting a mine of unproductive wealth, a mass of unrespected grandeur, a waste of unprofitable and uneducated genius, but presenting them we trust and believe, to the eye of thier regenerator. The island gem lies rude and useless on its ocean bed; it is for his regal hand to raise it to its station, to kindle its radiance, to call forth its beauty, and to place it pure and rich and splendid in the forehead of his diadem."

SATIRICAL BALLADS.—JUDY'S LAMENTATION ON THE DEPARTURE OF HIS MAJESTY FROM DUBLIN*.

And are you gone, and are you gone !
And left Poor Pat again for John,
    Oh wira sthru ! Oh wira sthru !
Oh ! sure we thought that here you'd stay,
And give us many a happy day ;
Och hone ! you turned our heads astray,
    Oh wira sthru ! Oh wira sthru !

Oh ! its you that praised Sir Bradley's† taste,
In laying out the city feast,
    Oh wira sthru ! Oh wira sthru !
And och ! you thanked the Lady Mayor,
For bringing all the damsels rare,
That at yourself did *gape* and *stare*,
    Oh wira sthru ! Oh wira sthru !

---

* Copy of an old ballad given to W. B. Kelly, Grafton-street, by — Myatt, Esq.
† Sir Abraham Bradley King. Lord Mayor of Dublin, in 1821.

And its you, that with a mighty whack,
Be-titled all the City Pack,
  Oh wira sthru! Oh wira sthru!
For with your sword you gave the lick
To *Jonas, George,* and *Billy Nick,*
That into *Knights* transformed them quick,
  Oh wira sthru! Oh wira sthru!

Oh! you would not hear that *Toast* notorious,
Nor let *Aby* give the *Mem'ry glorious,*
  Oh wira sthru! Oh wira sthru!
But Darley's* heart did for it pant,
When Sidmouth† say'd, "Indeed you shan't,"
For fear of vexing *Charley Grant,*‡
  Oh wira sthru! Oh wira sthru!

Oh! its you to Church brought Lord Fingall,
And its you that gave the grandest Ball,
  Oh wira sthru! Oh wira sthru!
But least that those should go astray,
Who were ne'er but *once* at Levee day,
You *invited* them to *stay away,*
  Oh wira sthru! Oh wira sthru!

Oh! its you that left the Bank in haste,
Nor neither bit or sup wou'd taste,
  Oh wira sthru! Oh wira sthru!
And its you that on Kildare-street plain,
Old D—x—n's *freedom* did restrain,
And then set off, post haste to *Slane,*§.
  Oh wira sthru! Oh wira sthru!

Oh! it is you that at your own Kingstown,
From Dan received the fine *Green Crown,*
  Oh wira sthru! Oh wira sthru!
And its then you say'd, alack, alack,
When seated in your fishing smack,
"*Sure I'll be here when I come back,*"
  Oh wira sthru! Oh wira sthru!

On presenting the city address, the Lord Mayor knelt, and had the honour of kissing his Majesty's hand. As he was rising, the King said: "Not yet, my Lord Mayor;" and holding out his hand for the Lord Mayor to kiss a second time, said: "Now rise, Sir Abraham Bradley King, Baronet of the United Kingdom."

 * Alderman Darley, a police magistrate of Dublin, after speeching for a while at the magnificent banquet given by the city of Dublin to his Majesty, was the first man to fling the apple of discord amongst the king's loyal subjects, by giving the "Glorious, pious, and immortal memory."
 † Lord Sidmouth, Secretary of State for the Home Department.
 ‡ The Right Hon. Chas. Grant, Chief Secretary for Ireland, 1821.
 § Slane Castle, the magnificent seat of the Marquis of Conyngham, near Drogheda.

THE VICTORIA PIER AT KINGSTOWN.

Pleasing recollections, historic remembrances, saddened memories, and hopeful anticipations invest this pier.

Twenty thousand men embarked, in 1854, at this place for an arid peninsula in the remotest extremity of the Black Sea, where they and their French allies wrote a new page in the history of Europe, on the battle-fields of the Alma, Balaklava, and Inkerman, and by the storming and fall of the fortress of Sebastopol.

The *Grande Armee Irlandais* (then stationed in this country) sailed from this pier for the Crimea, full of strength, full of life and hope for the future, full of heroism, proud of their past victories, so richly emblazoned on their colours, yet leaving many a mournful and saddened heart behind.

"*Eastward, Ho!*" was the watchword and reply on this pier for upwards of two years.

> The stormers of the breach pass on, the daring sons of Eire,
> Light-hearted in the bayonet-strife as in the country fair;
> The mountaineer who woke the lark on Tipperary's hills,
> And he who kiss'd his sweetheart last by Shannon's silver rills.
> The "Rangers" of our western land who own that battle-shout,
> That brings the "Fag-an-bealag" blow, and seals the carnage rout;
> Those septs of our old Celtic land, who stand with death abreast,
> And prove how glorious is the fame of Islesmen of the West.
> * * * * *
> Oh, England! in your proudest time you never saw such sight,
> As when you flung her gauntlet down to battle for the right:
> What are the Scindian plains to us, the wild Caffrarian kloof,
> That glory may be bought too dear that brings a world's reproof?
> The brightest deed of glory is to help the poor and weak,
> And shield from the oppressor's grasp the lowly and the meek;
> And that thou'lt do—for never yet you raised your lion-crest,
> But victory has blest your sons, the Islesmen of the West.
> —*Dublin University Magazine.*

At the Victoria Pier a portion of the victorious army, returning from the Crimea, arrived in 1856, sadly thinned in numbers, badly maimed, yet exulting in their past glories and newly-acquired laurels, they returned in triumph, crowned with victory, and forgetful of their past endurances. The citizens of Dublin gave a grand national banquet to upwards of 3,000 of these soldiers, at which the late well-beloved Earl of Carlisle, then Lord Lieutenant of Ireland, presided.

The following is a portion of his speech, when addressing those heroes of the East,—His Excellency said, with feelings of emotion:—" It is indeed a deep cause of thankfulness to see you thus—you, who have breasted the deep slopes of the Alma—you, who have dashed along the fatal pass of Balaklava—you, who have held the blood-red heights of Inkerman—you, who have survived the midnight trench, the thundering rampart, and the deadly hospital—it is a matter of deep gratitude to see you thus under a roof of peace, and before a board of plenty. In addressing the Regiment of the Royal Irish upon so interesting and happy an occasion, the first of the kind that has occurred in the ancient capital of Ireland since the close of the late memorable war, I almost feel that I might carry my view even beyond your own well-filled ranks, and include all your countrymen who, by the side of their intrepid brethren in England and Scotland, and of our brave allies, have maintained the honour of their Sovereign and their race, alike by their brilliant valour and their heroic endurance throughout every turn and period of the desperate struggle. The ridges and dales of the fair Crimea, the deadly trench and bloody parapet, all are crowned with their thousand proofs that the heroic courage of Ireland has exhibited no falling off in the very newest of her sons."

His excellency then presented new colours to the celebrated 18th Royal Irish.

THE LATE EARL OF CARLISLE'S DEPARTURE FROM KINGSTOWN.

Lord Carlisle had resigned; his official life had closed; in Kingstown Harbour, alongside the "Carlisle Pier," the vessel lay moored that was soon to bear from the shores of Ireland the "good and amiable Viceroy." Alas! how changed was the appearance of the gay and sprightly nobleman who, a few short years before, had landed here with firm step, and stately and graceful bearing, in buoyant spirits and healthful vigour, whom the people welcomed with hope and joy! He was now about to leave, in utter prostration, his physical powers wholly exhausted. This reflection affected and deeply moved an affectionate and warm-hearted people. They were sensible of their own great loss, yet deeply lamented the sad and afflicting cause; their sorrowing hearts sympathized with the sufferings of their friend and noble benefactor.

An immense concourse were assembled to bid their esteemed Viceroy farewell—a fond, and as it proved, a last farewell. The vast assemblage poured forth humble blessings upon him, and fervent hopes for his recovery, and that he would soon return, to assume again the office of Viceroy, with renewed health and vigour.

How overpowering must have been the emotions— what mingled feelings of sorrow, pride, and pleasure, must have pervaded the mind of Lord Carlisle at this, the closing scene of his bright, official career! His natural display of feeling on this affecting and memorable occasion, was felt to be no indication of physical weakness, but rather the farewell of tender regard. He appeared on the deck, leaning on the arm of Lady Elizabeth Grey, the sister whom he loved so well. His last words at the moment of parting were: "I leave, after my term of office, undimmed by one particle of personal bitterness, either on the present or the crowded memories of the past ;" and, the vessel proceeding on her way, he continually waved his adieus towards the receding shore.

Sir Robert Peel, speaking of the loss of Lord Carlisle, and his departure, well and vividly describes the interesting scene:—

"I do venture to say, that never did a man leave the shores of Ireland towards whom a deeper regret at the affliction which had befallen him was felt, than towards Lord Carlisle. I do not know if I may observe on one particular fact connected with his departure; but I would venture to say, that there was no person who witnessed the departure of Lord Carlisle from the shores of Ireland who was not affected at the spectacle that was presented. Crowds of people were assembled in Kingstown, in silent regret, to wish him good-bye; and I have been told, when my gallant friend, the Commander-in-Chief, advanced to bid him a last good-bye, and when he took his hand and grasped it for a few minutes, and said, 'God bless you, Sir!' I do believe—that there was not a dry eye in the crowded assembly that was there to wish Lord Carlisle farewell. He stood till the last moment on the deck of the vessel; and, as it was leaving the shore, he cast a long, lingering look behind him at that country where he had spent almost the whole of his public life, and where his public services had been given. Many a person in that assembly must have recollected those touching lines of Moore, where he says :—

"'As slow our ship her foamy track
Against the wind was cleaving,
Her trembling pennant still looked back
To that dear isle 'twas leaving :

> So loth we part from all we love,
> From all the links that bind us;
> So turn our hearts, where'er we rove,
> On those we've left behind us.'"

So parted the noble lord, amidst the regrets of the citizens of Dublin, of the people of Ireland, and their yearning for his return. He was certainly the most popular Viceroy that ever administered the affairs of Ireland, and his successor will find it difficult to rival him in those social and administrative qualities which marked the public conduct and private demeanour of Lord Carlisle.

KINGSTOWN HARBOUR.

The quarries of Dalkey supplied the granite* for the construction of the piers of this harbour, the first stone of which was laid in 1817, by Lord Whitworth, then Viceroy of Ireland. The East Pier stretches out into the Bay of Dublin 2,800 feet :—it affords a most charming promenade, particularly to convalescents who may require the invigorating sea breeze. A monument is erected on this Pier in memory of the heroic and intrepid Captain Boyd, who with a number of seamen of the "Ajax" lost their own lives while nobly trying to save the lives of others in a fearful storm, February 9th, 1861. He afterwards had a public funeral, and was buried in St Patrick's Cathedral, 1st of March, 1861.

The author who was present at Kingstown during this memorable storm, addressed several letters to the public journals on the sad and painful event. As these letters contained a description of the terrible scene and the effects of the storm—which made

* See Appendix for the particulars of the great granite chain which extends from Kingstown into the County of Waterford, read at the meeting of the British Association, August 1835.

a deep impression on his mind—and also some observations which he was impelled to make on the absence of all aid—of life-boats, and of any effective arrangements for the saving of life, he feels assured that he will be excused for reproducing here such portions of these letters as more particularly apply to the consideration of a subject of such vital importance and necessity; and he ardently hopes that his observations have attracted some attention, and that means, effective means, have been since provided for rendering assistance, in a similar crisis, for the preservation of life and property.*

At all events, these letters will serve as a faint narrative of the wild scene of confusion and ruin—written, as they were, under extreme excitement; when
"The angels of death spread their wings on the blast,"
and bore away the brave Boyd and his faithful followers.

To the Editor of the Freeman.
Kingstown, Saturday Evening.
February 9th, 1861.

DEAR SIR—Having heard early this morning of the melancholy accident which deprived my friend Captain Boyd and some of his gallant crew of their lives in endeavouring to rescue others from a watery grave, I visited the Eastern Pier while the storm continued to blow "wondrous strong" from the N.E., accompanied by rain, snow, and sleet, the tide was hissing, surging, and furiously battling with the outward barrier of artificial rock work which protects the Eastern Pier, over which this morning it completely swept, a receding wave engulphing gallant Boyd and his manly followers. The spectacle was truly awful, fragments of the wreck lay about in the

* A house for the life-boat has since been erected at Kingstown harbour, but unfortunately at the *wrong side* of the eastern pier.

most fantastic forms, the whole presenting the appearance of an immense box of matches crushed by a railway train. The first body was found at half-past two o'clock. On searching through the rocks near the *debris* of the wreck in company with Mr. Charles Nicholls the well-known artist, and a sailor boy, we discovered the body of an old man, closely held between the rocks, entangled in the cordage and a remnant of the sails of the ill-fated vessel. He was evidently at the helm when she struck, having the remains of a seacoat and large boots attached to his person, whilst his comrades, who were afterwards found, were nearly naked. We extricated the body with much difficulty from the wreck and rock work, placed it on the pathway of the pier, composed the limbs, and covered the face (which had been bleeding from a severe contusion) with his woollen tie. During the recent gales on the coast of England we were told that the entire fishing, seafaring, and naval population of the villages turned out and lined the coast and headlands anxiously watching to see if they could render any assistance to vessels in distress. Was such the case this day at Kingstown? Certainly not. It was a matter of much surprise to those gentlemen present that, out of the large nautical population of this rising town, there were only two men present who lent an assisting hand to recover the bodies of those who perished in the cause of mercy. At twelve o'clock a ship was seen in distress surging in towards the rock-bound coast where poor Boyd met his death. The moments were anxious and terrible. She was already given up as lost. The wind veered a point, the vessel answered her helm, and with a yard or so of canvas she drifted into the harbour. If she had struck on the rocks there were none present who could have rendered any material service either with ropes, boats, or life buoys. The police, tired and fatigued, were removing the bodies. Where was the lifeboat of which we have heard so much? A proper storm-proof building should be provided for its reception near the battery. When a gentle ripple agitates the waters of Kingstown harbour, the "*lifeboat is manned*" to astonish your suburban telescope sailors, nurse maids and old ladies in bath chairs, at an expense of ten shillings each man, but when the storm rages and every moment threatens death and desolation, the lifeboat is securely "housed." The ship which so narrowly escaped destruction had scarcely cast anchor in the harbour, when his Excellency the Earl of Carlisle arrived at the scene of wreck and devastation. His sympathies were awakened, and true and heartfelt sorrow was depicted on his countenance when he found that his gallant and pure-minded friend, Captain Boyd, was no more. A highly intelligent seafaring man explained the morning's disasters to his Excellency, who stood within a few yards of the dead body of an aged seaman,—made further inquiries relative to the melancholy incident, and shortly afterwards took his departure. The Eastern Pier is again left in comparative loneliness, the tide is on the rise, and the storm as boisterous as ever. A carriage approaches the scene —a lady, closely muffled—the wife of Captain Boyd, of the Ajax—steps out ; the boat of the Ajax is hailed; she enters—her heart "with silent grief oppressed ;" and as the boat puts off for the ship of mourning, exclaims, with mingled feelings of hope and anguish, " He cannot be lost, and, through the mercy of God, he will surely return." We had at this time occasion to visit Kingstown to change our clothes, which were completely saturated with rain, sleet, and seawater; at the corner of George's-street a group of idle men were " stopping the way," scarcely a mile from a scene of misery, where the least of them could have been of use. We returned to the wreck both sickened and saddened. Shortly afterwards the naked body of a fourth seaman was discovered. The police were now making every exertion to be of service ere the night closed on the scene of death. We again searched among the rocks and found a leg with a good boot and neat sock, protruding from a crevice, upheaved granite rocks concealing the remainder of the body. We immediately gave the alarm, thinking at the time it was Captain Boyd's body. A messenger was at once despatched to procure the attendance of the men of the "Ajax," who quickly came to the place, the body was extricated with the greatest possible difficulty from under the huge mass of rock-work, which must have been dashed about like small pebbles on the shore. It was found to be poor Curry, one of the finest and handsomest men in her Majesty's navy. The scene was truly heartrending when the men recognised their ship-mate, who left the "Ajax" that morning in the prime of life and manly heart, to lend a willing hand with his beloved captain in the cause of mercy. Curry's features were beautiful, even in death. Those honest, brave, and affectionate tars bore him on their shoulders, nearly a mile to the admiralty yard, which had now presented the appearance of a *morgue*. They had some refreshment, and afterwards returned in sorrow to the frigate. Night closed in, and storm and darkness took possession of the Eastern Pier—now the marine *via dolorosa* of Kingstown.

THE VICTIMS OF THE STORM—THEIR BURIAL.

To the Editor of the Evening Mail.

"Peace to the memory of the brave,
Tranquil may their slumbers be.
Peace to the dead beneath the wave;
Brave, gentle Boyd, peace to thee."

DEAR SIR,—It was a saddening sight to-day—the funeral of the drowned. The day, Ash

Wednesday; the occasion, the interment of the remains of fine and stalwart men—brave, gallant men—called to eternity in the midst of robust health, and under circumstances the mere contemplation of which would cause the stout-hearted to cower. But a few hours, comparatively, have passed since this harbour was the scene of a desperate riot of the elements. The angry wave which but yesterday carried 'murder unnatural' on its crest has subsided, (wearied and satiated with its work of destruction), into glassy smoothness. The apparently volcanic revellings on this rock-bound harbour are now numbered with the 'things that were.' All seems gentle, subdued, quiet. Melancholy broods over the scene—every one of the thousands who are assembled on the pier is impressed with a sad memory—all are silent—naught is heard but the altercations of the wreck gatherers (collecting the saturated fragments of the many "ill-fated ships,") or the shrill, sharp cry of the gull as it scuds by, and suddenly dives in search of its prey. But soon another sound is heard—'did you not hear it?' The cannon boom out the announcement that earth is about to receive its own.—The marine martyrs are being borne to the last resting-place.—The day is bright; yet all seems gloomy.—Ships wear their bunting half mast.—Grief is marked on every countenance as the mourners fall in to take part in the sad ceremony.—Nothing is left undone to testify the sorrow which they feel for the hard fate of the brave dead—military honours of the first-class are paid.—The officers of her Majesty's service, dressed in state, wear crape.—The procession forms, thousands join it.—Shops suspend their business,—Cannon continue to boom at regular intervals.—The marines, with inverted arms, take their place,—the 'Dead March in Saul' completes the saddening character of the ceremonial. With measured step and pent up grief the procession wends its way to the grave. Tears, friendly and sincere tears, dim eyes that had almost forgotten their use. The coffins, piled on the cannon carriages, (flags of heroic and glorious association enshrouding them), are drawn along by brave sailors, and the ministers of God of all denominations take part in the mournful proceedings. Still the procession is moving on—still the canon speaks out the public mourning, and silent, half-stifled supplications are sent forth. The graves at Monkstown are reached, the funeral ceremony performed, rounds fired, and then begins the heavy dead fall of earth, and the grave has received its first instalment of the many victims of the fearful storm of Saturday.

DUNLEARY HARBOUR—HISTORICAL ASSOCIATIONS.

The area enclosed by the two piers, East and West, covers 251 acres. Parliament advanced nearly a million of money towards the construction of this harbour, to be repaid by certain duties leviable off the vessels coming into it. Its situation is about half a mile eastward of the old harbour of Dunleary, at which the second Earl of Essex landed as Viceroy of Ireland in 1672, as did the Earl of Northington in 1783. Sir Anthony St. Leger, Viceroy of Ireland, sailed from Dunleary in 1554.* It is to be hoped

* Sir A. St. Leger built Maryborough Castle, now in ruins, A.D. 1547, in the reign of Queen Mary, to protect the English interests; and during the insurrection of the O'Mores, O'Dempseys, &c., in which the Earl of Essex was defeated at the "Pass of Plumes," 1559, this strong fort was held for the Queen's (Elizabeth) Majesty, by Captains Hartpole, Bowen, and Pigott, "all three ancestors of old country families in this land." In 1598, the castle of Lea was taken by the Irish chieftain O'More, who, having established a garrison, marched with a considerable force, and successfully attacked the Earl of Essex, then chief governor, at the pass of Ballybrittas. From the quantity of feathers taken from the gay soldiers of the English favorite, the field of action was called "The Pass of the Plumes."

the day is not far distant, when, through the energy of her local merchants, the harbour of Kingstown shall reflect the sails and funnels of a thriving traffic, and that the hum of busy labour shall musically resound on its Victoria, and Carlisle Wharfs, Landing Stages, and Eastern and Western Piers. Then Kingstown may become a youthful and aspiring rival of Liverpool.

Monkstown has had its "Tom Bradley," who raised that aristocratic and commanding pile "Longford-terrace." Bray has had its Quinn, Dargan, Breslin, and Brennan, men of progress who have left their mark on the stately buildings of that fashionable watering place of the first resort. Kingstown has its Gresham and Bryan,* who have erected beautiful terraces, magnificent parks, fringed by first-class modern houses, and palatial residences. A most commanding view of the Bay of Dublin is to be had from the "Royal Terrace," and "Gresham-terrace," so called after the worthy and estimable Mr. Thomas M. Gresham, who built a hotel in Sackville-street, Dublin, of world-wide reputation. This terrace with its spacious and elegant hybrid hotel (the Royal Marine), in front of which is Victoria Square, with its beautifully ornamented walks, statues, flower knots, and sparkling fountains, that is, *when* the Kingstown Commissioners succeed in inducing the bubbling brook, which passes through and near the Druid's and Bride's Glens, to change its course,

* The Messrs. Gresham and Bryan are gentlemen who have stood out from the canvass of their age in this locality. They are decidedly the most public spirited men in the Kingstown Township. Mr. P. W. Bryan, T.C., has spent £80,000 in building Clarinda Park, and upwards of 100 first-class houses in Kingstown. He has applied the energies of a vigorous mind, and the wealth acquired by an industrious life, to beautify this charming place—with marine villas, which he may now look upon with justifiable pride. This gentleman and Mr. Gresham (the father of Kingstown) possess that genial kindness of heart which must make mankind their well-wishers and friends.

the source of which they *discovered* after a *diligent* search, at a corporate pic-nic, in a tiny and secluded well, in a ravine of the "Three Rock Mountain;" while at their own doors, in old Dunleary, in the parish of Monkstown, the ancient and famous "Juggy's Well" discharges more delicious water in a year into natural conduits passing to the sea, than would supply the Orientals of Pekin, the most populous city in the world for a season—*mais tel est le monde.* The Victoria Gardens nearly extend to the new and handsome Gothic Church, with its light and graceful steeple (a welcome beacon to the tempest-tossed mariner)—immediately in the foreground, on the verge of the shore, are the Royal St. George and Royal Irish Yacht Clubs—*le tout ensemble* presenting a most picturesque and magnificent appearance when viewed from the sea.

At the Royal Yacht Clubs the *creme de creme* of the aristocracy and gentry assemble during the Kingstown Regatta, which generally takes place every August. The usual gaiety of the place during this aquatic carnival is much increased by the brilliant appearance of the harbour, which contains an immense assemblage of elegant pleasure vessels of every size and rig, from the ship and steamer of 500 tons burthen to the yawl of only ten; while in the sanctuary of the harbour, securely moored from all northern and eastern winds, the "war vessel" of the station (at present the Royal George) calmly and nobly floats on its peaceful waters, forming a charming and attractive addition to this highly interesting picture, a royal salute is fired, "all hands on board man the yards" amidst a profusion of bunting and flags of every nation, on the arrival or departure of Viceroys.

KINGSTOWN.

Kingstown owes its present proud position and growing prosperity to its having the Model Railway of the British Empire, and the most perfect Mail Service in the world, in connection with Holyhead.

On Saturday, October the 4th, 1834, the first trial of the steam engine "Vauxhall," with a small train of carriages filled with ladies and gentlemen, was made on this railway from Dublin to the Martello Tower at Williamstown. Large crowds of people were assembled at various points to witness the passing of the engine. The experiment is said to have given great satisfaction, not only as to the rapidity of motion, ease of conveyance, and facility of stopping, but the celerity and quickness with which the train passed (by means of the crossings) from one line of road to another. The distance—about two miles and a-half—was performed four times each way, at the rate of about thirty-one miles per hour. The control over the machinery was complete, the stopping and reversing the motion was effected without a moment's delay.

On the 9th of October, 1834, a train of carriages, crowded with ladies and gentlemen, proceeded the entire length of the line from the station-house at Westland-row to Salthill. There were eight carriages attached to the train; one of the first class, three second, and four of the third class. The first trip was made by the locomotive engine called the Hibernia, and with the many disadvantages attendant on a first starting, the trip from the station-house to Salthill, was performed in fifteen and a-half minutes, and again back to Dublin in twenty-three minutes.

A second trip was made by the Vauxhall locomotive engine, which performed the journey to Kingstown, in fourteen minutes and a-half; and back to Dublin in twenty-two and a-half minutes.

Several other trials were made with the different engines; all proved eminently successful. The application of steam—that subtile and mysterious vapour—as a motive power, was now, for the *first time*, on trial *in Ireland*. Hopes, fears, and feelings of danger, alternately prevailed.

Success, however, is the crown of every social revolution. The great problem of steam, as a motive power, was solved in Ireland, beyond the hopes of the most sanguine. Suspense, doubt, and danger were dispelled. The minds of all who occupied the experimental trains were filled with admiration, as the train from Dublin rolled majestically on its iron way—smoothly, rapidly; all, *una voce*, expressed their pleasure and delight at the perfect ease, rapidity, and imperceptibility of the movement, so that it was possible to read, and even write, with convenience.

Whirled along by the stupendous though invisible agency of steam, the astonished passengers (as has been happily observed) glided, Asmodeus-like, over the summits of the houses and streets of a great city—were presently transported through green fields and plantations of trees—skimmed across the surface of the sea—then, taking shelter under the cliffs, coasted by marine villas—passed through rocky excavations—and finally found themselves in the centre of a great seaport town, which unites, with pleasing variety, the bustle of a commercial city with the amusements of a fashionable watering-place.

To those who have not seen the beauties of Dublin bay and its vicinity, it is impossible to convey an adequate impression of the effect produced on the mind of the spectator from the moving railway train.

The following description of the Kingstown Railway Works is taken from *The Dublin Penny Journal*, 1834:—

"The character of the works, the variety of the different constructions, and the costly expenditure upon the Dublin and Kingstown railway, contrasted with the uniform level appearance which the country presents to the eye of a casual observer (glancing over the level ground, between the south side of Dublin and the shores of the bay), prompt the not unnatural remark of the cheapness and facility with which a railway might have been constructed. But many causes have concurred in requiring a continual change in the transverse sections of the railway, which have, certainly, greatly added to the novelty and interest of the work, though, at the same time, difficulties have been increased, and expenses augmented far beyond what has ever been required to form a level passage through the most difficult districts where railways have been introduced.

Among those causes may be enumerated the expediency of penetrating deeply into the centre of the metropolis; the attention requisite to be paid to public safety, and to vested and incorporated rights; the great value of the property, whether as building sites or suburban grounds; the interposition of secluded demesnes; the preservation of the bathing, boating, and other accommodations of individuals, and of the public along the coast; the necessity of making the course of the road as direct as possible, and of connecting the several changes of direction by easy curves; the caution to be exercised in tracing a complete and isolated route for the peculiar machines to be employed (through the rich and populous district in the vicinity of a large commercial city), to a termination on the quays of the finest artificial harbour in the world—where the smallest nautical conveniences had to be preserved from interference, or to be amply compensated for and replaced—close to the streets of a rising and populous borough, the conveniences and even the apprehensions of whose inhabitants had to be consulted.

The original intention was to have commenced the railway at the rere of the college buildings, and to have skirted the college park, parallel to Great Brunswick-street. This would have made the starting point about the Clarendon stables, and within a very short distance of the very centre of Dublin business. Vague fears, misrepresentations, and other causes, created an outcry against such a proposition, which, it is hoped, at a future and not distant period, may still be realized.

THE HOLYHEAD PACKETS AND MAIL SERVICE.

The noble and graceful looking steamers that sail from Kingstown Harbour twice every day, are unequalled in any other British or foreign port. A *quartette* and harmonious commercial union of really splendid vessels, commanded by gentlemen, whose courtesy and kindness to tens of thousands of passengers who annually travel with them across Channel, are only equalled by their great efficiency as first-class seamen in the most unqualified sense of the words, and by their anxiety for the preservation of life, and vast property entrusted to their safe keeping, by the energetic and spirited Directors of the

"CITY OF DUBLIN STEAM PACKET COMPANY,"

who deserve the thanks of the nation at large, for having placed on this great international transit and connecting link, steam vessels of such enormous power, vast proportions, and perfect nautical construction, unsurpassed in luxurious elegance and home comforts, as that to be found in the *Leinster*,

Munster, Connaught, and *Ulster,* now commanded by Captain Rogers, Captain Kendal, Captain Slaughter, and Captain Triphook

---

DUBLIN AND LONDON, 1793.

The following extracts from a report, relative to shortening the time in transmitting the mails from Dublin to London, was presented to the Irish Parliament, in 1793, by the Chief Directors of Inland Navigation. They will be read with much interest by the gentlemen interested in the transit of Her Majesty's Royal Mail at the present day.

"Look upon this picture, and upon this."

"The communication between London and Dublin may be shortened in point of time nearly one-half: to judge of this, it is necessary to see how the mail is despatched at present (1793); it is sent to the packet at different hours, from six till twelve in the evening, according as the tide serves; but when the tide serves between twelve and six, it waits for the tide: so that, taking the average, there are three hours here lost for one-half of the year. It is put on board the packet at the Pigeon-house Dock. If the wind blow fresh from the east, or north-east, the packet cannot sail; and thus an entire tide, sometimes two tides, or twenty-four hours, are lost. If the wind happens to blow fresh from the north at neap tides, the packet is sometimes neaped in the dock, as happened last summer, and, therefore, cannot sail; all this to the very great injury of trade. When the packet sails, unless the wind be to the westward, she has considerable difficulty in working out, to the great loss of time. When she arrives at Holyhead, which, taking an average of nine hours, is, perhaps, too short a time, the mail there waits for the coach to go out in the morning, and crossing two ferries, and passing over several mountains, and the sands of Cheshire, forty-seven hours are allowed for its arrival in London, but in general it takes forty-eight. When the mail returns to Holyhead, nearly the same delays arise there again, (for that also is a tide harbour,) so that, taking the average, a letter written from Dublin to London is in general not answered in less than a week; but, supposing the packet to lie and take in the mail at the Sound of *Ireland's Eye*, the mail would then be despatched at a certain hour every night, for the packet could sail at any given hour, and with any wind that blows, and could go out in weather that she could not work out in from the Pigeon-house Dock, and in fifteen minutes from the time the mail is put on board, she would be completely at sea, lying her course. When the mail arrives at Holyhead, if, instead of sending it across two ferries to Chester, it were sent from Bangor ferry, along Lord Penryn's road, coming out at the head of the valley of Llanroost, to Shrewsbury, by paying a little attention to shortening the road through Anglesea, and finishing Lord Penryn's road about four miles, the distance might be shortened by twenty-four miles. The distance between Holyhead and Shrewsbury at present is one hundred and fourteen miles; shortened by twenty-four, it would be ninety. The expenses attending the completing this line of road would not exceed £4,000. The distance between Dublin and Ireland's Eye might be shortened half a mile, and make the distance six miles and a-half. Supposing, then, this mode adopted, the mail cart might run from Dublin to Ireland's Eye in one hour; from Ireland's Eye, the packet being near two leagues to the eastward of the Pigeon House, and being so readily at sea, by giving a little premium to the captain and crew (supposing a guinea a trip), for

each time the mails were landed in twelve hours
after delivered, this being little more than the rate
of four knots (or miles) an hour, five times out of six
the mails would be delivered in time; and if, instead
of sacrificing the interest of the public to the convenience of mail coach travellers, their interest were to
give way, and the mails be sent forward in a lighter
carriage, carrying two passengers only, and the coachman and guard, with a little encouragement the mails
might be pushed from Holyhead to Llangollen (sixty
miles by the short road), at the rate of seven miles
an hour, and from Llangollen, the difficulties of the
Welch road being surmounted, and the road from
thence through Shrewsbury to London (one hundred and eighty-six miles) good, the mail might be
pushed at the rate of eight miles and a-half an
hour (the mails to Shrewsbury formerly ran ten
miles an hour), the account of time would then stand
thus—

	Hours
From Dublin to Ireland's Eye,	1
Putting mails on board,	0¼
From Ireland's Eye to Holyhead,	12
Landing mails,	0¾
From Hollyhead to Llangollen, allowing for cross-ing Bangor ferry,	10
From Llangollen to London,	23
Total,	47

"Supposing, then, the mails to leave Dublin at
eight in the evening, they would be at Holyhead a
quarter past nine in the morning; leave Holyhead
at ten, be at Llangollen at seven in the evening, and
in London at five the next evening, and letters might
be answered by that night's post; and, supposing the
Irish mails to leave London also at eight, and allowing one hour more for coming from Llangollen by
night, the mail would be at Dublin at six the fourth
evening. Upon return of the mail from London, in

order to avoid any delay arising at Holyhead from waiting for the tide, a short pier should be run out from the rock near the light-house, at which the packet next in order for sailing should lie afloat, and which would be then ready for sea at any time of the tide, and thus the communication between the two countries would be completed, without losing time on either side; the expense of this pier would amount to about £4,000. The advantages of such expeditious communications are too obvious to need argument.

"Another advantage arising from the adoption of this plan would be the speedy dispatch of government expresses, which at present are frequently delayed for hours together on account of the tide."

DUNLEARY.

LORD CLONMEL—THE SHAM SQUIRE AND MAGEE—"TEMPLE HILL" (OTHERWISE FIAT HILL)—MAGEE'S FETE AND PIG HUNT.

At Dunleary is "Temple Hill," once the favourite country seat of Chief Justice Clonmel, a personal friend of Mr. J. Fitzpatrick's immortal "Sham Squire," where the highly popular journalist, Magee of the *Dublin Evening Post*, got up his celebrated "Olympic Pig Hunts," &c., to worry his enemy, Lord Earlsfort, afterwards Earl of Clonmel, of Irish *lettres de cachet* notoriety.

The Sham Squire and Chief Justice Clonmel were chums in early life, and the judge constantly went out of his way on the bench to decide unconstitutionally in favour of Higgins, and to the prejudice of Magee of the *Evening Post*, who, with a courage unapproached, denounced the dark doings and the pernicious influence of the Sham Squire, to whom it really seemed the country was bowing down as to Baal. Higgins put Magee in dungeons on successive fiats of Lord Clonmel; but when he regained his liberty, on enormous bail, he resolved in turn to be revenged on the chief justice, who lived at Temple Hill, Monkstown, now the seat of Robert Gray, Esq. It was magnificently planted and laid out in costly pleasure grounds. Magee hired the fields adjoining, where he advertised foot-races, ball-kicking, running in sacks, and pursuing pigs with soaped tails, which were to become the property of the winner. A fine fat boar was christened Shamado, and other pigs, wearing wigs of different forms and hue, were known to personate Lord Clonmel, Daly, and others of that clique. Eight thousand people assembled, the great bulk of whom were supplied with porter by Magee. The pigs having been let loose, burst through the fences into Lord Clonmel's pleasure grounds, followed by the mob, who utterly destroyed its beauty, on which the chief justice expended several thousand pounds, and many an hour of his precious time in superintending.

The following is a copy of the original placard in which Magee announces to the citizens of Dublin, washed and unwashed, the forthcoming fetes at Fiat Hill. The intimation that this festivity was in honour of the birth of George, Prince of Wales, was an ingenious pretext, framed by legal advice, with the object of averting renewed strokes of vengeance from " the Premier of the King's Bench." Magee's real object, it is hardly necessary to repeat, was to worry Lord Earlsfort, for his lordship had not, for a month later, obtained the earldom of Clonmel, a sop thrown, as he himself confesses, to allay the ruffled feelings which Magee's persecution caused. Here is the placard, but in the original every line was, as is technically termed, " displayed :"—

" Magee, of the Arms of Ireland, Steward of the Irish Festivity, or Lau Braugh Pleasura in honour of the Birth of George, Prince of Wales, on old Lammas Day, Wednesday, August 12th—Presents his grateful acknowledgments to the men of Ireland, and most respectful compliments to those who are the fairest objects of this creation—the lovely daughters of Hibernia—that every preparation is made, and will be positively ready for their reception, to grace with their presence and honour by their appearance, the Irish Festivity, or Lau Braugh Pleasura, which will commence with a Boat Race—the Boats all ranged and to start from the Pier of Dunleary to a minute at 11 o'clock. At one o'clock the Ball will be kicked on Fiat Hill, the grounds adjoining John Scott, Baron Earlsfort, Premier of the Court of King's Bench, his magnificent seat at Marino, late Lord Tracton's. Dinner on the tented field at three o'clock. The Table D'Hote for ladies and gentlemen. Cudgel playing at five on a proper stage, with cool umpires to prevent ill temper and preserve good humour. At seven o'clock his worship, the Sham, will be coursed over the grounds. To close with harpers and pipers for the boys and girls. Printed directions will be ready for delivery on Monday for the disposition of the carriages. Ground will be allotted for the tavern keepers and publicans who choose to erect tents, which must be well and handsomely covered and ranged, so as to produce effect and accommodate the assembly. No person will be suffered to erect a tent on Fiat Hill but those who have characters; these must be real, not Sham. The cold collation, it is expected, will be such as ought to be placed before Hibernians, and served in that clean, regular manner, which must be creditable to the host. Fiat Hill will be open to every publican who engages to the steward to bring on the tented field wines good in their kind—native punch—nectar-ambrosial—nectar and provision—the best Dublin markets supply. As some honest people at present have the grass of the grounds, and will to the 25th of March, from the late proprietor, it is submitted whether some small compensation should not be made for trespass; therefore, suppose each tent pays 2s. 8¼d., carriage, 6½d., Berlin, 3d., and horse, 2d. Proper persons to be appointed to take care of the cattle and carriages. Fiat Hill is the ground lately held by Lady Osborne, and stretches from Lord Earlsfort's demesne wall along the Blackrock road, leading to Dunleary. Lady Osborne has leased the lands in perpetuity to Magee, of the Arms of Ireland, late Fiat Dungeon Cell No. 4 in the new Bastile opposite the Courts of Irish Justice, Steward of the Irish Festival, or Lau Braugh Pleasura, at Dunleary, in honour of George, Prince of Wales, on Lammas Day."

The *Dublin Evening Post* of August 13, 1789, has the following remarks on the Fiat Hill fete:—

"The foot ball agitated the whole field into exertion; not a pedestrian who did not throw in his might, and gave a hearty and unlimited kick to the fiat ball, which was lined with a bladder of fetid gas; this, with the unanimous approbation of a million, was footed up to Marino, and kicked into the premises of the Premier of the Court of King's Bench."

Magee's triumph was complete.

"When the free spirits of Irishmen," records a journal of the day, "shall have nobly burst the shackles forged for their dearest privileges, when Bastile law shall exist only amongst us in an indignant recollection, and when Irish fiats shall be cast into the same oblivious gulf with French *lettres de cachet*, it will be remembered that the standard of resistance was erected on Fiat Hill, under the very ramparts of the enemy, by a citizen of Dublin."

Thus it seems that Lord Clonmel, as well as Lord Norbury, exercised, unwarrantably under colour of law, the power of issuing fiats, whereby, in order to gratify private malignity and spleen, personal liberty was wantonly invaded. Lord Norbury, indeed, was the chief object of public odium and ridicule in the public journals, for the abusive exercise of this power. A rather impious parody on the Nicene Creed, beginning—" I believe in Judge Bladderchops, the Father of 'Fiats,'" appears in *Cox's Magazine* for February, 1810. "Bladderchops" was a nickname applied to Lord Norbury, in allusion to his Eolus-like cheeks.* But this practice of issuing fiats had at length become so odious and intolerable, that it was summarily checked by Parliament.

TOPOGRAPHY OF DUNLEARY AND KINGSTOWN.

On almost every map of Ireland which has been published during the last two centuries, a place called the "THREE CHURLS," appears marked on each map, near Dunleary. The author sought information in vain from the "*oldest inhabitant*" as to the present locality of the *Churls*, until he forwarded a letter of enquiry to the *Irish Times*, to which he received the following courteous and interesting reply:—

"THE THREE CHURLS.

"*Blackrock, Dublin, July 7th*, 1868.

"DEAR SIR,—In reply to your favour of this day, I regret much that I did not keep any copy of my

---

* "Ireland before the Union," by Mr. J. Fitzpatrick, the eminent biographer of Dr. Doyle, Lord Cloncurry, Lady Morgan, and author of the justly celebrated works "The Sham Squire," and "Ireland before the Union;" works replete with the most interesting features of Ireland's past history.

note to you in reference to the 'Three Churls.' However, I shall try to comply with your request in this letter as far as I can. On reading a letter from you in a number of the *Irish Times* newspaper of last week, requesting information as to the locality of the 'Three Churls,' it gratified me to be able to point out, by modern names, the exact place referred to. In the year 1826, the Tithe Commissioners then acting, described in the tithe composition assessment book of the parish of Monkstown, under the column of *townlands*, the 'Churls,' and of owners, 'Lords Longford and De Vesci.' My personal knowledge of this part of the country enables me to acquaint you that the 'Churls' comprise that portion of Kingstown extending from Old Dunleary harbour, by Clarence-street, to Lower George's-street, thence by the left-hand side, to a point in Upper George's-street nearly on a line with the east pier, and thence to the sea. These lands were formerly in the possession and occupation of the then tenants of the Messrs. Walnutt, Hanlon, and Sexton, and are now familiarly known as *Gresham Terrace*, and the lands in front of it to the sea. The lands embracing and adjoining the police-office, formerly the nunnery, and the lands belonging to the Commissioners of Kingstown Harbour, also the 'Quarry Field,' belonging to the Corporation of Dublin Port, Crofton Terrace, Mr. Walsh's hotel, now known as the 'Anglesea Arms Hotel,' Plunkett Lodge, and the land belonging to the Harbour Commissioners of Kingstown. It may also be interesting to you to know, that in the key to the print of King George the Fourth's embarkation at Kingstown, on the 3rd September, 1821 (now in my possession), by John Lushington Reilly, Esq., the following description is given:—'No. 16, J. L. R., Esq., taking his sketches from the *Churl Rocks*.' The spot indicated appears to be just about where the Kingstown Railway terminus now stands. This description fully supports

my statement, and may be satisfactory to you. If I
can be instrumental in affording you any further information as to the topography of Kingstown or
Dalkey, I shall be very glad, indeed, to do so.—I remain, dear sir, yours very truly,
"EDWARD L. ALMA.
"J. J. Gaskin, Esq."

O'Connell was accompanied by upwards of 100,000
persons, marching in procession from Dublin to
Kingstown, on going to take his seat in Parliament,
as M.P. for Clare, after the passing of the Emancipation Bill, in 1829. On the evening of the day on
which he left for London, a great fall of snow took
place, by which many persons lost their lives.

"ANCIENT AND MODERN TIMES."
*From the Portfolio of an Artist. Written on George the
Fourth's Visit to Ireland, 1821.*
To the air of *"The Old English Gentleman."*

*   *   *   *   *   *

In this posture of affairs, his gracious Majesty George the Fourth
intimated his intention of visiting his Irish dominions at no very
distant day,
Then each party call'd a meeting that preparation might be made
for his reception, so that when he should come, they would
know what to do and what to say;
The Catholics rehearsed their complaints, intending to make them
a subject (after salutation) for the royal ear, by the way,
When fresh advices declared that the king would set off immediately for Dublin, that is, with the least possible delay
AFTER THE CORONATION, CORONATION, THE WONDERFUL CORO-
NATION.

The good sense of the Roman Catholics caused them to change
their intention of annoying, with their complaints, the royal ear;
And they propos'd having a public dinner to celebrate the coronation, at which was expected the very best of good cheer;

The King expected at Dunleary.

Then an unexpected proposal came from the Protestants to the
 Catholics so very distinct and clear,
That all hostilities and jealousies should cease, and both parties
 assemble at dinner without any doubt or fear
AT THE CELEBRATION, CELEBRATION, OH ! THE WONDERFUL CELE-
 BRATION.

This proposal was accepted, the parties reconciled, and nothing
 but the general happiness was then in view,
When, lo! on the 12th of July, King William was dressed up as
 usual, in orange and in blue ;
The Catholics, filled with disgust and horror, proceed by revoking
 their compromise, and forming resolutions anew,
When the lord mayor declared it was done in defiance of his
 orders, without his knowledge, and by some persons that nobody
 knew :
THIS CAUSED RECONCILIATION, RECONCILIATION, OH ! WONDERFUL,
 RECONCILIATION.

Then came the great and aggregate meeting at the Royal Exchange,
 which took men of all parties into the ring,—
There was such shaking and squeezing of hands between the
 Roman Catholic advocate, O'Connell, and the lord mayor,
 Abraham Bradley King ;
Then came Sir E. Stanley dressing councillor O'Gorman in blue
 silk, like King William. This was really an excellent thing.
And master Ellis, caressing Ned Conlan, the brewer. At this
 sight you could not, if you had a stave left, refuse to sing
TERGIVERSATION, TERGIVERSATION, OH ! WONDERFUL TERGIVER-
 SATION.

And now the king is expected to land at Dunleary, great preparations are made all along the shore,
Engineers are moving mountains, levelling roads, raising fences,
 erecting scaffolds, seats, pavilions, and twenty thousand things
 more.
The commissioners, swelled with importance, look big at their
 officers; the officers, in their turn, swell at the people; at which
 the people feel uncommonly sore ;
AND THIS WAS ALL BUT EXPECTATION, EXPECTATION, OH ! IT WAS
 WONDERFUL EXPECTATION.

And now the long wish'd for day is come. His Majesty's fleet is
 seen off Dunleary, where you'd think half the world had collected.
The fleet have come to anchor under the salutation guns of
 batteries and cruisers, when all eyes on the Royal George Yacht
 were turn'd and directed.
But no king appearing on board, it is surmised that his Majesty
 has put in at Howth ; and at ten o clock at night this wonderful
 step is much more than suspected.

His Majesty lands at Howth. 147

The King's landing at Howth is confirmed. It gives a death-blow to the hopes of the south-side company; the disappointment is felt the greater, as it was so unexpected.
THIS MAY BE CALLED EXTRA VEXATION, EXTRA VEXATION, OH! IT WAS WONDERFUL EXTRA VEXATION.

His Majesty's reception, on landing, was so flattering that he was induced to extend on all sides his royal hand.
The people throng'd and press'd around him, anxious to see their sovereign on so good a footing in their devoted land.
And, tho' evidently fatigued, he, with the greatest affability, did for several minutes stand.
At length he gain'd his carriage, which bore him off amidst the proudest cheers to his palace in the Phœnix Park, where he was to take the command.
THIS WAS CONSUMMATION, CONSUMMATION, OH! 'TWAS WONDERFUL CONSUMMATION.

The King's grand entry into Dublin next takes place, attended by his noble peers and all the officers of state.
The procession moved on in regular order, without impediment, until his Majesty and suite had arrived at the City Gate,
When Athlone, herald-at-arms, made proclamation that King George the Fourth into the City of Dublin desired to be admitted straight.
Then you could see the army, navy, church, bar, college, custom-house, with all the attendants and dependants that on their betters wait,—
A TRICK OF THE CORPORATION, CORPORATION, OH! 'TWA A WONDERFUL CORPORATION.

And now the lord mayor presents the city keys, and on his knee doth humbly bend;
His Majesty, tho' teased and tired, submits with courteous patience; yet seems anxious that this city mummery would have an end.
Then the lord mayor and his party, common council and citizens, with the procession unite and blend.
The recorder speaks a speech, by way of address, to his Majesty, to which the king did most graciously attend,
TO THIS EXHORTATION, EXHORTATION, OH! 'TWAS WONDERFUL EXHORTATION.

Of the city now made free, his Majesty proceeds in open carriage, happy at being relieved from the usual precautionary cares and fears.
He passes thro' a multitude of his joyous people of all classes arranged in the streets; some on benches; others in windows and tops of houses, in rows and tiers,—
A spectacle so splendid (if ever) hath not been seen for some hundreds of years;—

148 A Royal Levee—Presentation.

A great and mighty king visiting his subjects in Ireland, and finding such unfeigned and hearty welcome made known by their shouts and cheers.
IT WAS ACCLAMATION, ACCLAMATION, A HAPPY AND WONDERFUL ACCLAMATION.

His Majesty is next seen on horseback viewing his troops in the Phœnix Park, and occasionally giving the royal word,
Which showed (if necessity required) the king was as well acquainted with the use as the power of the sword.
He was pleased to compliment the officers and men on their skill and quickness of manœuvre, which, to his Majesty and to thousands of spectators, did such great entertainment afford,
That again did his Majesty repeat his praise to the officers, to whom he gave a dinner that day at his splendid board.
NOW, THIS WAS TRULY APPROBATION, APPROBATION, OH! IT WAS WONDERFUL APPROBATION.

The next day, being Sunday, his Majesty attended divine service at church ; after which he held a royal levee, at which many of motley character attended.
The chamberlain's order for the next evening was, in consequence, ordered to be amended.
It was expected no gentleman would come but such as had to attend ladies. This kept the vulgar at home,—many of whom it most sorely offended ;
But it enabled his Majesty to receive the ladies that attended with more ease when the ceremony of presentation ended.
THIS WAS ROYAL PRESENTATION, PRESENTATION, IT WAS WONDERFUL PRESENTATION.

His Majesty next visited some public establishments; and first, that very useful one, called the Linen Hall.
Then did the king go to view the National Bank, formerly the House of Parliament, but now used as a house of call ;—
With these points in mind, he expected to have met the governors, directors, with their attendants, clerks, and all ;
Instead of which he beheld a tavern, and, in the former House of Lords, a house of ladies dressed out as if for an assembly or ball.
THIS PRODUCED CONSTERNATION, CONSTERNATION, OH! 'TWAS WONDERFUL CONSTERNATION.

The Dublin Society now prepare a breakfast, and receive his Majesty in the tented field.
The king most graciously attended, and not to be offended at what he found the people's *liking, was induced his own taste to yield ;
Yet plainly showed by his manner of tasting, that feeding was not the chief consideration of every king that doth a sceptre wield.

Embarkation at Kingstown. 149

To convey reproof, yet avoid showing disgust, he shortened his visit, which saved him from extra feeding, and from indigestion did his royal stomach shield.
YET IT SHOWED HIS DISAPPROBATION, DISAPPROBATION, OH ! WONDERFUL DISAPPROBATION.

The King was induced (though reluctant to feeding) to dine at Trinity College, where he met the best of good fellowship, with plenty of excellent malt,
He was addressed by a very *odd fellow*, who, though a good scholar, could not entertain his Majesty with either poetic taste or attic salt.
The address, though it came off but lamely, was amply made up in feeding, which did in no instance either limp or halt.
All went off smoothly; the dinner was well served, and better eaten; the wine of the purest quality, brought directly from a long and cool repose in the sunken vault.
THIS WAS MASTICATION, MASTICATION, OH ! 'TWAS WONDERFUL MASTICATION.

The lord mayor and aldermen, though well affected to church and king, have great reliance upon the good things of *this life*, and also to avoid getting thinner,
Resolved on building a circular room, capable of entertaining his Majesty, and permit themselves and the corporate bodies to expand at dinner.
This cost several thousand pounds; but, whoever lost, the worshipful lord mayor, by getting a baronetcy, became a winner.
This made him smile, and made his Joan a lady. The two sheriffs, in being knighted, each, in addressing his wife, became a grinner.
OH ! THIS WAS ROYAL REMUNERATION, REMUNERATION ; OH ! IT WAS WONDERFUL REMUNERATION.

His Majesty, having promised relief to the Roman Catholics, fixed upon his return to England; and on the third of September it accordingly took place from Kingstown, where some fifty thousand persons had collected.
There was O'Connell on his knee, with a laurel wreath in his hand, and an address in his mouth. The one was not spoken, nor the other presented, as his Majesty and the other party were inseparably connected.
The king thus escaped this and many other addresses, by making a most gracious speech to his affectionate people, whom he visited with pleasure, and parted from with regret; this was as much as could reasonably be expected.
The crowd closing and pressing about the king, he hasten'd to the boat, which conveyed him to the yacht, as it was order'd and directed.
THIS WAS EMBARKATION, EMBARKATION, OH! IT WAS WONDERFUL EMBARKATION.

KILLINEY.

SECTION V.

Killiney, my earliest memories
To thy shores are bound;

* * * *

A mountain scene with
Sylvan grandeur crowned.

There are three hills in the Rochestown range, all rising abruptly from the sea. Upon the summit of the centre one, at a height of 475 perpendicular feet from the sea, stands an obelisk, erected by Colonel Malpas, in 1741, after a severe and continuous frost (for the same excellent purpose which induced Sir Pigot Piers to build the more beautiful pillar at Stillorgan, in the year 1740), to give employment to the people, and thus mitigate the general distress then prevailing. Killiney was subsequently planted and greatly beautified by Viscount Loftus, who, as well as many of our Viceroys, resided there.

In the year 1831 a stone coffin, containing a perfect skeleton and numerous ancient coins (Saxon and Danish), were found by a ploughman at Quatre Bras, in a field which then belonged to a Captain Richardson, near Killiney.

J. Aspin, in his systematic Analysis of Universal History, speaking on the subject of coins and medals, observes, that "few studies are of more importance to history than that of coins and medals. Amongst the Greeks and Romans, no war was declared, no peace concluded, no colony founded, no magistrate entered on his functions, no prince ascended the

throne, but a medal was struck, commemorating the event. They are, therefore, in the absence of other documents, of the first importance to the chronologer in enabling him to fix the dates of such events as they were designed to perpetuate." On a medal of Alexander the Great, which was found under the foundation of the gateway of the Abbey of Ferns, county Wexford, it has on the obverse, the head of that prince in fine relief, crowned with the chaplet of ivy leaves and berries, which was the symbol of Bacchus, and which Alexander assumed on his conquest of India. There is also a ram's horn (the symbol of strength and power ascribed to Jupiter Ammon, whose son Alexander was ambitious of being thought), twisting round from the back of the ear. This horn was also an attribute of Bacchus, and it might be, that he took it together with the chaplet; or it might be the goat's, which was the symbol of Macedon. However, the former is the most probable supposition. On the reverse is the figure of Hercules, clad in the skin of the Nemean lion, and having the club in his hand." Aspin says the figure of Hercules is common on the coins of Alexander the Great. Partly round the margin, and on the exergue, is a Greek legend in very old characters, and in the Doric dialect, the first two words of which run from left to right in the usual manner, while the last word is from right to left. Now, Froelick, quoted by Pinkerton, remarks—" Coins of the most remote antiquity may be distinguished by certain infallible characteristics;" amongst which he enumerates "their not being exactly round—of a globous swelling shape —antiquity of the alphabet—the letters being retrograde, or the first division of the legend in the common style, while the rest is retrograde."

A rare and valuable Saxon coin of the time of Edgar, was recently found near Dalkey, by one of Mr. J. W. Paine's Sons, of Sandycove Avenue.

A writer of great power, whose works are to be found in that sanctuary of Irish literature, and Museum of Irish Antiquities,

THE ROYAL IRISH ACADEMY,

in describing Killiney and its unrivalled beauties says :—

"I have been a traveller for some years, and have cast not a listless eye over not only the British Isles, but over much that is beautiful and grand on the European and American continents. I have not only passed over the spires and ridges of the Alps and Pyrenees, and listened with delight to the shepherd's pipe, at evening's close, rising from the vine-covered hills of Auvergne and the Bourbonnais, but I have heard the downright dart of Niagara, and seen where the Potomac and Shenandoah burst their united waters through the pine-covered ridge of the Alleghany mountains; but, after all, I know not any landscape that ever came under my eye so rich, so various, so comprehensive, as the view from Killiney Hill. The whole valley of the Liffey, with the rich and wooded plains of the county Dublin under my feet, the Mourne mountains in the far northern distance rising in serrated peaks, the hills of Kildare in the far west, and just as it were beneath, the mighty city, covered with its wreathed smoke.

"The peculiarity of the spot on which I stood was, that, turning round on your heel, your eye opened on almost as different a prospect as if you were transplanted into a different clime, or as if looking into a showman's box, the rapid and voluble man had, with a turn of a pin, discarded one picture and substituted another; so, here by looking to the south, you have a different sea, shore, valley, hills, mountains; nay, even the character of the air, and sky, and clouds seemed changed. And as before you had the counties of Dublin, Kildare, and Meath before you, with the grand city in repose, land-locked bay, and the pier of Kingstown, and Howth, and Lambay reposing on the waters like *couchant* sentinel sea monsters; so now you have the silvery shore of Killiney, bending its graceful crescent line until it terminates in one of the finest of all Irish promontories, Bray Head—and then the narrow quiet valley, and the mountains, pile on pile, above it, the Sugar-Loaf piercing its white silicious head over all." *

Pause for a while, from the contemplation of nature in all its grandeur and wild sublimity, and take a passing glance at a not less interesting but more material prospect, the condition of the people. The author forbears alluding to the past; let all bitter memories, party dissensions, and animosities, be buried in oblivion. As to the present, by the bounty of Providence, the promise of a rich and abundant

---

* There is no city in the British Empire whose environs afford more various and attractive scenery than our beautiful city of Dublin, whose street and shop architecture will vie with any city in the United Kingdom. Thanks to the wise managers of our local railway companies, the poorest artisan can, in less than an hour, wander in the romantic glens of Howth, ascend the sea-cliffs of Bray, Dalkey, Killiney, and Bullock, meditate in the dark glen of the Dargle, or wander up the lovely banks of the Liffey, *via* the Phœnix Park; while the inhabitants of London, Liverpool, &c., may actually pass out of life without having cast one admiring look at a mountain prospect, with all its peaks, ridges, waterfalls, and glens, and while he may have no idea of the sea but what the tide waters of the muddy Thames present. The pleasure-seeker or antiquarian may direct his jaunting-car along the lower road that leads to Lucan—admire, perhaps, the finest river landscape in the world—observe cultivation carried forward with the greatest accuracy, and in keeping with the greatest beauty. He may spend his day at the Salmon Leap at Leixlip, or proceeding farther, admire the thousand and one acres in the centre of which Ireland's beloved Duke resides Or, if it should better please him, he can go northward, and exercise his antiquarian propensities and recollections, while admiring the venerable remains of Fingallian grandeur, as exhibited in the old Parliament House of Swords—its round tower—or the still more beautiful one at Lusk. He may venture to Holm-Patrick, and see the Church built by St. Patrick. He may thence return home, and on his way observe the ancient stone roof and crypt of St. Doulough, only inferior in antiquity to Cormac's chapel, on the Rock of Cashel.

harvest is most cheering: let us hope that happiness and prosperity is yet in store for Ireland, and that a land teeming with fertility will henceforth abundantly supply the wants of the population, and stay the evils of excessive emigration, that so the people may be happy at home in their own lovely land.

It has been well said that the future is in our power. United and combined, let our exertions be solely directed to the material progress and regeneration of Ireland. Let us knock loudly at the gate of the British minister (no matter who he may be), and demand practical measures, that our commercial and industrial resources may be fully and fairly developed. The minister must hear the voice of a united people ringing in his ears, unless he stubbornly and wantonly close them, like Ulysses of old, who sealed up his ears in order not to hear the songs of the syrens, thus eluding the effects of their charms.

AND OUR QUEEN,

"Whose welcome visits, like those of angels,
Are few and far between."

Why is there no royal residence in this country? This question admits of one solution only. We have been neglected. Our gracious Queen's visits endeared her Majesty to the people. The Prince of Wales and his lovely consort honoured us lately with a more extended sojourn; but these transient visits are calculated, as it were, to make darkness visible; the light effectually to dispel the darkness, should be more enduring and permanent, and not a mere transitory scintillation, however brilliant.

There should be a royal dwelling at once erected near Dublin, worthy of the sovereign: where our gracious Queen and the members of the royal family might sometimes dwell amidst the sublime scenery, but still more so in the hearts of her attached subjects, the people of Ireland, and where could such a residence be erected if not within the compass of the bright and glorious scenery lying between Killiney Hill and the vale of Shanganagh?

"Ever charming, ever new, the landscape never tires,
The windy summit wild and high, roughly rushing to the sky."

Killiney is a hill of considerable height, about seven miles from Dublin, and so situated as to command an extensive and varied prospect on every side from the summit.

Immediately in front of the spectator (looking northwards), beyond a luxuriant valley, stands the city, the white buildings contrasting well with the rich intermediate scenery. To the right opens, superb and unrivalled, Dublin Bay, stretching into the Irish Sea, a noble expanse of water, blue and placid, melting into the almost cloudless sky; the sails of many vessels, faintly discernible in the extreme distance, alone direct the eye to the nearly imperceptible line of the horizon. To the north of the bay stands, boldly prominent, the Hill of Howth, its rugged outline, reduced by distance to an almost level plain, whence the low sandy isthmus of Howth (above which is seen the craggy rock called Ireland's Eye)* sweeps towards the city, studded with villages, villas, and white cottages to the water's edge.

The view towards the south includes Blackrock, Kingstown, Bullock, and terminates, nearly at the feet of the spectator, at the picturesque island of Dalkey; still further south, Killiney Bay displays another bold sweep to the conspicuous head-land called Bray Head —altogether presenting a line of shore about twenty miles in extent, of a most interesting description.

* Ireland's Eye (*Oculus Hiberniæ*) where, as John Allen, (who was Archbishop of Dublin in the reign of Henry VIII.) observes "St. Nessan anciently was frequent in prayers, fasting, and watching."—Registrum Nigrum, or Black Book. This island is supposed, by some, to be that which Ptolemy calls "Adri Deserta," Pliny "Andros," and Richard of Cirencester "Edria."

Turning westward, the eye ranges over a rich and diversified country, the view being closed, at a great distance, by a range of mountains finely grouped, and skirting the horizon with the most picturesque outline imaginable; consisting of the Wicklow Mountains, rising in great majesty, the conical hills called the "Sugar Loaves," continued by the Douce, Three Rock, and Dublin mountains, which constitute an unbroken chain to the almost indistinct azure of the remote summits of the Mountains of Mourne, seen beyond the city. Every part of this beautiful scenery is so complete, as to leave nothing to the fancy to fill up; every object combines magnificently to promote a general harmony, to produce one grand and exquisite effect, and excite in a contemplative mind sentiments of pleasure, admiration, and profound reverence.—"Gaskin's Geography and History made Interesting."

Crithmum maritimum, the samphire immortalized by Shakspeare, grows on the cliffs and rocks of Killiney, as well as on the Hill of Howth.

"Half way down
Hangs one that gathers samphire—dreadful trade!"*

KILLINEY AND THE ROCHESTOWN HILLS

were much resorted to in the last century by the young men and boys of Dublin, and the adjoining towns and villages, on each St. Stephen's Day (December 26),

"TO HUNT THE WREN."

"The wren, the wren, the king of all birds,
On Saint Stephen's Day was caught in the furze."

---

* The celebrated firm of "Cross and Blackwall" consider this a most valuable plant for pickling. It is one of the rarest and dearest in their London establishment.

The following interesting and highly descriptive letter was written by a Cork "Wren Boy" in 1834 :—

SAINT STEPHENS'S DAY—HUNTING THE WREN—
HOLLY AND IVY, ETC., ETC.

Reviewing the many strange and apparently unmeaning customs which characterize a people, the superficial observer will see only what may be laughed at, as ridiculous and absurd; whilst the antiquarian or philosopher, diving beneath the surface, and comparing the present with the past, is frequently enabled to separate, in wisdom's crucible, the dross from the finer metal, and thus to trace these customs to their true origin.

Ireland is a spot peculiarly marked by such customs; some derived from the earliest annals of Druidism—others coeval with Christianity, all richly deserving the enquiry of the critic, or the ingenious conjecture and research of the antiquary. The antic mummeries of a rude, unpolished peasantry—the boisterous and hearty mirth that at certain periods of the year bursts forth through every impediment, levelling the barriers that modern refinement would interpose, and giving full scope to the strong ebullition of national feeling, show, that in sunshine or storm—in times of dearth or plenty—in the calm and sluggish stillness of debasing servitude, or the hurricane of political agitation—under every vicissitude or clime, the Irish peasant is the Irish peasant still—the light-hearted, generous, enthusiastic lover of his father-land—the ardent panegyrist of the olden time, and the scrupulous observer of the various fetes of fun and superstition handed down through a long series of years; no matter how inconsistent with reason or common sense they may be—whether the cause of their institute be remembered or forgotten.

From the fire of Baal, at Summer's dawn, to the

158 All-Hallowed-Eve and Shrovetide.

Brideog, of Bridget's night—from the startling rites of All-Hallowed-Eve to the pancake tossing of Shrovetide, we have seen comments and discussions, from Vallancey to the present day; but why, in the festivals of Christmas, the holly and ivy should, in preference to all other shrubs, adorn the house or embower the dresser; or, huddled together and hung with ribbons, become the throne of a murdered wren, no attempt has yet been made to explain.

It appears to me a very reasonable supposition that, in a season of universal gladness, sensible and mercurial people, who knew the value of the senses as conduits of information, would avail themselves of the opportunity of blending instruction with amusement, and thus point out to the aosóg of that day, whilst they carolled and gambolled round the object of their delight, its grand and mysterious associations. Like the Jews and Egyptians, the Irish were extremely fond of figure and hieroglyphic; and like the old Fire-worshippers of Persia, in their May-eve fire (Baalteine is the name of May) worshipped Baal or the Sun, who was considered the supreme dispenser of life and light to this nether world. On the introduction of Christianity, as may well be conjectured, they naturally looked around for suitable emblems to represent the object of their new faith. As an illustration of the Trinity, the Shamrock was immediately adopted; whilst the wren, embedded in holly and ivy, might not be considered an inappropriate type of the incarnation. Indeed they could scarcely have chosen a more expressive symbol of the wondrous humility of the Deity in taking the helpless form of infancy than the wren, the smallest and most despicable of the feathered race in our island. The chilling wind and piercing cold of winter, with the various circumstances of poverty and humiliation which attended a Saviour's birth, are not inaptly denoted by the prickly roughness of the holly, which circles the poor persecuted wren,

The Value of a Good Conscience. 159

hunted down, as was its Creator, by the unreflecting votaries of false, misguided zeal. But, whilst the holly reminds us of the stings and crosses of a wicked and cantankerous world, the smooth, unruffled surface of the ivy must also bring to our recollection the peace and goodness announced in the mild tenets of the Gospel to man, and the value of a good conscience, which, though bound up too often through life's journey with the holly of turmoil and disappointment, yet strengthens and supports its possessor, like the ivy that clasps and shelters some aged oak or venerable pile, adding lustre to its beauty, and protecting it from ruin.

The bush, then, is emblematic of the crib of Bethlehem; the ribbons that embellish it represent the swaddling clothes that wrapped the tender limbs of the Redeemer; and the glad and merry notes of the wren-boys, chaunting the praises of "the king of all birds," may denote, though feeble and immeasurably distant indeed, the sweet melody of the angelic choir announcing the glad tidings of redemption; and, to pursue farther the illustration, the rich offerings of gold, frankincense, and myrrh, of the Eastern wise men, may be typified by the willing contributions given in honour of the little feathered monarch to his numerous and devoted followers, who generally retire at the close of e'en, to enjoy that social happiness which, to them, as individuals, their comparatively cheerless dwellings are too often incapable of affording:

" For Christmas comes but once a year,
And when it comes it brings good cheer."

Such, I conceive, is a true interpretation of these annual displays; which, however solemn and instructive their origin may have been, yet, now-a-days, form a portion of those superstitious observances that, in many places, disgrace our country, being succeeded by scenes of vice, riot, and intemperance. However, there can be no doubt that the character of our people is fast improving—education is making rapid strides—the thirst for information is abroad, and crime must necessarily give way to the steady advance of that light and genial instruction which is now spreading over every portion of our island.

THE OBELISK ON KILLINEY HILL.

From the *Dublin Penny Journal*, 1835. Edited by the late Dr. PETRIE, M.R.I.A., LL.D.

Who is there living in Dublin, but has visited this delightful spot, so rife in fine views and pleasing prospects? And who is there that has visited Killiney, and ascended its summit, that has not felt gratified and pleased at being allowed to rest his wearied limbs, after toiling up the hill, in the little reception room in the obelisk, which was some time raised by Mr. Boucher, to commemorate *nothing!* but to point out to the stranger in search of the picturesque, a spot from which he can at once obtain, by merely turning on the pivot supplied by the heel of his shoe, some of the finest views of maritime and inland scenery to be met with in our island.

Approaching from the Dublin side, and ascending the hill, a sudden view is gained of Killiney bay, with its glittering semicircle of water and smooth zone of sand sweeping round to Bray-head, from which the graceful cones of the greater and lesser Sugar-loaf, ethereally tinted through the half-dozen miles of intervening air, terminate the view. Turning round and looking along the coast, a scene of inexpressible richness, variety, and grandeur, bursts upon the eye: beneath is Kingstown, no longer the poor residence of fishermen, but a large town, or rather an infant

city, built in the most ornamental style, and still
enlarging into the dimensions of maturity; stretching away beyond its picturesque pier, the most
splendid bay in Europe spreads for miles its vast
and lake-like level, adorned with all imaginable
objects that can animate and diversify; the towns
and shining outlets—the piers, docks, batteries, and
beacons—the sail of every form, the darkening curve
of steam, the cloud-like canopy of Dublin—and
Howth,
'Like a Leviathan afloat on the wave,'
shutting in the bay at the distance of a dozen miles."

PETRIE.—THE ANCIENT MUSIC OF IRELAND.

The author, who had the honour of enjoying the
personal friendship and patronage of this great antiquarian, artist, and musician, initiated and conducted
(under his auspices) the first and only concert ever
given in Ireland, the programme of which consisted
entirely of the *Ancient Music* (vocal and instrumental) of the country—the unwritten music of the
people, which was collected and saved from oblivion
by Petrie and Bunting. The following formed the
principal features of this *repertoire* of ancient
song.

PROGRAMME.

"*The Fairies' Invitation,*" with an Introductory Notice, by Petrie,
very ancient; author and date unknown.
Air, . . "*I'm a Lady of Honour that Lives in the Sea.*"
Song, . . "*I'm obliged to you, Madam.*"
Reverie, . "*Beautiful Shore.*"
Bardic Caoine, "*O, Son of Connal, why didst thou die?*" with
an Introductory Notice by Petrie; highly expressive; very
ancient; author and date unknown.*

---

* A concert, *In Memoriam*, to Dr. Petrie, was given in Dublin,
at which this celebrated Bardic Caoine was sung, with solemn

"*The Jolly Ploughboy,*" with chorus; very ancient.
"*The Spinning Girl's Song;*" author unknown.
"*O, wearily, wearily, lags the Day,*" W. Connallon, 1670.
"*Love's a tormenting Pain,*" Bunting.
Fairy Chant, "*Dia Luna Dia Mort,*" author and date unknown.
Connaught Caoine, "*O, Thou art gone;*" with Introductory Notice, by Petrie; rich in wild harmonies; very ancient.
Ancient Irish Song, "*Shule Aroon;*" with the Irish burthen, "*Iuh go deay, Mavourneen Slaun;*" very ancient; author and date unknown.
"*Lullaby, sweet Babe, a Golden Cradle holds thee;*" with the burthen, "*Shuheen Sho, Lulo Lo.*"
Song and Chorus, "*Thy welcome O'Leary,*" translated from the Irish, by Curry; very ancient.
"*Alexander MacDonnell's March,*" (the March of the Pipers of Munster).
"*The Peacock,*" with burthen; author and date unknown.
Ancient Irish Air, "*We'll tell the World we're Irishmen.*"

Many old authors, from the tenth to the sixteenth century, speak in the highest terms of the music of Ireland.*

The world is indebted to Dr. Stokes, a physician of European reputation, for his invaluable work on the antiquarian history of Ireland, in connexion with his dear friend, the late Dr. Petrie, President of the Royal Irish Academy. The moderate and retiring scholar.—The courteous and accomplished editor of the *Freeman's Journal*, John O'Donohoe, Esq., in the opening part of an able review of this work, says:—

effect, by one hundred voices. The words chanted on the occasion were—

> O! son of Erin, why didst thou die? gentle, revered
> Scholar, Artist, Poet, Painter, Minstrel—
> Thou of the Round Towers—why didst thou die?

---

* Ireland and Scotland far excel England in those compositions, for which she has been denied the gift of melodious utterance. Ireland and Scotland, though less favoured in other respects, teemed with the harmonious productions of bards who have left no other monument behind them,—not even, in most cases, their names.

"This graceful and friendly tribute to the memory of a good man will be enduring as the fame of the author." It had its origin in affection; its completion is worthy the motive, the subject, and the writer. The life of an unworldly, diffident man, has been written by a philosophic and independent thinker; who knew his duty and loved it for its own sake, who was not impelled by gain or incited by ambition, and whose every page breathes a refined nationality and a moderate, yet firm, profession of faith. There were few quiet contemplative men who had won more friends than George Petrie—friends of whom any man might be proud. The troop included scholars, antiquarians, artists, poets, divines, and men of various kinds of learning. The man who was revered by Lover and Otway, O'Curry and O'Donovan, Anster and M'Cullagh, Todd and Graves, Ferguson and Stokes, Dr. Russell and Lord Dunraven, can hardly have been called poor. Some of those had passed away before Ireland had lost Petrie; some now enjoy an *otiose* retirement. But it remained for one whose days are spent in relieving human suffering, to devote the nights of his advanced years to the memory of his friend. * * * Dr. Stokes, by his life of Petrie, has established a claim to the gratitude of every Irishman; he has placed the diadem on a reputation built up by earnestness, and truth, and charity; and has given proof of the maintenance of that singular devotion and unselfish diligence which marked the vigour of his early manhood. The following notice and summary of Dr. Stokes's great work appeared in the *Belfast Northern Star*:—

Dr. Petrie.—Art and Archæology in Ireland.*

"When Dr. Petrie established his fame in 1845, by the publication of his first volume on the mysterious Round Towers of Ireland, the late Dr. Matthew Kelly, of Maynooth, in an article in the *Dublin Review*, after giving an abstract of the labours and authorities adduced by the former, and expressing his high opinion of the results, wrote :—' In France a work like his would be a patent of nobility—a seat in the Chamber of Peers; and in Ireland, if we had a Government that wished to rally around it the national associations, and strike its roots deep into the national heart, encouragement to men like Petrie would be sound policy, as it certainly is common justice. For our own parts, fervently hoping that he may be enabled to complete his glorious task, we venture the Popish wish, that he may have the blessings of all the saints in the Festilogium of Aengus.' In this language Doctor Kelly simply echoed the feelings, not only of the scholars and people of Ireland, but of the entire scholars and archæologists of Europe, without exception. It is the life of this man we have now laid before us in the present volume, the record of whose labours and works forms the history of his life—a life that was destined not only to resuscitate the long-neglected fine arts of our country, but more especially and beneficially to lay on a sure and solid, clear and simple foundation, its general and special history. The author was well fitted for the task ; but we should obliterate the word, for with him it has surely been a labour of love ; for as he says in the preface, he 'had the ad-

* The Life and Labours in Art and Archæology of George Petrie, LL.D., M.R.I.A., and Member of many learned societies. By Wm. Stokes, M.D., D.C.L., Oxon., Physician to the Queen in Ireland, and Regius Professor of Physic in the Dublin University. London : Longmans, Green, & Co.

vantage of having been long one of the most intimate friends of Petrie, whose confidence in him is now among the happiest, as well as the proudest recollections of his life.' He had also had the advantage of having accompanied him in some of his wanderings through the sacred and historic parts of our olden country, investigating her antiquities, not with the passing glance of the tourist, but with the critical eye of the artist, the loving reverence of the pilgrim, and that perfect knowledge of her language, traditions, and history, which by long study and assiduity he had acquired. In the biography of such a man, unmixed with the party politics of the day, his hours spent in his *studio* and study, in wild glens, island-solitudes, or the bosom of his family, little of stirring incident was to be expected, and little came, and yet what we catch of adventure and romance in his journeyings in search of the beautiful and true, whether in Scotland, Wales, or his own loved island, will be read again and again with pleasure.

"Doctor Petrie was the son of James Petrie, a portrait painter in Dublin, whose father, a native of Aberdeen, had settled in Ireland some time early in the last century. He was born in Dublin in 1789, his mother, a Miss Simpson, of Edinburgh, being, we are told, a lady of great beauty. When about ten years old he went to the well-known school of Mr. White, in Dublin, at which Sheridan, Moore, and several others of our distinguished countrymen were educated, after which, his tastes and feelings impelling him to an artist's life, he began his special education under his father's guidance, in his father's *studio*. And here it was, about this time, that an incident occurred, which we have ourselves heard him narrate with the deepest emotion, as one whose painful recollections could never be obliterated, and which, perhaps, gave the key-note to many things in his after life. It occurs at the end of the volume, but is more properly connected with his early days. Of the eminent men of the day whose portraits his father had painted, were Lord Edward Fitzgerald, Emmet, and Curran. 'After the execution of Emmet, he was requested to paint a portrait of him from memory, with the aid of such studies of the head and face as he had by him. It is needless to say from whom this order came. When the work was finished the artist wrote to Miss Curran, requesting her to come and see it. He was out when she called, but she entered his studio notwithstanding. Petrie, then a young boy, was sitting in a corner of the room, when he saw a lady, thickly veiled, enter, and walk straight to the easel on which the work rested. She did not notice the boy, and thought herself alone with the picture of her buried love. She lifted her veil, stood long and in unbroken stillness gazing at the face; then suddenly turning, she moved with an unsteady step to another corner of the room, and, bending forward, pressed her forehead against the wall, heaving deep sobs, her whole frame shaken with a storm of passionate grief. How long this agony lasted the boy could not tell. It appeared to him to be an hour; and then, with a sudden effort, she controlled herself, pulled down her veil, and as quickly and silently left the room as she had come into it. She was unaware of his presence, unconscious of the depths of silent sympathy she had awakened in the heart of the boy, whose sensitive and delicate nature kept him from intruding on her grief.' That grief that mourned so deeply her buried love, will live for ever, embalmed in song and story by the hearts and pens of Moore and Washington Irving.*

* In reference to this tearful event, and to the surpassing skill she was known to possess in attuning the harp of her country, Moore composed this exquisite *morceau* :—

"She is far from the land where her young hero sleeps,
And lovers around her are sighing;
But coldly she turns from their gaze, and weeps,
For her heart in his grave is lying.

"*She is Far From the Land.*" 167

"We next find him at the drawing school of the Dublin Society, obtaining the silver medal in his fourteenth year; and next, in 1808, in the Dublin and Wicklow mountains, sketching, collecting the ancient music of his country, examining its remains, and discussing their origin and uses, 'starting at nightfall, that he might reach before sunrise some chosen spot for study among the mountains,' and there gaze on their undimmed beauties in all their freshness the Sabbath stillness and glory of the morning. In the following years he visited Wales and London, and in the latter, through the influence of Sir Benjamin West, enjoyed full opportunities of examining the public, as well as many private collections of paintings in the metropolis. But he soon returned to Ireland, and spent the next five years in landscape drawing, principally from studies in Leinster and Kerry. For many of these he had to study architectural drawing, which afterwards proved of inestimable value in forming his style, adding accuracy and faithful delineation to his easy, graceful manner. These studies were chiefly for engravers, supplying ninety-six illustrations to 'Cromwell's Excursions in Ireland,' twenty-one to 'Brewer's Beauties of Ireland;' sixteen to 'Fisher's Historical Guide to Ancient and Modern Dublin,' besides contributions to 'Wright's Tours,' and 'The

"She sings the wild songs of her dear native plains,
Every note which he loved awaking;
Ah! little they think, who delight in her strains,
How the heart of the minstrel is breaking.

"He had lived for his love, for his country he died,
They were all that to life had entwined him :
Nor soon shall the tears of his country be dried,
Nor long will his love stay behind him.

"Oh! make her a grave where the sunbeams rest,
When they promise a glorious morrow;
They'll shine o'er her sleep, like a smile from the west,
From her own lov'd island of sorrow."

Guide to Wicklow and Killarney.' This was followed by illustrations of these popular Annuals and Guide Books—a movement of which Turner was the exponent in England, and Williams and Thompson in Scotland. Particularising some of his works, Dr. Stokes says that of Puck's Castle, county Dublin, in its moorland and mountain solitude, 'is truly a painted poem;' and he speaks with special commendation of the drawing of the shattered ruins of Clonmacnois, the Churches of Deral-Ossory, and St. Fechin of Fore, all ,being distinguished for truthfulness, beauty and finish.

"In 1829 the Royal Hibernian Academy opened their first exhibition, to which Petrie contributed one of his largest and finest works, "Ardfinnan Castle," as he did in each successive year, all of historic interest and illustrative of the antiquities and ancient legends of the country. In 1827 he had been enrolled an academician, and in 1830 was appointed librarian, in which year he exhibited no less than six pictures, one of which, that of kneeling pilgrims at the Holy Well of St. Bridget, county Clare, is thus described :—' A rapid rivulet runs round the steep banks of a little promontory, clothed on one side with wild wood. Behind this is the holy well, surrounded by kneeling figures. In the back ground, their soft and golden hues changing into purple with the fall of the valley, rise the green hills of Clare. A pillarstone, bearing an inscribed cross, crowns the promontory, round which groups of pilgrims, in the old dress of red and purple, are in attitudes of prayer, or standing in meditation. This picture is a gem of colour—a history, not only of days gone by, but of the lasting hold which the early faith has taken on the hearts of the people in the present day. For these wells, originally belonging to pagan times, have a double claim to popular worship. They were places of healing in pre-Christian ages, and were sanctified by the blessing of the early missionaries; and the reverence still paid to them, marks, not only the piety of the people, but the tenacity with which the Celtic races, when undisturbed, cling to their ancient customs.' In 1831 he exhibited, amongst other pictures, that of Gougane Barra, the scene of which has been immortalized by the poet Callanan:

> There is a green island in lone Gougane Barra*
> Where Allua of songs rushes forth as an arrow;
> In deep-vallied Desmond a thousand wild fountains
> Come down to that lake from their home in the mountains.
>
> There grows the wild ash, and a time stricken willow
> Looks chidingly down on the mirth of the billow;
> As like some gay child, that sad monitor scorning,
> It lightly laughs back to the laugh of the morning.
>
> How oft when the summer sun rested on Clara,
> And lit the dark heath on the hills of Ivera,
> Have I sought thee, sweet spot, from thy home by the ocean,
> And trod all thy wilds with a minstrel's devotion!
>
> And thought of thy bards, when assembling together,
> In the cleft of thy rocks, or the depths of thy heather;
> They fled from the Saxon's dark bondage and slaughter,
> And waked the last song by the rush of the water.

"The subject is the hermitage of St. Finbar, situated on a lake between Cork and Bantry. The lake is surrounded by hills, whose apparent height is increased by a shrouding veil of mist while the sky is overcast with dark clouds. There is a partial break in this gloomy canopy overhead, through which a sunray falls perpendicularly on the still waters of the lonely lake, on the ruins, and the wild wood

---

* Gougane Barra, the Gap of Dunloe, Clonmacnoise, Killiney, its circling Bay, and primitive Church in ruins, &c., have been painted by our highly-talented resident artist, B. Colles Watkins, R.H.A., at the special request of his great friend and patron, Dr. Petrie, for the Annual Exhibitions of the Royal Hibernian Academy. Mr. Watkins has made himself famous by his Killarney Sketches and Southern Landscapes, many of which have graced the walls of the Royal Academy, London.

which hangs above them, as if to show that even its desolation and ruin, and in storm and darkness, some light from heaven still falls on this old scene of Christian worship. We cannot afford space for many of the other paintings described, all dedicated, as every creation of his genius was, to the illustration of Ireland, yet one, as connected with Ulster, we cannot pass over. It is that of the Caah Hill, near Dungiven, in the county of Londonderry, a monumental circle of stones, where lie interred some of the great Milesian chiefs on the field of their triumph and defeat, and which, with others of the same kind, have erroneously been designated Druidic temples. 'The circle is one of several still remaining on the mountain, which, according to the tradition of the peasantry of the district, are the tombs of the chiefs slain in a great battle fought here, and from the mountain has received its name of Caah, or Battle-hill. The tall stones raise their dark forms against the saffron sky, through which the evening star is just appearing, and shedding its soft light, while a few cattle stand perfectly motionless on the horizon. The sense of solitude and breathless silence conveyed in this picture, and the deep poetry in the simple treatment of the whole, can be felt only by those who have seen it.' In 1820 and subsequent years he visited Clonmacnoise and the Isles of Arran, in the former of which he was so singularly fortunate as to discover several monumental inscriptions of the sixth and seventh centuries, which, as he wrote, went farther towards establishing the truth of our ancient records than all the writings of the learned for the preceding two hundred years. He kept journals of these tours, which he intended to publish, a design never realised, though, as Dr. Stokes writes, the information collected was in part used in his greater scientific works, 'while the beautiful descriptive passages—the little touches of human feeling and sympathy with all that is simple and holy in nature—have lain for forty years unknown and forgotten.' We are much disposed to extract some of these charming pictures, so highly interesting in every point of view, and so characteristic of the feelings of the man, and select the following from many others we had noted. How very graceful and beautiful is the following description of the pilgrims at Clonmacnoise, how full of sympathy, reverence, and truth :—

"'It will be seen from the above outline that the scenery of Clonmacnoise is of a character altogether lonely, sublime, and poetic. These qualities are rather enhanced than abated by the appearance of the figures usually found here, and which are so identified in character with the ruins that they may be truly said to belong to each other. These figures are of pilgrims who came hither from various and frequently the most remote parts of Ireland, to court the favour or avert the displeasure of God by a long and painful penance. Their simple costumes, of every varied colour, give animation to the landscape, while the character of their countenances presents subjects for observation of the deepest interest. They consist chiefly of females and men of middle age, in whose physiognomies the indications of intense devotion or despairing guilt are often strongly defined. Characters of a most pleasing kind, however, are by no means uncommon. The anxious mother may be seen endeavouring to procure health for her decaying child; the blind and decrepid to obtain deliverance from their ailments; the unfortunate to obtain a cessation of their afflictions; and the aged, with their white locks floating on the wind, shortening their road to a better world by a toilsome penance in this. Their attitudes, too, and the situations in which they are grouped, are often in the highest degree picturesque and striking—sometimes kneeling or prostrated round a grassy hollow—

the ruins of some holy shrine; at other times creeping on their bare knees to some place of still higher sanctity; now arranged in silent prayer round the rude but gorgeously sculptured stone cross, which they afterwards kiss with the utmost fervency of devotion; and now hurrying rapidly along to some more distinct object of worship. In all their movements there is an abstracted intensity of feeling that carries the mind back to remote times, and a rapturous expression of devotion and holy love may occasionally be observed, which a philosophic observer might, perhaps, envy or wish to participate in. The casualties of season or weather are wholly disregarded, and the observations of strangers unnoticed. Figures of a higher rank and less picturesque costume seldom appear here, and such indeed, I have seen but once. They were a lady and her two daughters, habited in elegant mourning dresses, who, entering the graveyard with hurried step, advanced to a tomb of recent erection, round which they knelt in silent prayer for an hour or two, while the tears, which flowed continually down their cheeks, showed the intensity of the sorrow which brought them hither. After they retired, I had the curiosity to examine to whom the monument had been raised. He was a gentleman of the name of Coghlan, a descendant of the ancient princes of the country. . . . Few days, however, pass over in which Clonmacnoise does not for a while present a scene of wild commotion, when the silent solitude is disturbed by the *relligaun* or death-cry, raised as some peasant of the country is borne to the grave of his ancestors. On these occasions the sorrowing kindred give full vent to their excited feelings of grief and affection at sight of their graves, throwing themselves on the grassy hillocks, which they kiss and press with melancholy ardour, now praying fervently, and now making the most distressing lamentations.'

The Ancient Melodies of Ireland. 173

"Petrie was from his earliest youth passionately fond of music, but more especially of the wild strains of his own native land, and during his professional tours he never failed to garner up all the old airs he heard sung or played, or versions he considered superior to those already printed. And thus it was that his collection became so extensive that when the Society for the Preservation of the Ancient Melodies of Ireland, of which he was President, published its first volume, containing one hundred and forty-seven airs, with a supplement containing thirty-six additional; all had been contributed by him, and noted by himself from the singing of the peasants and wandering musicians. What added considerably to the value of the work were the historic notes appended to each air. It is very interesting to learn what, in some cases, for instance in the remote islands of Arran, was the procedure he adopted to obtain pure and authentic settings. In 1857, after the visit of the British Association to those next neighbours of America, Dr. Petrie remained for some time with the author, Mr. Ferguson, and the late Professor O'Curry, to examine in detail some of the relics of the past, and particularly some monumental inscriptions, the readings of which had been debated. The village of Kilronan was their head-quarters, near which an appointment would be made to meet parties known to possess and sing some of the old airs. 'To this cottage, when evening fell, Petrie, with his manuscript music-book and violin,' (on which he was an accomplished performer) and always accompanied by his friend O'Curry, used to proceed. Nothing could exceed the strange picturesqueness of the scenes which night after night were thus presented. On approaching the house, always lighted up by a blazing turf fire, it was seen surrounded by the islanders, while its interior was crowded with figures, the rich colours of whose

dresses, heightened by the fire light, showed with a strange vividness and variety, while their fine countenances were all animated with curiosity and pleasure. It would have required a Rembrandt to paint the scene. The minstrel—sometimes an old woman—sometimes a beautiful girl, or a young man—was seated on a low stool in the chimney corner, while chairs for Petrie and O'Curry were placed opposite; the rest of the crowded audience remained standing. The song having been given, O'Curry wrote the Irish words, when Petrie's work began. The singer recommenced, stopping at a signal at every two or three bars of the melody to permit the writing of the notes, often repeating the passage until correctly taken down, and then going on with the melody, exactly from the point where the singing was interrupted.' The entire air being obtained, the singer, gave the song continuously, and then Petrie played the air on the violin, as he alone could play it, the people listening with rapt pleasure, and, when the music ceased, murmuring their delight in their own native language. We would willingly copy the entire chapter on the ancient music of our country, but it is too long for our pages, and we can only refer to parts. It contains many interesting strictures on the peculiar qualities and composition of Irish music, as of itself, and whether of common origin with Scottish, on the genuineness of the Harp of Brian Boroimhe, on the melody of Robin Adair, which is shown to be the Irish composition of Aileen Aroon from the corrupt version of 'You're welcome to Puckstown, Johnny Adair,'* and of the discussion between Petrie and Bunting, whether the words of the song were adapted to the air, or the air composed

---

* Oh ! you're welcome to Puckstown,
    Johnny Adair, Johnny Adair !
Oh ! you're welcome to Puckstown,
    Johnny Adair.

to give expression to the words, it being the decided opinion of the former, that the air was originally made for the words, and that the metrical arrangement and sentiment gave them their peculiarity, beauty of form, and expression. But for the present we hasten on to give some extracts from his journals as to that music which, in his opinion, stood pre-eminent among those of all other Celtic nations, in beauty and power of expression in her caoines, lamentations, and love songs—the latter by their strange fitfulness and sudden transitions from gladness to pathos and longing, marked by a character peculiarly their own :—'The music of Ireland has hitherto been the exclusive property of the peasantry—the descendants of the ancient inhabitants of the country. It is characteristic of their ardent and impassioned temperament, and expressive of the tone of feeling that has been for ages predominant. The upper classes are a different race—a race who possess no national music; or, if any, one essentially different from that of Ireland. They were insensible to its beauty, for it breathed not *their* feelings; and they resigned it to those from whom they took everything else, because it was a jewel of whose worth they were ignorant.—He, therefore, who would add to the stock of Irish melody, must seek it, not in the halls of the great, but in the cabins of the poor. He must accept the frank hospitality of the peasant's humble hearth, or follow him as he toils at his daily labours; but he must choose a season to do so—unlike the frightful

How does Will Aldigar do ?
Johnny Macarrot, too,
And all the girls, we drained
Many a barrel to.
  Oh, oh, why came they not
  With you, Johnny Adair ?
Old song from memory, written by Mrs. Fitzpatrick (aged 80), mother of Mr. Fitzpatrick, the popular author of "The Sham Squire."

summer of 1822—when even 'the song of sorrow' was only heard embodied with the song of death! Dear music of my country! I cannot speak of it without using the language of enthusiasm; I cannot think of it without feeling my heart glow with tenderness and pride! Well may Ireland exult in the possession of such strains; but she will exult more when freedom shall bid her indulge the proud feelings that of right belong to her. If the character of a people were to be judged by the national music—and is there a truer criterion?—where in the world would there be found a people of more intense sensibility—that sensibility, which, though it may, in its unconfined expansion, often exceed the limits within which cold prudence would confine it, is still the root of all genius, and the source of every generous feeling. Could we suppose a being of another planet come down to live among the inhabitants of this, ignorant of every language but music—that language of the heart—what strains would allure him like those of the green island? In what region would he be addressed with such eloquent language, whether of gaiety or tenderness, of sorrow or of joy, as in this bright land of song? Alas for those who are insensible to its beauty! It is among them that the dull and ungenerous bigots will be found who spread poison on the land which they tread. Could music penetrate their stony hearts, the melodies of Ireland would make them weep for the ill they were the means of perpetuating on this unhappy island; and they would embrace that ill-treated people with a generous affection, anxious to make reparation for past injuries."

"These are noble sentiments eloquently expressed, and every generous heart, which can appreciate the Irish people and their glorious music, will respond to them."

IRELAND.—MEMORIALS OF HER EARLY HISTORY.

*Thus often shall memory, in dreams sublime,
Catch a glimpse of the days that are over;
Thus sighing, look through the waves of time,
For the long-faded glories they cover.*

MOORE.

"Ireland is rich in the possession of memorials of her early history. The Museum of the Royal Irish Academy is, in the matter of antique gold ornaments, one of the richest and most valuable in Europe. Articles of other materials and uses, to illustrate more ancient and more modern epochs, are not wanting—monumental stones with the strange Ogham marked on their angles, decorated urns containing the ashes of the pagan dead and their necklaces of shells, flint arrow heads, graceful bronze blades, and steel weapons, square bells, crosses and croziers, and gospel shrines adorned in precious metals with the intricate designs characteristic of ancient Irish art. The country itself is singularly illustrated by monuments of distant and greatly differing ages: sepulchral caves and mounds, forts of clay and dry stones, round towers, ecclesiastical ruins, and feudal castles, abound on every side. Relics are to be found which show the presence of many races, and reveal their varying degrees of civilization. They are mingled, but not confused. Like the ripple on the shore-sand and the shell-print in its surface, they have been made perpetual, through a process which obviates the danger of destruction; reverence and superstition have peopled and preserved them. If these were all that remained, a historian, gifted with scientific instinct, might, perhaps, obtain results as satisfactory as those of a geologist; but the difficulties to be overcome would be great, and the false starts and lost lines of pursuit many, before a historical event could be divested of speculative vagueness. Happily for students of Irish history, Ireland can produce documentary testimony of very ancient date to certify occurrences, and has preserved the code of ancient laws, as revised by the earliest Christian missionaries, to guide speculation as to her former modes of thought, action, and comparative civilization. It is likewise a fortunate circumstance for the historian that the course of events has brought her into contact with many other races, so that he can test, and if needful modify, the statement of native annalists by the records of friendly or hostile observers. At many important epochs of her history Ireland can be seen, not only as she saw herself, but as others saw her—the Scandinavian, the Anglo-Saxon, the Anglo-Norman, the kindred inhabitants of Scotland and Wales, the ecclesiastic from Italy, and the statesman or tourist from England and France. Often, in fact, it is not the poverty but the wealth of materials which constitutes the historian's embarrassment when he has to deal with Ireland. The views taken of certain facts are sometimes so conflicting that it becomes necessary to trace out their history as well as that of the matters to which they refer."

Close to Killiney, on one of the Rochestown Hills, a pillar has been raised to the memory of the Duke of Dorset, on the spot where he was killed by a fall from his horse in hunting.

THIS PILE
Was raised to mark the fatal spot where, at the age of 21,
GEORGE JOHN FREDERICK
The Fourth Duke of Dorset,
Accidentally lost his life, 14th February, 1815.

The following are extracts from a poem written by Lord Byron, suggested by the receipt of intelligence reporting the death of the young Duke of Dorset. He was one of Lord Byron's most constant and attached associates:—

THE DUKE OF DORSET.

Dorset ! whose early steps with mine have stray'd,
Exploring every path of Ida's glade ;
Whom still affection taught me to defend,
And made me less a tyrant than a friend.
Though the harsh custom of our youthful band
Bade *thee* obey, and gave *me* the command ;*
Thee, on whose head a few short years will shower
The gift of riches, and the pride of power.
E'en now a name illustrious is thine own,
Renown'd in rank, nor far beneath the throne.
Yet, Dorset, let not this seduce thy soul
To shun fair science, or evade control,
Though passive tutors, fearful to dispraise
The titled child, whose future breath may raise,
View ducal errors with indulgent eyes,
And wink at faults they tremble to chastise.

When youthful parasites, who bend the knee
To wealth, their golden idol, not to thee—
And even in simple boyhood's opening dawn
Some slaves are found to flatter and to fawn—
When these declare, ' that pomp alone should wait
On one by birth predestined to be great ;
That books were only meant for drudging fools,
That gallant spirits scorn the common rules ;'
Believe them not ;—they point the path to shame,
And seek to blast the honours of thy name.
Turn to the few in Ida's early throng,
Whose souls disdain not to condemn the wrong ;
Or if, amidst the comrades of thy youth,
None dare to raise the sterner voice of truth,
Ask thine own heart ; 'twill bid thee, boy, forbear ;
For *well* I know that virtue lingers there.

---

* At every public school, the junior boys are completely subservient to the upper forms till they attain a seat in the higher classes. From this state of probation, very properly, no rank is exempt ; but after a certain period, they command in turn those who succeed.

"I love the Virtues which I cannot claim."

Yes; I have mark'd thee many a passing day,
But now new scenes invite me far away;
Yes; I have mark'd within that generous mind
A soul, if well matured, to bless mankind.
Ah! though myself by nature haughty, wild,
Whom Indiscretion hail'd her favourite child:
Though every error stamps me for her own,
And dooms my fall, I fain would fall alone;
Though my proud heart no precept now can tame,
I love the virtues which I cannot claim.

* * * * * *

Fain would I view thee, with prophetic eyes,
Exalted more among the good and wise,
A glorious and a long career pursue,
As first in rank, the first in talent too;
Spurn every vice, each little meanness shun;
Not Fortune's minion, but her noblest son.

Turn to the annals of a former day;
Bright are the deeds thine early sires display.
One, though a courtier, lived a man of worth,
And call'd, proud boast! the British drama forth.*
Another view, not less renown'd for wit;
Alike for courts, and camps, or senates fit;
Bold in the field, and favour'd by the Nine;
In every splendid part ordain'd to shine;
Far, far distinguished from the glittering throng,
The pride of princes, and the boast of song.†
Such were thy fathers; thus preserve their name;
Not heir to titles only, but to fame.
The hour draws nigh, a few brief days will close,
To me, this little scene of joys and woes;

---

* Thomas Sackville, Lord Buckhurst, was born in 1527. While a student of the Inner Temple, he wrote his tragedy of "Gorboduc," which was played before Queen Elizabeth, at Whitehall, in 1561. His tragedy, and his contribution of the Induction and Legend of the Duke of Buckingham to the "Mirror of Magistrates," comprise the poetical history of Sackville. The rest of it was political. In 1604, he was created Earl of Dorset by James I. He died suddenly at the council table, in consequence of a dropsy on the brain.—CAMPBELL.

† Charles Sackville, Earl of Dorset, who flourished *temp.* Charles II. and William III. and who was as remarkable for his valour, as for his talent, taste, and patronage of literature. See the casual poems of Dryden, Prior, Pope, Congreve, and others of that period

Each knell of Time now warns me to resign
Shades where Hope, Peace, and Friendship—all were
  mine:
Hope, that could vary like the rainbow's hue,
And gild their pinions as the moments flew ;
Peace, that reflection never frown'd away,
By dreams of ill to cloud some future day ;
Friendship, whose truth let childhood only tell ;
Alas ! they love not long, who love so well.
To these adieu ! nor let me linger o'er
Scenes hail'd, as exiles hail their native shore ;
Receding slowly through the dark-blue deep,
Beheld by eyes that mourn, yet cannot weep.
Dorset, farewell ! I will not ask one part
Of sad remembrance in so young a heart ;
The coming morrow from thy youthful mind
Will sweep my name, nor leave a trace behind.
And yet, perhaps, in some maturer year,
Since chance has thrown us in the self-same sphere ;
Since the same senate, nay, the same debate,
May one day claim our suffrage for the state ;
We hence may meet, and pass each other by,
With faint regard, or cold and distant eye.

For me, in future, neither friend nor foe,
A stranger to thyself, thy weal or woe,
With thee no more again I hope to trace
The recollection of our early race ;
No more, as once, in social hours rejoice,
Or hear, unless in crowds, thy well-known voice :
Still, if the wishes of a heart untaught
To veil those feelings which perchance it ought,
If these—but let me cease the lengthen'd strain
Oh ! if these wishes are not breathed in vain,
The guardian seraph who directs thy fate
Will leave thee glorious, as he found thee great.

Near Druid Lodge, Killiney, are traces of a curious relic of antiquity. In the *Dublin Examiner*, published in 1816, is an etching of a rude stone, of mountain granite, deeply inscribed with a circle, and a segment of a circle, supposed "to represent the sun and moon," deities of the pagan Irish. This stone, together with another of nearly the same size, quite plain, "and a stone seat or chair, constitute the remains of an antient temple, near the village of Killiney. This temple not very many years since, contained two other chairs, similiar to the one remaining, one of which we have seen in an adjoining field, and was encompassed by a circle of stones, eighteen or twenty in number. These stones have either been removed, or are covered with an embankment which appears to have been thrown up round it. The area outside the circle has been converted into a kitchen-garden ; and when first turned up, some ornaments, celts and spear heads, were discovered. About 1790, a number of rude slate coffins, containing skeletons, were found between the temple and the shore ; and about ten years since (1813), five large urns of baked clay, containing calcined bones, were dug up in a field near the village of Killiney."—*Brewer's Beauties of Ireland.*

The much-lamented Lord Edward Fitzgerald, a descendant of the historic Geraldines, resided at Frescati, Blackrock. His favorite drive with his wife, Pamela, daughter of the Duke of Orleans, and other friends, was to Killiney Hill.

In a posthumous work written by Dr. Peter Lombard, Roman Catholic Primate of Armagh, who died in Rome, A.D., 1625, the title of which is: " De Regno Hiberniæ, Sanctorum insula, Commentarius : in quo, præter ejusdem insulæ situm, nominis originem, &c., piiconatus et res a Principe O'Neillo ad fidem Catholicam propagandam feliciter gestæ continentur Lov., 1632." At page 11 the following appears relative to the Geraldines :—"Giraldini, ex Brittannia huc venerunt, origine vero sunt Itali, nempe Vetustiffimi et Nobilissimi Florentini."

That the princely house of Fitz-Gerald came from Florence, is a very ancient tradition. Alluding to this are the following pretty verses in *Hollinshed*, by Lord Surrey.—

> "From Tuscan came my lady's worthy race,
> Fair Florence was some time her ancient seat,
> The Western Isle, whose pleasant shore doth face
> Wild Camber's cliffs, did give her lively heat.
> Foster'd she was with milk of Irish breast,
> Her sire an earl, her dame of prince's blood,
> From tender years in Britain she doth rest,
> With kinges child, where she tastes costly food
> Hunsdon did first present her to mine eine,
> Bright is her hue, and Geraldine she hight,
> Hampton me taught to wish her first for mine,
> And Windsor 'las! doth chase her from my sight.
> Her beauty of kind, her virtues from above,
> Happy is he that can obtain her love."

This beautiful Geraldine, as Lord Oxford in his Noble Authors ascertains, was lady Elizabeth Fitz-Gerald, second daughter of the tenth Earl of Kildare.

Of the illustrious mother of many fair Geraldines, another poet thus sings :—

> "For Venuses the Trojan ne'er
> Was half so puzzled to declare ;
> Ten Queens of beauty sure I see !
> Yet sure the true is Emily.*
> Such majesty of youth and air,
> Yet modest as the village fair :
> Attracting all, indulging none,
> Her beauty like the glorious sun,
> Thron'd eminently bright above,
> Impartial warms the world to love.
> —*Dodsley's Collec.*

---

* The Duchess Dowager of Leinster, who was alive in 1793.

SHANGANAGH.*

SECTION VI.

There are echoes in this beautiful vale, with its grey ruins of the ancient castles of the Walshes and Lawlesses, Druid's seat, solitary cromleach, and close by the Danish remains at Rathmichael, the "Druid's Glen," Puck's Castle, and the "Sanctuary" of Tullagh, which, if

"Waked by some hand less unworthy than mine,"

could be woven into tales of interest, interlaced with sadness and legendary lore; for, as an eminent writer in the *University Magazine* says—"Sadness is the badge of our country's whole history. Many of our Irish counties, such as Galway, and its Athenry and its Aughrim; Dublin, and its Clontarf; Kilkenny, with its thrice noble Ormondes and busy Confederates; Kildare, and its patriotic Geraldines; Kerry, and its Desmonds; Armagh, and its Ecclesiastics; Tipperary, and its Cashel and her Councils; Derry, and its Maiden City; and Louth, with its Boyne and its battle; and Leigh and Ossory, all of which boast of a large measure of historical association, invested with memories of sadness."

THE VALE OF SHANGANAGH.
BY DENIS FLORENCE M'CARTHY.

WHEN I have knelt in the temple of Duty,
Worshipping honour and valour, and beauty—
When, like a brave man, in fearless resistance,
I have fought the good fight on the field of existence:

---

* "Our shores, particularly from Shanganagh to Bray, abound with pebbles of all colours, and often beautifully variegated, so that they might contend with the Egyptian. They all strike fire with steel, and cause no ebullition with acids. They bear the polish, and serve to make the tops of snuff-boxes, seals, heads of canes, sleeve-buttons, and handles of knives."—Rutty's Natural History of the Co. Dublin, 1772.

When a home I have won in the conflict of labour,
With truth for my armour and thought for my sabre,
Be that home a calm home where my old age may rally,
A home full of peace in this sweet pleasant valley!
    Sweetest of vales is the Vale of Shangànah!
    Greenest of vales is the Vale of Shangànah!
    May the accents of love, like the droppings of manna,
    Fall sweet on my heart in the Vale of Shangànah.

Fair is this isle—this dear child of the ocean—
Nurtured with more than a mother's devotion;
For see! in what rich robes has Nature arrayed her,
From the waves of the west to the cliffs of Ben Edar,*
By Glengariff's lone islets—Killarney's weird water,
So lovely was each, that then matchless I thought her;
But I feel, as I stray through each sweet-scented alley,
Less wild but more fair is this soft verdant valley!
    Sweetest of vales is the Vale of Shangànah!
    Greenest of vales is the Vale of Shangànah!
    No wide-spreading prairie—no Indian savannah,
    So dear to the eye as the Vale of Shangànah!

How pleased, how delighted, the rapt eye reposes
On the picture of beauty this valley discloses,
From that margin of silver, whereon the blue water
Doth glance like the eyes of the ocean foam's daughter!
To where, with the red clouds of morning combining,
The tall "Golden Spears"† o'er the mountains are shining,
With the hue of their heather, as sunlight advances,
Like purple flags furled round the staffs of the lances!
    Sweetest of vales is the Vale of Shangànah!
    Greenest of vales is the Vale of Shangànah!
    No lands far away by the calm Susquehannah,
    So tranquil and fair as the Vale of Shangànah!

But here, even here, the lone heart were benighted,
No beauty could reach it, if love did not light it;
'Tis this makes the Earth, oh! what mortal can doubt it?
A garden with *it*, but a desert without it!
With the lov'd one, whose feelings instinctively teach her,
That goodness of hear. makes the beauty of feature,
How glad, through this vale, would I float down life's river,
Enjoying God's bounty, and blessing the Giver!
    Sweetest of vales is the Vale of Shangànah!
    Greenest of vales is the Vale of Shangànah!
    May the accents of love, like the droppings of manna,
    Fall sweet on my heart in the Vale of Shangànah!

---

* Ben Edar is the Irish name for the Hill of Howth.
† The Sugar Loaf Mountains, Co. Wicklow, according to some antiquarians.

SHANGANAGH CASTLE.

No sooner had the Norman knights set their feet upon the verdant island, and gazed around upon its golden valleys and fertile pasture lands, than they at once found themselves filled with an inordinate desire to become possessed of something more than the mere vision of such luxuriance. They smacked their lips at the glittering prospect, and, in the abject subserviency of selfish expectation, prostrated themselves before their gracious and beneficent monarch. Henry received these advances with complacency; he was desirous of rewarding the services of his faithful knights; and, as he had no land to spare in England, he gladly distributed amongst them, with a lavish hand, the Irish manors, which he only knew by name.

One there was, situated in the vicinity of Dublin, that made the Norman mouth of Sir Hugh de Lawless water. It went by the name of the Manor of Shanganagh, and was, in sooth, a most ethereal spot. Slumbering beneath the mountain parish of Killincy, and sheltered by the umbrageous foliage of Old Connaught, the vale of Shanganagh, with outstretched arms, while embracing a creek of the dark blue ocean, grasped into a focus all the naturally picturesque beauty of that eminently rich district.

Sir Hugh de Lawless heard of the exquisite scenery of Shanganagh; he resolved to test the truth of these reports, and made a personal pilgrimage to the spot. To modify the words of Cæsar, he came, saw, and (was) conquered. Yes! The Norman found himself speechless with admiration before its beauties. Shanganagh had taken his heart by storm, and he would that very day wait upon King Henry and conjure him to make it his for evermore. His majesty heard the request, complied with it, and from that moment Shanganagh became the property, or, as the attorney said, who drew up the deed of settlement, the *fee-simple* of Sir Hugh.

The old age of Sir Hugh Lawless did find a home in the vale of Shanganagh, and what is more, " the accents of love fell sweet on his ears "' the while. He married, erected a castle near the water's edge, and lived and died, after a long life of labour, within it."

* * * * * * * *

In 1354, Stephen Lawless was consecrated Bishop of Limerick, and died on Innocents' Day, 1359. The family were then in possession of large estates in Dublin and Wicklow. "In the fourteenth and fifteenth centuries," observes Dalton, in his History of the County Dublin, " the Lawless family were in possession of Shanganagh, Kilruddery, Corkagh, and Old Connaught; but in 1473 the Vicars of St. Patrick's Cathedral, Dublin, petitioned Parliament, stating that they and their predecessors were seized of the seigniory of Shanganagh from time immemorial, had leased it to Thomas Lawless, and had also leased eighty acres within said seigniory to Edmund Walsh, who disowned their authority, and would pay no rent."

Shanganagh about this time, 1473, passed out of the family; but the Lawlesses were too much attached to the old property not to re-establish themselves as soon as possible in its immediate vicinity. This they did by erecting a castle at Shankhill, and a dwelling-house at Cherrywood, townlands situated within a stone's throw of Shanganagh. In the fifteenth century, the Lawlesses were in possession of considerable landed property in Kilkenny.*

* "Cloncurry and His Times," with the permission of the author, W. J. Fitzpatrick, Esq., J.P.

At the head of the verdant Glen Druid, near Shanganagh, is the site of the ruined castle of Carrickmines, on which a lofty pleasure turret was erected by Mr. Barrington. Carrickmines Castle belonged to the Walshes, a family or sept whose history is most interesting.*

In 1642, Sir Simon Harcourt marched hither to dislodge the Irish garrison of Carrickmines. He was shot in the attack and died the following day at Merrion, at the house of Lord Fitzwilliam, whither he had been removed.

Borlase, in his "Irish Rebellion," says, that Lieutenant Colonel Gibson, Sir Simon Harcourt's Lieutenant, thereupon stormed this castle, and his soldiery put them all to the sword, sparing neither man, woman, nor child.

The waters of the Bride's Glen flow into the stream which passes through Glen Druid, and fall into the Shanganagh rivulet, before it reaches Killiney Bay. The interesting valley of the Druid's Glen—the sequestered retreat where the priests of Odin celebrated their mysteries and imposing rites 2,000 years ago, was also looked upon by the ancient Irish as a

---

* The Walshes were the former proprietors of Old Connaught, the seat of the great and illustrious Lord Plunkett. From the distracted state of the country in 1641, the Walshes of Old Connaught and Shanganagh, disposed of their lands, which were not forfeited, and withdrew to France.

The final desertion of the abode of their ancestors took place in 1691, immediately after the *Treaty of Limerick.* There is a small chapel, draped in ivy, with a favorite and much revered Cemetery, in Old Connaught Avenue—This chapel was of similar design, and its dimensions equal to those of the little cell at the foot of Bray Head. Wright, an eminent writer, in his tour through Wicklow, in speaking of Old Connaught Chapel, says, "The ruin is *preserved* in all its interesting picturesque solemnity, by a gentleman not less remarkable for purity of taste, and acuteness of judgment in elegant literature, than for a dignified, yet unaffected, unassuming, yet assiduous, discharge of the clerical duties of the populous parishes of Bray and Old Connaught; of which he, the Rev. Mr Plunkett, was then the incumbent.

highly favoured spot, where fairies, genii and elves held their midnight and moonlight revels.*

* The idea prevalent among the peasantry of Ireland, Great Britain, and most of the northern nations of Europe, relative to preternatural beings inhabiting woods, mountains and wastes, and denominated in the English language *Fairies*, originated in the tenets of Polytheism, or that sect of paganism professed by all the ancient inhabitants of Europe, before the light of the Gospel shone among them.

Our ancestors, not content with deriving the origin of nature from an eternal almighty Being, delegated the works and operations of nature, to subordinate divinities of different orders and degrees; some having immediate intercourse, and ultimately connected with the Divine Being, from whom they originated, whilst others, though far superior to mankind, were only ministering spirits to those of higher dignity. In every order and degree, myriads of these spiritual existences were supposed to inhabit all parts of the universe; some dwelt in the sun, some in the moon, and others in the planets and stars; whilst others again were stationed on earth, superintending not only the affairs of mankind, but every animal and vegetable production; nay, rivers, lakes, plains, vallies, rocks and mountains, were under their protection, and even the elements have their guardian genii. The descriptions given of these aerial beings, in the traditions and superstitions of the people, are elegant and pleasing. They are generally defined blooming in full perfection of youth and beauty, enjoying the most elegant and finished forms, and clothed in loose and flowing garments of azure, blue or purple, skirted with gold and silver, whilst chaplets of the most beautiful and odoriferous flowers of the different seasons, adorn their heads, necks and arms; and gems, which exceeded in brilliance the pellucid drops of early dew, gave a lustre to their elegant golden tresses. Of these beings some sported in living crystal waters, rivers and fountains; others presiding over groves, forests and plains, reposed on carpets of violets and primroses, in bowers of jessamines, woodbines and roses; whilst others, furnished with gold plumed wings, rode through the regions of the air in cloudy chariots of the most splendid hues, where they directed the winds, rain, storms and tempests.

Those which were supposed to preside over the forests and vegetable productions of the earth, the Irish and Britons denominated *Feadh-Ree*, pronounced *Fairy*, or woodland divinities. They were supposed to hold their habitations under the ground and in the bodies of trees; to them appertained the care of corn, fruit and cattle. They were generally favourable to the human race, though when through the ingratitude of mankind, they were injured in any of their charges, they frequently notified their resentment on several subjects committed to their charge; the springs became turbid, the corn and fruit blasted, and the cattle

Puck's Castle—The Loughlinstown Camp.

Not far from Brennanstown House, Cabinteely, is the plain or area where 4,000 were encamped in 1795, commonly called Loughlinstown camp. Here, also, the army of King James encamped for five successive days after the battle of the Boyne. On one of the intervening nights the King slept at *Puck's Castle*, upon the side of Shankill, which overlooked the camp.[*]

The following extract is from Wright's Wicklow, published many years ago:—" In this edifice called Puck's Castle,[†] the unhappy monarch, James, slept sickened and died. On which account great care and attention were employed to merit the favour of these guardian spirits; and no small degree of homage was paid to them. The ancient Irish generally sacrificed to them by pouring a part of what they drank upon the earth; and so firmly did they believe in their existence, that there were persons in rural districts called Fairy Doctors, who were supposed to hold immediate intercourse with them, and prevented them from not only injuring the cattle, corn and trees, but cured them of such diseases as they were supposed to have inflicted on them.

Those imaginary beings among different nations have various names and employments, according to their situation and mode of life. Among the northern nations they were called *Aafe, Fairies* and *Elves.* With the Greeks, *Nomes :* with the Romans, *Naiads, Nymphs, Silvans, Satyrs,* &c., and with the Hebrews, among whom they make a considerable department in their theology. From whence it is evident that the opinion respecting Genii, Fairies, Spectors, and Apparitions, so prevalent amongst most nations, arose from this ancient doctrine.

[*] There is a house at the village of Chapelizod, Phœnix Park, Dublin, which was occupied by King James in the morning, and by King William in the evening of the same day.

[†] The very peculiar state of Irish scenery in the fourteenth, fifteenth, and sixteenth centuries rendered such strong frontier residences as Puck's Castle necessary. It was customary, at these periods, for hordes of men, under the O'Toole, to leave their territories and march on the palesmen of Loughlinstown, Shanganagh, Shankhill, and Bray, very much, it may be supposed to their annoyance and discomfiture. These harrassing incursions appear to have been kept up until James the First ascended the throne. A flight of stone steps leading to the roof of Puck's Castle, is still in excellent preservation. A fine view of land and sea is commanded from the summit.

Robert Cowley, writing to Lord Cromwell, in 1537, speaks of the O'Toole as a sept "who most noyeth about Dublin."

the night after his defeat at Oldbridge, while his army bivouacked in front. Tradition states, that James, being apprehensive of an ambush in the woods of Windgate, took a boat at Killiney Bay, and coasted to the town of Wicklow, where he slept in a house afterwards occupied by a Dr. Smith. This anecdote relative to King James, rests on the authority of an unpublished M.S., in the possession of a private individual. From the town of Wicklow, King James must have proceeded to Shelton Abbey, in the Vale of Arklow, which was the last place he slept at in the county of Wicklow."

CROMLECHS,* NEAR SHANGANGH AND KILLINEY.

One of the most perfect and magnificent cromlechs in the kingdom (of extraordinary dimensions) within a short distance of Shanganagh and Killiney, is at "*Glen Druid*," the lovely residence of the much-respected Mr. Manliffe Barrington,—an extremely beautiful and picturesque spot—situated opposite to "Brennanstown House," adjoining Cabinteely, one of the charming country seats of those *progressive* and truly *independent* Irishmen,

"THE PIMS,'

who have already done so much for the material prosperity of their country.

The cromlech consists of a prodigious altar stone,

---

* These cromlechs or altars are thoroughly Eastern and primitive. Such an altar Noah "builded unto the Lord;" such an altar God himself commanded—"If thou wilt make Me an altar of stone, thou shalt not build it of *hewn* stone, for if thou lift up the tool upon it, thou hast polluted it." Cromlechs similar to those in Ireland exist in Syria. (Kemp's "Monumenta Antiqua.") Several cromlechs are still to be found in the East, which are commonly called "Altars of the Gentiles."

six feet thick at the upper part, its length being eighteen feet and width fifteen, leaning on four slabs of rock.

The cromlech at Shanganagh rests on three grey stones, the under surface being quite level.

At Killiney, behind Mount Druid House, which was occupied for some time by the late much-lamented J. B. Dillon, M.P., may be seen a well-preserved Druidical circle with the high priest's chair and sacrificing stone. Some small plantations appear around this mystic scene, the humble successors of those venerated oaks that shaded the Magi centuries ago.*

There is another very fine cromlech, which some think larger than the one at Glen Druid, on the hill behind the Golden Ball, a mile and a-half from Cabinteely, at a place called Kilternan.† Near Kil-

* The " Hill of Ward," which is near Athboy, was the ancient *Slacht-ga*, or Royal Seat of the Pagan Irish Kings, and a stronghold of Druidism, where annually, on the last night of October, the sacred fires were lighted and victims sacrificed.

† The cromlech at Kilternan was considered the largest in Europe, until the following appeared in the *Illustrated London News* :—

" Among the most interesting Druidic remains in Brittany is the gigantic "dolmen," called La Roche aux Fées, or the Fairies' Rock, situated in the Commune of Essé, twenty miles from Rennes. We are indebted to Mr. G. A. Mevius, of that city, for two photographs and description of this extraordinary building. It is, as shown in our illustrations, a long covered avenue, formed of forty-two stones of various sizes. Of these stones, seventeen are placed along the south-west side, and fifteen along the northeast, all planted upright in the earth, and composing the two walls of the abbey ; their height above the ground, ranges from 4ft. 11in. to 7ft. 3in. The other nine stones which form the roof, are enormous blocks laid across, with their ends resting on the tops of the walls on each side. Several of these huge pieces are from 5ft. to 7ft. in thickness ; and one of them is estimated to weigh about forty-five tons. The stone above the entrance is it the length of 18ft., and about 4ft. in width and thickness ; of forms, with the two pillar-stones on which its front is supported, a gateway, 11ft. 6in. wide, and 4ft. 4in. high. We do not know whether the height may not have been somewhat greater in former

ternan and the Golden Ball is the "Scalp," a very extraordinary natural pass through the mountains which divide the counties of Dublin and Wicklow. It is situated about two miles from Enniskerry. The opposite hills appear to have been rent asunder by some tremendous convulsive shock, and being composed of granite strata, the internal structure, when exposed to view, presents the secret recesses of nature in an awful and appalling point of view. Enormous masses of granite, many tons in weight, are tossed about in the most irregular manner, and so imperfect and unfinished was the effort of nature in creating this gulf, that the opposite sides of the pass are distant only the breadth of a narrow road from each other; in some places enormous masses actually interrupt the continued regularity of the limit of the road.

ages, when the level of the ground was, perhaps, lower than at present. This entrance is at the south-east side. At the north-west side, the temple, if such it was, is closed by a single block of great size. The total length of the edifice is 64ft. 2in., and its greatest height externally is 13ft. 2in. The interior is divided into two chambers, which are separated from each other by two stones, forming a sort of doorway. The first chamber is 14ft. 2in. long, and 9ft. wide; the second chamber is more than 48ft. long, and its width varies from 14ft. 6in. to 12ft. 2in.; it is subdivided into three compartments, or cells, by three projecting stones which run part way across from the south-east wall. The height of the interior, from the floor to the roof, now varies between 4ft. 11in. and 6ft. 6in.; but it was probably sufficient, in the original structure, for men to stand upright in every part. A few paces off, near the singular building described, lie two blocks of the same kind of stone—one to the west, the other to the east—under the shade of a venerable chestnut-tree, which shelters with its thick foliage the entrance to the temple. It is worthy of remark that the rock, a reddish coloured schist, of which this temple is built, is only found at a place about four miles distant, named Belle Marie, to the south-west of Essé, and fragments of this stone are found lying about on the road between these places. A stream, called the Rousseau de Sang, or Blood Brook, in the channel of which are some Druidic stones, runs not far from the Roche aux Fées; and in the small forest of Theil, which is in the same neighbourhood, is a "Menhir" of considerable dimensions.

THE "ANTIQUITIES OF TULLAGH," NEAR CABINTEELY, COUNTY DUBLIN.

The ancient burial-place of "Tullagh," near the village of Cabinteely, in the county of Dublin, contains within its precincts many objects of interest to the antiquarian. The ruins are approached from Cabinteely by a winding green lane, which, from its elevated position, presents some charming views of the surrounding country, that will amply repay the visitor, irrespective of the time-honored associations of the place. The church of Tullagh, i.e., "of the green eminence," is supposed by Dalton to have been originally built by the Danes, and dedicated to their king and patron, St. Olave, who became a martyr in 1030. In 1178, Archbishop O'Toole confirmed the church to the Priory of the Holy Trinity; and the taxation roll of 1306 shows that there was a certain portion of land next the church appropriated to St. Patrick's Cathedral, valued at £6 per annum. Dalton also states that in the Irish Chancery Rolls of 1370, there is an entry that Matthew, the son of Raymund de Bermingham, was despatched to Tullagh by the Lord Deputy to oppose the Kavanaghs, O'Byrnes, O'Nolans, and other "Irish enemies" of the English Pale. It is the opinion of the same historian that the church and its surroundings were formerly a sanctuary or asylum founded to protect the persecuted and penitent, similar to those mentioned in sacred and profane history. The numerous crosses or portions of same which still may be seen at a distance from the ruins of the church, favour this idea; as it is reasonable to suppose that sanctuaries were in many cases surrounded by certain outposts, such as crosses or other symbols of Christianity, which formed a sacred line or boundary for the better protection of those who fled there for refuge.

Of the church, only what was probably the choir now remains, which is of small proportions, and presents but few features worthy of notice, further than a well-built and perfect semi-circular arch. At the entrance of this apartment lies a tombstone of large dimensions, which denotes the grave of the Mercer family. It may be interesting here to remark that from the date, and one of the names, Mary Mercer, on the slab, it is not unlikely that Miss Mary Mercer, of charitable memory, who in 1734 founded "Mercer's Hospital," one of Dublin's noblest institutions, found here her last resting place. In the grave-yard, close to the ruins of the church, at its western side, is a very curious monumental stone of great antiquity, having on its upper surface a cross carved in bold relief with sunk panels. It is supposed that this stone originally formed a portion of the lid of a stone coffin in which an ecclesiastic of note was buried. Next to this stone lies a remarkable monument of a very remote period of this island's history; on its smoothest face appears a triple set of well defined, of what are called annular inscriptions. They differ in size, and each set is composed of four or five circles, with a boss in the centre. Mr. Henry Parkinson, who first drew attention to this curious monument, read an interesting paper on it and some other stones with similar inscriptions he found in Rathmichael church-yard,* at a recent meeting of

* In this old churchyard are six monumental stones, with annular inscriptions; two of them were found by the late Dr. Petrie, in 1815; the remaining four were recently discovered by Mr. H. Parkinson. Close to the churchyard, stand in a very perfect condition, the ruins of the well-known Puck's Castle. A gentleman, who has taken the farm of Rathmichael, discovered, a short time ago, the remains of a subterraneous passage evidently communicating between the Castle and the old church at Rathmichael. The country people think that a quantity of treasure will be found in the passage some day or other. It may not be known that the ancient town of Bray was at Rathmichael, and not on the sea shore.

the Royal Irish Academy. Dr. Graves, Bishop of Limerick, has written an instructive article on this class of inscriptions. The late Dr. Petrie also describes, in the *Dublin Examiner* for October, 1816, two of these stones he found at Rathmichael.

Mr. Henry Parkinson, Barrister, author of that beautiful work, the "Illustrated Record of the Dublin International Exhibition" of 1865, thinks that the following conjecture is worthy of consideration, namely, that the inscribed stone at Tullagh, was the monument of some former chief, and the carving, representing perhaps three shields were the symbols of his name, rank, and tribe. In the Irish grammar it is stated that "Fiacra was slain at the battle of Conry, his uacht or funeral stone, was erected, and on his tomb was inscribed his ogum name." Outside the grave-yard of Tullagh, on the roadside, stands a fine specimen of the ancient Irish cross belonging to the order which Ledwich calls that of Odin. A few yards from this latter may be seen in a field another cross, which Dalton describes as belonging to the Maltese pattern, with a good deal of carving on its shaft, and although greatly mutilated, is a most interesting relic. Next to this are the stone pedestals of two crosses which have disappeared. At first sight one is led to think that this triple group of crosses was erected as symbolical of Calvary; but on consideration it is manifest that these crosses were removed to their present position at no very remote period, and they once stood, together with the cross first described, in the four cardinal points of the compass, at some distance

---

The foundations of the houses can still be traced. Stretching up the hill at the back of the ruins of Rathmichael lies one of the finest fair greens in Ireland, and there are people alive who remember fairs being held there not far inferior to the now famous Ballinasloe. At the head of the fair green, on the top of the hill, are two Danish raths.

from the church, so as to form a line of outposts, and increase the security of the sanctuary.*

In the immediate neighbourhood of Tullagh is Rathmichael, a place of great antiquity, where the confederate forces of Strongbow and Dermod M'Morogh secretly passed from Waterford for the relief of Dublin, when besieged by the native princes. At Rathmichael are the ruins of an old church, and the lower section of a round tower, seven feet high, and twenty yards in circumference, called by the people of the district the "Skull Hole." On an eminence of Rathmichael is the *finest* Danish Rath in Ireland, which is really worth the notice of all antiquarians. It extends over an area 86 feet in diameter, the circumference of which was marked by a circle of stones, most of which are now nearly sodded over. Below this the Rath was encircled by a deep fosse of a much wider range, parts of which are still discernible. A wall and mound of an immense circumference enclosed all. The position of this fort was most commanding. Almost every Dane who arrives in this country visits this great military station of their ancestors. A few hundred yards from the fort in a hollow may still be traced the remains of another Rath, but of smaller dimensions.

Moore, in his history of Ireland, says—" It has been conjectured, however, and with much probability, that the stone circles of the Druids were employed, no less as rude observatories, than as places of judicature and worship; and the position in both of them of the great perpendicular stones, of which some, it is said, are placed generally in or near the meridian of the spot,

---

* In Mervyn's "Letters on Ireland," is quoted the following epitaph on a tombstone in Tullagh churchyard:—
Ye, who the power of God delight to trace,
And mark with joy each monument of grace,
Tread lightly o'er this grave, as ye explore
"*The short but simple Annals of the Poor.*"

while others are as carefully stationed to the right or left of the centre, would seem to indicate in their construction some view to astronomical purposes."

ROCHESTOWN AVENUE AND HOUSE.

ROCHESTOWN AVENUE AND HOUSE—"SQUIRE MAPASE"—FINE SPECIMENS OF THE QUERCUS VIRENS, OR EVERGREEN OAK—THE KILL OF THE GRANGE AND ITS OLD ABBEY—THE LATE MATHIAS J. O'KELLY, ESQ.—SPLENDID SPECIMENS OF EVERGREEN OAKS AT DELVILLE, GLASNEVIN—THE ONCE CLASSIC RESIDENCE OF THE CELEBRATED DEAN DELANY, NOW IN THE POSSESSION OF P. J. KEENAN, ESQ., NATIONAL EDUCATION BOARD.

Adjacent to the point, where the Killiney road intersects the famous "Rochestown avenue," one of the finest roads in the kingdom, and a favourite walk in summer owing to its being over-arched with trees from one end to the other, stands a quaint old rambling mansion called Rochestown house; the favourite residence, for many years, of the late respected and ever to be lamented Mathias J. O'Kelly, Esq., the eminent Naturalist.[*] The house from its

[*] Mr. O'Kelly was one of the founders, and honorary Secretary for some years to the Company which formed Glasnevin Cemetery, the Pere La Chase of Dublin, and though not forty years established, yet a vast Necropolis where close on three hundred thousand sleep their last sleep. Here the immortal Curran, O'Connell, and others, who in their life time were able "listening Senates to command," have found their final resting place. The Cemetery is really worth a visit, being tastefully laid out with plants and evergreens, and abounds in beautiful monuments. Mr. O'Kelly was a member of the Royal Irish Academy, and on the Council of the Royal Zoological Gardens Society, and a member of many other Societies in Dublin. Mr. Kelly was the author of what is written on Irish shells, in Whitelaw's "History of Dublin."

pointed gables, and high pitched roof presents rather an imposing specimen of what may be called the Dutch order of architecture, much in vogue in Queen Anne's time, and that of the early Georges; and was once the country seat of the Malpas family. In Burke's *Landed Gentry*, we read in the history of the Byrnes of Cabinteely, of one Walter Byrne marrying Clare, daughter of Christopher Malpas, of Rochestown, in or about the year 1700. John, known as the *Squire Mapase*, who erected the obelisk on Killiney hill, to provide employment for the people on his estate, during a year of scarcity, resided there His daughter and heiress, Catherine, was married in 1789 to Lord Talbot de Malahide, and brought with her the broad acres of the Malpas estate into the Talbot family. The Honourable Captain Richard Talbot, brother to the present Lord Talbot de Malahide, resides on this portion of the estate, at Ballinclay, Killiney, a handsome modern mansion.

On the death of Squire Malpas, the last of his race, Rochestown house gradually went into decay, till at length it fell into the hands of an aspiring dominie who sought to convert its classic groves into an. Irish Rugby. The speculation seems not to have been successful, for, after a short campaign the dominie retired, and the fine old place was again deserted. Finally, Mr. O'Kelly came to the rescue; not a moment too soon, for the axe was already laid at the roots of its stately trees; which however, the "Woodman had to spare," for Mr. O'Kelly purchased all the timber as it stood. The trees in return afforded for many years their grateful shade to their kind-hearted preserver. The house is still in the possession of the O'Kelly family, and contains among many other curiosities, a large portrait of Squire Malpas, in the entrance hall; and a fine collection of Irish shells, the result of a life time spent by Mr. O'Kelly, in patient research on our coasts and inland waters. The grounds must have once been very extensive, but field after field having from time to time been added to adjoining farms, they are now sadly curtailed; even the old entrance gateway on Rochestown avenue, and a portion of the ancient stately drive has been converted into a farmyard. In front of the house there is still standing an old ivy covered tower, which tradition points out as the place where a private marriage was celebrated at the witching time of night—while a ball was going on—between a trembling maiden of the house of Malpas and her lover true.

In a field adjoining the house are fine specimens of the Quercus Virens, evergreen oak. One of them rears its magnificent head above the rest of the trees, and is a beautiful object covered with its masses of dark green foliage, from the base to the summit; especially when nature has assumed her winter garb, and the fallen leaves are covered with snow. Rochestown avenue terminates at the Kingstown side, in the little hamlet of the Kill-of-the-Grange, which has sprung up round the extensive tile and pottery works of the Messrs MacCormick. Brick clay has been found in large quantities in this locality from time immemorial; some are of opinion that the first portion of the name kill was derived from the kilns that have been at work for years. It is, however, more probable that it was from Kill the Irish for a burial place. Close to the village, there is an interesting old ruined church and burial place, no longer used; the remains of two or three ancient crosses, and other relics within the enclosure recommend the place to the notice of antiquarians. In the chancel of the church is an old monument said to be that of a bishop, and in the south-west corner of the church-yard may be seen the tomb of one of the Byrne family of Cabinteely, decendants of the once powerful chieftains of that name. The tomb bears the following inscription: "Sacred to the memory of Robert Byrne, Esq., of Cabinteely, who was born in Dublin, on the 20th of May, 1748, and died at Buenos Ayres, in Lisbon, on Monday, the 7th of January, 1799, after a long and tedious illness, which he bore with christian fortitude; he was married on Sunday, the 7th of January, 1790, to Mary, the only daughter of Robert Devereux, Esq., of Carigmenan, county Wexford, by whom he had issue, Mary Clare, Clarinda Mary, and Georgina Mary Byrne." Within a few yards of the gate of the church-yard stands Kill Abbey, the residence of Richard Espinasse, Esq., J.P. one of the oldest houses perhaps in Ireland, for according to the date over the entrance door it was erected or repaired in the year 1595, Queen Elizabeth's reign; the house is of peculiar construction, consisting of a groupe of pointed gables, each of them terminating with a finial or pinnacle of a granite ball; most of the doors and windows are lancet-shaped, which give the building an ecclesiastical appearance. Kill Abbey it seems was famous in olden time, as one of the principal stations of an influential order of Monks, many of whom, no doubt, sleep peacefully under the shadow of the adjoining church. The vaults under Kill Abbey are very extensive, and communicate it is said with the church, reaching even as far as Kingstown itself.

DELVILLE.—GLASNEVIN.

Delville with its groves of evergreen oaks, and yew and mulberry trees, is situated in the classical village of Glasnevin. It was once the residence of the celebrated Dr. Delany, Fellow of Trinity College, where that "learned divine assembled his coterie of wits in the Augustan Age of Queen Anne; where the patriot Dean, and the beautiful and enduring Stella have charmed the feast; where Southern has frequently sojourned, and in whose immediate vicinity Addison, Sheridan, Parnell, and Tickell* have resided." Dalton, in his "History of the County Dublin," in describing Delville House, Glasnevin, the present residence of P. J. Keenan, Esq., says : "A tall close gate and wall conceal it from the view of prying curiosity ; but these obstacles once removed, and the mind's eye is rapidly attracted by the ancient edifice, with its bower window—the old garden walls thickly flowering with the snap-dragon—the gracefully undulating grounds—the broad terrace, on which the peripatetics of another day have glided and philosophized—the magnificent trees on the bank of the rivulet ; the fine mount, and the turret overlooking the Bay of Dublin and distant city ; the beauties of the intervening country, and more solemnly glancing over the churchyard,† where its remembered owner lies ; the dark vault beneath that turret, where the first impression of the "Legion Club ‡" is supposed to have been printed ; the temple, with its fresco painting of St. Paul, and its medallion bust of Stella, by Mrs. Delany ;§—the inscription on the frieze at its front—

Fastigia despicit urbis,

written by Dean Swift, and supposed to allude to the situation of this villa—the temples scattered through the demesne the rustic bridges : the bath—the lonely willow dropping its feathery wreaths into the water, amidst the

---

* The present Botanic Gardens at Glasnevin, was once the demesne of Tickell, the poet, the literary executor of Addison, who came to Ireland as his assistant, when he was secretary to the Earl of Sutherland, in 1714. In 1725, Tickell was himself appointed secretary, an office which he filled until his death, in 1740. His demesne was purchased, subject to a ground rent, for the sum of £2,000 by the Royal Dublin Society.

† Dr. Delany and the learned and eccentric Dr. Barret, who wrote memoirs of Swift, are buried in the old graveyard of Glasnevin. Many are of opinion that Robert Emmet was also buried in this churchyard.

‡ Dean Swift spent the summer of 1735 at Delville. Some time since a printing-press and type was discovered in a room under the temple, on the walls of which Mrs. Delany painted St. Paul and the medallion bust of Stella. It is supposed that the first edition of Dean Swift's "Legion Club" was printed in this room, as it is generally understood that this bitter satire was not printed in Dublin, as no one would undertake its publication.

§ These charming paintings are now being restored by Mr. B. C. Watkins, R.H.A., for Mr. Keenan.

lilies that floated round it—the venerable mulberry tree—
its surrounding compeers of aged elms, and yews, and evergreen oaks;—all powerfully marked the taste and elegance
that formed and enlivened this scene.

" Perhaps the *first* attempt at modern gardening in Ireland
was made by the Rev. Dr. Delany, at Delville, near Glasnevin. Like Pope, he impressed a vast deal of beauty on a
very small spot of ground. Nor is it improbable that Pope,
with whom he lived in habits of intimacy, taught him to
soften into a curve the obdurate straight line of the Dutch,
to melt the terrace into a swelling bank, and to open his
walks to catch the vicinal country. These gardens at Delville still remain a monument of Delany's taste.* Swift has
left a humourous poetical description of them, in which,
though he has contracted the features, he has preserved the
likeness."

"Would you that DELVILLE I describe ?
Believe me, sir, I will not gibe;
For who would be satirical
Upon a thing so very small!
You scarce upon the borders enter,
Before you're at the very centre ;
A single crow would make it night,
If o'er your farm he took his flight.
Yet, in the narrow compass we
Observe a vast variety ;
Both walks, walls, meadows, and parterres,
Windows and doors, and rooms and stairs,
And hills and vales, and woods and fields,
And hay and grass, and corn it yields ;
All to your haggard brought so cheap in,
Without the mowing or the reaping ;
A razor, though to say't I'm loth,
Might shave you and your meadow both.
Tho' small your farm, yet here's a house,
Full large—to entertain a mouse ;
But where a rat is dreaded more
Than furious Caledonian boar ;
For if 'tis entered by a rat
There is no room to bring the cat.
A little riv'let seems to steal
Along a thing you call a vale,

---

* Essay on the Rise and Progress of gardening in Ireland, by
J. C. Walker, M.R.I.A. From the "Anthologia Hibernica,"
1793.

Like tears a-down a wrinkled cheek,
Like rain along a blade of leek;
And this you call your sweet meander,
Which might be suck'd up by a gander,
Could he but force his rustling bill
To scoop the channel of the rill;
I'm sure you'd make a mighty clutter
Were it as big as city gutter.
Next come I to your kitchen garden,
Which one poor mouse would fare but hard in;
And round this garden is a walk
No longer than a tailor's chalk;
Thus I compute what space is in it,
A snail creeps o'er it in a minute!
One lettuce makes a shift to squeeze,
Up through a tuft you call your trees;
And once a year a single rose
Peeps from the bud, but never blows;
In vain, then, you expect its bloom;
It cannot blow for want of room.
In short, in all your boasted seat
There's nothing but *yourself* is—great."

"*Delville*, 28*th June*, 1744.*

"We arrived at Delville, our own pleasant dwelling by eleven,—and never was seen a sweeter dwelling. I have traversed the house and gardens, and never saw a more delightful and agreeable place.

"I have a most extensive and beautiful prospect of the harbour and town of Dublin, and a range of mountains of various shapes.

"Delville stands on a rising ground, and the court is large enough for a coach-and-six to drive round commodiously."

"*Delville*, 19*th July*, 1744.

"I wish I could give you an idea of our garden, but the describing of it puzzles me extremely: the back part of the house is towards a bowling-green, that slopes gently off down a little brook that runs through the garden; on the other side of the brook is a high bank with a hanging wood

---

* The autobiography and correspondence of Mary Granville, (Mrs. Delany), with Interesting Reminiscences of King George the Third and Queen Charlotte. Edited by the Right Hon. Lady Llanover. London: Richard Bentley.

of evergreens,* at the top of which is a circular terrace that surrounds the greatest part of the garden, the wall of which is covered with fruit-trees, and on the other side of the walk a border for flowers, and the greatest quantity of roses and sweet briar that ever I saw: on the right hand of the bowling-green towards the bottom is placed our hay-rick, which is at present making, and from our parlour window and bed-chamber I can see the men work at it, and have a full view of what I described; and beyond that pleasant meadows, bounded by mountains of various shapes, with little villages and country seats interspersed and embosomed high in tufted trees: to complete the prospect, a full view of Dublin harbour, which is always full of shipping, and looks at this instant beautiful beyond description: these are the views from the house *next* the gardens. On the left hand of the bowling-green is a terrace walk that takes in a sort of a parterre, that will make the prettiest orangery in the world, for it is an oval of green, planted round in double rows of elm-trees and flowering shrubs, with little grass walks between them, which will give a good shelter to exotics. The terrace I just mentioned is bounded at one end by a wall of good fruit, in which there is a door that leads to another very large handsome terrace-walk, with double rows of large elms, and the walk well gravelled, so that we may walk securely in any weather.

"On the left hand the ground rises very considerably, and is planted with all sorts of trees. About half way up the walk there is a path that goes up that bank to the remains of an old castle, from whence there is an unbounded prospect all over the country; under it is a cave that opens with an arch to the terrace walk, that will make a very pretty grotto; and the plan I had laid out for my brothers at Calwich I shall execute here. At the end of this terrace is a very pretty portico, prettily painted within and neatly furnished without; you go up a high slope to it, which gives it a mighty good air as you come up the walk; from thence you go on the right hand to the green terrace I mentioned at first, which takes in the whole compass of this garden; in the middle, sloping from the terrace, every way, are the fields, or rather paddocks, where our deer and our cows are kept, and the rurality of it is wonderfully pretty. These fields are planted in a *wild way* with *forest-trees and with bushes*, that look so naturally you would not imagine it the

---

* The finest collection of the Quercus Virens, or evergreen Oaks in Ireland, are growing in Delville demesne.

work of art. Besides this, there is a very good kitchen-garden and two fruit gardens, which, when proper repairs are made, and they are set in order, will afford us a sufficient quantity of everything we can want of that kind.

"There are several prettinesses I can't explain to you—little wild walks, private seats, and lovely prospects. One seat particularly I am very fond of, in a nut grove, and '*the beggar's hut*,' which is a seat in a rock: on the top are bushes of all kinds that bend over; it is placed at the end of a cunning wild path, thick set with trees, and it overlooks the brook, which entertains you with a purling rill.

"The little robins are as fond of this seat as we are. It just holds the Dean and myself, and I hope in God to have many a tête à tête there with my own dear sister; but I have had such a hurry of business within doors, and so many visitors, that I have not spent half as much time in this sweet garden as I want to do. I am afraid this will prove an incomprehensible description; but if it does but whet your desire of seeing it, that is sufficient for me. Monday I visited all the Barber race,* and our good old friend.   *   *   *

"Adieu,
"Yours with everlasting love,
"MARY DELANY."

"*Delville, Glasnevin*, 13*th Feb.*, 1745.

"The Dean has subscribed to some philosophical lectures. Last Monday I was at Mrs. Clayton's *drum*, which was *very magnificent;* her apartment is very fine, and she had a great deal of good company. D. D. Bushe and I dined there. To-morrow I go to the "Fair Penitent,"† to see our three famous actors together. Garrick‡ performs the part of Lothario;

---

* Mrs. Barber of Glasnevin was the same Mrs. Barber so often mentioned as the poetess so much patronized by Dean Swift, who visited England to obtain subscribers for her productions.

† "The Fair Penitent," a tragedy by Nicholas Rowe. He was born 1673, and died 1718.

‡ David Garrick, born 28th February, 1716, died 20th January, 1779. He twice visited Ireland. A short poem in his praise, called "The Stage," is dated Dublin, 14th February, 1746, and printed in the *Gentleman's Magazine*.

Sheridan,* Horatio; and Barry,† Altamont. Sheridan I have not seen; my brother has; he is here in great reputation. Barry is the handsomest man and figure altogether hat I ever saw upon the stage, and a promising actor."

"*Delville*, 15*th Oct.*, 1745.

"Mrs. Clayton's house is very magnificent, but *more for show* than *comfortable living*. I would not give up my sweet Delville for it; no, nor for *any palace I ever yet saw*."

---

* Thomas, third son of Dr. Thomas Sheridan, was born at Quilca, near Dublin, in 1721. He was educated at Westminster School, and Trinity College, Dublin, which university he suddenly quitted, after having graduated M.A., and turned actor, in which profession he obtained great celebrity. He died on the 14th of August, 1788. He was the father of the celebrated Richard Brinsley Sheridan.

† Barry was the son of a silversmith, and born in Werburgh-street, Dublin, on the 20th of February, 1719. He determined to try his success on the stage, and accordingly in 1744 he made his debut on the Irish boards, in the character of Othello. He afterwards played at Cork with equal applause, and thence returning to Dublin, made one of that galaxy of talent which drew such full houses in the summer, that it was very common to say that a person had *died of a Garrick, a Quin, or a Barry fever*. In 1746 he went to London, and was engaged at Drury Lane, where he performed both in tragedy and genteel comedy with much approbation; After having for some time divided the applause of the town with Garrick, Barry removed to Covent Garden in 1749, when a decided competition took place between the two great actors, each playing against the other their principal characters, with various success. The grand struggle made by both was in the part of Romeo, in which the majority agreed in awarding the palm to Barry. He died January 10th, 1777. The admirers of Garrick were in the habit of allowing Barry every physical and denying him every mental qualification. They sneered at him as "the silver-toned lover," "the elegant automaton," &c.; but there is no doubt "in the silver scenes of dramatic love, conjugal tenderness, and agonizing distress, Barry was Garrick's master.' Victor, in his History of Theatres (1761), states that on January 20, 1745-6, he went over to Ireland, and when he arrived in Dublin he found "his good friend Mr. Garrick" at the Theatre Royal with Mr. Sheridan, as sharers and adventurers, and Mr. Barry engaged at a salary by the proprietors. There were several tragedies, in which Victor had the pleasure of seeing these three performers appear together, as, in "The Fair Penitent," Garrick acted Lothario, Sheridan, Horatio, and Barry, Altamont; and, he adds, in his belief, "that he was much envied that happiness."

The Earl of Chesterfield visits Delville.

"*Delville, Oct.* 22, 1745.

"Yesterday we were honoured with a visit from our Viceroy* and Queen. They sent over early in the morning to know if we were disengaged, as they would breakfast. To work went all my maids, stripping covers off chairs,† sweeping, dusting, &c., and by eleven, my house was as spruce as a cabinet of curiosities, and well bestowed on their Excellencies, who commended and admired, and were as polite as possible. They came soon after eleven in their travelling coach, with only two footmen. Mr. Bristol and Mrs. Chenevix‡ in the coach with them. They were first carried into the drawing-room, examined every room in my apartments above, delighted with the situation, liked the furniture, but were impatient to see my own works, upon which the Dean conducted them to the MINERVA, where I had two tables covered with all sorts of breakfast. When breakfast was over, they made me play on the harpsichord, which I did with a very ill grace. When that was done we went into the garden and walked over every inch of it ; they seemed much surprised with the variety they found there, and could not have said more civil things had it been my Lord Cobham's Stowe ! To-day we dine at the Bishop of Clogher's, tomorrow at Lord Grandison's."

"*Delville*, 16*th Nov.*, 1745.

"Pray have you read the four sermons by Swift that were published last year ?§

"They are very fine and worth the reading. There is just published a humorous pamphlet of Swift's, I think called 'Advice to Servants ;' it is said to be below his genius, but comical.—I have not yet seen it. Surely I wrote you word a month ago of his death. It was a happy release to him

---

* The celebrated Earl of Chesterfield.
† These "*Chairs*" were doubtless her own marvellous chenille embroidery of flowers of nature.
‡ Mrs. Chenevix, wife of the Bishop of Killaloe, afterwards Bishop of Waterford, grandmother of the beautiful Mrs. St. George, afterwards Mrs. Trench, mother of the Dean of Westminster, now the Protestant Archbishop of Dublin.
§ According to Dr. Johnson, Dean Swift gave up mental labour in 1736, though some works previously written were subsequently published. In 1741, he was placed under legal guardians and personal restraint; and after years of raving, alternating with speechless fatuity, he died in October, 1745.

(I hope), for he was reduced to such a miserable state of idiotism that he was a shocking object; though in his person a very venerable figure, with long silver hair and a comely countenance, for being grown fat, the hard lines, which gave him a harsh look before, were filled up."

Dr. Barber on D.D.:

> Let others gain from power a titled name,
> Unconscious of the noble rights to fame!
> On the mitre could reflect no light,
> Where learning, genius, virtue, taste unite,
> Circling the head with glory's brightest rays,
> Viceroys can neither give nor damp that blaze.

"*Delville,* 21*st December,* 1745.

"Last Monday the Dean and I went to the rehearsal of the Messiah for the relief of poor debtors. It was very well performed, and I was much delighted.*

"*Delville,* 20*th June,* 1747.

"I have just had a visit from the Dowager, Lady Kildare, and the Duchess of Manchester. Yesterday we spent a very pleasant day in the country with Mr. and Mrs. Lawe, at their bleach green, near the famous Salmon Leap of Leixlip.†

"*Delville,* 15*th October,* 1748.

"Last Monday we set out for Dangan, Lord Mornington's. He is now the same good-humoured, agreeable man he was seventeen years ago, when I made him my last visit. Miss Wesley‡ did the honours of the table; my godson, Master Wesley,§ is a most extraordinary boy; he was

---

* The Messiah was first performed in Dublin, on the 12th of April, 1742; when Mrs. Cibber executed her airs so pathetically, that Dr. Delany is said to have exclaimed, as he listened,

"Woman, for this, be all thy sins forgiven."

† Leixlip Castle was erected by Adam FitzHereford, one of the Anglo-Norman conquerors. Its antique towers, mantled with ivy, rise above the surrounding trees and rivers. Immediately adjoining Leixlip is the Salmon Leap, where the Liffey, falling over a ledge of rocks, forms a beautiful cascade, up which the fish, at certain seasons, are seen to spring. The town of Leixlip is in the county Kildare, and situated on the River Liffey, about ten miles from Dublin. Near Leixlip is Celbridge, where *Vanessa* died.

‡ Frances, second daughter of Richard, first Lord Mornington, who married, in 1750, William Francis Crosbie, Esq.

§ Garrett, only son of Lord Mornington, born July 19th, 1735, afterwards created Viscount Wellesley and Earl of Mornington He was father of Arthur, the celebrated Duke of Wellington.

thirteen last month; he is a very good scholar, and whatever study he undertakes he masters it most surprisingly. He began with the fiddle last year, he now plays everything at sight; he understands fortification, building of ships, and has more knowledge than I ever met with in one so young. Daugan is really magnificent, the old house that was burnt down is rebuilding. They live at present in the offices; the park consists of six hundred Irish acres; there is a gravel walk from the house to the great lake, fifty-two feet broad and 600 yards long. The lake contains twenty-six acres, is of an irregular shape, with a fort built in all its forms; there are islands in the lake for wild fowl, and great quantities of them embellish the water extremely. I never saw so pretty a thing. There are several ships, one a complete man-of-war; my godson is governor of the fort and lord high admiral; he hoisted all his colours for my reception, and was not a little mortified that I declined the compliment of being saluted from the fort and ship. The part of the lake that just fronts the house forms a very fine basin, and is surrounded by a natural terrace wooded, through which walks are cut, and a variety of seats placed, that you may rest and enjoy all the beauties of the place as they change to your eye. The ground, as far as you can see every way, is waving in hills and dales, and every remarkable point has either a tuft of trees, a statue, a seat, an obelisk, or a pillar.

*　　*　　*　　*　　*　　*

Lord Harrington is not going to Delville; the Lord Chancellor* has prevailed with him to go to his country seat at Merrion."

The following are extracts from a poem by Dean Swift, said to have been printed at Delville:—

TO DR. DELANY, ON THE LIBELS WRITTEN AGAINST HIM.

　　Tanti tibi non sit opaci
　　Omnis arena Tagi.—Juv.

*　　*　　*　　*

'Tis eminence makes envy rise;
As fairest fruits attract the flies.
Should stupid libels grieve your mind,
You soon a remedy may find;

---

* Robert Jocelyn, appointed Lord Chancellor of Ireland on the 7th September, 1730; created, 29th November, 1743, Baron Newport; and 6th November, 1755, Viscount Jocelyn; and died October 25th, 1756. His son was created Earl of Roden.

Lie down obscure like other folks
Below the lash of snarlers' jokes.
Their faction is five hundred odds;
For every coxcomb lends them rods;
And sneers as learnedly as they;
Like females o'er their morning-tea.
  A *genius* in the rev'rend gown
Must ever keep its owner down;
'Tis an unnatural conjunction,
And spoils the credit of the function.
Round all your brethren cast your eyes,
Point out the surest men to rise;
That club of candidates in black,
The least deserving of the pack,
Aspiring, factious, fierce, and loud,
With grace and learning unendu'd,
Can turn their hands to every job,
The fittest tools to work for Bob:
Will sooner coin a thousand lies,
Than suffer men of parts to rise;
They crowd about preferment's gate,
And press you down with all their weight.
For, as of old, mathematicians
Were, by the vulgar, thought magicians;
So academic dull ale-drinkers
Pronounce all men of wit *freethinkers*.
  Wit, as the chief of virtue's friends,
Disdains to serve ignoble ends.
Observe what loads of stupid rhymes
Oppress us in corrupted times:
What pamphlets in a court's defence
Shew reason, grammar, truth, or sense?
For tho' the muse delights in fiction,
She ne'er inspires against conviction.
Then keep your virtue still unmixt,
And let not faction come betwixt:
By party-steps no grandeur climb at,
Tho' it would make you England's primate:
First learn the science to be dull,
You then may soon your conscience lull;
If not, however seated high,
Your genius in your face will fly.
  When Jove was from his teeming head
Of wit's fair goddess brought to bed,
There follow'd at his lying-in
For after-birth a Sooterkin;
Which as the nurse pursued to kill,
Attain'd, by flight, the muses' hill,
There in the soil began to root,
And litter'd at Parnassus foot,

From hence the critic vermin sprung
With harpy claws and pois'nous tongue,
Who fatten on poetic scraps,
Too cunning to be caught in traps.
Dame Nature, as the learned show,
Provides each animal its foe:
Hounds hunt the hare, the wily fox
Devours your geese, the wolf your flocks:
Thus Envy pleads a nat'ral claim
To persecute the muses' fame;
On poets in all times abusive,
From Homer down to Pope inclusive.
   Yet what avails it to complain?
You try to take revenge in vain.
A rat your utmost rage defies,
That safe behind the wainscot lies:
Say, did you ever know by sight
In cheese an individual mite?
Show me the same numeric flea,
That bit your neck but yesterday:
You then may boldly go in quest
To find the Grub-street poet's nest;
What sponging-house in dread of jail
Receives them, while they wait for bail;
What alley are they nestled in,
To flourish o'er a cup of gin:
Find the last garret where they lay,
Or cellar where they starve to-day.
Suppose you had them all trepann'd,
With each a libel in his hand,
What punishment would you inflict?
Or call 'em rogues, or get 'em kick't?
These they have often try'd before:
You but oblige 'em so much more:
Themselves would be the first to tell,
To make their trash the better sell.
   You have been libelled—Let us know
What fool officious told you so?
Will you regard the hawker's cries,
Who in his titles always lies?
Whate'er the noisy scoundrel says,
It might be something in your praise:
And praise bestowed in Grub-street rhymes
Would vex one more a thousand times.
Till critics blame, and judges praise,
The poet cannot claim his bays.
On me, when dunces are satiric,
I take it for a panegyric.
Hated by fools, and fools to hate,
Be that my motto and my fate.

SECTION VII.

THE O'BYRNES AND THE O'TOOLES.

. HISTORIC ASSOCIATIONS.

THE O'TOOLES, PRINCES OF IMAIL; AND THE O'BYRNES PRINCES OF GLENMALURE, AND THE ENTIRE SEA COAST OF WICKLOW, AT ONE TIME EXTENDED THEIR POWER OVER THE SOUTHERN PARTS OF THE COUNTY DUBLIN, INCLUDING AND COMMANDING THE ENTIRE DISTRICT UNDER THE THREE ROCK MOUNTAIN TO THE SHORES OF DUBLIN BAY.

The O'Byrnes and O'Tooles were two powerful Septs who owned the greater part of the county Wicklow. The castles and strongholds of the O'Byrnes were situated in the romantic valley of Glendalough, while those of the O'Tooles were situated in the lovely and picturesque glens of Imaile, Glenmalure and Anamoe.

"Bright shines the morn on Carrickmuir,
And silvers every mountain stream;
The autumnal woods on Glenmalure
Look lovely in the slanting beam."

In 1173, Strongbow, on the part of Henry II., gave to Walter de Riddlesford, Bray and the land of the sons of O'Toole, with all their appurtenances.

In 1297, Theobald le Botiller, ancestor of the Earls of Ormond, after accompanying and aiding Edward I. in his expedition against Scotland, purchased the manor of Bray, with all the estates of the O'Byrnes.

In 1312, the O'Byrnes and O'Tooles made an incursion into Rathcoole and Saggard, in the neighbourhood of the city, in the absence of the chief force sent from thence to quell an insurrection of the De

Verdons in Louth and Ergallia. These brave and hardy Septs, whose territories were in Wicklow and Kildare, although so near the capital, preserved their independence for three centuries after the Anglo-Norman invasion, and continued to harass and annoy the English government and the city. From time to time the citizens sallied out, and carried the war into their mountain districts; these were called "hostings," in which they were occasionally successful, but were more frequently obliged to return with considerable loss.*

In 1331, O'Toole of Imaile, at the head of a numerous train of armed followers, plundered the palace of Tallagh, carried away a prey of 300 sheep, slew many of the bishop's servants, and defeated, in a pitched battle, Sir Philip Brett and a body of the citizens of Dublin that came out against him. Watch and ward were constantly kept here and at Bray, to repel similar attacks.

In 1349, the abbot of the religious house of the Blessed Virgin, of Dublin, on his part, freely and voluntarily consented to find, at his own cost and charges, two complete horsemen and six hobillers, to assist the King's warders at Bray, in protecting the country from the O'Tooles and O'Byrnes, the king declaring, and it being understood, that such voluntary act of the abbot should not be drawn into a precedent to the prejudice of future abbots.

In 1355, a strong ward was placed at Ballymore Eustace, to guard the Marches from the O'Byrnes and O'Tooles. In the following year, the king commanded Maurice, Earl of Kildare, to strengthen and maintain his possessions at Kilkea, Rathmore, and Ballymore, under penalty of forfeiting the same and all other estates granted to his grandfather.

In 1356, in consequence of an expected invasion of

* Marmion's "Maritime Ports of Ireland."

the county of Dublin by the O'Byrnes, John, the son of Geoffry le Brett, was commanded to defend the pale at his manor of Rathfarnham.*

In 1356, William de Barton had a liberate or money-order on the treasury, for fortifying certain places on the Marches of Dublin against the O'Byrnes, and for furnishing food and provender to the garrisons.

In 1361, Robert de Hollywood was one of those, "the worthiest then in chivalry," who were knighted by Lionel Duke of Clarence, in 1377. He was obliged to march with his retinue against the O'Byrnes and O'Tooles, county Wicklow.

In 1379, Richard Talbot of Malahide was at the parliament, or rather council, convened to Baltinglass for the purpose of treating on terms of peace with the O'Byrnes, O'Tooles, O'Nolans, and MacMurroughs. He was afterwards sheriff of the county Dublin.

In 1402, John Drake, mayor of Dublin, with a strong body of well-armed citizens, marched against the O'Byrnes and O'Tooles, whom he encountered in battle near Bray, where 400 of the Irish were slain. For this service the citizens re-elected Drake their mayor for the ensuing year, while Daniel O'Byrne tendered his allegiance and his castle of M'Kinegan, near Delgany, to the king.

In 1419, O'Toole "took 400 cows belonging unto Ballymore, thereby breaking the peace contrary to his oath."†

In 1422, the council in Dublin directed that, on account of "the notorious war, engaged by the O'Tooles on the liegemen of the counties of Dublin and Kildare, the same forces of men-at-arms and archers should be continued as theretofore to oppose them, and the same subsidy raised."

In 1429, by writ reciting that Sir John Sutton, Lord Lieutenant of Ireland, had lately made a suc-

* Rot. in Canc. Hib. † Marlburgh's Chronicle.

cessful incursion on the O'Byrnes of the county Wicklow, at his own expense, for which the sheriff of this county and its crosses* was ordered to provide 100 "carts" of victuals, 800 men with axes and bundles of wood, 100 men with "iron tools," and 200 with " caltrops," together with victuals for six days, under certain penalties which had been incurred by his neglect in that behalf: all said penalties were directed to be forthwith paid to the said Lord Lieutenant.

In 1429, the sheriff of Dublin was commanded to provide from the county and cross lands of Dublin 100 carts' load of victuals, 800 men with axes and bundles of wood, " fasciculis," 100 men with spades,

---

* Dalton, in his " History of the County Dublin," says:—
" Some few centuries after the establishment of Christianity in Ireland, in the fifth century, those districts of the country known by the name of croceæ or cross lands, were dedicated to the Church, and most extensive jurisdiction was given to the abbots and bishops therein. Such were the croceæ of Ulster, Kilkenny, Meath, Kildare, Louth, Kerry, Navan, Ferns, Carlow, Wexford, Leighlin, &c., and such were the croceæ or liberties of the cross of the Archbishop of Dublin ; and as in England the symbol of triumphant Christianity was frequently set up to mark the boundaries of civil districts, so in Ireland, with more propriety, crosses, some of them very handsomely ornamented, were erected to distinguish the ecclesiastical possessions.

"The cross lands of Dublin appear to have been partly in the northern, and partly in the southern sections of the county. The northern croceæ retain some of the actual crosses, as at St. Doulogh's and Finglas ; while another, called pardon cross, is particularly recorded as having been erected at Swords, Clondalkin, Tullagh, St. Ann's, the Kill of the Grange, Kiltuc, and Rathmichael. Similar emblems seem to demarcate somewhat of the extent of the southern croceæ.

"Crosses were, in truth, the first objects to which it was sought, by various inducements and associations, to attach the reverence of the people, and were multiplied according to the facility of collecting Christian congregations. As they demonstrated ecclesiastical retreats and possessions, so did they also assert the dignity of ecclesiastical jurisdiction ; and, when the guilty fugitive placed himself within the circle of their authority, and sat down in sin and sorrow beneath their shadow, municipal punishment and private revenge were alike disarmed."

"vangis," 200 with machines for hurling stones, "tribulis," and full provisions for the whole force for six days, all which men, arms, and supplies, were directed to be at Bray on a day named, under heavy penalties, as the same were urgently required for service against the O'Byrnes.

Puck's castle was one of the frontier residences of the Pale, on the Marches of the O'Tooles, who ceased not to harass the palesmen down to the time of James I.

In 1534, the citizens of Dublin, having received advice that the O'Tooles were conducting a prey from Fingal to the mountains, sallied out to intercept them at Kilmainham-bridge. They met at the wood of Salcock; but being overpowered by numbers, the former were routed, with the loss of 80 men.

In 1537, Robert Crowley, writing to Lord Cromwell, says, " Ballymore and Tallagh, 'longing to the Archbishop of Dublin, standeth most for the defence of the counties of Dublin and Kildare against the O'Tooles and O'Byrnes: be it therefore ordered, that the commissioners shall see such farmers or tenants there as shall be hardy marchers, able to defend that marches."*

The district of Glendalough, or the Valley of the Seven Churches, though within twenty-five miles of Dublin, and surrounded by the English of the *Pale*, was held by the O'Tooles, who maintained possession of it with uncontrolled authority till the 17th century.

Mr. Anthony O'Toole, of Raheny (the eminent public contractor), is one of the few descendants of that great Irish Sept, the O'Tooles, Princes of Imail.

* State Papers, temp. Henry VIII.

IRISH VARIETIES.

THE
KINGDOM OF DALKEY,

(AS IT WAS IN THE LAST CENTURY:)

ITS SUMMER REVELS, RE-UNIONS, AND MOCK PAGEANTRIES,
POLITICAL ASSOCIATIONS,
AND INTERESTING REMINISCENCES.

STEPHEN THE FIRST,

AND THIS

"ELECTIVE AND LIMITED! MONARCHY,"

CORONATION ODES AND SERMONS.

THE "KINGDOM OF DALKEY," AND ITS OFFICERS OF STATE, ETC., ETC., EIGHTY YEARS AGO.

IN the last century, a curious convivial society or club was established in Dublin, which existed for a considerable time, until it became the parent of secret democratic societies, in connexion with the French revolutionists. Most of the wits and gay fellows of the middle and liberal class of society were members of it. Its president was styled "King of Dalkey, Emperor of the Muglins, Prince of the Holy Island of Magee, and Elector of Lambay and Ireland's Eye, Defender of his own Faith and Respecter of all others, and Sovereign of the Most Illustrious Order of the Lobster and Periwinkle." Proclamations in connexion with this mimic kingdom were issued from "The Palace, Fownes'-street."* The last and most popular King of Dalkey was a very respectable bookseller and pawnbroker of Dublin—Stephen Armitage, who reigned under the title of

"King Stephen the First."

"George has of wealth the dev'l and all,
Him we may King of Diamonds call ;
But *thou* hast such persuasive arts,
We hail *thee* Stephen, King of Hearts."
MOORE.

The members of this society met once a year on Dalkey Island, to choose a king and state officers, the

---

* The following are extracts from the *Dalkey Gazette Extraordinary:*
"The meeting at Dalkey to-morrow is expected to be the fullest and most splendid that has occurred in the kingdom for half a century.—Stephen Rex. Given at our Palace, Fownes'-street, 23rd June, 1791, in the third year of our reign."
"The birth-day ode, written by the celebrated Countess of Laurel, will be read in Council previous to its being set to music by Sir Jno. Handel."
"The deputation from the states of Lambay, Ireland's Eye, and the Muglins, and from the Holy Knights of the Magee, came to lay their annual tribute at his Majesty's feet, consisting of three milk white rabbits, three young sea-gulls, three large lobsters, a firkin of mushrooms, a firkin of oysters, do. cockles, an antique mether of whiskey, a wreath of misletoe, and a robe of sea-wrack.—September 22nd, 1792."
"Last night (September 28th, 1792) came on the election for Lord Mayor and Sheriffs of the kingdom of Dalkey for the year ensuing, when Alderman Warren was elected Lord Mayor, and Sir Patrick Marlay and Sir Joseph Wilcock were elected Sheriffs, took the test, and sworn in."—*Dalkey Gazette.*
From the *Dalkey Gazette,* August 26, 1793 :—"Yesterday her Most Affable Majesty departed this life. Her last moments were marked by firmness and resignation. The greater part of her personal property she has left in different donations to the poor. Her five millions in the Bank of Amsterdam are to return to the island from which they were produced, and to be expended in Christmas beef for such manufacturers as are at present destitute of employ ; notwithstanding which his Majesty Stephen the First has declared that he shall have no occasion to call on his people to pay his debts.
"On this calamitous event the court has been thrown into the

monarchy being elective. Strictly limited—that is, in extent— the people were averse to foreign conquest and standing armies. The point and intention of this original travestie of fun and festivity, was to revive, in a humourous and satirical vein, the events of the past year, and to discuss the questions of interest affecting political topics of the day, the shortcomings of the government, and the state of European affairs generally. All the nobility of this *petit* kingdom were at one time wits, orators, and generally first-rate vocalists, and the royal visitors were supposed to be similarly gifted. The proceedings of these summer *réunions*, with a full report of the coronation sermons, as preached in the ruined church on the island, which was called Dalkey Cathedral, were published in most of the Dublin papers—more especially in *Cooney's Morning Post*, the politics of which were very democratic. The *Dalkey Gazette* formed a portion of this journal. This paper is now difficult to be met with. At the conclusion of the coronation revels, which generally took place on a Sunday in the end of August or beginning of September, an ode, composed for the occasion, was sung by all the people, and the whole ceremony finished

profoundest grief. The Marchioness of Mushroom, who was to have had a drawing-room, shut herself up with no other company than her Prayerbook and 'Hoyle upon Gaming.' Lord Periwinkle forgot to feed his pet monkey, and the dear creature expired through the neglect. Six Commoners—Oyster, Scollop, Kelp, White Rock, Muglin and Surge—who were said to be engaged to vote against their country in the evening, could not, through decency, appear in public, and were honest through regard to ceremony ; and all the officers of the court appeared to be daily affected with a sense of their loss."

"The Chamberlain has issued orders from the Royal Court at Armagh for a suitable dress. Full dress: Black calimancoe, trimmed with sea-weed. Undress: Grey frize, and weepers of the muslin of fish skin."

"Royal Palace, July 13th, 1797.—This day his Majesty was pleased to appoint the Right Hon. Sir John Despatch to be Postmaster-General of Dalkey."

Mrs. Battier, "Countess of Laurel." 221

by a feast on the rocks; after which his Majesty and his officers of state embarked in pomp, followed by his people.

What glorious days these must have been for the boatmen of Bullock, Dunleary, and Dalkey! Generous fellows! they would cheerfully take over his Majesty's liege subjects from "Dalkey stone common" to the seat of empire for *nothing;* but being determined enemies to *absenteeism* (the greatest grievance Ireland ever had), they would not allow them to depart on such easy terms, but would mulct with a heavy penalty all those who desired to abandon their country. The last royal procession, levee, and coronation anniversary of the "Kingdom of Dalkey," were held on the 20th August, 1797, the year immediately preceding the rebellion of '98, on which occasion upwards of 20,000 persons were present. At the time martial law was proclaimed; the prisons were full of persons suspected of treason; the United Irishmen were held in suspicion by the Lord Chancellor Clare and the Government; the mutiny at the Nore had been put down a month previous to the Dalkey revels in 1797, by reason of which numbers of soldiers and sailors were shot and hung, alluded to in the ode, written for the occasion by the satirical poetess, Mrs. Battier* ("Countess of Laurel").

* "The notoriety I had already acquired by my little attempts in literature, as well as my own ambition to become known to such a person, brought me acquainted, at this time, with Mrs. Battier, the "Countess of Laurel," Poetess Laureate to the Kingdom of Dalkey, an odd, acute, warm-hearted, and intrepid little woman, the widow of a Captain Battier, who, with two daughters and very small means, lived, at the time of my acquaintance with her, in lodgings up two pair of stairs, in Fade-street; and acquired a good deal of reputation, besides adding a little to her small resources, by several satirical pieces of verse, which she from time to time published. Her satires were chiefly in the bitter Churchill style.

"As Mrs. Battier was much older than my own mother, and, though with a lively expression of countenance, by no means

222 *The Druids*—" *Druid's Head*" *and Major Sir.*

It is stated in *Cooney's Morning Post*, September 10th, 1792, that—" The long coronation sermon recited by Gillespey, Chief of the Druids,* and Primate of 'the Kingdom of Dalkey,' was one of the

good-looking, it is some proof of my value for female intellect, at that time (though I have been accused of underrating it since), that I took great delight in her society, and always very gladly accepted her invitations to tea. One of these tea-parties I have a most lively remembrance of, from its extreme ridiculousness. There had lately come over from some part of England one of those speculators upon Irish hospitality and ignorance, which at that period of Dublin civilisation were not unfrequent—a Mrs. Jane Moore, who had come upon the double speculation of publishing her poems, and promulgating a new plan for the dyeing of nankeens. Whether she had brought letters of introduction to Mrs. Battier, or had availed herself of their common pursuit (in *one* at least of their avocations) to introduce herself, I cannot now say; but having expressed a wish to read her poems to some competent judges, she was invited by my friend to tea for the purpose, and I was, much to my gratification, honoured with an invitation to meet her. I rather think that poor Mrs. Battier was reduced to a single room by the state of her circumstances, for I remember well that it was in the bed-room we drank tea, and that my seat was on the bed, where, enthroned as proudly as possible, with these old poetesses (the new arrival being of the largest and most vulgar Wapping mould), I sate listening while Mrs. Jane Moore read aloud her poems, making havoc with the *v*'s and *w*'s still as she went, while all the politeness of our hostess could with difficulty keep her keen satirical eyes from betraying what she really thought of the *nankeen* muse."—*Moore's Memoirs, &c.*

* About the year 1792 the order of knights designated "The Druids" was founded by the then King of "Dalkey." The Druids soon became an important body; their place of meeting was at "The Druid's Head," in George's-street, South, a house kept by John Sweeny. He had the two houses now numbered 8 and 9. A large carving of the Druid's Head was placed on the pier of the house No. 9; the holdfasts still remain. The house for some years previous to '98 was the rendezvous of United Irishmen. They met as Druids, and for a length of time eluded the notice of the government. John Sweeny opened the Druid's Head Tavern in 1792, and continued in occupation till 1798. Major Sir then made his acquaintance, seized him and his chief waiter, and also a quantity of pikes in the waste ground next to his house, on which the present No. 10 is built. "Phil.," the waiter, was severely flogged in Exchange Court, and I think Sweeny also. The house was never after re-opened.—*Personal Recollections of Dr. Willis, senior, Ormond-quay, Dublin.*

richest treats of the day, and produced effects such as sermon never produced before."
This part of the proceedings was very objectionable, in treating with levity sacred subjects.* The

* While these cowardly and malignant attacks on religion and its ministers were appearing from day to day in the public journals of Dublin, a set of men, under the title of "Philosophers," or Freethinkers, were trying to establish a new system of civil society in France. In order to realize this dream of their vanity, it was necessary for them to overturn and destroy all the received notions of subordination, morality, and religion, which forms the safety, the happiness, and the consolation of mankind. Their projects of destruction were unfortunately attended with too much success. The events which so rapidly succeeded each other in France at that time, surpass, in atrocity, all that ever stained the page of history. Property, liberty, safety, and life, became a sport to the rage of unbridled passions, to the spirit of party and hatred, and to the most cruel and unbounded ambition. The annals of the human race do not present an epoch, when, in so short a space of time, so many crimes were committed, so many misfortunes occasioned, and so many tears caused to be shed. On the 20th of January, following the date of this "Coronation Sermon," Louis XVI. of France, an amiable and innocent monarch, was publicly *murdered* by the hands of these most relentless monsters, execrable and sanguinary regicides, Robespiere, Pelletier, Legendre, Lacroix, Lasource, Thuriot, Barbaroux, Rubel, Barere, Petion, Merlin, Saint Just, Breard, Danton, Herbois, and a hundred and seventy-eight other blood-hounds. In the following October, 1793, the queen of France, the beautiful Marie Antoinette, of Austria and Lorraine, daughter of the great and immortal Marie Theresa, queen of Hungary, and of Francis I, emperor of Germany, was guillotined by a blood-thirsty set of maddened wretches, in the face of an astonished, sorrowful, and indignant world; and in defiance of the conscious terrors of God's awful and avenging justice. Marie Antoinette was born Nov. 2nd, 1755; married, May 10th, 1774, Louis 16th, then Dauphin of France. She died with a spirit and greatness of mind far above her misfortunes.

An Irish priest, the Rev. J. Edgeworth, prepared Louis the 16th for death. The following letter was written from Paris to a Rev. Mr. Massey, P.P., six weeks before the execution:—
"You are undoubtedly surprised, my dear and honoured friend, that whilst the clergy of France are flocking to England and Ireland, for Christian shelter and support, I should remain here, amidst the ruins of this persecuted and afflicted church; indeed, I have often wished to fly to that land of true liberty and solid peace, and to share with others your hospitable board; where, to be a stranger in distress is a sufficient title; .... but Almighty God has

following coronation sermon is said to have been written by the celebrated John Philpot Curran :—

A SERMON,

Preached September 9th, 1792.

BEING THE

ANNIVERSARY OF THE CORONATION OF

Stephen I., King of Dalkey.

"Love God above all things, and your neighbour as yourself."

"Dearly beloved,—We are this day met to celebrate the anniversary of an event auspicious to these realms—an event which the happy people of Dalkey Island and their fellow-subjects in the neighbouring states do hail, I am sure, with all that loyal gladness that does become the hearts of subjects loving, not dreading, the prince by whom they are ruled, not with a rod of iron, but with the peaceful olive-branch; a prince, to whose auspicious reign the good fellow-

baffled my measures, and ties me to this land of horrors by chains which I have not the liberty to shake off. . . . . The case is this :—the wretched Master charges me not to quit the country, as I am the person whom he intends to prepare him for death. And should the iniquity of the nation commit that last act of cruelty, I must also prepare myself for death ; as, I am convinced, the popular rage will not allow me to survive an hour after the tragic scene ; but I am resigned ; my life is of no consequence ; the preservation of it, or the shedding of my blood, is not connected with the happiness of millions : . . . could my life save him, I would willingly lay it down, and I should not die in vain. . . . Receive this unfeigned assurance (perhaps for the last time) of my respect and affection for you, which, I hope, even death will not destroy." *See Appendix* for a short sketch of the last Twenty-four Hours of the Lives of Louis the Sixteenth and Marie Antoinette.

ship, brotherly love, and festive mirth, pervading every quarter of his happy dominions, give the truest marks of wise councils, and his benevolent sway—a prince, whose tranquil and happy subjects, equally distant from that indigence ever consequent to those oppressive taxes imposed by the avarice of weak princes, the corrupt luxuries of courts, or the insatiable rapacity of our court minions—from which, thanks to bounteous heaven! the virtuous government of Dalkey Island is free—and from that hell-begotten pride and restless ambition, which, in every other nation of Europe, tempts a few worthless beings, with no other merit than a casual pelf, to assume not only a superior rank over other men, their betters in every characteristic that can dignify human nature, but to usurp a privilege of insulting and oppressing them—a prince, I say, whose fortunate subjects, keeping the medium between these extremes, move in that temperate centre, where virtue and wisdom have ever found happiness; whilst wars, revolutions, carnage, plunder, and destruction, with all the dire and dreadful evils of Pandora's fabled box, distract the great continent of Europe. Such are the baneful effects of those greatest of all national curses, from which we, happy islanders of Dalkey, are exempt—the wicked ambition of princes, and the insatiable rapacity of their corrupt minions.

"Could the chief pastor, whom the wise and illustrious ruler of Dalkey has chosen to superintend in these islands the religion of his people, forget so far the great object of his mission on the service of the Most High, as to devote to the flattery of an earthly prince, the day and the occasion set apart for a nobler purpose, infinitely more honorable to the prince himself, the beautiful and sublime of the Old Testament might afford me abundance of grand and high-sounding texts and pompous epithets wherewith to decorate the royal character, and adulate the royal mind into imaginary possession of virtues and reflections, seldom the lot of man, even in his remotest recesses of retirement and reflection, but much seldomer that of princes, surrounded by all the temptations of power, of wealth, of ambition, and more than all, of self-flattery, from those vassal sycophants who pander for the unseemly caprice of princes, and while they tempt it to tyranny, or, what is the same thing, the exertion of inordinate power, they become themselves the ready ministers of royal vice, in order to become sharers anew in royal protection and favour.

"But, no; if I could profanely forget, that the great occasion of this day is to glorify the King of kings for those blessings we enjoy under the ruler He hath set over us, or to devote to the adulation of a mortal the praise consecrated to the Great Eternal, I should, on a moment's reflection, blush for the rashness and folly of my error, when I know that I am speaking in the presence of a prince, who forgets not that the trappings of royalty are not proof armour against mortality; and who is mindful that, although we are subject to those laws over which he presides, yet that he is as responsible for his mission as I am for mine, and that he is subject, in common with us all, to the laws of the same great Creator, and the power of doing good or evil to his subjects, instead of being an helmet against the wrath of the Most High, will serve but to aggravate the omission of the one, or the commission of the other, before the great tribunal of 'Heaven's Chancery.'

"Governed by such sentiments of my episcopal duty on one hand, and my reverence for the wisdom, benignity, and Christian modesty of a good-humoured, facetious, and unassuming prince on the other, I have chosen that text above all others which contains at once the essence of true religion and social happiness; which enjoins our first duties to the great Author of

our being; and the Giver of all good unto us, and then
counsels, as children of the same great parent, to
'love one another,' not as modern brothers sometimes
do, with an adulterated affection, alloyed with jealousies, policy, or what the sordid world calls prudence, but
tells each to measure his affection for his neighbour
by the love which he bears to himself—a love to be
modulated under the first injunction of my text, by a
preference to everything, for the justice, the piety,
and the beneficence of the divine law. And thus,
this brotherly love, stamped with the sterling touch
of a heavenly mint, becomes currency suited to the
commerce of Christianity and true friendship, and
not like that shining dross which the misers of other
countries, like the thievish jackdaws, filch from the
common service of mankind, and hide in their sordid
coffers; for which lawyers combat truth and reason,
and pervert justice and mercy; for which soldiers
engage in the sanguinary trade of war, butcher their
fellow-creatures, and call it glory and valour; for
which senators betray the dearest rights of their
country, the most solemn confidence of their fellow-
citizens; and for which admirals and generals sometimes betray the safety of their country, and surrender to defeat and slaughter whole fleets and
armies; for which, oh, worst of abominations! the
clergy betray the faith and conscience of their flock,
and sound the trumpet of prejudice and discord from
the seat of meekness and peace, and wink at the
vices of the great, the proud, and the wealthy, for
interest or gain. No, my beloved brethren, but a
currency which, like the manna in the wilderness,
nourisheth all to whom it passeth, cheers the heavenly
spirit of mutual love, harmony, and good fellowship,
and chases from the social soul the gloom of ill-nature,
of pride, of peevishness, and misanthropy. In a word,
it is the great golden rule laid down by the Divine
Author of our religion, the Prince of Peace—'Love

God above all things, and your neighbour as yourself.'

"With regard to the first part of my text, it is not my design to enter into learned and unintelligible illustrations from the writings of the Holy Fathers, nor yet exhibit an ostentatious variety in displaying my own depth of reading, by ringing the changes on various texts of Scriptures, from *alpha* to *omega*. The diction is so plain, so perfectly comprehensible, and withal, so consonant to that gratitude for numberless benefits, inseparable from the manly, social, and generous heart, that I am sure, even though some of you, in human frailty, may have been omissive in your duty, you would feel your good sense offended, if I thought it necessary to explain that which none can misapprehend.

It occurs, however, that he who loves not in his heart justice, mercy, good-nature, honest fellowship, good living, peace and plenty, which are amongst the attributes and best gifts of the Deity, cannot be expected to extend them to his neighbour; and this observation brings to me the second part of my text —*Love your neighbour as yourself.*

This precept of Him who suffered and sacrificed so much for the love of mankind, seems so admirably calculated for both the general and particular happiness of man in a social state, that it may be accounted the only sovereign antidote against avarice and ambition, and the only balm for those grievous wounds inflicted by both upon the peace and happiness of nations.

"But the duties of this heaven-descended maxim are no more fulfilled by the insipid civilities of a ceremonious intercourse, garnished with bows, grimaces, and unmeaning compliments—the mere dead-letter of friendship—than due obedience to the former part of my text consists in the mere, cold, church-going formality of frog-hearted hypocrites, who put on the grave cloak of eternal sanctity, like shop-lifters, in order the more effectually to purloin the confidence and good opinion of their neighbours.

"Who is he, that, forgotten by the ingrate world, pierced by the freezing wounds of indigence, and cast by the storm of adversity on the bleak sands of neglect, scorn, and despair, and who feels not in the benignant glance of one pitying friend, the emanation of the divine spirit of brotherly love, that banishes his sorrows for the moment, resuscitates his departed hope, and recalls his disgusted affections to the great purpose of creation—Society?

Where is the generous soul that has quaffed from the chalice of Christianity the celestial nectar of beneficence, and reveled in the god-like luxury of doing good, that does not see in this divine precept of my text, a jewel worth all the gold of Ophir, all the diamonds of Golconda, all the sordid treasure of misers, who, destitute of benevolence, yield not a ray of happiness to the honest heart?

"Where is the hospitable man, whom heaven hath blessed with plenty, and who sees around his friendly board, not the saucy rich, the swollen proud, the haughty upstart, or the worthless, hungry-hearted niggard, called there not for the purposes of harmony and happiness, but to forward some mean, avaricious object—not the contemptuous great, courted to condescension by lavishing on them those kindnesses which were better bestowed in cultivating social happiness, and cementing the bonds of equal and honest friendship, but whose festive table reflects the smiles of his friends, like a mirror; all of whom merit, and some of whom, perhaps, may want his bounty? Ask him, for he knows, in the core of his worthy and benevolent heart, what is the invaluable blessing of the precept of my text,
Love thy neighbour as thyself.

"Point out the man, and I will hail him as the noble of nature.

"Where is the liberal man, whose godlike mind, untainted by the narrow bigotries of politics or religion, glows with the heavenly fire of charity towards all the children of Adam, and who can admire the virtues, pity the failings, relieve the distress, and espouse the natural rights of every citizen of this world, alike regardless of complexion, country, sect, or party, and by no means daring to assume a self-dubbed rank of superiority in the favour of heaven, much less to wrest from the hand of Omnipotence the scale of eternal justice, and attempt to weigh on the feeble fulcrum of human discernment the secrets of hearts, or the truths of speculative creeds, in whose mystic altitude, above the reach of our comprehension, consists the whole merit of our faith? Point me out the man, and I will hail him as the noblest work of God. He will tell you, for he enjoys it with the purest ecstacy, the blessings of compliance with the precept of my text,

Love thy neighbour as thyself.

"And where is the sordid wretch, in the frigid regions of whose gloomy bosom the genial rays of heaven-born friendship never shed their cheering light, but on whose flinty heart the cold icicles of apathy continually trickle their gelid distillations, while the noxious mists of envy and distrust hover round his brain, and shed their slumbering influence on his torpid nerves? He is an outcast from that heaven which the precept of my text opens to man upon earth. Even great crimes, and bold enterprising villanies, are above his grovelling soul; and if he dares not act the footpad or the pickpocket, I suspect honour or honesty have nothing to do with his forbearance, and his avarice only wants courage to lead him to plunder.

"The gay flowerets of cheerfulness, the balm of friendship, the jessamine of taste, the myrtle of love, or the sweet rose of fruition, take no root in the barren, blighting climate of his dark soul. The rue of envy, the abortive savine of distrust, the rank hemlock of murky avarice, and the deadly nightshade of chill penury, are the native vegetations of that ungenial soil. A Gordian knot for ever binds up from pity and from friendship his relentless purse-strings, while he skulks with downcast look of conscious ingratitude by some reduced heartbroken worthy, who, perhaps, has often assuaged his youthful hunger, or benevolently raised him from rags and beggary, to the comforts of whole clothes and the first step of the ladder to affluence; or else struts on with awkward saucy importance, scowling at modest worth in threadbare garb, and thus sets up the shield of impudence against the shafts of contempt.

"His sordid hand, fitted only to the filthiest and most degrading offices of nature, was never extended to wipe away the widow's tears, the orphan's hunger, or lift the load of affliction from the heart of a distressed friend. To him the poverty of others is pestilence; for though, like the poison of a serpent, it abounds in his own blood without injury, yet he instinctively shuns the semblance of it in an old companion, as the rattlesnake shuns the asp or the toad a spider.

"Who ever saw his board crowned with plenty, or surrounded by the smiles of cheerful festivity? Who ever beheld an altar raised to hospitality within his damp walls, or smoke with the savoury incense of roast beef or plum-pudding, of white plum-gravy, teeming legs of mutton, or well fed turkeys, or delicious hams? *No one!*

"Who, with thirst-parched lips, has ever blown the yellow froth from his foaming tankard of rich brown stingo, the native cordial of honest hearts? *No one!*

"Who has ever heard the cheering sound of a cork drawn from his sixth bottle, or beheld with a gladdened eye the liquid ruby flow in brimming bumpers round his board? *No one!*
"In vain for him does plenty pour out on the earth her copious horn. In vain does Ceres show her yellow fields, with teeming crops of ripening corn. In vain do the fleecy flocks and lowing herds bear twins, the goodly feathered race of the farm-yard bring forth doubled broods, and pregnant nature load the earth with abundance. In vain Pomona decks her verdant trees with tempting fruits. In vain does Bacchus bepurple his Gallic fields with blushing clusters, and shed on his favoured clime a flowing vintage. In vain the hardy and adventurous sons of our happy isles elude the keen vigilance of revenue spies, and yield us at half-price the nectarious juice of France, the cordial pass-gruck of the plodding Dutch, or the flagrant rum of Western India. In vain might the lords of the revenue remit all taxes on the articles of good cheer, and the markets reduce their rates one-half. Still would sordid, worthless Gripus be the same. Still would his beer grow sour, his wine be pries, his bread mouldy, his meat musty, and the keys of his cellar and pantry rust in his pocket; and while the wretch would starve the world and himself, he would substitute his fancy in the place of his palate; and by the combined strength of avarice and imagination, transubstantiate his cucumbers, cold mutton, and small-beer, to ideal pine apples, venison, and Burgundy. But away with this horrid picture, which for you, happy subjects of this social realm, I have drawn as a contrast to your virtues, and as a hateful deviation from the benignant precept of my text. By you, disciples of cheerfulness, and children of friendship, the shrine of hospitality has never been impiously profaned. May you long enjoy the hal-

lowed blessings of this happy reign, and never may you know the want of a friend, a bottle, or a splendid guinea! May you ever wear around your hearts the oaken wreath of manly fortitude, entwined with the sacred mistletoe of friendship and druidical piety. The blessings of the beggar and of the clerk of the crown attend you all in your adventures in this life, and the last prayer of the Recorder and of all the judges of crown circuit attend you in the next.

"A word now to the clergy, my fellow-labourers in the vineyard, and I have done.

"To you, venerable Druids, the exemplary clergy of these happy isles, let me, on this auspicious occasion, pay the tribute of just applause for the great and important share your wise precepts and pious examples have borne in the good morals, harmless mirth, cheerful demeanour, and singular contentment which reign throughout the festive kingdom of Dalkey. To your laud be it spoken, that while the chosen ministers of the Gospel in the surrounding nations have abandoned the primeval simplicity and exemplary lives of the primitive Apostles—while they have quit the pious labours of the Gospel vineyard, to launch into the regions of speculative controversy and polemical discord—while they have rent the seamless garments of their Divine Leader, and instead of conciliating among mankind the precept of charity and brotherly love laid down in my text, they have sown amongst them hatred and disunion; instead of infusing into their souls the meekness of Christianity, they have inflated them with the rage of furies and the phrenzy of fanaticism, and taught them to manifest their piety, their charity, and their love to an omnibeneficent Creator by all the horrors of fire and sword, of devastation and massacre—while they themselves, instead of illustrating their avowed faith and the truth of their doctrines by the humility, meekness, and purity of their lives, have built hierarchy upon hierarchy, grasped at all the pomps, vanities, and vices of this wicked world, rioted in all its luxuries, or wallowed in all its carnalities, and ground the face of the poor to raise revenues for the purpose of administering to avarice and extravagance; preaching at the same time, in solemn mockery, from their stalls or pulpits, which, as they never practised, so nobody would suppose they believed.

"Thus, true virtue and piety were forgotten, brotherly love and Christian charity were exploded, and men taught to contract mutual attachments or implacable hatreds to each other and posterity, not upon the merits or demerits of conduct or morals, but on the nature of mere speculative opinions in religion.

"In the meantime, you, ye venerable successors to the Druids of old—ye gentle missionaries of concord and peace—have followed with pious steps the example of the primitive apostles, teaching to your disciples the saving truths of Christianity, and not the polemical substitutes of fantastical schoolmen—the charity and brotherly love of your Divine Leader, and not the rancours of bigotry. You have not ground the face of the poor with oppressive tithes, nor torn from the oppressed husbandman. You have scorned to live as idle drones in the social isle; and generously preferring to live on the bounty of Providence, drawn from the plenteous ocean with the labours of your own hands, and have become, like the first disciples, fishermen.

"Pursue, ye ministers of peace, labours worthy of yourselves, and befitting the meekness of your mission. Continue to hold up to the churches that have strayed, examples worthy of imitation.

"Point out to the distracted nations of the earth a system of equal representation in the senate, equal liberty under the laws, and equal happiness in the several ranks of society throughout these happy isles, whatever may be the diversities of religious persuasion. On this score we are answerable alone to the great Searcher of hearts, and not to short-sighted men, who would foolishly set bounds to the imprescriptible franchises of the mind, yet who cannot restrain from their error the acts of the body.

"Go, show the triple-crowned pontiffs, the mitred dignitaries, and full-fed pastors of the earth, the wild folly and presumption of measuring the mercies of the God of the universe by the narrow policy of prejudiced mortals.

"Which of them, in collecting the general tribute of his popedom, his priority, his bishopric, or his rectory, would reject the pence of Peter or the proctor's arrears, because they were offered in silver money, and not in gold? Or who amongst them would refuse a tithe pig because it was not a sheaf of corn, or a sheaf of corn because it was not a lamb? Tributes to the Church, however various in kind, are all acceptable, because all converted to one aggregate revenue. Why, then, Church deny to the Deity the power of receiving the tribute of adoration from His creatures in such language and form as nature or education may have taught them? or cut off from eternal salvation nineteen-twentieths of mankind for differing in opinion from certain principles they never had an opportunity to learn?

"Narrow prejudice! uncharitable thought! With regard to worship, too silly for serious attention; and with relation to policy, too preposterous and absurd to meet the test of reason.

"The impiety and injustice of the system which the impolicy of a neighbouring kingdom founds upon this principle, is the best illustration of its folly. There the atheist, who denies all religion, and the apostate, who regards none, require no other title to the rights and immunities of citizens than the highest trusts and honours of the state, and swearing, in solemn mockery, upon the Gospels they don't believe, while three-fourths of the people, who have conscience enough to abide by the faith in which they were educated, and honesty enough to decline the impious prophanation of a false oath, are treated with all the diffidence of aliens, enemies, or thieves, and cut off, not only from the humblest offices of trust or emolument in the state, but from the common birthright of subjects.

"To you, liberal Druids, such doctrines are abomination. You have wisely taught your flocks to separate their temporal from their eternal concerns, to live in harmony, in charity, and brotherly love—'to render unto Cæsar those things which are Cæsar's, and unto God those things which are God's.' Your happy prince and wise senate, satisfied that all an earthly government can reasonably wish, and all that good subjects can fairly render as the best test of of their loyalty, is a strict and cheerful obedience to the laws of God and of the realm—they hold no other title necessary to the equal rights of subjects, and they resign the jurisdiction of men's minds and opinions to the great Searcher of hearts, to whom alone it belongs.

"Let us, then, rejoice this day, and be exceeding glad. Let us commemorate with joy and festivity the coronation of a prince, at once the father, the friend, and the respected favourite of his people. Let us eat, drink, and be merry. Long may his facetious Majesty reign over his kingdom and states of Dalkey; and long may the delicious Dublin Bay herring, the fine black sole, the delicate salmon trout, the charming large haddock, the rich lobster and high-flavoured crab, the nice mullet, mackerel, knowd, gurnet, and John Dory, in successive seasons, spread plenty round your coast, and give health, vigour and activity to you and ninety-nine generations of your children's children ! May your days be employed profitably in industry, and your nights in harmony, good-fellowship, and love ! May you long smoke together the calumet of peace, and quaff nectarious whiskey from the meather of friendship ; and bound together like the famed faces of the Romans in the brotherly belt of wampum ! May you ever, unbroken, resist your foes, and united in truth, harmony, and good fellowship, may you live all the days of your lives !"

"The extraordinary demand for our account of the proceedings of the ancient kingdom of Dalkey on the anniversary of King Stephen's coronation, and also the very elaborate and edifying sermon of his Grace the Lord Primate of all Dalkey on that occasion, has induced us to comply with the entreaties of many of our readers, by publishing the whole in our next."*

ODE,

BY HENRIETTA, COUNTESS OF LAUREL,†

TO BE

Performed on Sunday the 20th of August 1797.

ON THE CORONATION OF

Stephen I., King of Dalkey.

I.

Again the glorious sun
His annual course has run,
To bring about this festive day,
Which recognizes Stephen's sway.

* *The Morning Post*, September the 20th, 1792.
  † Royal Palace 22nd August, 1197.
At a full meeting of the Kingdom of Dalkey.
Present—The King's Most Excellent Majesty, in Council.
RESOLVED—
That the thanks of the King, and subjects of Dalkey, be given

"Happy Dalkey, Queen of Isles."

Ever gracious, ever gay,
King of all those happy isles,
O'er which imperial Dalkey smiles
With brow serenely great ;
While rising from his watery bed,
The sun lifts up his regal head,
With cloudless countenance to view our state.

II.

Happy state ! where worth alone
Gains admission to the throne ;
Where our King's his people's choice, —
And speaks but thro' his people's voice ;
Where election is the test
Of public virtue in the breast ;
And where electors and elect
Their sacred trust alike respect.

III.

Hail, happy Dalkey, Queen of Isles !
Where justice reigns, and freedom smiles.
In thee we realize the Arcadian scene,
And dance on velvet of perpetual green.
In Dalkey justice holds her state,
Unaided by the prison gate ;
No subjects of King Stephen lie
In loathsome cells, they know not why.
Health, peace, and good humour, in music's soft strains,
Invite and unite us on Dalkey's wide plains.

IV.

No flimsy sheriff enters here ;
No trading justice dare appear ;
No soldier asks his comrade whether
The sheriff has yet cleaned his feather ;
Our soldiers here deserve the name,
Nor wear a feather they don't pluck from fame.
Time-honor'd Dalkey ! at thy silver spring,
The votive muse presumes to sing
The guiltless greatness of thy state and king.

---

to Henrietta, Countess of Laurel, and that a gold medal be presented to her, in the name of the kingdom, by Earl Posey, as a small token of the high sense, which the King and subjects of Dalkey entertain of her unrivalled talents and unwearied exertions in the cause of freedom.

V.

How much unlike those wretched realms,
Where wicked statesmen guide the helms!
Here no first-rate merchants breaking;
Here no first-rate vessels taking;
Here no property is shaking;
Here no shameful peace is making;
Here we snap no apt occasion
On the pretext of invasion;
Here informers get no pensions
To requite their foul inventions;
Here no secret dark committee
Spreads corruption through the city.
No placemen or pensioners here are haranguing;
No soldiers are shooting, or sailors are hanging;
No mutiny reigns in the army or fleet,
For our orders are just, our commander discreet."

VI.

Hail! then hail this happy day,
That recognizes Stephen's sway—
Ever gracious, ever gay.
Illustrious Stephen! hail to thee,
Whose virtues guard the sacred tree
Of Heaven-implanted liberty.
May sacred science ever shed
Her influence on King Stephen's head,
Long, long may his harmonious voice
His happy subjects' hearts rejoice;
  Whilst round they throng
  To claim the song,
The sweetly, sweetly warbled lay,
Which crowns the joy of this auspicious day."*

"Dalkey: Printed (by permission) by Sir Peter Type, price Sixpence-halfpenny."

---

* A Muglin Knight, on reading the Ode on King Stephen's birth-day, asked one of the Dalkey nobles what was the reason it was so much superior to any that ever had been written on a similar occasion in a neighbouring kingdom? The wit replied: "*That poets always succeed best in fiction.*"

A SERMON,

Preached on Sunday, August 20th, 1797.

BEING THE

ANNIVERSARY OF THE CORONATION

OF

Stephen I, King of Dalkey.

In the third chapter of Ecclesiastes, and the first verse, are these words :—

"TO EVERY THING THERE IS A SEASON, and a time to every purpose under the Heaven."

These are the words of King Solomon, surnamed The Wise. Yea, he was a wise man, indeed; he was wiser than any alderman of Dublin—nay, than any of the aldermen of Dalkey—nay, than the sapient privy counsellors of this realm, or any man, excepting our sovereign, who is wisdom itself.

Now, what does this wise King teach us? Why, in the words of my text, that there is a season for everything, and a proper time for every purpose. Thence we may conclude that everything is right that is done in season, and at a fit and proper time; and, therefore, there is a fit time for the celebration of the high festival we now commemorate, and that we aught in it to give way to every kind of festivity. To this we are urged by the words of the same wise King, who, in other parts of the same chapter, expressly declares, "there is a time to laugh;" therefore let us laugh. "There is a time to dance;" therefore let us dance. "There is a time to embrace;" therefore let us embrace, whenever opportunity offers. And, also, "that every man should eat and drink, and enjoy the good of all his labour;" therefore, let us eat and drink and be merry; for that purpose we are all come hither.

Every man knoweth the strict alliance between *church* and *state*, and that the *crown* and *mitre* are the natural supports of each other; therefore, whilst the King of this realm has bestowed on me the archiepiscopal mitre, it is fitting and proper that I, out of just return, should do my endeavours to support the interest of his crown, and this I cannot do better than in exhorting you all to due obedience, and to exert yourselves to promote the happiness of this extensive kingdom.

* * * *

So, praying for the health and prosperity of our King, and all who are put in authority under him, I recommend you to the practice of what you have heard this day.

To the Printer of the *Dalkey Gazette*.

SIR,—Yesterday a very numerous deputation sailed for the island of Dalkey to present the enclosed address to his Majesty, but unfortunately the wind and tide were against us, and prevented our vessel getting to the sound; we were obliged to cast anchor, and were under the painful necessity of returning without effecting our purpose. You will be pleased to lay it before his Majesty at the next Privy Council.

I am, sir, your very humble servant,

THO. KINGSMERRY,

Seneschal of Ireland's Eye.

August 15, 1796.

At a general meeting of the inhabitants of the land of Ireland's Eye, held the 13th day of August, 1796, the following address was unanimously agreed to, and a deputation consisting of Tho. Kingsmerry, Esq., and twenty-four burghers were appointed to present the same to his sacred Majesty, at his palace in the ancient kingdom of Dalkey, on the 14th of August, 1796.

"To the King's most excellent Majesty, Stephen the First, of the Kingdom of Dalkey, Ireland's Eye, the Muglins, and their dependencies.

"WE, your Majesty's loyal subjects of the island of Ireland's Eye (convened by public notice), have beheld, with admiration and gratitude, the wisdom and justice which reigned in your Majesty's councils for some time. After we had the happiness of being placed under your protection, we have experienced the blessed effects of the most salutary laws, administered equally to every description of your Majesty's subjects without partiality or prejudice. We have seen your Majesty's choice of Government and magistrates, meet the most cordial approbation of your subjects; and while the former administered the laws of wisdom and mercy, the latter cheerfully submitted to those decrees, that had no other object in view than the public good. But, alas! those halcyon days are past. Your Majesty's unsuspecting nature has been imposed upon, and those good ministers that preserved peace and happiness to your subjects, were disgraced, and a set of men placed in their situation, remarkable only for their effrontrey, inordinate ambition, avarice, and a thirst for blood; for they care not what streams flow, what human misery they create, so as they shall retain their places; and though your Majesty's subjects are driven to the greatest distress, to pay the ponderous taxes, which weighed them down beyond their strength of bearing—yet your ministers and their numerous dependants, declare 'your subjects to be happy and your nation rich and powerful, and able to continue what they call—this just and necessary war.' We must say, indeed, if widows and orphans constitute the wealth and power of a nation, your's is the most rich and powerful in the world. We therefore beseech your Majesty, to remove from your councils those weak and wicked ministers, that have brought your kingdom to the brink of destruction, and call on men who possess the loves and confidence of all your people, we may then hope for a speedy termination to this calamitous war!—a war founded on principles of despotism, and ending we fear, in the subversion of monarchy. Your Majesty by this means will destroy that weak and wicked system of policy which heretofore divided and coerced your people, you will command the unequivocal blessing of their hearts, and the irresistible support of their hands.

"Signed by order,

"THOMAS KINGSMERRY, Seneschal."

Supplement to the *Dalkey Gazette.*

BANQUET.

Previous to dinner, a discharge of three rockets. After dinner, on the King's health being drank, a discharge of three rockets and nine cannon. Signal to prepare to leave the island, a rocket. His Majesty going on board the royal barge, a discharge of three rockets, to be answered by twenty-one guns.

The procession to be as follows :—
Two gentlemen with white rods.
The deputy gaoler, Sir James Watch, dressed in a proper habit, &c., &c.
Such members of his assistants as can be provided.
The high gaoler, Mimkin.
Two gentlemen with white rods.
The Sword of State to be borne by Lord Quebeck.
The Crown, on a cushion, to be borne by two Esquires.
The Royal Banner.
Two Knights with white rods.
His Majesty, attended by two Pages.
Two Esquires with white rods.
The Primate.
The Chancellor.
The Officer of State, Lord Poscy (Gold Stick in waiting.)
Dukes.
Marquisses.
Earls, Lords, &c., &c.
Knights.
Esquires.
Two gentlemen with white rods to close the procession.

THE CROWN OF DALKEY—ITS LOSS.

Monday night, August 15, 1796. From the *Morning Post.*

It is with infinite concern we state (from authority) that the report of this morning respecting the CROWN of DALKEY, is but too well founded. The particulars are as follow :—
His Majesty, attended by Lord Poscy and Sir Thomas Trump, crossed the sound in a private gondola, got refreshment, and walked to Bullock, *in cog.* At Bullock, being a good deal fatigued, they rested, and drank three tumblers each, and then proceeded on their rout. It was observed that they not only measured the length but the breadth of

the road ; at the last mentioned place the King entrusted the Crown to the care of Lord Posey, but before they reached the Black Rock, his lordship first lost the King upon the road, and afterwards the crown ; on his examination at the Secretary of State's office, this day at noon, in the presence of the Privy Council, he solemnly declared, that he was inclined to think he had lost it ; he, however, candidly admitted, that it might have been stolen, for he observed a great many *Bloods* on the road. His Majesty, King Stephen, is so well convinced of the loyalty and integrity of his people, that *though it is the richest crown in Europe*, he does not intend offering a higher reward than

HALF-A-CROWN.

Dalkey Gazette—Extraordinary. August 16, 1796.

Never was there a day of greater festivity and harmony. His Majesty, by the advice of able ministers left politics entirely out of the question, and on the singing of "God save the King," it was received with the most enthusiastic demonstrations of joy.

Among the variety of deputations to the King of Dalkey, a very respectable one from the clergy deserves particular notice, as follows : " The Commissioners having adjusted to the mutual satisfaction of both parties, the contested rights of presentation to the Deanery of the Muglins, and having superseded the ponderous of political discussion, the clangor of the trumpets proclaimed the approach of an harbinger preceding an herald, who demanded an immediate audience of the King.

"This being by the proper officers communicated to the lords in waiting, and by their lordships announced to his Majesty, He, with his accustomed condescension was graciously pleased to command the herald to be conducted into the royal presence, which being done, and his credentials duly examined and ascertained, the Lord High Chamberlain was ordered to enquire into the nature of his mission, and silence being proclaimed, he thus unfolded the subject of his dispatch—' Please to inform the most august and happy of the European powers, that I am charged by that beneficent prelate, his Grace of Lambay and Kilbarrack, to signify that he is perfectly satisfied with the equitable determination which his Majesty and Council have made, respecting his Grace's claim to the Deanery of the Muglins, and he drinks his Majesty's health, and wishes that God may long preserve the royal family.'"

This was received with every demonstration of unfeigned pleasure by the King and nobles ; and his Majesty facetiously observed "the herald who bears Cousin of Kilbarrack's greeting does in no wise disgrace his Lord's diocese—for by holy Paul he is as fat as butter, and will, in our mind, fitly become our noble order of the Scollop ; I do, therefore, direct that a chapter of emergency be forthwith holden."

Proclamation being accordingly made, the herald was in due form invested with the ensigns of the order, and the sword of state being presented to his Majesty, he gently laid it on the herald's head, and dubbed him Sir Harry Icikle, amid the plaudits of surrounding millions.

His Majesty having drunk the health of his Grace, and prosperity to the united dioceses of Lambay and Kilbarrack, was pleased to direct same conduct to Sir Harry, and to order the Attorney-General, the Speaker, and Sir James Turf, to bear his gracious greetings, to his trusty Cousin, and assure his Grace that every right, royalty, and privilege of his should be preserved inviolate.

Dalkey Gazette—Extraordinary. August 16, 1796.

On Sunday morning, at the dawn of day, his Majesty King Stephen, came in a private coach to the palace in Eustace-street, attended by their Graces, the Dukes of Glosdoon and Stoneland and Lord Posey (goldstick in waiting), and held a grand council to adjust the weighty affairs of the kingdom, after which his Majesty, attended by the great officers of state, and a splendid suit, preceded by the royal band, marched in procession to Sir John Rogerson's-quay, and embarked on board a fleet of light brigantines, under the command of Lord Neptune, Lord High Admiral of Dalkey. His Majesty's arrival was announced by firing of rockets, discharges of artillery, and the most unbounded shouts of applause from the surrounding multitude. His Majesty entered his dominions at Dalkey, at one o'clock, and was received as the father of a country ought to be, with adoration. A grand procession took place ; and on arriving at the council chamber, the foreign ambassadors, &c., were introduced ; different processions round the dominions afterwards took place, when was performed the following Ode :—

246 *Dalkey—" Happiest Island of the Main."*

ODE
On the King of Dalkey's Birth Day,
WRITTEN BY HENRIETTA, COUNTESS OF LAUREL,
POETESS LAUREAT.

Now let each scollop swell,
Within its loyal shell,
To greet the flowing tide,
On which doth ride,
The state barge that brings,
So many pretty things—
The PEERS OF DALKEY and the best of KINGS!

Happy island, free from guilt,
In which no subject's blood is spilt,
Free from knaves, and free from fools,
In which no proud plebeian rules;
In which no rent-wreck'd peasants sweat,
Beneath a nations sizeless debt,
In which the nobles are *indeed*,
All of true patrician breed;
Happiest island of the main,
Free from every venal strain,
And trebly blest in good KING STEPHEN's reign.

While kings of iron heart,
Their savage will impart,
That subjects all
Both great and small
Should march away to slaughter;
Our gracious king employs
His time in harmless joys,
And on his *natal* day,
He comes to make his subjects gay,
In spite of wind and weather.

Then may no heavy rain
Descend upon the plain,
Till all the weighty cares
Of Dalkey's state affairs,
Are settled to King Stephen's mind,
And all his trusty citizens have dined;
And may no envious cloud,
Our ceremonies enshroud.
That all around may flock,
As at the opening of the Dock,
When fish and flesh stood gazing on;
While Camden* laid
The glittering blade,

---

* Earl Camden, Viceroy of Ireland in 1795.

Across the back
Of dapper Jack,
And bid him rise—Sir John.
Thus shall the honours given,
By order of King Stephen,
Whether of Knights, or Dukes, or Lords,
Be entered on the tower records
  Of Muglin or Magee.
And from palace sent,
By charge of our good government,
  Gazetted they shall be ;
And then 'tis eight to one but Captain Trolope
Begs for the nobler order of the Scollop ! ! !

Thus on Dalkey's fertile plains
The all-illustrious Stephen reigns,
And while the rocks and mountains ring
The praises of a patriot king,
His subjects round him throng ;
Not with petitions to redress
The grievance of some made cess,
But with the ancient charter of the land,
By which his people all demand

King Stephen's favourite Song.—" LOVE'S MY PASSION AND GLORY."

The dinner was sumptuous ; great conviviality prevailed; when the cloth was removed, the following toasts were drank—
  " The Kingdom of Dalkey."
" Stephen, King of Dalkey, and a long and prosperous
  reign to him."
On which, his Majesty arose, and with great dignity gave—
" His brother, George the Third, King of Great Britain
  and Ireland, and long may he reign."

A royal salute of twenty-one guns.

His Majesty then accompanied by the whole Board, and the royal band, sung " God save the King."

The next toast given by King Stephen was—
" His Majesty of Great Britain's forces, by sea and land."

Then " Rule Britannia," which was sung by his Majesty, accompanied as before.

  Supplement to the *Dalkey Gazette.*
  Dublin Morning Post, August 20, 1796.
    ORDERS FOR THE DAY (SUNDAY, 14TH INST.)

[The following is the arrangement for the coronation, as struck out by *Sir John Hasler*, of Dalkey.]

Leaving the quay, three rockets and nine cannon to be discharged.

His Majesty, on his arrival at the island, to be saluted

with twenty-one guns and nine rockets, then to proceed to the royal tent, where after the ministers of state forming a council, his Majesty will receive all foreign ambassadors, and such noblemen and gentlemen of his kingdom, as come to pay their respects. The city to march in form, preceded by a band, to the levee ; the Lord Mayor and Aldermen in their wigs and gowns, after which his Majesty, attended by the whole kingdom, in their proper regalias, to proceed to the cathedral (the crown, &c., carried on a cushion before the King). After the sermon to proceed the usual bounds of the kingdom, and in the most convenient part, the whole to draw up, and the band to be disposed of in the most judicious manner, for the purpose of singing the ode, and after the necessary proclamation, the whole to proceed in the most regular manner to partake of the royal banquet.

Prerogative was an assumption of undefined power, which could not be suffered in any country where there was law and reason. And patronage, as it should never be exerted but for the public good, was a dangerous instrument in bad men's hands—he therefore thought it safer for this end—that official *department* (qr.) should always depend on known talents and popular election, rather than the partiality or caprice of an individual.

Lord Seaview moved that his Majesty's proposal be accepted, and the question being put, was carried unanimously.

His Majesty then returned without crown or sceptre to the bar of the Assembly.

By order of the Assembly the Viceroy of Ireland's Eye, King at Arms, went forth to the people, preceded by an herald—and proclaimed the King's resignation of the crown and sceptre, with the nature and causes of his resignation, and demanded of them to nominate a king from amongst the great body of the nation whom they would choose to rule over them, in consequence of his resolution—and the whole, with one voice, named their beloved monarch—

STEPHEN I.

Ireland's Eye returned to the Convention, and reported the choice of the people, which was forthwith confirmed by the unanimous vote of the Assembly, and his facetious Majesty was again invested with the ancient crown and oaken sceptre ; and after being consecrated by the Primate, and having taken the oaths of festivity and public justice towards his people, upon a bowl of grog, was again proclaimed—King.

Lord Minikin, Keeper of the Tower, by order of his

Majesty, went forth with a herald trumpeter, and declared to all the people, that his Majesty, in open senate, was now ready to hear their complaints, and grant the reasonable and just desires of his people. If any, therefore, were aggrieved, they were desired to come forward, and they should be heard.

A deputation from the order of Periwinkle immediately came to the bar of the assembly, and presented four articles of impeachment against the Lord Chancellor.*

First, for *corruption* in a former official capacity.

Secondly, violating a sacred and solemn obligation, taken on his being appointed one of his facetious Majesty's most good humoured privy council.

Thirdly, mal-administration of justice in his capacity of Chancellor, and—

Fourthly, his late unconstitutional conduct in using undue influence, as a peer of the realm, at a meeting of the order of the *Scollop*, to make them declare contrary to the known laws of the empire, that the members of the orders of the Periwinkle had no right, individually or collectively, to petition the King and Senate for a redress of grievances.

Those articles being read, the Lord Chancellor was called upon by his Majesty, to answer those several charges, when his lordship, not being prepared for trial, made the following affidavit.

WE, the Right Hon. J. Lord High Chancellor of the Empire of Dalkey, maketh oath and saith, that the several persons following, viz., Henry Stevens Rielly, Esq., Alderman, Wm. James, Wm. Napper, Esq., and John Walter, Esq., are material witnesses for dept. on the trial of the articles of impeachment exhibited against dept. And dept. not having received information of the items of said articles, so as to have an opportunity of summoning said persons to attend on this day, means and intends to use every exertion to procure their attendance on the day appointed for his trial before the National Convention, now agreed upon by his Majesty, and all the people, and does not mean any affected delay, &c. Sworn before me,

LAUGHABLE, Lord Mayor.

In consequence of which, his Majesty and the assembly were pleased to order that the trial be postponed until the next National Convention.

The Grand Committee appointed to inquire into the interior state of the nation brought forward articles of impeachment

---

* John, first Baron Fitzgibbon, afterwards Earl of Clare, was Lord Chancellor of Ireland when this was published in the *Dalkey Gazette*.

against Lord Glassdone, Tony Laughable, Lord Mayor, and the Lord Chancellor, as guardians of the empire during his Majesty's absence, for high crimes and misdemeanours—first, in neglecting all inquiry into the government of the several interior departments of the kingdom, by which his Majesty's subjects were oppressed, good humour and harmony interrupted, and his Majesty's revenues considerably impaired. Ordered to be tried at the next general Convention.

The Committee of Finance also exhibited articles of impeachment against the Lords of the Treasury for the embezzlement of the sum of £200,000 in good and gingerbread money of the realm, entrusted to their care, and also against the Chief Commissioner of the Revenue, and his accomplices, in aiding and abetting therein. Ordered that the investigation do stand over till the next general Convention.

NEW ORDER OF NOBILITY.

Lord Jocular observed, that it had been frequently remarked, and with too much justice, that titles of nobility, instead of being considered as the rewards of the past, and the inducements to future virtues and great actions by their possessors, were too often used as substitutes for virtue itself, and only served as the empty supporters of ignorant pride, of vicious and tyrannical principle; no man could consider the dignity of a mere titular distinction in a more frivolous light than himself, and no man more pointedly despised the owner, if his actions were not such as marked the superiority of his virtues, as well as his title did that of rank.

His lordship observed, that the monarch of the country had nobly come forward, and disclaimed all hereditary pretensions to distinction, placing his claims to the rank and power on the most honourable of all foundations, that of *personal virtue* and *merit*, he therefore thought the least that should be expected of the nobles, was to follow the example of their king, and subject their titles to annual appointments, and their conduct to annual revision. Titular honours, he said, were the strongest sarcasms on demerit, and the very pillory of vice, for who but an idiot, or an atheist, would wish to be blazoned in titles, that are supposed to distinguish superior virtue, yet whose notoriety in the lowest vices sunk him to the level of abandoned reprobacy. A rascal in robes, said his lordship, is a character infinitely more ridiculous and contemptable, than a bedlamite emperor or a mountebank buffoon.

His lordship said, that though he did not wish, like the

French Assembly, to abolish all titular distinctions, he would not wish to settle a *lease* of titular honours upon any man longer than he should deserve it ; much less entail on his posterity, without proviso or condition. Human nature was frail, and in nothing more than ambition. If a man must need wear a title, he should wear it like a gentleman, and keep it *clean*, like his coat ; and the best way to insure his *decency* in this respect was, to subject him to annual revision ; his lordship concluded by moving, that no titular honours be enjoyed longer than one year without a revision of the conduct of those who wore them, before a committee of honour, to be chosen from the members of the Convention. Carried unanimously.

His lordship then moved, that the title *virtuous citizen*, do henceforward stand as the highest rank of noble distinction in the state next to royalty. Carried unanimously.

After which, with his Majesty's concurrence, the Convention adjourned, *sine die*.

His Majesty, attended as before, returned to the great hall, where a sumptuous banquet was prepared ; and in the meantime, the Lord Mayor and municipality, attended by Lord Seaview, and several other noblemen, knights, and squires, perambulated the franchise of the city of Dalkey. They were met at Stormy-gate by a party of the Liberty boys of Dalkey, who, according to custom, took the sword from his lordship's sword-bearer in triumph to the great mole, from whence his lordship threw the civic dart into the sea, and then returned to the royal hall and participated in a most sumptuous repast, in the course of which a plenipotentiary arrived from the Grand Duke of Bullock, with a present of potatoes ready boiled for his Majesty's table, which was most graciously accepted ; and his Majesty was pleased to confer the honour of knighthood on the ambassador.

After dinner a council of war was held, in which it was resolved, that the thanks of his Majesty in council, be returned in the name of the king and people of Dalkey, to Captain Wm. Power Keating French, of Dublin garrison, for his politeness and assiduity in endeavouring to obtain musicians from the garrison to supply the deficiencies of the royal band of Dalkey, and that the messengers who bear the said thanks be instructed to express to Colonel York of that garrison, the *proper* sense which the court of Dalkey entertains of his Yorkshire politeness, in a surly refusal of his permission for any of the military bands to attend.

It was also resolved, that the thanks of his Majesty in council be returned to the captain, officers, and seamen of his Britannic Majesty's frigate lying off Dunleary, and also

252 The King's Song—"Love's my Passion, etc."

those of his Britannic Majesty's yacht, the "Dorset," in Dublin Bay, for their polite and honourable attentions to the Dalkey squadron, on passing them. The council having broken up—

The grand chambers of hilarity were thrown open, the royal band filled the orchestre. His Majesty was graciously pleased to sing the first song, "Love's my Passion and Glory," the Lord Mayor the second, and the evening concluded with a grand ball, to which the fair visitants of the island were invited; while the exhilerating cup went round and the loyal subjects of the empire of mirth, jovially supported the honours of their facetious government.

The remarkable toasts on this occasion were as follows:—

By the King—The people and constitution of Dalkey, with a grand signal of rockets, by a party of fireworkers, under the direction of Lord *Portfire*, Master-general of the Ordnance, and three cheers by the people.

May the will of the people be the law of the land. Three cheers.

Prosperity to the commerce, and lasting happiness to all the subjects of the Empire of Dalkey. Three cheers.

Lord Seaview then gave, on the part of the people, "A long life and prosperous reign to the King of Dalkey." Three cheers, uncovered.

Equal liberty, political and religious, to all the sons of Adam. Three times three.

The fair visitants of the island, and all the fair sex of the earth. Three times three, uncovered, and with flowing bumpers.

The ball and entertainments being ended, his Majesty retired towards his yacht, and all the subjects of his kingdom formed around him a circle, and performed a festive dance, after which his Majesty embarked, and his example was followed by all his subjects, who went on board hundreds of vessels, and the whole fleet immediately weighed and sailed for Dublin.

The following interesting notice of the Kingdom of Dalkey in the last century, is taken from Herbert's "Recollections for the last Fifty Years," a rare book, published many years ago:—

THE KING OF DALKEY.

"A party of high-bred wits formed, by what accident chronology has not promulgated, but as long as I can remember any public occurrence worthy of notice, I recollect The King of Dalkey, his court, and adherents, going to spend a day every summer at this charming place, and the sayings and doings of that day have been echoed and re-echoed in my ears.

"My reader shall be made acquainted with the subject as far as I can relate. In the first place Dalkey Island, in Dublin Bay, is a small piece of land, which in fine weather is invitingly eligible to pass a day and partake of a cold collation, and it is frequented by citizens, particularly on Sunday, for that purpose. One of those parties, becoming numerous, formed a government, and elected a king and court. All the officers of state, the military, the church, and the bar, furnished places, or at least titles ; and the same ceremonies practised at courts were observed, and the respectful homage paid to rank and station ; the speeches used, and the mode of addressing, copied from the court, senate, bar, and church ; these were strictly attended to : the whole was a playful burlesque upon forms and prescribed rules. Stephen Armitage, of vocal memory, was king when I first witnessed this scene of hilarity and mockery. I obtained a ticket, and was permitted to land, for they had even land-waiters, who were very strict ; all officers were kept on the alert.

"Kane O'Hara was poet laureat of the mimic kingdom at the time—I believe he obtained that high favour for "My Lord Altam's Bull ;" "The Night before Larry was stretched," another song from his pen. In the course of the day, while business was transacted, many subjects were discussed before his majesty ; those subjects were questions on some public measure that was perhaps not decidedly passed, and therefore such objections as might be made were slily introduced ; but the gravity of the speaker, the whim, the satire, were beyond endurance, without bursts of laughter. Never had comedy and farce, or burlesque, such fair display ; when business ended and refreshments were administered, then came the tug of war ; but all was in good humour, every one was served, and there were great numbers admitted as visitors. After dinner, and drinking a few glasses, his majesty, king Stephen, honoured his subjects by singing. He had a good voice, and gave his song with great energy, which the open space where we were assembled required. Then followed calls, and many excellent songs, duets, catches, glees, slang, and other humorous compositions, perhaps matchless in any other assemblage, entertained us the whole evening. The party then retired, boats in requisition surrounded the island, and we all got home generally without accident. I had the pleasure of enjoying this occasionally whilst it continued a custom.

But King Stephen died, and John West, brother to my worthy master, Francis Robert West, was chosen king. This new monarch came into power too near the Rebellion in Ireland, 1798, so that the satire was not deemed such a safe conductor of sentiment as it had been in more peaceable times. The kingdom of Dalkey was therefore neglected, and the government died a natural death on the demise of King John. Oh, Rebellion! thou destroyer of all the social virtues! I saw one rebellion, and I never shall, I hope, see another."

Among the persons who took part in the convivialities of the Kingdom of Dalkey, was the celebrated T. O'Meara. As the times became menacing, and Ireland infected with French principles, the Lord Chancellor Clare was vigilant in watching every society which was formed, and, among the rest, the kingdom of Dalkey and its Druids attracted his notice. O'Meara was personally known to him, and supposing he could enlighten him, Lord Clare sent for him.

"You, sir," said the Chancellor, "are, I understand, connected with the kingdom of Dalkey."

"I am, my lord," said O'Meara.

"Pray, may I ask what title are you recognized by?"

"I am Duke of Muglins."

"And what post do you hold under the government?"

"Chief Commissioner of the Revenue."

"What are your emoluments in right of your office?"

"I am allowed to import ten thousand hogsheads duty free."

"Hogsheads of what, Mr. Commissioner?"

"Of salt water, my lord."

The chancellor was satisfied without further question.

O'Meara was an attorney well known at that time,

as many of the same profession were, for his conviviality, spirit, wit, singularity and good nature. Among other anecdotes told of him was one very characteristic. An Englishman of rank and fortune visited Ireland, and accidentally met him at dinner at a friend's house. It was then the hospitable custom for every person who met a stranger at a friend's house, to ask him to dinner, and show him every attention. This was done with more than usual attention by O'Meara, who attached himself to the Englishman, invited him to his house in the country, and, in the display of his good-nature and sense of hospitality, gave up his time and business to make the visit agreeable and instructive to his acquaintance, who left Ireland with many expressions of obligation for the kindness and attention he had received. Soon after, O'Meara for the first time visited London, and being a total stranger there, was well-pleased to see one day his English acquaintance walking on the other side of Bond-street; so he immediately crossed over, and with outstretched hand declared how delighted he was to see him again. The gentleman was walking with a group of others of a high aristocratic cast, and dressed in the utmost propriety of costume; and when he saw a fine-looking man, with soiled leather breeches, dirty top-boots, not over clean linen, nor very close shaven beard, striding up to him, with a whip in his hand and the lash twisted under his arm, he started back, and with a look of cold surprise, said—

"Sir, you have the advantage of me."

"I have, sir," said O'Meara, looking at him coolly for a moment—" I have, sir, and by —— I'll keep it;" and turned from him, casting such a look of contempt and superiority, as the other did not think it prudent to notice.

Moore, in his Memoirs, edited by Lord John Russell, in speaking of the anniversary of this convivial society (1796), at which he was present, says :—" My recollections of poor Mrs. Battier have brought back some other events and circumstances of this period, with which she was connected. There was a curious society or club established in Dublin, which had existed I believe for some time, but to which the growing political excitement of the day lent a new and humorous interest. A mere sketch of the plan and objects of the club (to which most of the gay fellows of the middle and *liberal* class of society belonged) will show what a fertile source it afforded not only of fun and festivity, but of political allusion and satire. The island of Dalkey, about seven or eight miles from Dublin, was the scene of their summer *réunions*, and here they had founded a *kingdom*, of which the monarchy was elective; and at the time I am speaking of, Stephen Armitage, a very respectable pawnbroker of Dublin, and a most charming singer, was the reigning king of the island. Every summer the anniversary of his coronation was celebrated, and a gayer and more amusing scene (for I was once the happy witness of it) could not be well imagined. About noon on Sunday, the day of the celebration, the royal procession set out from Dublin by water; the barge of his majesty, King Stephen, being most tastefully decorated, and the crowd of boats that attended him all vieing with each other in gaiety of ornament and company. There was even cannon planted at one or two stations along the shore, to fire salutes in honour of his majesty as he passed. The great majority, however, of the crowds that assembled made their way to the town of Dalkey by land; and the whole length of the road in that direction swarmed with vehicles all full of gay laughing people. Some regulations were made, if I recollect right, to keep the company on the island itself as select as possible; and the number of gay parties there scattered about, dining under tents, or in the open air (the day being, on the occasion I speak of, unclouded throughout), presented a picture of the most lively and exhilarating description.

"The ceremonies performed in honour of the day by the dignitaries of the kingdom, were, of course, a parody on the forms observed upon *real* state occasions; and the sermon and service, as enacted in an old ruined church, by the archbishop (a very comical fellow, whose name I forget) and his clergy, certainly carried the spirit of parody indecorously far. An old ludicrous song, to the tune of "Nancy Dawson," was given out in the manner of a psalm, and then sung in chorus by the congregation; as thus—

> "And then he up the chimney went,
>   The chimney went—the chimney went;
> And then he up the chimney went,
>   And stole away the bacon."

"There were occasionally peerages and knighthoods bestowed by his Majesty on such 'good fellows' as were deserving of them; on this very day which I am describing, Incledon the singer, who was with a party on the island, was knighted under the title of Sir Charles Melody. My poetical friend, Mrs. Battier, who held the high office of poetess laureate to the Monarch of Dalkey, had, on her appointment to that station, been created Countess of Laurel. I had myself been tempted, by the good fun of the whole travestie, to try my hand (for the first time I believe) at a humorous composition in the style of Peter Pindar, and meant as a birthday ode to King Stephen. Of this early *jeu d'esprit* of mine, which I remember amused people a good deal, I can recal only a few fragments here and there. Thus, in allusion to the precautions which George III. was said to be in the habit of taking, at that time, against assassination, I thus addressed his brother monarch, Stephen:—

" Thou rid'st not, prison'd in a metal coach,
To shield from thy annointed head
Bullets, of a kindred lead,
Marbles and stones, and such hard-hearted things."

But *hæ nugæ seria ducent in mala*. Most serious and awful indeed was the time which followed these gay doings. The political ferment that was abroad through Ireland soon found its way within the walls of our university; and a youth destined to act a melancholy but for ever-memorable part in the troubled scenes that were fast approaching, had now begun to attract, in no ordinary degree, the attention both of his fellow-students and the college authorities in general. This youth was Robert Emmet, whose brilliant success in his college studies, and more particularly in the scientific portion of them, had crowned his career, as far as he had gone, with all the honours of the course; while his power of oratory displayed at a debating society, of which, about this time (1796-7), I became a member, were beginning to excite universal attention, as well from the eloquence as the political boldness of his displays. He was, I rather think, by two classes, my senior, though it might have been only by one. But there was, at all events, such an interval between our standings as, at that time of life, makes a material difference; and when I became a member of the debating society, I found him in full fame, not only for his scientific attainments, but also for the blamelessness of his life and the grave suavity of his manners.

On the very morning after the celebration at which I was present, there appeared in the newspaper which acted as his Majesty's state gazette, a highly humourous proclamation, offering a reward of I know not how many hundred crobanes or Irish halfpence, to whatsoever person or persons might have found and would duly restore his Majesty's crown, which, in walking home from Dalkey the preceding night, and "measuring *both* sides of the road," according to custom, he had unfortunately let fall from off his august head.

THE DALKEY KINGDOM, 1797.

GRAND ANNIVERSARY OF THE CORONATION OF HIS FACETIOUS MAJESTY STEPHEN I., KING OF DALKEY, EMPEROR OF THE MUGLINS, PRINCE OF THE HOLY ISLAND OF MAGEE, AND ELECTOR OF LAMBAY AND IRELAND'S EYE, 1797.

From the *Dalkey Gazette.*

"Sunday morning, at six o'clock, his Majesty, having spent the whole of the preceding night in the grand Chamber of the Carousal, at the Royal Palace of the Revels, in Eustace-street, in adjusting some important matters of state with the officers of his kingdom, and in preparing for his intended visit to his royal dominions, went in grand procession to the quay of St. George, attended by the privy council, his great officers of state, the lord mayor, and municipality of the capital of Dalkey, and a vast concourse of cheerful citizens, and embarked on board the royal yacht, attended by a squadron of light frigates, under the command of Commodore Byrne, who, on a signal gun from the royal yacht, immediately orderered a grand salute of three rounds from all the guns of the squadron.

"The fleet immediately weighed anchor, sailed down to Poolbeg, passed the Hills of Howth, and tacking on the starboard, stood right for Dalkey Sound, which, we understand, they reached after a voyage of three hours. We since learn of an officer on board the fleet, that as the royal yacht of Dalkey passed the *Dorset* yacht belonging to his Britannic Majesty, his Majesty, standing on the forecastle, sung the song of 'Rule Britannia,' accompanied by all the officers of state, the choir of Dalkey Cathedral, and the royal band of the household, in grand chorus; and was complimented in turn by three cheers from the *Dorset's* ship's company.

"His Majesty, with the same politeness, paid a similar compliment to a British frigate of war lying off Dunleary, which was most politely returned by her commander with every degree of respect to his Dalkeian Majesty. The shrouds of the frigate were instantly manned from the deck to the round top; and her fore and main mast presented two heroic pyramids of brave, honest fellows, who hailed with three cheers the King of Dalkey and fleet."—

Cooney's *Morning Post or Dublin Courant*, September 2nd, 1797.

FURTHER PARTICULARS RESPECTING THE BUSINESS OF DALKEY, FROM THE "DALKEY GAZETTE EXTRAORDINARY," DATED MONDAY, SEPT. 10TH.

"Yesterday morning, at nine o'clock, the royal yacht of Dalkey, with his facetious Majesty on board, conveyed by a squadron of frigates, under the command of Commodore Byrne, entered the Sound, and came to anchor opposite the royal stairs. The barges of the fleet were immediately manned, and his Majesty, attended by all the great officers of state, the lord mayor, and municipality, were immediately landed, and were received in the great valley of liberty by all the citizens of Dalkey, with three cheers that rent the vaults of heaven with the sound of gladness. His Majesty then procceeded to the great hall of the palace, where he took his seat on the royal throne of granite, under a canopy of celestial blue ether, surrounded by the officers of state in the robes and ribbons of their respective orders.

"The great verdant table of nature was then spread in the royal hall of hospitality for a grand *dejuner*,

and instantly covered by the royal sutlers with
abundance of hams, sheeps' tongues, roast mutton,
and other cold viands, and two tuns of nutbrown
stingo from the royal cellars were broached in the
grand saloon.

"A herald sounded the trumpet of hospitality, and
invited all the world to come and partake of the
good cheer of the king's table. After which, grace
being said by the lord primate (very contrary to
the custom of surrounding nations at breakfast), the
assembly seated themselves on the green sod, and
manifested the gladsome coalition of those long contending parties, appetite and good cheer, while the
royal band struck up

'O'Rourke's Noble Feast.'

"Breakfast being over, his Majesty, attended by his
court and state officers, and the municipality, perambulated the boundaries of his capital, and then
attended divine service in the cathedral, where a
most excellent sermon was preached by the lord
primate of Dalkey, and the service concluded by a
grand anthem performed by the whole choir. Service being over, his Majesty held a levee at the
palace, at which were present several of the nobility
of the empire, and a great number of illustrious
foreigners from Bullock, Dunleary, Howth, Kil-
barrak and Ireland's Eye, and other parts of the
neighbouring continent.

"His Majesty then ascended the great rock, and
entered the senate-house, where the states of the
empire were assembled, and being led to the foot of
the throne by the chancellor and the primate, and
proceeded by the lord mayor, as representatives of
the municipality, his Majesty declined ascending the
royal seat. But turning round to the assembly, and
pulling off his royal diadem, he laid it with his oaken
sceptre on the table of the assembly, and addressed
them in the following speech:

"'My Lords and Gentlemen, and Citizens of Dalkey and her States—

"'I come this day, to commemorate with my cheerful people, the occasion which raised me, by the unsolicited honour of their suffrages, to the throne of their realms. And I rejoice most exceedingly that nothing like hereditary pretensions are quartered in my scutcheons, or ranked amongst my claims to that dignity; that I hold it not as an heritance from ancestors who attained it by injustice, rapacity, or bloodshed, but that I enjoy it by the most honorable of all claims, the unsolicited choice and that unfeigned confidence and affection of a free, a generous, and a happy people.

"''Tis my glory that I love you all; 'tis my pride that you are happy, and my joy that you think so. And to manifest my sincerity on this head, it is my wish this day to establish, in the happy constitution of Dalkey, for ever, a principle which shall place its liberty and happiness above the power of permanent tyrants; and by depositing in the people of this happy realm a controlling discretion, which shall for evei preserve to them the privilege of recalling power and dignity from their king, so soon as they shall be found unworthy to hold either, to give them some hostage for the honesty of crowned heads.

"'The crimes of royalty, its tyrannies, its treacheries, and its rapacities, have rendered it suspicious everywhere—from that suspicion it is my wish to vindicate for ever him who wears the crown of Dalkey. Feeling no interest or happiness separate from yours, there is nothing in the title loyalty that can tempt me to wear it tarnished by the general suspicion. A king should be like Cæsar's wife, not only *virtuous* but *unsuspected;* and where reasonable doubt or suspicion can find footing in the character, I shall for ever hold, that " the post of honour is a private station.

"'Take back, then, my people, this crown and this sceptre, types of that power which is yours, and which you have only delegated to my hands for your own welfare and good government, and not for my ambition or aggrandizement. I desire not to hold longer the weight of the trust than I shall have done my duty. If you return them to me, it will be a manifestation that you approve my past government, and thus renovate the covenant in expectation that I shall continue to deserve your confidence, and in this trust I shall never deceive you; but if you choose a worthier ruler, I shall rejoice.

"'For your parts, I advise you, trust not the promises of any mortal in the station I here fill, beyond your own power of control; and I, for mine, have but one ambitious wish left to exist, before your wisdom may judge it right to accept this day my resignation for ever, and dismiss me from the crown of those realms, and it is this: "That the last act of my regal life should be to join with you this day in adding to the great charter of your freedom, a clause which shall make the election of your king annual, and that no ruler be permitted to hold your confidence more than one year without being re-chosen by you."

"'I am not an advocate for the prerogative of kings against the rights of the race of Adam; but my ambition was always to reign over your hearts and affections, and not above your liberties.

"'Your wisdom, I am sure, will see the good purposes of my proposal, and suggest the necessity of your joining with me this day in securing for you the liberties of Dalkey.'

"The lord chancellor immediately rose, and, in a speech of considerable length, disadvised his Majesty from soliciting that which must for ever circumscribe the rights attached to the crown of Dalkey, and resigning that penance of power, of prerogative and patronage, which his predecessors had maintained with becoming dignity, regardless of the notions of that long-eared mobocracy, called the people; and which future princes might highly value, though his Majesty's taste might not be in the splendour of royalty. His Majesty shortly thanked the noble lord for his advice, and replied, he knew of no rights of royalty paramount of that power who made it—the power of the people."

Moore wrote the Dalkey Coronation Ode for 1797. The poems composed for these commemorations had various degrees of merit. The following are two verses of the Ode of 1793 :—

> "Lord of all Dalkey lands,
> Chief of our jovial bands,
>   Are you not man?
> With you though peace doth reign,
> Nor blood your isle doth stain,
> Nor famine here complain,
>   Are you not man?
>
> What though the realms rejoice
> In your melodious voice:
>   Kings are but men!
> And while each subject sings:
> 'God made us men, not kings!'
> With echo Dalkey rings:
>   'Kings are but men!'"

The following curious letter on political secret societies (the United Irishmen, Defenders, and the French Revolutionists of 1792), the style of which the celebrated " *Terry O'Driscoll* " seems to have adopted in his famous letters to the *Warder*, appeared in most of the leading papers in Ireland, almost at the same time with Gillespie's Coronation Sermon on Dalkey Island, in 1792. It was afterwards copied into the *Anthologia Hibernica*.

MY DEAR MISTER PRINTER,—Ime a very plane man, I hav no Lattin, and verie littel English, tho' I can tauke Irish as fast as any man in Munster, except my weif, who, to be sure, can tauke me def ; and afterwards tauke on till Ime tired of hearing hur. But tho' Ime not book-larn'd, yet Father Tedy O'Rourke, who is a deep Scollard, offten tells me, when Ime giving him a jorum of whiskey punch, that tho' Ime ignorant, yet I have a good understanding. But if this be all blarny, and if I hav no understanding at aule, this need nat hinder me from riting abaute pollyticks, becaise this is a thing that everybodie understands. But it is time for me to be aftur telling what it is I mane. The Society of United Irishmen are sartingly mity fine people ; they cant but noe everything, for they hav among um aule profissions, atturnies, and bruers, and steymakers, und docturs, and grand jontlemen, who ware formerly parliament men, and if they wer able to by burroes, wud be the seme agen ; and they hav likeweys among um, preests and prospiterion ministers, and ethiests, and all the other religions in the kingdom. Now this Society tells us that the Frenshe revolushon is the most charmin, vartuous, nobel biznisse that the world ever sawe, and that we aut to immitate it as faste as we can. But, on the other hand, there ere topping makers who swere that it is the most abominable, hellish worke, that ever was done sense Adam was cristened ; and that if we attempt any such thing, we shall distroy all Irelond, and what is worser, destroy ourselves. Now by the vessment, these great people bodder me so by their palauvering on both sides, that I don't noe what to think of it, at all, at all ; and, therefore, I send you my own thauts upon the subject. I thinks then that tenn years is littel enuff for giving the Frensh Revolushon a fare triel. If we find in the year 1800, that it has brout to the Frenshmen, riches and honour, and happyness, and all that, then in the name of —— let us aule drawe our spedes and flauns, and shilellies, and hav a grand bodderation of our one. But iff we see that it has maid the Frenshmen poor and infimous, and wicked, then lett us remane snug and pasible, and content ourselves with wolunteering, and singing trezion and ranking rebellion, jest to sho that we are brave Irish boys, but not come the joak any further. In the manetime, until that happy yeer shal come, in which we may posibly have the plesure of cutting one anoders troats, let us be indistrous, and ern a grete dele of money, and seve more. For tho' England, to be shure, is not a match for us, yet in case of a war with hur, we shood want some mony. War is like a law-shute; and I know, to my grief, what a law-shute is; for I was almost ruineted by ganing a cauze against a gossup of mine, that cheeted me; butt the divel shal hav all my gossups, men, women, and childrin, befoar I go to law with one of urn agen. War requiers money as bad as a law-shute; without mony our generuls, and cornits, and granydeers wood'nt fire; without money our preests woodn't prey us out of purgatury, when we were kilt; nay, our drummors wood no moar rattle their sticks without mony, than Counsillor Currin or Counsillor O'Driscoll wood rattle their tongues without their hire. When we have got mony, then will be the time to invaid Englond, take Lonnon, bring it hoam with us, and build et in Belfast.

My deer countrymen, everyone of you noes parfitly, that you are a wize nashon; herfoar, my sweet duils, take a fool's advice, and be quiet.

I am, deer printur, your sarvent to command till death,
PATRICK O'FLAHERTY
BALLYBOOITY, NEAR TIPPERARY,
Oggus the First, 1792.

PROCEEDINGS AND DEBATES OF THE PARLIAMENT OF PIMLICO.*

[NO. XIX.]

LOWER HOUSE, 23rd and 25th of Jan. 1799.

The follwing is an extract from a supposed speech, by one styled Lawyer George, on the proposed union :—

"Sir, the varieties of shapes and colors this proposed measure of union with Oxmantown has assumed, since its first introduction in Pimlico, and the multiplicity of opposite pretences with which it has been covered, create some difficulty as to the choice of points in which it is to be attacked, though

* Tripoli; Published by the executors of Judith Freel, late printer to his Dalkeian Majesty: and sold at No. 5, College Green, and by all the flying stationers; price, four camaos.

"*My Nobs and Gentlemen.*" 267

at all points it seems to me equally weak and untenable; it is a measure not to annihilate or diminish the independence of the Pimlico parliament, but to concentrate, confirm, and eternise that independence, and to give it a proportionate sway over the whole Dalkeian empire."

EXTRACT FROM THE PROCEEDINGS AND DEBATES OF THE PARLIAMENT OF PIMLICO, ON THE LAST SESSION OF THE EIGHTEENTH CENTURY.

HOUSE OF NOBS, *Die Stephani*, 1799.

Their Wigships being assembled in their best *bibs* and *tuckers*, his honor, the *Seneschal*, who had in the morning taken the diversion of *bull-beating*, came down to the hall in great *snuff*. His honor was attended in the *State Jingle*, by *Nob Nothingworth*, commander-in-chief to the Pimlico guards, who bore the *cap and bells*, and *his grace, Moses, Marquis* of *Truck-street*, who bore the *axe* of *state*.

His honor entered the hall about five o'clock, ushered by CROSS PODDLE, *king-at-arms*, and being seated on the *great stool*, (after three solemn reverences thereto made), a message was sent to the lower assembly by the *gentleman usher of the oak stick*, requiring their attendance forthwith. The lower assembly being accordingly come to their place, preceded by Mr. *Orator Mum*, their chairman, his honor, *the seneschal*, was pleased to deliver the following most facetious speech to both houses.

MY NOBS AND GENTLEMEN.—

The Secretary commands me to inform you that the long, arduous, and ruinous contest, in which he has been graciously pleased to involve these realms, jointly with our *good allies*, the *Emperor of the Muglins*, the *Czar of Lambay*, and the *grand Duke of Bullock*, against the *impious republic of Skerries*, is just about as far from termination as ever, notwithstanding all the threatened *growlings* and *prowlings* of the *great and invincible generalissimo*, Rusty Fusty; and that our said good *allies*, having for their *most generous and disinterested* aid, fleeced us of every camac and cronbane they could, are now resolved to follow the adage.—" No *longer pipe, no longer dance,*" and are about to reneague from the contest, leaving to us the *honor* of fighting it out alone, or getting out of the scrape in any manner we can; possessed, however, of an *inexhaustible fund of experience* and a most *elaborate* system of *finance*, the *advantages* of which will be fairly divided with his Majesty's *Pimliconian subjects*, so soon as this GREAT MEASURE shall be established, whereby the most permanent advantage will accrue to the great virtues of temperance and economy in this realm of Pimlico.

The brilliant successes which have so recently distinguished the arms of Dalkey and her allies against the *Zooder-Zealanders;* the *cheap* bargain we have bought of their *bumb-boats,* and, above all, the *splendid retreat* secured for our gallant legions ; a retreat unincumbered by *horses, artillery, camp equipage, stores,* or other such *trumpery* as must have proved highly embarassing to that singular and unparalleled manœuvre, beggars everything told in history of the races of *Dunkirk* or Ballinamuck; and gives the strongest pledge of indubitable success in our new expedition to the Fingallian coast, and the brightest promise to our hopes, that *some time in the course of the new century,* such order of things may be established amongst the Skerrinians as may warrant the Dalkeian cabinet in condescending to listen to terms of peace.*

* Throughout the Pimliconian debates, which extend to a considerable length, there is frequent allusion to the King of Dalkey, and other mock titles from that quarter.

BULLOCK,*

SECTION VIII.

"BOULEK," OR "BLOYKE."

THE village of Bullock, with its remains of an ancient castle, and pier of Danish erection, commands a grand view of the Bay of Dublin. In 1307, the advowson of the rectory and vicarage of this place, consisting of fifteen acres, was granted to the prior of the Monastery of St. John the Baptist, Dublin, by Sir John Asyk, then Lord of " Boulek ;" and certain religious houses in the city were entitled to receive, from every fishing boat entering the harbour, one of their best fish, herrings excepted ; and from every herring boat a meise annually.

The village of Bullock was formerly defended by a fortified castle and watch-towers. A great portion of the wall that connected the barbican with the castle is still perfect. It also had a bawn of considerable extent. Grose, in his "Antiquities of Ireland," states that he could not discover who constructed this castle, which was formerly of an octangular shape, with few windows, and surmounted by a granulated parapet. Some writers suppose the castle of Bullock to be coëval with those at Dalkey,

---

* Bullock is a corruption of the proper name ; and, probably, the great and well-known sandbanks on either side of Dublin Bay (the North and South Bulls) were so called from a like corruption. The name Bullock is derived from the word "Bloyke," the *little bank.*

270 *Trim Castle and Ross in the Olden Time.*

Carrickfergus, Shankhill, Puck's castle, Trim,* Carlingford, and Ross† in the County Wexford.

"ROSS IN THE OLDEN TIME"—ITS FORTIFICATIONS—
CASTLES, &C.

Curious account of the erection of the walls and fortifications of New Ross, in the year 1265, founded on an ancient French poem, supposed from the pen of Father Michael Kyldare, who was an eye witness, and therefore of undoubted authority.

Among the Harleian MSS. in the British Museum is preserved a highly curious volume, towards the

---

* Trim castle, standing on the banks of the Boyne, forms a pleasing object in the landscape. Sir R. C. Hoare says, that it "is almost the only building in Ireland that deserves the name of *castle.*" It was originally erected by Hugh de Lacy, to secure his large possessions in Meath, or, as Camden asserts, by William Peppard, previously to the grant of Meath to De Lacy, and continued during successive centuries to be the most important stronghold of the English Pale. According to an historical fragment by Maurice Regan, published by Harris in his "Hibernica," Hugh de Lacy on completing the building, departed for England, leaving it in the custody of Hugh Tyrrell, "*his intrinsicke friend.*" The King of Connaught, taking advantage of De Lacy's absence, assembled all his powers with a view to its destruction; and though Tyrrell, advised of his coming, dispatched messengers to Strongbow for assistance, and though the earl marched towards Trim in all haste, yet Tyrrell, seeing the enemy at hand, and thinking himself too weak to resist their numbers, abandoned the castle, and burnt it; upon which the Irish Monarch, satisfied with the success of his expedition, returned home. Strongbow, however, pursued him, and falling upon the rear of his army, slew 150 of the Irish; which done, he retired to Dublin, and Hugh Tyrrell to the ruined castle of Trim, to re-edify it before Hugh de Lacy should return from England. The castle was built in a much stronger manner, upon the ruins of the old one. Here, in 1399, Richard II. who was then in Ireland, hearing of the progress of the Duke of Lancaster in his English dominions, imprisoned the sons of his rival and of the Duke of Gloucester; the former of whom was afterwards drowned on his passage to England. In 1423, Edmund Mortimer, Earl of Meath and Ulster, who had possessed the inheritance of Trim, and, as Lord Lieutenant of the island, had enjoyed more than customary authority in that office, died of the plague in this castle.

† Sir James Ware calls him Earl of Desmond, and says he was drowned in 1263, while crossing from Ireland to Wales; but both these errors are corrected by Cox. The first Earl of Desmond was Maurice Fitzthomas, created by Edward the Third, August 27, 1329.

close of which occurs an interesting poem, written in the Norman, or ancient French language, contributing, in a remarkable degree, to throw an illustration on the early topography and history of the town of New Ross, county of Wexford, Ireland.

The poem is founded on a quarrel which occurred there between Sir Morice and Sir Walter, A. D. 1265. This is not a very accurate description, since the object of the writer was not to relate a quarrel between two anonymous knights, but to give a detailed narrative of the erection of the fortifications and walls of Ross, occasioned by the dread felt by the inhabitants, lest the unprotected and open situation of the place might cause them to suffer from a feud, then raging with violence, between two powerful barons, Maurice Fitzmaurice, the chief of the Geraldines, and Walter de Burgo, Earl of Ulster, whose deadly wars, in the year 1264, brought trouble throughout the realm of Ireland.

So little is known of the early history of New Ross, it is merely described by all topographers as having once been a place of great strength and extent, situated in a large ravine, formed by the junction of the rivers Barrow and Nore. Of its high walls and frowning towers and gates, some remains continue until the present day. It was a place of considerable trade so early as the reign of Henry the Fifth, and obtained charters from several of the English sovereigns, the earliest of which is supposed to be that of Henry the Fourth. Its port is so capacious, that ships of nine hundred tons burden may come up to the quay; but the commerce of the town decreased, subsequently, to such a degree, that in 1776 we only find five or six brigs were to be seen in it. It has since rapidly improved, for upwards of thirty large ships, chiefly employed in emigration, belong to the merchants of the town. The port has also been lately opened, as previously it was in dependence to Waterford.

Among the collection of the second Randle Holmes M. for the city of Chester, (MS. Harleian, 2173, fol. 42,) is a copy of "a certyficate from the soveraine (Mayor) of New Ross, alias Ross Ponte, in Ireland, to show how we be free with them, and they with the city of Chester, of all customs," 29 Eliz. 1587, A.D. A seal was appended to the document, with the arms of Ross, being a greyhound pulling down a stag, and beneath, a bridge raised on several arches, from which bridge the appellation of *Ross Pont* was doubtless derived. Round the edge we read, " S. Office, ... superiour, Newe Ross." In 1257, the Franciscans are said to have settled there; and a convent of St. Augustine's was founded in the reign of Edward the Third. Sir John Devereux subsequently erected the convent of St. Saviour on the site of the Franciscan monastery, and part of it is still appropriated to the use of a parish Church. The more modern history of this place is chiefly remarkable for the defence made against the "United Irishmen" and misguided peasantry on the 6th of June, 1798, by the garrison under the command of General Sir William Johnson, Bart.

The author of the poem commences in the following abrupt manner: "I have an inclination to write in romance, if it pleases you to hear me; for a story that is not listened to is of no more value than a berry. I pray you, therefore, to give attention, and you shall hear a fine adventure of a town in Ireland, the most beautiful of its size that I know of in any country. Its inhabitants were alarmed by the feud existing between two barons, whose names you see here written, Sir Maurice and Sir Wauter. The name of this town I will now disclose to you—it is called Ros—it is the New Pont de Ross." He then proceeds to relate how the principal men of the town, together with the commonalty, assembled to take measures for their safety; and they resolved to sur-

round the town with mortar and stone. They commenced, accordingly, on the feast of the Purification, (February 2, A.D. 1265,) and marked out the fosse or line of circumvallation. Workmen were speedily hired, and above an hundred each day came out to labour, under the direction of the Burgesses. When this step was taken they again assembled, and determined to establish a bye-law, such (says the poet,) as was never heard of in England or France; which was publicly proclaimed the next day to the people, and received with applause; this law was as follows:
—"That on the ensuing Monday, the vintners, the mercers, the merchants, and the drapers should go and work at the fosse, from the hour of prime till noon." This was readily complied with, and above one thousand men, (writes the poet,) " went to work every Monday with brave banners, and great pomp, attended by flutes and tabors. So soon as the hour of noon had sounded, these fine fellows returned home, with their banners borne before them, and the young men singing loudly and caroling through the town. The priests, also, who accompanied, fell to work at the fosse, and laboured right well, more so than the others, being young and skilful, of tall stature, strong, and well housed.

The mariners, likewise, proceeded in good array to the fosse, to the number of six hundred, with a banner preceding them, on which was depicted a vessel; and if all the people in the ships and barges had been hired, they would have amounted to eleven hundred men," a convincing proof of the importance of the town, at that time, as a mercantile port. On the Tuesday this party was succeeded by another, consisting of the tailors and cloth-workers, the tent-makers, fullers, and celers,* who went out in a similar manner as the former, but were not so numerous,

* " Celers," mean saddlers, from the French word "selliers."

2 L

amounting only to four hundred men. On the Wednesday, a different set was employed, viz., the cordwainers, tanners, and butchers; many brave bachelors were among them, and their banners were painted as appertains to their craft. In number, I believe, they were about three hundred taken together, little and great; and they went forth, caroling loudly as the others did. On the Thursday came the fishermen and hucksters. Their standards were of various sorts; but on one was painted a fish and a platter; these, five hundred in number, were associated with the wainrights, who were thirty-two in number. On Friday went out the ...... (illegible) in number three hundred and fifty, with their banners borne before them, unto the border of the fosse. On the Saturday succeeded the carpenters, blacksmiths, and masons—in number about three hundred and fifty. Lastly, on the Sunday, assembled in procession the ladies of the town! Know, verily, that they were excellent labourers, but their numbers I cannot certainly tell; but they all went forth to cast stones and carry them from the fosse. Whoever had been there to look at them, might have seen many a beautiful woman—many a mantle of scarlet, green, and russet—many a fair folded cloak, and many a gay coloured garment. In all the countries I ever visited never saw I so many fair ladies. He should have been born in a favourite hour who might make his choice among them." The ladies also carried banners, in imitation of the other parties; and when they were tired of the duty assigned to them, they walked round the fosse, singing sweetly, to encourage the workmen. On their return to the town, the richer sort held a convivial meeting, " and," as we are told, "made sport, drank whiskey, and sang," encouraging each other, and resolving to make a gate, which should be called the ladies' gate, and there would fix a prison. According to the poet, " the fosse was made twenty feet in depth, and its length extended above a league." "When it shall be completed," adds the writer, "they may sleep securely, and will not require a guard; for if forty thousand men were to attack the town they would never be able to enter it, for they have sufficient means of defence; many a white hauberk and haubergeon—many a doublet and coat of mail, and a savage Garcon—many a good cross-bow-man have they, and many good archers. Never, in any town, beheld I so many good glaives, nor so many good cross-bows hanging on the wall, nor so many quarrels to shoot withal, and every house full of maces, good shields, and talevases. They are well provided, I warrant you, to defend themselves from their enemies; for the cross-bow-men, in reality, amount to three hundred and sixty-three in number, as counted at their muster, and enrolled at their muster-roll. And of other archers have they one thousand two hundred brave fellows, be assured; and besides these there are three thousand men, armed with lances or axes, in the town; and knights on horseback one hundred and four, well armed for the combat."

The poet then assures us that the object of the inhabitants was by no means to court an assault," but simply for their own protection; "for which," says he, "no one ought to blame them:" they appear however, to have amply provided for their safety; for the writer continues, "when the wall shall be completely carried round and fortified, no one in Ireland will be so hardy as to attack them; for by the time they have twice sounded a horn, the people assemble and fly to arms, each anxious to be before his neighbour, so courageous and valiant are they to revenge themselves on an enemy. God grant they may obtain revenge, and preserve the town with honour! And let all say amen, for charity! for it is the most hospitable town that exists in any nation ; and every stranger is welcomed with joy, and may buy and sell at his will without anything being demanded of him. I commend the *town and all who inhabit it to God, amen." This was done in the year of the Incarnation of our Lord, 1265.

The ancient family, " Fagan of Feltrim," were the owners of Bullock and the adjoining lands. In 1611, John Fagan was possessed of one castle, one ruinous tower, thirty messuages, ten acres of meadow, 200 acres of pasture and furze, with the fishing and haven to the main sea. In a survey of 1654, it states, that Bullock, in the parish of Monkstown, containing ninety acres, of which sixty were arable, twenty-three rocky pasture, and seven meadow, was the property of Christopher Fagan, of Feltrim. At that time, there were, on the premises, a fine slated castle, a good haven, and bawn ; the chief fish, tithe fish, custom fish, and corn tithes, belonged to the proprietor of the castle.

The King's (Henry IV.) son, Thomas of Lancaster, landed at the old Danish pier of Bullock, as Lord Lieutenant of Ireland, in 1402. Bullock was included, in 1448, as one of the places on the bounds of " the four obedient shires." In the year 1559, the Earl of Sussex landed at Bullock haven as Lord Deputy of Ireland.

The whole district is an inexhaustible bed of granite.

Goshawks were found, in the last century, in the immediate neighbourhood of Bullock. Ware, in his "Antiquities of Ireland," says : " Among the feathered kind, there breed in Ireland eagles—hawks, which, from their preying upon wild geese, are called in English gos-hawks, of which those that breed in the north of Ireland are reckoned the best."

There was formerly at Bullock one of those remarkable rocking stones, which are asserted to have been used for divination by the pagan priesthood of Ireland, and are additional evidence of the eastern colonization of this country, being identically the same as the bœtylia—the animated stones of the Phœnicians, mentioned by historians, as moving or rocking in the air. It is supposed the Bullock rocking-stone was destroyed at the same time that the Druids' circle on Dalkey Common disappeared.

About the year 1797, on that part of the common opposite Dalkey Sound, near Bullock, stood a circle of granite blocks in a rough state, enclosing within its area a cromleach. At that period the upper stone or slab had slipped off the perpendicular rocks or pillars which originally supported it, except at one end, where the passage was still left sufficiently wide under the upper flag. The stones were overgrown with fern.

When the martello towers were being erected, the stones composing the ring, which were from ten to fourteen feet square, together with the cromleach, were blasted and quarried, under the special directions of the late General Fisher, who had the management of the line of military stations then being erected between Bray and Dunleary, along the coast. The antiquarian or lover of Ireland's "by-gone days," must ever regret this destruction of an interesting relique of antiquity, so worthy of preservation; and this vandalism was perpetrated with the miserable object of obtaining some few hundred loads of stone, comparatively of little value.

Bullock, Dalkey, Killiney, and Rochestown, were favourite places of resort, during the "long vacation," by O'Connell, whose remains were recently removed from their temporary tomb at Glasnevin to the magnificent mausoleum, erected from designs by the late Dr. Petrie.

PUNCH'S OFFERING TO O'CONNELL.

"The remains of the Liberator were this day

transferred from their temporary resting-place, where they have reposed since 1847, when he died, with great pomp, to the tomb raised for him by national contribution in Glasnevin Cemetery."—*Dublin News of May 14th*, 1869.

Bear his bones, with all pomp, from the place they have kept
For the twenty-two years that have pass'd since he slept,
To the tomb that his Erin has painfully reared
For the champion she loved and her enemies feared.

There's a time to note sharply, a time to pass by,
The flaw in the brilliant, the cloud in the sky:
There's a time to be gen'rous, nor narrowly scan
The stains on a mem'ry, the faults in a man.

Standing now by his tomb, who devoted his life
With wrong and oppression to wage deadly strife,
Till from Captive, Emancipate, Erin he saw,
In the liberty won by the triumph of Law.

Why gauge the alloy that was mixed with his gold?
Earth and matrix why weigh 'gainst the gems in their hold?
A great work was laid on him, and that work he wrought;
He'd a battle to fight, and that battle he fought.

And he wrought to good end, and he fought till he won,
And the sun of injustice was less 'neath the sun;
Let what smallness or selfishness darkens his name
Be drunk up and drowned in the light of that fame.

Let us think of the warm heart, still open, at need,
To the wronged of his race, the oppressed of his creed:
Untempted by pelf, and undaunted by power,
Too noble to crawl, and too daring to cower.

Let us think of the big brain, and eloquent tongue,
That like Erin's own *clair-seach** now wailed and now rung,
O'er the wrongs of the slaves he was vowed to set free,
Or in praise of his green isle, his gem of the sea!

On the bier that is borne to Glasnevin to-day,
One offering the hand of the Saxon can lay—
The Bill that the Church of the stranger strikes down—
Of the work of *his* life consummation and crown!

Last link of the chain, once red-rusted with gore,
Forged by Saxon for Celt, in the ill-times of yore,
At whose crushing coil, forty long years ago,
His hand struck the first and the deadliest blow!

Punch, May 22, 1869.

---

* The ancient Irish harp.

THE DEPARTURE OF HIS EXCELLENCY LORD VISCOUNT
TOWNSHEND* FROM BULLOCK HARBOUR.
26th Debember, 1771.
"To Bullock† the mock-monarch flees,
In ev'ry bush a dagger sees,
But safe beneath thy‡ auspices,
Escapes the indignant rabble."

The following letter appeared in the *Freeman's Journal*, December 23rd, 1771:—

"SIR,—If you can find room for the inclosed inscription, you will much oblige your constant reader, "Lapidarius."

AN INSCRIPTION ON A PILLAR WHICH IS SPEEDILY TO BE
ERECTED AT THE TOWN OF BULLOCK.
This column was erected at the private expense
Of good Men,
To stand a monument of Irish Story, and
A Memorial to Posterity

---

* So, to effect his monarch's ends,
From hell a viceroy devil ascends,
His budget, with corruptions cramm'd,
The contributions of the damn'd,
Which, with unsparing hands he strews,
Round COURTS and SENATES as he goes,
And then at Belzebub's black hall
Complains his budget was too small.—SWIFT.

† "Bullock is a village on the sea-coast (Dublin Bay), in the neighbourhood of Rockfield, a villa of Lord Townshend's, where (these lines were first published in 1771) it was conjectured, from his love of *privacy*, and aversion to all kind of ostentation, he would have embarked for England. But the night before his departure, having employed the fidus Achates, his companion and panegyrist, to hire a mob in the city, he the next day *ventured* to proceed publicly through the streets; and being accompanied by Lord Harcourt, escorted by the military, and protected by the ruffians whom he had paid to huzza him, he got to the water-side without any *considerable* indignity being offered to him."—*Baratariana*.

‡ "Wagstaffe I sing, notorious name."
—*Horace*, book i., ode x., imitated.
During the administration of Lord Townshend in Ireland, an essay in defence of his measures was regularly inserted in the *Dublin Mercury* newspaper, under the heading of "*The Bachelor, or Speculations of Jeoffry Wagstaffe*," for which his excellency very generously paid him out of the public money. Jephson and Nimcox were the writers who advocated Lord Townshend's policy in the *Mercury*.

Of our happy deliverance from the scourge
Of insolence and oppression,
By the unexpected, but not unwished for, departure
Of George Lord Viscount Townshend ;
Who resided in this land, as Chief Governor,
For the space of four years : But at length
Departed on the 26th day of December, in the year
1771.
Having on that day, being St. Stephen's day,
The 15th day after his obtaining a victory,
(Which the *wise* called a defeat)
And the 2nd day after he pass'd the Moneybills,
(Which *he* thought an exploit)
Embarked *without ostentation*,
At this little Port of Bullock.
He came to Ireland professing and practising
Every mystery of corruption—
Waging war against
Power, abilities, and *integrity;*
And accordingly his administration was
Absurdity, Impotence, and *Profligacy.*
During his residence, the *powers* of his office
Frequently compell'd him to confer favours,
But a capricious nature and barbarous manners
Defend him from the returns of
Friendship and Gratitude :
He therefore never made
A friend.
So that in a country, in which any misfortune
Calls forth the affection of the people—
Where they drop tears at the execution of
Every malefactor,
He, however, was
Unassisted in his difficulties,
Unpitied in his disgrace,
And unlamented in his departure.
He uttered falsehood from the throne,
In the name of the king.
From his closet did he promise
The things which never were performed—
His conduct in government was
A disgrace to him whom he represented,
A reproach to those who appointed Him,
And a scourge to those whom he governed.—
He was a Mimick,
A Scribbler,
A Decypherer of features,

But he was not
A Delineator of corporeal infirmity;
A Statesman,
A Governor,
A Soldier,
A Friend,
Or a Gentleman:
He was victorious only when he involved
His cause with the cause of
Private persons—
And the ordinary effects of
Sympathy and Affection,
(Usually so strong in this country)
Became weak or doubtful,
As they were damp'd by the influence
Of his co-operation.
His wisdom, was fraud;
His policy, corruption;
His fortitude, contempt of character;
His friendship, distrust;
His enmity, revenge;
And his exploit, the ruin of a Country.
—"BARATARIANA."

The following letter signed *Fabricius*, addressed to Lord Townshend after his departure from Bullock harbour, in 1771, is taken from *Baratariana*:—*

"*Jacet ille nunc, prostratusque est, Quirites, et se perculsum atque abjectum esse sentit; et retorquet oculos profecto sæpe ad hanc urbem, quam ex suis faucibus ereptam esse luget: quæ quidem lætari mihi videtur, quod tantam pestem evomuerit, forasque projecerit.*—CIC.

"TO LORD TOWNSHEND.

"MY LORD,—After all the chances and changes of your political life, you have at length *escaped* to Holyhead. That theatre of modern chivalry opened its arms, no doubt, to the successor of Wolfe. Alexander visited the tomb of Achilles, and an old field of battle has always arrested the notice of a military genius. In the same spirit, I suppose

---

* "Baratariana."—A collection of fugitive political pieces, published during the administration of Lord Townshend in Ireland.

Præsenti tibi maturos largimur honores.—HOR.

The collected edition of these fugitive pieces has no printer's or publisher's name to it.

your lordship will reconnoitre all the stations of combat in that celebrated spot, and examine every rock at which that gun-powder Galwayman, Mr. Blake, discharged a pistol, in his morning exercise, upon a late excursion. Like Scipio, too, you may occupy yourself a while in the innocent recreation of collecting pebbles on the shore; not forgetting that the meanest and basest of the Roman governors did the same; that he brought back some cockle-shells to the Capitol, as trophies of his success; and claimed, and obtained a triumph for having extended the empire of Rome. The ceremony of a triumph, indeed, is out of date, my Lord; the Ordnance and a Marquisate must suffice you.

"By command of your Sovereign, you remained in Ireland till you were publicly stripped of your temporary distinction, and ordered *to return to the place from whence you came:* but you could scarce bring yourself to comply with the sentence; you lingered, like a discontented spirit, and hovered over the grave of your former dignity. Your friends boasted, that if you could not, like Fabius, retrieve the state, you would give a specimen of your valour by *delay.* How did the experiment answer? It is true, that now and then, with nerves unstrung, and with a countenance that more than insinuated embarrassment, you sallied into the streets; but your flights were short, and your season *twilight.* An opportunity which a brave, but *blemished,* soldier would have solicited, offered itself to you. Instead of seizing the armour of valour, you forgot, in your disturbance, the *refuge* of station. Day after after day, your door was *dunned* by Mr. Lowther, on behalf of his friend;* like an importunate creditor, he grew clamorous at length; by accident you became visible to him; but, a bankrupt in honour, instead of *discharging,* you *compounded the debt.*

"The new viceroy† declared, that whilst you continued in Ireland you were to be his guest; he, therefore, stopped the circulation of public dinners, which are a matter of *precedent,* on the arrival of a lord lieutenant. To pay a greater compliment, by a further accommodation to your lordship's genius, he proclaimed an *armistice* of business. There could not be a more decent exhortation to your departure. But Candy's chop-house, and the gratuitous hotel of Mr. Montgomery, stood in your way. From the intenseness of

---

* The Honourable Robert Rochefort, from whom Mr. Lowther carried a challenge to Lord Townshend, about a fortnight before his departure from Ireland.
† Simon Harcourt—First Earl Harcourt.

your dissipation, a stranger might have thought that you were indemnifying yourself in some sort, for a former contrast of toil and industry; but the people of Ireland were not to be so deceived; they did not wonder that you should continue to *impede* the national business, which you had so long *disgraced* and *confounded*. The charms of the Miss M—ntg—ys might have attracted the honourable attention of the most elegant nature; but yours, my lord, was out of their reach. An eleemosynary bottle with their cheerful father, a little time to negociate away an altercation or two, together with the dear delight of playing at *hide and seek* with the expectations of the public, and of doing every thing but what you ought to do, were the principle of your stay. The army was ordered out every day to escort you, and sometimes more than once. All was uncertainty, and the citizens were at a loss when your lordship would require their attendance. You never appeared a greater general, my Lord, than in this instance; you effectually harassed your enemy—*the people*.

"In the prime and strength of your government, you affected to despise the most respectable popularity; but when the period of its expiration drew near, you grew solicitous for the *hired* huzza of the lowest of the rabble; a sort of death-bed repentance, my Lord, which can operate little to your political salvation; the sickly suffrage of a mercenary mob is not the voice of heaven. But a fatality peculiar to the contrivances of your lordship, even their miserable cry, for once, became the vehicle of truth; for after all the farcical preparation of the matter, by your city agitators, the salutation, which you purchased, proved but a *shout for your departure*.

"But if the presence of the new Chief Governor, who accompanied you to your ship, and of whom the public have favourable hopes—if the threats of intimated vengeance—if the terror of a military power—if the vileness of bribes operating upon the hunger of necessitous miscreants—if any, or all of these, had stifled public imprecation for a moment, or procured your Lordship the echo of a counterfeited applause, you must confess it would be no proof of your merit, however it might be an aggravation of your guilt. Verres, the persecutor of Sicily, had public thanks decreed, and public statues erected to his honour, by the cities which he had plundered, and which afterwards impeached him. Thanks to the dignity of my countrymen, in their collective capacity, you have no such scandalous compliances to boast. They have no inconsistency, no ingratitude to you, in their way. Their justice may pro-

perly overtake your crimes, for their wants rejected your
charity.* But though they should abandon your person to

---

* "*Dublin, Monday Nov.* 23, 1772.
"At a post-Hall of the Master, Wardens, and Brethren of the
Corporation of Sheermen and Dyers, pursuant to a public notice,
the following resolutions were unanimously agreed to:—
Resolved—"That the spurious Address or Petition advertised in
Hoey's *Dublin Mercury* of Saturday last, and said to be presented
to George Lord Viscount Townshend, Lord Lieutenant-General
and General Governor of Ireland, by the journeymen weavers of
the worsted and woollen branches, was entirely unknown to, and
is highly disapproved of by, this corporation.
Resolved—"That the *two hundred pounds* given by his Excellency to be distributed among the poor manufacturers, was
intended as a *bribe* to obtain addresses of approbation from the
two Corporations of Weavers, and Sheermen and Dyers, for his
Excellency's past conduct as Chief Governor of Ireland.
Resolved—"That it appears to this Corporation that the two
hundred pounds so given was at the request, and by the influence
of, some person or persons who are not well-wishers of, or attached
to, the Protestant interest of Ireland.
Resolved—"That it is the request and desire of this corporation,
that the Master of the Weavers do immediately return to his Excellency the said two hundred pounds; and at the same time do
let his Excellency know that if he really wishes that sum to be
distributed, he will please to put it for that purpose into the hands
of some of the people (*if any there be*) who have approved of his
Excellency's conduct as Chief Governor of Ireland.
"Resolved—That these resolutions be printed in the public
papers of this city.

JAMES YEATES, *Master,*
HAMILTON WEST, } *Wardens.*
ROBERT BEASLY,

"*Dublin, Monday, Nov.* 23, 1772.
"By the Master and Wardens of the Corporation of Weavers,
at this Hall assembled, pursuant to public notice.
"The Master of the Corporation laid before the body a letter in
the words and figures following:—
"SIR,—His Excellency my Lord Lieutenant desires the favour
of seeing you, with your Wardens, Members, and Clerk, at the
Castle, to-morrow morning at eleven o'clock.
"I am, sir, your obedient humble servant,
"THOMAS WAITE.
"*Thursday, Nov.* 19, 1772.
"Mr. John Wiseheart,
"Master of the Corporation of Weavers, Corn Market."

your own care, your name at least they will brand, and your image they have already brought to a public and ignominious execution. Æneas sighed when, turning towards Carthage, he saw from shipboard the flames of the funeral pile of Dido. His heart gave intimation of the disaster which had befallen. Did any similar misgiving vibrate at your lordship's breast, or did any sympathic presage melt you into tears, when, looking to the shore you beheld from deck the conflagaration of your effigy ? The whole town, with countenances expressive of peculiar gratification, beheld the spectacle of your lordship in procession. Even in your *natural* person you never thridded so many passages, and alleys, nor explored so many nooks and recesses of the metropolis, as you did *in that your counterfeit presentment,* during this solemnity. Had your friend, the late lord mayor, presided over the pomp, you could not have perambulated the city more completely.

"At length, however, you have made your ever-memorable retreat; not, indeed, like Xenophon with the ten thousand Greeks, but, like yourself, with Courtney and with Frazer. Is it not strange, that wheresoever we survey you, whether in your stay or in your departure, in the camp or cabinet, in your own character, or in any which you assume, you should still present us with some perverse incongruity, some contemptible caprice, or some indignity not to be paralleled. Go, then, thou wretched commander, and thou still more miserable viceroy, go then, thou unworthy man, bury thyself, if thou can'st, in oblivion. If thou can'st be consistent in anything, be so in that despicable buffoonery, in which

And also a bank note of £200 given to him by the Lord Lieutenant.

Resolved unanimously—"That it is the opinion of this Corporation, that from the past conduct of his Excellency George Lord Viscount Townshend, Lord Lieutenant, and General Governor of Ireland, in repeatedly refusing admission to deputations from this body, particularly when applied to for assistance to relieve the poor in a time of real distress and public calamity; and also, from the manner in which the present donation of two hundred pounds appears to have been procured, that this Corporation cannot receive or assist in the distribution thereof, although it would at all times give this Corporation the greatest pleasure, on every occasion, to be instrumental in relieving the necessities of the poor; and they do hereby direct the said sum to be *returned* to his Excellency.

Resolved—"That the above be published in the public papers.

"Signed by order,

"JOHN GELLING, *Clerk of Guild.*"

alone thou can'st be eminent. Be uniform in that, for it may shut out reflection, which, if it comes, must come with scorpions to thee. Thou hast the violation of the entrusted rights of a nation to answer for. Heaven and earth condemn thee. What must be thy portion?"

"The papers in *Baratariana* will reach you, my Lord, in another country. They will contribute to amuse those leisure moments when you reflect on transactions that must once have agitated your bosom. They will recall those motley times of embarrassed indolence, of broken councils, of sordid society, when business waited, while Denis jested, and Cunningham advised; you will look back to the sea on which you once were tossed, and feel a joy to be on shore, though naked, *and without a friend*. In those moments of reflection and of *safety*, you will recollect that you have introduced into this country a long train of mischiefs;—that you have left a name as little to be forgotten as it can be beloved;—that the men who opposed you were not your enemies, nor the men who supported you your friends;—that your *largesses were rejected* by the spirit of indignant poverty;—that your favours, when they were received, were written in the sandy memory of disgusted hirelings, but your injuries engraven on the marble of the constitution. Softened and stung by these considerations, you will lament the time when you were called *from the rank to which you belong*, and, from the singularity of your genius, transplanted to a station where honours did not grow around you, and where, of all whom you have served, and of all whom you have injured, your adversaries are those alone of whom you cannot complain."

*Extract from the dedication of "Baratariana" to Lord Townshend.**

LORD TOWNSHEND'S ADMINISTRATION—SATIRICAL AND POLITICAL BALLADS.
To the Printer of the "Freeman's Journal."
"February 6, 1772.

"SIR,—The ballad which I sent you a few days ago, having, I find, gone through a second edition, I make no doubt you will give a place in your entertaining paper to two others sent herewith. They are not, indeed, enriched with

---

* Flood's letters to the *Freeman* appeared under the signature of "Syndercomb;" they were reprinted in "Baratariana."

such *learned* and *curious* notes, and they relate chiefly to transactions which happened somewhat more than a year ago, the ever-memorable *protest* and *prorogation:* but they exhibit very striking likenesses of some eminent personages, and a lively picture of the early part of Lord Townshend's administration. In that light, perhaps, they deserve to outlive the occasions that produced them. If the Muse should again inspire the bards of Fishamble-street, you may, perhaps, hear once more from

"Your Constant Reader,

GREEN MAN,   "CANTILENA."
Fishamble-street.

"A LIST OF THE PACK."

Tune, *Ballynamony.*

I.

Fellow-citizens all, to my ballad give ear,
That we must be undone I will make it appear,
Unless in defence of our Freedom we stand,
'Gainst Townshend, that dunce, and his damnable band.
    Then kick out those rascally knaves, boys;
    Freemen we'll be to our graves, boys;
    Better be dead than be slaves, boys;
      A coffin or freedom for me!

II.

But plainly to prove what I here have set down,
Regardless and fearless who smile or who frown;
As a palpable proof that all must go to rack,
I'll give you their marks, and a list of the pack.
    Then kick out those rascally knaves, boys;
    Freemen we'll be to our graves, boys;
    Better be dead than be slaves, boys;
      A coffin or freedom for me!

III.

At the head of the list set down A——y* first;
The chief of his favourites, because he's the worst
To show himself worthy and fit for his trust;
Without judgment a judge, he makes justice unjust.
    Then kick out those rascally knaves, boys;
    Freemen we'll be to our graves, boys;
    Better be dead than be slaves, boys;
      A coffin or freedom for me!

---

* The Right Hon. John Lord Annaly, Lord Chief Justice.

IV.

Frank A——s comes next, of corruption the sink,
What a dog must he be, who's a rogue in his drink!
No wonder he's fat, since our mis'ry's his food,
And he daily gets drunk with poor Ireland's life-blood.
    Then kick out those rascally knaves, boys;
    Freemen we'll be to our graves, boys;
    Better be dead than be slaves, boys;
        A coffin or freedom for me.

V.

Lo! T——l* whose looks would make honest men start,
Who hangs out in his face the black sign of his heart;
If you thought him no devil, his aim he would miss,
For he would, if he could, appear worse than he is.
    Then kick out those rascally knaves, boys;
    Freemen we'll be to our graves, boys;
    Better be dead than be slaves, boys;
        A coffin or freedom for me.

VI.

Yet T——l unfeeling, and void of remorse,
Is still not the worst—H——y H——n'sț worse;
Who feels ev'ry crime, yet his feelings defies,
And each day stabs his country with tears in his eyes.
    Then kick out those rascally knaves, boys;
    Freemen we'll be to our graves, boys;
    Better be dead than be slaves, boys;
        A coffin or freedom for me.

VII.

See squinting T——e, from the Primate's black school,
Whom merciful nature designed for a fool;
T——e, whom not even his folly can save,
For in nature's despite he will needs be a knave.
    Then kick out those rascally knaves, boys;
    Freemen we'll be to our graves, boys;
    Better be dead than be slaves, boys;
        A coffin or freedom for me.

VIII.

If a sinner repentant can angels delight,
To Devils and apostates as pleasing a sight,

---

* The Right Hon. Philip Tisdall, attorney general.
† The Right Hon. Hely Hutchinson.

Nor has there been ever such bonfires in hell
Since Judas's fall, as when O——e fell.
    Then kick out those rascally knaves, boys ;
    Freemen we'll be to our graves, boys ;
    Better be dead than be slaves, boys ;
        A coffin or freedom for me !

IX.

But why must I mention the knight of *three crows?*
His name is unworthy of verse or of prose ;
To lash such a reptile would satire disgrace,
'Tis but *ex-officio* he here has a place.
    Then kick out those rascally knaves, boys ;
    Freemen we'll be to our graves, boys ;
    Better be dead than be slaves, boys ;
        A coffin or freedom for me !

X.

Shall such wretches as these o'er our patriots prevail,
And be suffer'd to set our poor country at sale?
No ;—let us all join in defence of our right,
And let Ponsonby, Shannon, and Leinster unite.
    Then kick out those rascally knaves, boys ;
    Freemen we'll be to our graves, boys ;
    Better be dead than be slaves, boys ;
        A coffin or freedom for me !

ADVICE FROM THE LIBERTY :[*]
OR, THE WEAVER'S GARLAND.

I.

My dear fellow-subjects, who love to be free,
Despise not my ballad, but listen to me,
Accept good advice from a brother, a friend,
Who writes for your good, and for no other end.
    Derry down, down, down, derry down.

II.

My name is Dick White, I'm a weaver by trade ;
I hide not my name, since of none I'm afraid ;
And though I want wit, and my verse rudely jingle,
I'll tell you a story shall make your ears tingle.
    Derry, &c.

III.

Our king, heaven bless him and keep him from ill !
Our friend has been ever, and would be so still ;
A curse on those traitors who make him appear
At odds with his people that hold him so dear.
    Derry, &c.

---

[*] Formerly the principal manufacturing district of Dublin, which belonged to the Earl of Meath.

IV.

This rascally herd, to the devil I pitch 'em,
(Must we toil, and labour, and sweat to enrich 'em?)
To serve their own purpose and mischievous ends,
First strive to enslave our American friends.
    Derry, &c.

V.

Nor even of our brethren of England afraid,
With Star Chamber warrants their rights they invade;
And to bring all their villanous schemes to perfection
They strike at the root and the right of election.
    Derry, &c.

VI.

And next at poor Ireland they level their blows;
Poor Ireland, that still has been led by the nose;
And to show they resolv'd both to ruin and fool her,
They send over Townshend, that blockhead, to rule her.
    Derry, &c.

VII.

This Townshend, they knew, would their purposes suit,
For the creature he was and the tool of Lord Bute;
To wade through their dirt he could never refuse,
For, *his character lost*, he had nothing to lose.
    Derry, &c.

VIII.

But lest we should struggle, the villains determine
To add to our number of red-coated vermin;
And swearing 'twas all for the good of the nation,
They got us to yield to their curs'd *Augmentation*.
    Derry, &c.

IX.

And now we have granted them all they could ask,
They laugh at our folly, and throw off the mask;
They aim a bold stroke, all at once to undo
Our honour, our freedom, and property, too.
    Derry, &c.

X.

The Commons, you know, who to us owe their station,
Are our stewards to guard the purse of the nation;
But now they declare, when our money is wanted,
That the Council as well as the Commons shall grant it.
    Derry, &c.

XI.

But G— bless our Commons, I mean the majority,
For Dick would not cry if he damn'd the minority ;
At once they perceived what a mischief was brewing,
And flung out* the bill that was meant for our ruin.
Derry, &c.

XII.

There's Lanesb'rough, and Shannon, and Leinster unite ;
Brave Leinster, our patron, whom none could affright ;
All their friends to the House in a hurry they send,
Who, with Ponsonby joined, may our freedom defend.
Derry, &c.

XIII.

And Charlemont firm, may the Heavens reward him !
Whose heart is still open to us like his garden ;
And Loftus† so powerful, and Longford so true,
All bring up their squadrons the fight to renew.
Derry, &c.

XIV.

O'Brien, and Bingham, and Hussey, and Bushe,
With Flood at their head, the court parricides push,
And Brownlow, and Pery, who reason so just,
And Lucas,‡ our Lucas, still true to his trust !
Derry, &c.

---

* In November, 1769.
† This noble lord, after the transaction here alluded to, in contempt of every social tie, deserted his country and his friends.
‡ " Lucas, for whose unwearied care
To heaven ascends the general prayer,
Whose patriot heart with honest pride
For years hath stemm'd corruption's tide ;
Say thou, 'in various nature wise,'
What boots how pure the fountain rise,
If, tainted by the course it came,
We loathe the violated stream."
 " *The Viceroy*," a Poetical
Caricatura, 1773.

Dr. Charles Lucas, whose statue is placed next to Grattan's in the Royal Exchange, Dublin, now the City Hall, was M.P. for the city of Dublin in the Irish Parliament. His most embittered enemies were compelled to allow him a consistency and uniformity of parliamentary conduct, in which he stood without a rival.

XV.

In fine, the court's routed, and Ireland is sav'd,
With such champions as these we can ne'er be enslaved!
But now, see the spite of this rascally crew,
To the devil I pitch them, and give him his due!
    Derry, &c.
       BARATARIANA.

"Good heav'n! for what peculiar crimes
Beyond the guilt of former times,
Is Ireland ever doom'd by fate
To groan beneath oppression's weight?
To nourish with her best increase
The fell destroyers of her peace?
Domestick traitors to her cause,
Who sell her rights and spurn her laws;
And alien vermin, who devour
Her ripen'd fruit and opening flow'r;
Yet, with illiberal selfish aim,
Confine and circumscribe the stream,
Which bounteous heav'n ordain'd to run
Free as thy beams, all cheering sun!
Insatiate pests of human kind,
Whose poison taints the royal mind,
Corrupts the fountain at its source,
And turns each blessing to a curse!
What crimes, I say, hath Ireland shown
Which Britain claims not as her own?
Hot from the violated bed
Doth rank adultery rear her head
With fouler stains?—'No,' Grafton cries ;*
'No,' Grosvenor for the herd replies.
Or hath some bold bad man appear'd,
To every touch of conscience sear'd,
Form'd by some demon in his rage,
A chosen curse to mark the age,
Who, singular in vice and odd,
Disdains the paths by others trod,
Whose giant guilt hath soar'd so high
It madly rushes to the sky,
And calls from heav'n's vindictive hand
The full perdition on our land?
To Britain turn—there Rigby† thrives;

---

* The breaches of matrimonial contract here pointed at occurred in 1771.

† Rigby thrives—" To preserve unperished the infamy of these detested names (amongst many others equally illustrious), and to hand them down to posterity in their native colours, without diminution or impair, an ingenious gentleman is now (1771)

> Weymouth his country's wreck survives,
> Dashwood yet lives, and Sandwich still
> Claims the pre-eminence in ill :—
> Fall'n as we are, a set so vile
> Was ne'er the produce of *our* Isle.
> Yet, thanks to Russell's generous care,
> This isle her crop in time may bear ;
> In time—but distant be the hour !—
> May nurse a March or boast a G— — r,
> And rival on the rolls of shame
> A Norton's execrable name ;
> Thanks, Russell,—thanks ! the mighty debt
> Ierne never shall forget !
> Safe treasured in her grateful breast
> Thy unexampled bounties rest,
> Thy efforts for her wealth's increase,
> Thy fond attention to her peace ;
> But, chief of all, thy skill refin'd,
> To open and enlarge her mind !
>   *   *   *
> Illusions vain !—Tho' Townshend calls,
> Nor darkness comes, nor mountain falls ;
> Still faithful to her task, the Muse,
> With watchful eye, thy walk pursues ;
> Hangs thee aloft to public scorn,
> The curse of ages yet unborn !
> With Strafford's rolls thy hated name,
> And damns thee to eternal fame."*
>   "*The Viceroy*," *a Poetical Caricatura,
>   Addressed to a certain great Lord.*

IRISH HOUSE OF LORDS—LORD TOWNSHEND'S ADMINISTRATION.

PROTEST I.
IRISH HOUSE OF LORDS.
Dies Veneris, Dec. 22, 1769.

A motion being made, that the Speaker of this House be desired to direct that no protest of any person whomsoever who is not a Lord of Parliament and a member of this

---

preparing for the press a work entitled, 'An History of the British Worthies of our own Times.' In this will appear a full display of the hallowed mysteries of the Monks of Bedmenham Abbey, some anecdotes of the Beefsteak Club, never before published."
—*Baratariana.*

* See Cromwell damn'd to everlasting fame.—POPE.

house, and which doth not respect a matter which hath been previously in question before this house, and wherein the lord protesting had taken part with the minority either in person or by proxy, be entered on the journal of this house, which Lord Townshend did on the 26th of December, 1769.

And a debate arising thereupon, the question was put, and the house divided.

It passed in the negative. The following are the names of the noblemen who signed the protest :—

Lowth, Mountmorris,
Charlemont, Longford.
Powerscourt,

On Friday, the 22nd of December, 1769, the above protest was entered ; notwithstanding which, on the Tuesday following, the Lord Lieutenant went down to the House of Lords, and entered a protest on the Lords' journal against the proceedings of the Commons, in rejecting the Privy Council Money Bill, and alleging their reason for so doing. The House of Commons gave orders to their clerk that the Lord Lieutenant's speech or protest should not be entered upon their journals.

PROTEST II.
IRISH HOUSE OF LORDS.

Dies Lunæ, 4 Martis, 1771.

A motion being made that the paragraph in the address to the King, returning thanks to his Majesty for continuing Lord Townshend in the government, be omitted—it passed in the negative.

* * * We cannot, without violation of truth and justice, return thanks to the King for continuing a chief governor, who, in contempt of all forms of business and rules of decency, heretofore respected by his predecessors, is actuated by the most arbitrary caprice, to the detriment of his Majesty's interests, to the injury of this oppressed country, and to the unspeakable vexation of persons of every condition.

Louth, Moira,
Leinster, Molesworth,
Westmeath, Shannon,
Lanesborough, Mornington,
Powerscourt, Bellamont,
Bective, Longford,
Mountcashel, Baltinglass,
Charlemont, Lisle.

PROTEST III.
IRISH HOUSE OF LORDS.

A motion being made that the protest of Lord Townshend, entered upon the journals of this house on the 26th December, be now expunged ; it passed in the negative.
The following noblemen voted in favour of the motion :—

Lowth,   Molesworth,
Leinster,   Shannon,
Westmeath,   Mornington,
Lanesborough,   Bellamont,
Powerscourt,   Knapton,
Bective,   Longford,
Mountcashel,   Baltinglass,
Charlemont,   Lisle.
Moira,

PROTEST IV.
IRISH HOUSE OF LORDS.

Protest on the institution of a new board of accounts.
The seventeen noblemen who voted in favour of Protest No. III., supported also this motion, with the addition of Lords Sydney and Wandesford.
The protest was negatived.

IRISH HOSPITALITY IN THE LAST CENTURY.
SECTION IX.

DEAN SWIFT, DR. T. SHERIDAN, AND THOMAS MATHEW, CO. TIPPERARY.

THE HUGUENOTS INTRODUCE A SUPERIOR CLASS OF FLORICULTURE INTO IRELAND—AUDOEN'S CHURCH, DUBLIN, AND THE AUDAIN FAMILY—WILLIAM III. AND THE DUTCH STYLE OF GARDENING—SPLENDID GARDENS AT THOMASTOWN, THE COUNTRY SEAT OF MR. MATHEW IN THE LAST CENTURY.

The year after Dean Swift had left Delville, Glasnevin, where he was on a visit with Dr. Delany, he was induced to visit the celebrated Mr. Mathew's place at Thomastown, County Tipperary, where his Royal Highness Prince Arthur, in his recent tour through Ireland, stayed a few days with the noble proprietor. Thomastown castle is the present residence of Major-General the Viscount Chabot, K.C.H., and is supposed to be the Thomastown where Swift and Dr. Sheridan enjoyed themselves for four months.

Mr. Mathew was possessed of a large estate in Tipperary, which produced a clear rent of £10,000 a year. As he delighted in a country life, he resolved to build a large, commodious house for the reception of guests, surrounded by fifteen hundred acres of his choicest land, all laid out upon a regular plan of improvement, according to the then adopted mode of English gardening (which had supplanted the bad Dutch taste, brought in by King William), and of which he was the first who set the example in Ireland; nor was there any improvement of that sort then in England which was comparable to his, either in point of beauty or extent.* As this design was formed

---

* Gardening is entitled to a place of considerable rank among the liberal arts. It is as superior to landscape painting as a reality to representation.—WHEATLY.

The English introduced the *formal* style of gardening into Ireland. Of this style several specimens remained till 1790. Dr. Smith, writing in this year, says:—"At Ballybeggan, in the county of Kerry, there are some good old improvements which escaped the universal devastations of the times, particularly some fine avenues of walnut, chestnut, and other trees, with a large, old, but thriving orchard, planted in a rich limestone ground, beneath which are several subterraneous chambers, lined with stalactitical exudations."[1]

The same author states that, at Bangor, in the county of Down, "there are gardens which are large and handsome, and filled with noble evergreens of a great size, cut in various shapes."

The pensile gardens of *Thomastown*, in the county of Tipperary, were laid out in the reign of Charles II. They lie principally on the gentle declivity of a hill, resting on terraces and filled with

"Statues thick as trees."

---

[1] "History of the County Kerry."—Subterranean structures of high antiquity abound in Ireland; but the vaults at Ballybeggan were probably coeval with the gardens, and built in imitation of the ancient English bower. Rosamond's bower is supposed to have been of that kind. See *Anecd. of Paint. in England*, vol. iv., p. 263.

early in life, in order to accomplish his point, without incurring any debt on his estate, he retired to the Continent for seven years, and lived upon six hundred pounds a year, while the remaining income of his estate was employed in carrying on the great works he had planned at Thomastown. When all was com-

A long fish-pond sleeping under "a green mantle" between two rectilineous banks, appears in the midst. And in one corner stands a verdant theatre (once the scene of several dramatic exhibitions), displaying all the absurdity of the architecture of gardening.

In the reign of Charles II. we find some of the clergy of the Established Church content to forego the academic shade and the luxury of pleasure-grounds, soliciting permission of Parliament to turn their gardens to account. Their prayer being propitiously heard, an act was accordingly ordained, enabling the *Precentor* and *Treasurer* of the Cathedral Church of *St. Patrick's*, Dublin, and the *Archdeacon* of Dublin, to make leases of part of their yards and gardens for sixty years.

The French and Italian mode of gardening, which had been introduced by the English, continued to prevail in Ireland until the arrival of William III., when it soon yielded to the Belgian style.[1]

Such of his followers as settled here indulged their passion for "trim gardens;" instead of mending, they changed the features of nature, totally regardless of this golden precept—
"Consult the genius of the place in all."

Extensively acquainted with the vegetable kingdom, to them we probably owe the introduction of flowers. These they displayed in giant knots, designed with geometric skill, and edged with box.[2]

Moryson says that, in his time, "Ireland was not quite destitute of flowers," and instances the county of Kilkenny as most abounding in them.[3]

A few flowers might, perhaps, have been propagated by the

---

[1] Of this style a specimen was given under his Majesty's auspices in his gardens at Chapelizod, near Dublin, which are now (1740) a scene of desolation. In the year 1717, an overseer of these gardens was placed on the Civil establishment, with a salary of £120 per annum.

[2] Barras, or box, employed in edging the knots, was an article of importation in the reign of Charles II.

[3] It is recorded that when the Earl of Essex, in his progress through Ireland, in the year 1520, visited Kilkenny, amongst other demonstrations of joy, the streets were strewed with flowers.—*Anthologia Hibernica.*

pleted he returned to his native country; and after some time passed in Dublin, to revive the old, and cultivate new acquaintance, he retired to his country seat, to pass the remainder of his days there. As he was considered one of the finest gentlemen of the age, and possessed of so large a property, he found no difficulty, during his residence in Dublin, to get access to all those whose character, for talents or probity, made him desirous to cultivate their acquaintance.

Out of these he selected such as were most conformable to his taste, inviting them to pass such leisure time as they might have upon their hands at

English settlers; but it is to the Huguenots we are to attribute their diffusion through the kingdom.[1]

It was principally exotics they introduced. Walker in his *Progress of Gardening in Ireland*, says, that in the reign of George I., "Many a beautiful flower grew spontaneously in several parts of this kingdom, where the human foot has seldom made an impression."[2]

To the Huguenots, too, we are chiefly indebted for our knowledge of the use of the shears, that enemy "to the long wildness of form with which nature (says the elegant Walpole) has distinguished each various species of trees and shrubs."

This direful engine began its depredations in the neighbourhood of Dublin, and continued them, with unremitting fury, amongst all the noblemen's and gentlemen's seats in the kingdom. Neither

---

[1] In the reign of George I. some of the Huguenots of Dublin, together with a few citizens, formed themselves into a club, called "The Florists' Club," for the purpose of furthering the cultivation of flowers in Ireland. They held their meetings for many years at the Rose Tavern, in Drumcondra-lane (now Dorset-street, Dublin), where they adjudged premiums to the members who produced the most beautiful flowers to the club on given days. This club existed till the close of the reign of George II. The Rose Tavern was in being up to 1793.

[2] Mr. Leslie, in his poem of "Killarney," speaks of several flowers and shrubs growing naturally on the mountain of Mangerton, in the early part of the 18th century, which hold a distinguished place, rank amongst the favourite productions of the modern gardens in 1792; but he omits the myrtle, which flourishes not only in the wilds of the counties of Wexford and Wicklow, but on several islands in the Lakes of Killarney.

Thomastown. As there was something uncommonly singular in his mode of living, such as was never carried into practice by any mortal before in an equal degree, the reader will not be displeased with an account of the particulars, the first account of which was published in 1761.

His house had been chiefly contrived to answer the noble purpose of that constant hospitality which

a box nor a yew tree was now to be found which had not assumed the human shape, or that of some inferior animal.[1]
Like Milton's genius of the woods, to
"———————— curl the grove
With ringlets quaint,"
was now the business of every gardener. Even water was no longer permitted to flow in the undulating line of nature; checked in its course, it was spread into an expanse, which a mathematical figure was taught to circumscribe. Such is the powerful influence of custom, that though "the mind of man (says Addison) naturally hates everything that looks like a restraint upon it, and is apt to fancy itself under a sort of confinement when the sight is pent up in a narrow compass," yet these formal followers of King William, strangers, perhaps, or averse to the sunk fence, rear lofty walls around their improvements, and unkindly shut out the view of the neighbouring country. However, they are to be excused:

[1] "An old gentleman of my acquaintance (J. C. Walker, M.R.I.A., 1792), remembers to have seen in Mr. Forteck's garden, near Drumcondra, Dublin, the figures of men with their arms in various positions, cut in yew and box; and the figure of a colossal goose in the latter. He recollects, also, to have observed, in the garden of Beamore, in the county of Meath, the representation of a large cock, with bristled feathers, cut in yew. In the gardens of Bullen, New-street, Dublin (now O'Keefe's nursery), which were laid out in the reign of Queen Anne, there was a bare hunt and a boar hunt in box. The first pine apples produced in Ireland were raised by Bullen, a native of Westmoreland, who settled in the vicinity of Dublin in the reign of Queen Anne. He had a a nursery in New street, consisting of four acres, which he rented from one Rowe, who had been his predecessor in that line. It is supposed that the fantastical fashion of cutting yew and box, so as to represent the human figure, &c., was in earlier date in Ireland than 1700. An anonymous traveller, in describing Bishop Usher's Palace at Drogheda, says, 'here is a prettie neat garden, and over against the window, in the gallery end, upon a bank, these words in fair great letters are written—
'Oh, man, remember the last great day.'"

he intended to maintain there. It contained fifty commodious apartments for guests, with suitable accommodations to their servants. Each apartment was completely furnished with every convenience that could be wanted, even to the minutest article. When a guest arrived, he shewed him his apartment, saying, " This is your castle, here you are to command as absolutely as in your own house ; you may breakfast, dine, and sup here whenever you please, and invite such of the guests to accompany you as may be most agreeable to you." He then shewed him the common

they came from a country incapable of landscape. But they did not confine their constraint of nature to the limits of the garden ; they trammelled her wherever they attempted to heighten her charms. The whole demesne confessed their tyrannic power. Even the avenue assumed the gloom and appearance of the Gothic cloister; the stately pine, the murky fir, or the "star proof" elm, were marshalled in fraternal rows, nodding at each other, until their intermingled branches formed a verdant canopy, excluding the face of Heaven.[1]

Passing from this gloom, you ascended to the dwelling-house "with aching feet," terraces piled on terraces, covered with green parterres "buttoned round" with flower-pots, and bearing on pedestals in their centres the whole progeny of the heathen deities.

But nature, with the aid of taste, has at length prevailed, and proclaimed, with an exalted voice, her proud behests through the land :—

" ———— At the awful sound
The terrace sinks spontaneous ; on the green,
Broidered with crisped knots, the tonsile yews
Wither and fall ; the fountain dares no more
To fling its wasted crystal through the sky,
But pours salubrious o'er the parched lawn
Rills of fertility."
—*Mason's* "*Eng. Garden,*" cant. ii.

Walker, in concluding his admirable essay on the Rise and Progress of Gardening in Ireland, says :—

"Did I not fear I should exceed the limits which I have prescribed to this Essay, I would give a descriptive enumeration o

---

[1] "Some years since (1792) I saw in the Earl of Clanbrassil's garden, near Dundalk, a walk answering the description. It reminded me of the long vista through a Gothic Cathedral ; and might, I think, be safely adduced in support of Bishop Warburton's ingenious conjecture concerning the original of Gothic architecture."— *Walker.*

Rise and Progress of Gardening in Ireland. 301

parlour, "where" he said, "a daily ordinary was kept, at which he might dine when it was more agreeable to him to mix in society; but from this moment,

several demesnes in this kingdom, which Browne, the successor of Kent (that great competitor of Nature), would be proud to number with the happiest proofs of his genius. It is, indeed, with much reluctance I lay down my pen without essaying to do justice to the beauties of Marino,[1] Castletown,[2] Carton,[3] Curraghmore,[4] the sweet sequestered seat of St. Wolstan's,[5] or the paradise which the Earl of Moira has opened in the County Down.[6]

It is recorded that the "Fagans of Feltrim" devoted much of their time to floriculture. This ancient Irish family are buried in St. Audoen's Church, Dublin,[6] with a number of other distinguished Irishmen.

---

[1] Lord Charlemont's country seat, near Clontarf.
[2] Near Leixlip, the country seat of Thomas Conolly, Esq., M.P.
[3] The country seat of His Grace the Duke of Leinster.
[4] The magnificent seat of the Marquis of Waterford.
[5] The charming residence of Edward Cane, Esq., J.P., Celbridge, Co. Kildare.

[6] AUDOEN'S CHURCH, DUBLIN.—THE AUDAIN FAMILY.

This edifice, from its remains, appears to have originally consisted of a "very extensive pile of building, which was divided in the centre by a range of eight pointed arches and their piers, extending from west to east. These arches appear of an equilateral shape, and of a regular uniform size. The mouldings, even now, bear evidence of very good workmanship, and the capitals of the piers are composed of mouldings nearly circular." The history of the Audoins or Audains, of which family the pious and illustrious St. Audoin, the founder of an order, to whose memory this church was built and dedicated, was so bright an ornament, is eminently characteristic of the strange vicissitudes of families. Audoin, the founder of the family, the guardian of the son of Walter, succeeded him to the throne of the Longobards in A. D. 548 (Valesius). He was celebrated for his justice, indomitable energy and fortitude (Gibbon's Fall and Decline of the Roman Empire), and was particularly memorable for having led the Lombards into Pannonia, part of which the Emperor Justinian ceded to him, giving him the Thuringian princess, Rodelinda, a daughter of King Hermanfrid, in marriage. Audoin conquered Thorissimus, the King of the Gepidæ, and was succeeded by his son, Alboin, who finally overthrew the Gepidæ, and with his victorious Lombards invaded Italy, and established himself at Milan, taking with him the celebrated Iron Crown, and forming an epoch in the history of the nation. The fate of Alboin was highly tragic. He was poisoned at Verona by his wife, Rosamond,

you are never to know me as master of the house, and only to consider me as one of the guests." In order to put an end to all ceremony at meal time, he took his place at random at the table; and thus all

the daughter of his foe, the last king of the Gepidæ, in revenge for having caused her to drink his health out of a goblet fashioned from her father's skull. The descendants of Audoenus were driven out of Italy by Charlemagne, when they settled in Normandy. There was a saint, besides a pope, bishop, archbishops, writers on divinity, military science, natural history, and other subjects, among the distinguished men of the family. St. Audoin was blessed by St. Columbanus, in requital for hospitality shown to the great Leinster missionary by the saint's father, a nobleman of Brie (Gilbert's History of Dublin). St. Audoin afterwards became highly eminent for piety, and acquired the favour of Clothaire II., to whose successor, Dagobert, he was appointed chancellor. A handsome abbey church was dedicated to St. Audoin, at Rouen, regarded as one of the finest specimens extant of pointed Gothic architecture, and in it were deposited the heart of Richard Cœur de Lion, and the remains of most of the early rulers of Normandy. In 918 the relics of Audoin and Langefrid were placed under the protection of St. Germain, in the delicious vale of Campaign Villiers, on the borders of his camp, near Port Orson. The period of the erection of St. Audoen's Church in Dublin, by the Anglo-Norman settlers, in honour of the patron saint of the capital of their original country, is not recorded, but the parish of St. Audoin appears to have been founded before the close of the twelfth century. This church was highly esteemed, and many important families made it their burial-place, including those of FitzEustace, Molyneux, Ball, Bath, Blakeney, Browne, Cusack, Desminier, Fagan of Feltrim, Foster of Ballydowd, Fyan, Gifford, Gilbert, Malone, Mapas, Molesworth, Pulteney, Perceval, Quinn, Talbot, Usher, Henrys, &c.

The subsequent history of the Audoins or Audains, as they came to spell their name, the old French (o) being changed into (a) is not uninteresting. They remained as a family of consequence in Normandy, possessing large landed estates at Rouen, at Caen, and Brotend, at which latter place was a "palace of chase, in the vast Arelaunensis silva," frequented by the kings of the Moravingian, or second race of Franko-Saxon kings—until the revocation of the Edict of Nantes, at which period, having embraced the new religious opinions of the Huguenots, they were forced to quit France, emigrating to the West Indies, where they purchased large sugar plantations. John Audain married while there the daughter of Lord Mulgrave, afterwards Earl of Normandy, and his son, who was married to a Miss Payne, heiress-at-law to Lord Lavington, was educated at Winchester by his uncle, Colonel Phipps, the intimate companion of the then Prince of Wales, afterwards George IV. He was distinguished succes-

ideas of precedence being laid aside, the guests seated themselves promiscuously, without any regard to rank or quality. There was a large room fitted up exactly like a coffee-house, where a bar-maid and waiters attended to furnish refreshments at all times of the day. Here, such as chose it, breakfasted at their own hour. It was furnished with chess-boards,

sively as a soldier, a sailor, and a large landowner in the West Indies, a mining capitalist in South America, a churchman, and eminent popular preacher in Bath, and president of the Republic of San Domingo or Hayti. This remarkable man, who could fight, write, preach, bargain and sell, or legislate, with equal facility, and could deliver an extempore address, or harangue a mob in several different languages, signalized himself by the exhibition of indomitable heroism, great fertility of resources, and military and strategic talent in numerous encounters with the Spanish and French expeditions against the West Indian Islands, voluntarily placing his privateering vessels and the tenants on his estates, in the hour of danger, at the service of the English Government. At the siege of St. Kitts, by a French fleet, he organized and headed the defence in person, and defeated the Marquis of Bouillé, who was so charmed with his gallantry and military skill that, afterwards learning he was of French extraction, offered him a high command in the army, and the restoration of his family property in Normandy, which had been forfeited to the French Government, if he would join the French, and that if he refused, his government contemplated converting the chateaux and estates into a model-farm. The offer to betray the country of his asylum, his adoption, and his inclinations, was rejected with scorn by the gallant emigré, who, some years afterwards, in accordance with the spirit of the lax and stirring age in which he lived, although at the time in holy orders, he headed the defence of the Island of Dominica, which was besieged by the French, and ably kept the enemy at bay until an English squadron came to the rescue. The published memoirs of this distinguished man, who, at different times, made and dissipated several fortunes (and of which Coleridge's "Six Months in the West Indies" is, in great part, a reprint), teemed with hairbreadth escapes and anecdotes of eccentricity; and several novelists, including Sir Walter Scott, have been indebted for some of the most trenchant episodes in their works to the facts and realities of his life. His grandson, Colonel Willett Payne Audain, at present residing at Fitzroy-avenue, Belfast, is the surviving representative of this historic family. He has in his possession several valuable memoirs, besides a rare collection of antique sculpture of great value, which his grandfather, the Rev. Dr. John Audain, purchased from one of Napoleon's generals, who had taken it out of the pope's palace at Rome.

back-gammon tables, newspapers, pamphlets, &c., in all the forms of a Dublin coffee-house. But the most extraordinary circumstance in his whole domestic arrangement, was that of a detached room in one of the extremities of the house, called the tavern. As he was himself a very temperate man, and many of his guests were of the same disposition, the quantity of wine for the common room was but moderate; but as drinking was much in fashion in those days, in order to gratify such of his guests as had indulged themselves in that custom, he had recourse to the above-mentioned contrivance; and it was the custom of all who loved a cheerful glass, to adjourn to the tavern soon after dinner, and leave the more sober folks to themselves. Here a waiter, in a blue apron, attended (as was the fashion then), and all things in the room were contrived so as to humour the illusion. Here every one called for what liquor he liked, with as little restraint, as if he were really in a hotel. Here, too, the midnight orgies of Bacchus were often celebrated, with the same noisy mirth as is customary in his city temples, without in the least disturbing the repose of the more sober part of the family. Games of all sorts were allowed, but under such restrictions as to prevent gambling; and so as to answer their true end—that of amusement—without injury to the purse of the players. There were two billiard-tables, and a large bowling-green; ample provision was made for all such as delighted in country sports; fishing tackle of all sorts; variety of guns, with proper ammunition; a pack of buckhounds, another of foxhounds, and another of harriers. He constantly kept twenty choice hunters in his stables, for the use of those who were not properly mounted for the chase. It may be thought that his income was not sufficient to support so expensive an establishment; but when it is considered that ten thousand a-year at that time was fully equal to double that sum at present; that his large demesne, in some of the richest soil in Ireland, furnished the house with every necessary except groceries and wine, it may be supposed to be easily practicable, if under the regulation of a strict economy; of which no man was a greater master. His plan was so well formed, and he had such checks upon all his domestics, that it was impossible there could be any waste; or that any article from the larder, or a single bottle of wine from the cellar could have been purloined without immediate detection. This was done partly by the choice of faithful stewards, and clerks of approved integrity; but chiefly by his own superintendence of the whole, as not a day passed without having all the accounts of the preceding one laid before him. This he was enabled to do by his early rising; and the business being finished before others were out of their beds, he always appeared the most disengaged man in the house, and seemed to have as little conduct of it as any of the guests. And, indeed, to a stranger he might pass for such; as he made it a point that no one should consider him in the light of master of the house; nor pay him the least civilities on that score; which he carried so far, that he sometimes went abroad without giving any notice, and staid away several days, while things went on as usual at home; and, on his return, he would not allow any gratulations to be made to him, nor any notice to be taken of him, than if he had not been absent during that time. The arrangements of every sort were so prudently made that no multiplicity of guests, or their domestics, ever occasioned any disorder; and all things were conducted with the same ease and regularity as in a private family. There was one point which seemed of great difficulty, that of establishing certain signals, by which each servant might know when he was summoned to his master's apartment. For this purpose, there was a great hall appropriated to their use where they always assembled when they were not on duty. Along the wall bells were ranged in order, one to each apartment, with the number of the chamber marked over it; so that when any one of them was rung, they had only to turn their eyes to the bell, and see what servant was called. He was the first to put an end to that inhospitable custom of giving vales to servants, by making a suitable addition to their wages; at the same time assuring them, that if they ever took any afterwards, they should be discharged with disgrace; and, to prevent temptation, the guests were informed, that Mr. Mathew would consider it as the highest affront if any offer of that sort were made.

As Swift had heard much of the place from Dr. Sheridan, who had been often a welcome guest there, both on account of his companionable qualities, and as being preceptor to the nephew of Mr. Mathew, he was desirous of seeing, with his own eyes, whether the report of it were true, which he could not help thinking to have been much exaggerated. Upon receiving an intimation of this from Dr. Sheridan, Mr. Mathew wrote a polite letter to the Dean, requesting the honour of a visit, in company with the Doctor, on his next school vacation. They set out accordingly on horseback, attended by a gentleman who was a near relation of Mr. Mathew. They had scarce reached the inn where they were to pass the first night, and which, like most of the Irish inns at that time, afforded but miserable entertainment, when a coach and six arrived, sent to convey them the remainder of their journey to Thomastown; and at the same time bringing store of the choicest viands, wine, and other liquors for their refreshment. Swift was highly pleased with this uncommon mark of attention paid him, and the circumstance of the coach proved particularly agreeable, as he had been a good deal fatigued with his day's journey. When they came within sight of the house, the Dean, astonished at its magnitude, cried out: " What in the name of God can be the use of such a vast building ?" " Why, Mr. Dean," cried out their fellow-traveller, before mentioned, " there's no less than forty apartments for guests in that house, and all of them, probably, occupied at this time, except what are reserved for us." Swift, in his usual manner, bawled out to the coachman to stop, and bade him turn about and drive him back to Dublin, for he could not think of mixing with such a crowd. " Well," said he, suddenly afterwards, "there is no remedy, I must submit; but I have lost a fortnight of my life." Mr. Mathew received him at the door with uncommon marks of respect, and then conducting him to his apartment, after some compliments, made him his usual speech, acquainting him with the customs of the house, and then retired, leaving him in possession of his castle. Soon after the cook appeared with his bill of fare, to receive his directions about supper, and the butler at the same time with a list of wines and other liquors. "And is all this really so," said Swift, "and may I command here as in my own house?" The gentleman before mentioned assured him he might, and that nothing could be more agreeable to the owner of that mansion than that all under his roof should live conformably to their own inclinations, without the least restraint. " Well, then," said Swift, " I invite you and Dr. Sheridan* to be my guests while I stay, for I

---

* Dr. Thomas Sheridan the personal friend of Dean Swift, who enjoyed Mr. Mathew's hospitality at Thomastown, published in 1719, with the concurrence of the Dean, his "Arts Pun-ica, sive Flos Linquarum in seventy-nine rules, for the further improvement of conversation and help of memory. By the labour and industry of Tom Pun-Sibi."—Dublin, 1719.

About this time, 1719, punning was so fashionable in Ireland, that ladies were as much infected with its contagion as the gentlemen ; it was the amusement of every party, and was a species of wit with which every one seemed to be bewitched. Dr. Sheridan

think I shall hardly be tempted to mix with the mob below." Three days were passed in riding over the demesne, and viewing the several improvements, without ever seeing Mr. Mathew or any of his guests; nor were the company below much concerned at his absence, as his very name used to inspire those who did not know him with awe; and they were afraid his presence would put an end to that case and cheerfulness which reigned among them. On the fourth day Swift entered the room where the company were assembled before dinner, and addressed Mr. Mathew, in one of the finest complimental speeches that ever

wrote this work, turning punuing into ridicule, as the only effectual means to cure this folly.

Dean Swift subscribed to the work, and addressed the following verses to the Author.

"Had I ten thousand mouths and tongues,
Had I ten thousand pair of lungs;
Ten thousand skulls with brains to think,
Ten thousand standishes of ink,
Ten thousand hands and pens to write,
Thy praise I'd study day and night.
O may thy work for ever live
(Dear Tom, a friendly zeal forgive).
May no vile miscreant saucy cook
Presume to bear thy learned book;
Or singe his fowl for nicer guest,
Or pin it on the turkey's breast.
Keep it from pastry bak'd or flying,
From broiling stakes and fritters frying;
From lighting pipe or making snuff,
Or casing up a feather muff.
From all the several ways the grocer,
Who to the learn'd world's a foe, Sir,
Has found in twisting, folding, packing
His brains and ours at once a racking.
And may it never curl the head
Of either living block or dead.
Thus when all dangers they have passed,
Your leaves like leaves of brass shall last.
No blast shall from a critic's breath,
By vile infection cause their death;
Till they in flames at last expire
And help to set the world on fire."

was made, in which he expatiated on all the beauties of his improvements, with the skill of an artist, and the taste of a connoisseur. He showed that he had a full comprehension of the whole of the plan, and of the judicious adaptation of the parts to the whole; and pointed out several articles which had escaped general observation. Such an address from a man of Swift's character, could not fail of being pleasing to the owner, who was at the same time the planner of these improvements; and so fine an eulogium from one who was supposed to deal more in satire than panegyric, was likely to remove the prejudice entertained against his character, and prepossess the rest of the company in his favour. He concluded his speech by saying: "And now, ladies and gentlemen, I am come to live among you, and it shall be no fault of mine if we do not pass our time agreeably." After dinner, being in high spirits, he entertained the company with several pleasantries. Dr. Sheridan and he played into one another's hands; they joked, they punned, they laughed, and a general gaiety was diffused through the whole company. In a short time all constraint on his account disappeared. He entered readily into all their little schemes of promoting mirth, and every day, with the assistance of his coadjutor, produced some new one which afforded a good deal of sport and merriment. Never were such joyous scenes known there before; for when to ease and cheerfulness there is superadded at times the higher enjoyment of gay wit, lively fancy, and droll humour, nothing can be wanting to the perfection of the social pleasures of life. When the time came which obliged Dr. Sheridan to return to his school, the company were so delighted with the Dean, that they earnestly entreated him to stay there some time longer; and Mr. Mathew himself for once broke through his rule of never soliciting the stay of any guest (it being the established custom of the house that all might depart when they thought proper without any ceremony of leave-taking), by joining in the request. Swift found himself so happy in his situation there, that he readily yielded to their solicitations; and, instead of the fortnight which he had originally intended, passed four months there, much to his own satisfaction, and that of all those who visited the place at that time. Having given an account of the owner of this happy mansion, I shall now relate an adventure he was engaged in of so singular a kind as deserves well to be recorded. It was towards the latter end of Queen Anne's reign, when Mr. Mathew returned to Dublin after his long residence abroad. At that time party spirit ran very high, but raged nowhere with such violence as in that city, insomuch, that duels were every day fought there on that score. There happened to be, at that time, two gentlemen in London who valued themselves highly on their skill in fencing; the name of one was Pack, of the other Creed; the former a major, the latter a captain in the army. Hearing of these daily exploits in Dublin, they resolved, like two knights errant, to go over in quest of adventure. Upon inquiry, they learned that Mr. Mathew, lately arrived from France, had the character of being one of the first swordsmen in Europe. Pack, rejoiced to find an antagonist worthy of him, resolved, the first opportunity, to pick a quarrel with him; and meeting him as he was carried along the streets in his chair, jostled the fore-chairman. Of this Mathew took no notice, as supposing it to be accidental. But Pack afterwards boasted of it in the public coffee-house, saying, that he had purposely offered this insult to the gentleman who had not the spirit to resent it. There happened to be present a particular friend of Mr. Mathew of the name of Macnamara, a man of tried courage, and reputed the best fencer in Ireland. He immediately took up the quarrel, and said he was sure Mr. Mathew did not suppose the affront intended, otherwise he would have chastised him on the spot; but if the major would let him know where he was to be found, he should be waited on immediately on his friend's return, who was to dine a little way out of town. The major said he should be at the tavern over the way, where he and his companions would wait their commands. Immediately on his arrival, Mathew, being made acquainted with what had passed, went from the coffee-house to the tavern accompanied by Macnamara. Being shown into the room where the two gentlemen were, after having secured the door, without any expostulation, Mathew and Pack drew their swords; but Macnamara stopped them, saying he had something to propose before they proceeded to action. He said in cases of this nature, he could never bear to be a cool spectator; so, Sir, addressing himself to Creed, if you please, I shall have the honour of entertaining you in the same manner. Creed, who desired no better sport, made no other reply than that of instantly drawing his sword, and to work the four champions fell, with the same composure as if it were only a fencing-match with foils. The conflict was of some duration, and maintained with great obstinacy by the two officers, notwithstanding the great effusion of blood from the many wounds they had received. At length, quite exhausted, they both fell, and yielded the victory to the superior skill of their antagonists.

Upon this occasion Mathew gave a remarkable proof of the perfect composure of his mind during the action. Creed had fallen the first, upon which Pack exclaimed, " Ah, poor Creed! are you gone?" " Yes," said Mathew, very composedly, and you shall instantly *pack after him*," at the same time making a home thrust quite through his body, which threw him to the ground. This was the more remarkable as he was never in his life, either before or after, known to have aimed at a pun. The number of wounds received by the vanquished parties was very great; and, what seems almost miraculous, their opponents were untouched. The surgeons, seeing the desperate state of their patients, would not suffer them to be removed out of the room where they fought, but had beds immediately conveyed into it, on which they lay many hours in a state of insensibility. When they came to themselves, and saw where they were, Pack, in a feeble voice, said to his companion, Creed, I think we are conquerors, for we have kept the field of battle. For a long time their lives were despaired of; but, to the astonishment of everyone, they both recovered. When they were able to see company, Mr. Mathew and his friend attended them daily, and a close intimacy afterwards ensued, as they found them men of probity and of the best dispositions, except in the Quixotish idea of duelling, whereof they were now perfectly cured.

Curran, in one of his celebrated speeches, thus beautifully described the *native* hospitality of his country: "The hospitality of other countries is a matter of necessity, or convention; in savage nations, of the first; in polished, of the latter; but the hospitality of an Irishman is not the running account of *posted* and *legered* courtesies, as in other countries— it springs, like all his other qualities, his faults, his virtues, directly from the heart. The heart of an Irishman is by nature bold, and he confides; it is tender, and he loves; it is generous, and he gives; it is social, and he is hospitable."

SECTION X.

BRAY.

"Bray's threatening top, high o'er the seas,
Appears to soar on yonder sky;
Lo! at his feet the trembling waves!
His brows the thunder's force defy!"

BRAY (the Brighton of Ireland and principal rendezvous of tourists visiting the charming and sublime scenery of the county Wicklow) has grown rapidly into great favour and importance, from the splendid improvements which have rendered it a choice suburban retreat of exquisite beauty and singular attractions.

The magnificent Esplanade, of considerable extent, and beautiful in the extreme, with a fine view of the sea coast, forms a grand, fashionable promenade.

It extends along the verge of the sunny shore, decorated in profusion with an endless variety of rare and curious pebbles and shells, nearly pellucid, and of every imaginable form and species. The sparkling, murmuring waves, crested with white silvery foam, gracefully lave the shore, and fringe the Esplanade, as with a border of silver, from the northern extremity of the cozy bay, nestling, as it were, beneath the venerable shadow of its "heath-crowned head," to the embouchure of the limpid and picturesque Dargle river, of "trout celebrity," where that stream unites its fresh, pure, and glistening waters with the briny waves.

Bray Strand, a shelving shore, with gracefully eddying billowy waves—the fine appearance of the adjacent country in the highest state of cultivation, having a surface-soil, rich and fertile, resting on a warm bed

of granite formation.* Beautiful and stately marine villas, well-arranged terraces, and mansions of noble proportions and architectural beauty, palatial hotels, oriental concert rooms.†
Rich and beautiful prospects of land and sea (charming views, which exhibit nature and art in the rarest combinations). Bray Head,‡ a commanding promontory, rising boldly from the sea to an elevation of 807 feet, with rugged, indented, storm-lashed creeks, and towering, beetling brow (over whose steep sides traverses the Dublin, Wicklow, and Wexford Railway), with Alpine loftiness, sharp curves, and serpentine sinuosity, where the

"Billowy anthems ne'er will sleep, until the close of time."

How glorious is the scene which the Bray Esplanade presents on a moonlight night, " ere the summer tints grow pale." Such scenes awaken in the reflecting mind, calm, pure, holy thoughts and aspirations, and emotions, whilst listening to the exquisite yet mournful music of the ever-chanting main.

* The granite of Wicklow covers an area of nearly 140 square miles or about 84,000 acres.—*Robert Frazer*, 1801.

† These elegant and curiously embellished structures were originally designed for Turkish baths, where invalids and convalescents might not only "face the breeze and catch its sweetness" (availing themselves of a change of air, most congenial to their delicacy of constitution), but revel in the luxury of an Eastern bath, with all its anodyne accompaniments and restorative qualities, whilst sojourning in the pursuit of health, pleasure, and relaxtion in the capital (so to speak) refined and aristocratic—of picturesque Wicklow, within an easy distance of the grand and wondrous scenery of this charming county.

‡ On the sides of the dark and precipitous cliffs of Bray headland, the curlew, cormorant, and gull, were wont formerly to build their nests, and in the winter months kept up a continual and clamorous chorus ; and by their discordant, melancholy screams, emulated the war of the elements, out-rivalling the boisterous howling of the wintry winds, and the hoarse solemn roar of the rolling waves. But now the march of improvement, and the rapid increase of population, have caused these birds to disappear, and retire to more congenial and wilder regions, so that they are rarely to be seen in the vicinity of Bray at present— "*tempora mutantur.*"

"The wind was hush'd,
And to the beach each slowly-lifted wave,
Creeping with silver curl, just kissed the shore,
And slept in silence."

The air (extremely salubrious, and most genial in the summer months) is, even in the depth of winter, comparatively mild and clear—bracing and invigorating.

The town itself—on one side open to the sea, and bounded on the south by the bold headland, "Bray Head," and the Sugar-loaf Mountains, overlooking the "Valley of Diamonds," in view—is encompassed by grand and beautiful scenery. All these attractions and advantages combine to render Bray a favorite place of abode with the nobility and gentry. No wonder that progress and prosperity should, in an eminent degree, result.

And now to speak of the enterprise and energy of the worthy and zealous men who designed and carried out, at vast labour and expense, the various and grand improvements, to whom Bray is principally indebted for its rising prosperity and proud position.

First and prominent, stands the name of the late noble-minded, generous, and good William Dargan, a man of nature's true nobility. By him the sea-beach, from the mouth of the Dargle river to Bray Head, was levelled, a good road formed, the Esplanade planned and perfected, and the Turkish baths built.

Sir William Wilde, the eminent physician, erected several ranges of first-class mansions along the shore, overlooking the Esplanade.

However, Bray, in a great measure, owes its present proud position to Quin,* Breslin, Fortune, and

* Mr. J. Quin may be justly styled the father of Bray. His hotel had a European reputation. He lived many years to enjoy the affectionate intercourse of his numerous friends. "Quin, of Bray," had a kindness of heart which made every tourist who visited Wicklow his well-wisher. He was also a celebrated agriculturist.

the much-lamented Brennan, who built the International Hotel, whose many useful and amiable qualities are recorded in the hearts of his friends. His successful exertions for the improvement of Bray, have left lasting testimonies of his merit with the public. Mr. Edward Breslin is now the ruling spirit of progress and the presiding genius of Bray's future prosperity. In his hands the *International Hotel* has risen, Phœnix-like, from the ashes of decay. The "Royal Marine Hotel," which faces the grand Esplanade of Bray, is also the sole property of Mr. Breslin, This aristocratic and fashionable marine residence is patronized by the nobility of Great Britain and Ireland, as well as of France, Italy, and Germany. These spirited and enterprising men, with sustained energy and noble self-reliance, performed their role in the drama of life ; and by their example, excited their countrymen to emulate their virtues and their worth.

A writer in the *Dublin University Magazine* truly says :—" Let Irishmen cease to revile or envy England, and seek to emulate, if not to equal her. With more native talent, if prudently directed, and as much energy, if properly sustained, we have but to try, to persevere, and to succeed. Let Ireland plant her young shoots henceforth rather in the soil of principle than that of impulse; let her girdle her loins with honourable endeavour ; and, above all, casting aside for ever the whine of entreaty and the rags of her mendicancy, let her weave for herself the rough but honest garment of independence—of the *true Dargan* pattern—the robe of self-respect, warmest near the heart, in which she will walk as a queen and a lady, amidst the applause of nations, and shine forth more 'great, glorious, and free,' than ever she could have done had she listened to the voice of agitation, and unsheathed the wild but fruitless sword of rebellion."

The pithy and brilliant Shiel, in his speech in the House of Commons upon the discussion of the " Repeal of the Union," emphatically exclaimed—"What! Repeal the Union! RESTORE the Heptarchy." The same illustrious orator termed the Repeal movement "*A splendid phantom;*" and truly the impolicy of that philosophy which seeks the unattainable, closely resembles the instance of canine sagacity in the fable—" The dog swimming in the river, grasping at the shadow, and losing the substance."

These worthy and true-hearted Irishmen, Dargan, Breslin, Putland, Quin, Wilde, Brennan, Radley, Kelly, Dr. Stewart, &c. (the founders of modern Bray), sought no visionary shadows; they effected substantial realities—and by their peaceful achievements for the advancement and prosperity of their native land, merit more justly *living honour*, and the grateful remembrance of posterity, than the proud and triumphant conqueror, who has risen on spoil, rapine, and desolation, to dignities, greatness, and fame.

Among the residents and visitors at Bray, the number of distinguished artists is worthy of special comment. When a country is progressing in opulence and civilization, Art progresses *pari passu*, and the residence of many of that honoured profession is presumptive, nay, conclusive evidence of the gradual increase of wealth and refinement. May we hope that Art will be more generally diffused through every part of our land.*

Bray, also, in addition to its natural attractions and the improvements referred to, owes its prosperity to a great extent in being blessed with a resident nobility and gentry. Bray and the surrounding

* At present Art is almost nothing in Ireland. It is unpatronised, undervalued, if not despised. Our great names adorn the English Academy; not that they prefer another country to their own, but because they are unappreciated at home. If, however, the love of Art should spread, and exercise as wide an influence among us as in some of the Continental states, then may we expect to mature a Maclise, a Foley, an Edwin Hayes, a Kendrick, a Charles Nicholls, a Marquess, a Brunton, and a M'Dowell, and retain them where all their sympathies are centred—in the land of their birth.

country has a large and beneficent band of *ever resident and generous landlords*,* who spend their income from year to year at home, in useful improvements for the fertilization of the soil from which they derive their rents. This is what gives to this part of Wicklow and Dublin that peculiar look of refinement, that happiness and high cultivation, which there generally prevail. Would to God that the same sentiments that animate and influence the minds of these good landlords were general among the proprietors of the soil in Ireland, and that absenteeism was the exception, residence the rule, as at Bray.†

Then, indeed, would Ireland become contented and happy under the fostering care of the proprietors of the soil The people of Ireland are proverbially attached to their native land, and when obliged to *emigrate*, feel the keenest pangs and sufferings. Why should not the landlords (who are under no obligation to reside abroad) live amongst their tenantry, and so promote, by the offices of mutual good-will and friendly feelings, general harmony and happiness?

Our country is rich, fair, and fruitful; our people are good-natured, grateful for kindnesses, and of generous impulses.

* Lord Viscount Powerscourt, Lord Viscount Monck, the Earl of Meath, Sir George Hodson, Bart., Charles Putland, Esq.; D. C. Latouche, Esq.; Alexander Boyle, Esq.; Phineas Riall, Esq.

† "As I stood leaning over the stone battlements of the bridge which spans the Bray river, musing and reflecting, I could not help devoutly wishing that the stream of my country's history henceforward might more and more resemble the track and passage of the tranquil river below me, no doubt at times to be fretted by rock or swollen by flood, or shoaled by drought—no doubt at times subjected to windings and to rapids, and exhibiting foam and bubbles; but on the whole, flowing calmly, fertilising its own banks with its own waters, and reflecting their prosperity, their industry, and their peace on its quiet bosom, and performing in the sight of nations its stated and steady course from fount to fall- from its rise amidst the rocks of the cycles of time till its flow into the broad main of eternity."

The following verses graphically and truly depict the feelings of every true Irishman with respect to the loved land of his birth:—

HOME PREFERENCE.

Oh! had I the wings of a bird,
   To soar through the blue sunny sky,
By what breeze would my pinions be stirred—
   To what beautiful land would I fly?
Would the gorgeous East allure,
   With the light of its golden eves,
Where the tall green palm, over isles of balm,
   Waves with its feath'ry leaves?
     Ah! no! no! no!
      I heed not its tempting glare;
     In vain would I roam from my island home,
      For skies more fair.

Would I seek a southern sea,
   Italia's shore beside,
Where the clustering grape from tree to tree
   Hangs in its rosy pride?
My truant heart be still,
   For I long have sighed to stray
Through the myrtle flowers of fair Italy's bowers,
   By the shores of its southern bay.
     But no! no! no!
      Though bright be its sparkling seas,
     I never would roam from my island home,
      For charms like these!

Would I seek that land so bright,
   Where the Spanish maiden roves,
With a heart of love and an eye of light,
   Through her native citron groves?
Oh! sweet would it be to rest
   In the midst of the olive vales,
Where the orange blooms and the rose perfumes
   The breath of the balmy gales!
     But no! no! no!
      Though sweet be its wooing air,
     I never would roam from my island home
      To scenes, though fair!

Would I pass from pole to pole?
   Would I seek the western skies,
Where the giant rivers roll,
   And the mighty mountains rise?
Or those treacherous isles that lie

In the midst of the sunny deeps,
Where the cocoa stands on the glistening sands,
And the dread tornado sweeps?
  Ah! no! no! no!
    They have no charms for me;
    I never would roam from my island home,
    Though poor it be!

Poor! oh! 'tis rich in all
That flows from Nature's hand,
Rich in the emerald wall
That guards its emerald land!
Are Italy's fields more green?
Do they teem with a richer store
Than the bright green breast of the Isle of the West,
And its wild luxuriant shore?
  Ah! no! no! no!
    Upon it heaven doth smile!
  Oh! I never would roam from my native home,
    My own dear Isle!

DENIS FLORENCE MAC-CARTHY.

BRAY—ITS HISTORICAL ASSOCIATIONS.

Sir James Ware, in his "Antiquities of Ireland," published in 1639, says, "Bray Head is a high and large cape, stretching a considerable way into the sea, on the south side of the Bay of Dublin, from which a river and town take their names. Perhaps it was so named from some fancied resemblance it bears to a neck, which is called Braighe in Irish, or from Bri, a hill. The country lying between this town and Dublin was, in the Danish times, called Dubh-Gall, or the lands of the Black Foreigners, who were the Danes, in opposition to Fingall, which lay on the north side of Dublin, and was inhabited by the Norwegians, or White Foreigners."

Maurice O'Regan, secretary and interpreter to Dermod Mac-Morough, King of Leinster, when writing the history of Strongbow's invasion, in the year 1177, says "Maurice Fitz-Gerald got the county of O'Felin, formerly the estate of Mac-Kelan, lying between Bree and Arcklow."

In 1173, the manor was granted by the Earl of Pembroke, Lord-Deputy, to Walter de Riddlesford, a Norman adventurer.

In 1215, the Abbot of the Monastery of St. Thomas obtained it at a fine of sixty, and an annual rent of three marks.

On the dissolution of the monasteries, the manor, with other lands of the above abbey, were granted to Sir Thomas Brabazon, an ancestor of the Earl of Meath, who is the present owner of the fee of the greater part of the town, which is situate in the counties of Dublin and Wicklow, the river Bray being the boundary between the two counties.

Bray town was frequently assailed by the powerful mountain septs, the O'Byrnes and the O'Tooles. On the 16th of April,

1316, they destroyed the castle, but were defeated on the same day by the English, under Edmund le Botiller. In 1402, a fierce battle took place in Bray between the citizens of Dublin (from the Pale), who were headed by John Drake, their provost. Camden, the historian, says 4,000 of the O'Tooles and the OByrne's were slain, but Hervey and Marlbrigg, other historians, say 400. Bloody Bank, at Bray, is supposed to derive its name from this battle.

THE DARGLE,

"A VERDUROUS WALL OF PARADISE UPRAISED."

As we stood upon an eminence near one of Lord Powerscourt's beautiful cottages, a new world of rural beauty opened upon us, of rich valleys and mountains covered with wood, melting into air, whilst below a serpentine river glistened in the sun, until it lost itself in the Dargle. Impossible as it is to convey, by verbal painting, a just idea of this exquisite scene, I approach an attempt to describe it with considerable apprehension. The Dargle is a deep glen, or narrow valley, of about a mile and a half in length. At the entrance where we approached it, opposite to us a beautiful little pleasure-cottage peeped over the ridge of one of the hills which form the green, heathy sides of this glen. It was just discernible in a little plantation which crowned the precipice upon which it stood.

This elegant and romantic little summer retreat was raised after the tasteful design of Mrs. H. Grattan, the lady of the illustrious member of that name, to whom it belongs. As we descended by the paths which have been cut through the woods, new beauties opened upon us. The hill, on the sides of which we stood, was covered with trees, principally young oak, projecting with luxuriant foliage from masses of rock half green with moss, which reminded us of Milton's description of the

"*Verdurous* wall of Paradise upraised."

Here, concealed by over-arching leaves, the river, like fretful man in his progress through this unequal world, was scarcely heard to ripple; there it flashed before the eye again, as if in anger at its concealment, rolled impetuously over its rocky bed, and roared down a craggy declivity. A little further, having recovered its calmness, it seemed to settle for a while, resembling, in sullen silence and placidity, a dark mirror; then never destined to long tranquillity, it proceeded, and was again lost in arches of foliage, under which it murmured and died upon the ear.

It was in this spot, under the green roof of native oaks starting from their rocky beds, sequestered from the theatre of that world upon which he afterwards sustained so distinguished a character, that GRATTAN, when a very young man, addressed the tumultuous waters as his auditory, and schooled himself, like Demosthenes, in that eloquence which was destined to elevate the glory of Ireland with his own.*

We ascended the Lover's-leap, a vast high grey rock, whose base is concealed by sloping trees: it rises higher than any other object, and commands a very extensive view of this verdant scenery, which travellers, who have visited Italy, pronounce to be equal to any spot in that lovely land.

Heavens! what a contrast to the luxuriant richness of this scenery has Mr. A. Young given us, in his clear and invaluable account of Ireland, when he speaks of that vast, wild, and impenetrable tract of mountain and bog, called the Barony of Erris.

THE DARGLE

With its romantic charms,
Where every form of Nature's loveliness
Wakes in the breast a thousand sympathies—
As music's voice in some lone mountain dell,
From rocks and caves around
Calls forth each echo's swell.

The Dargle is part of the ample and beautiful demesne of Lord Viscount Powerscourt, who, with a

* See *Appendix*, "Irish Eloquence"—Extracts from the Speeches of Grattan, Curran, and Flood.

liberality worthy of his rank and mind, permits every one to visit it, and has erected seats in various parts of it for the accommodation of the public.

Nothing can be more beautiful than the view of the Dargle from St. Valori and the river, which

    ——— ———leads you on
To the extreme bound
Of a fair flowery meadow, then at once,
With quick impediment,
Says stop, adieu, for now, yes now, I leave you;
Then down a rock descends.
There, as no human foot can follow further,
The eye alone must follow him, and there
In little space you see a mass of water,
Collected in a deep and fruitful vale,
With laurel crowned and olive,
With cypress oranges, and lofty pines—
The limpid water in the sun's bright ray,
A perfect chrystal seems."*

St. Valori, near the Dargle, is a beautiful spot. It was once the residence of the eminent Irish author, W. Cooper Walker, who was well known to a large circle of friends for the excellence of his heart, and to the world for the learned and elegant literary productions with which he gratified it. A variety of knowledge, ancient and modern, a long residence in Italy, a correspondence with the most distinguished literary men of the age in various parts of the world, a felicity of temper, and a resignation to the hand of Heaven, enabled this elegant scholar to support a long visitation of sickness with perfect serenity. He modestly but forcibly depicted himself in his sequestered retreat of St. Valori, which overshadows the romantic and picturesque cottage of Fassaro,† in his highly interesting " Historical Memoirs on Italian Tragedy."

* "*The Stranger in Ireland*," 1805.
† " Soon after my arrival in my native country, ill health obliged me to retire from the busy hum of men ; and I sunk into rural

The following beautiful lines were addressed to him at St. Valori, by that extraordinary, early but unfortunate genius, Dermody, the Chatterton of Ireland:—

> " 'Tis thine with fond research to trace
> The shrinking river's latent vein ;
> From dust to dig th' imperial face,
> Or raise to light the lofty strain.
>
> " Then, like the bee, full fraught return,
> Instruction pour from wisdom's urn,
> And bid the Alban Graces smile
> On lost *Juverna's* barren isle.
>
> " Oh ! could'st thou, from some gentle shade,
> Retrieve the lost, the priceless page,
> The depths of elder time invade,
> And brighten blank oblivion's age !
>
> " The wish is vain : What taste can do,
> What elegance with sense combin'd ;
> Thy learned toil shall bring to view,
> And nourish the abstracted mind."

Near St. Valori was an ancient cross, which was removed, in the early part of the 18th century, from the old church in the Glen of Ballyman. Between this cross and St. Valori there are the ruins of the Castle of Fassaro, which once guarded this pass into the mountains.

Dean Kirwan, one of the greatest devotional orators that ever appeared since the days of Massillon, was a constant visitor at St. Valori. This great man laboured under a weakness of constitution which conducted him to the grave in the prime of life, and in the full zenith of those powers which the Divine

seclusion in a verdant valley, watered by a winding river, at the foot of a range of lofty mountains. Here I summoned round me the swans of the Po and of the Arno, and whilst I listened to their mellifluous strains, time passed with an inaudible step; but, though I no longer sighed after the society which I had abandoned, I felt an ardent desire to increase its stock of harmless pleasures."

Author of his being had bestowed upon him, for the purpose of unfolding his glorious attributes, and unlocking the copious streams of charity. Dean Kirwan raised upwards of *sixty thousand pounds* by the influence of his sermons alone. A single discourse has frequently been followed by a collection of one thousand pounds. In speaking the cause of the wretched, he spoke as with the tongue of inspiration.

The following are extracts from his unpublished sermons :—

PULPIT ELOQUENCE.

HUMAN VANITY.

" Insects of the day that we are! hurried along the stream of time that flows at the base of God's immutability, we look up and think in *our* schemes and *our* pursuits to emulate his eternity.

INFLUENCE OF EXAMPLE.

" It is the unenvied privilege of pre-eminence, that when the great fall, they fall not by themselves, but bring thousands along with them, like the beast in the Apocalypse, bringing the stars with it.

RELIGIOUS LIBERTY.

" I will now more immediately call your attention to the institution for which I have undertaken to plead. The principle which forms its groundwork is, I am glad to inform you, of the most liberal and expanded nature. Children of all religious persuasions may be educated without any attempt on the part of their governors to instil sentiments contrary to the judgment and choice of their parents. Such perfect religious liberty must ever recommend similar establishments to men of enlarged ideas, who (be their own mode of worship what it may) will always unite in their support upon the broad and generous ground of philanthropy alone. *Philanthropy*, my friends, is of *no particular sect ; it is* confined by no paltry form of rule ; it *knows no distinction but that of the happy and unhappy ;* it is older than the Gospel, eternal as that great source from whence it springs, and often beats higher in the heathen's breast than in those of many who are called Christians, who, though under the influence of the most benevolent of all possible systems, yet not unfrequently refuse both relief and compassion to the petition of the wretched, and the entreaty of the unhappy. God forbid that the genuine feelings of the heart were confined to this or that mode of faith ! God forbid that any ridiculous prejudice should hinder me from reverencing the man (however we may differ in speculative notions) whose gentle spirit flies out to soothe the mourner ; whose ear is attentive to the voice of sorrow; whose pittance is shared with those who are not the world's friends; whose bountiful hand scatters food to the hungry, and raiment to the naked; and whose peaceful steps, as he journeyeth on his way, are blessed, and blessed again by the uplifted eye of thankful indigence, and the sounds of honest gratitude from the lips of wretchedness. Should such a man be ill-fated here, or hereafter, may his fate be light! Should he transgress, may his transgressions be unrecorded! Or, if the page of his great account be stained with the weaknesses of human nature, or the misfortune of error, may the tears of the widow and the orphan, the tears of the wretched he has relieved, efface the too rigid and unfriendly characters, and blot out the guilt and remembrance of them for ever.

WANT OF HUMANITY.

"The individual whose life is dedicated to a constant warfare with his passions, whose life is a scene of temperance, sobriety, assiduous prayer, and unremitting attendance on divine worship, such an individual is certainly entitled to all the merit justly due to such Christian works; but, my friends, if, under so fair and plausible a surface, there be a dark and frightful void; if, under the show of virtue, the stream of sensibility does not flow, if such a character, pure and evangelical as it may appear, has never been marked by one solitary act of humanity, by any instance of that brotherly affection and mutual love which hourly breaks out into offices of mercy and useful beneficence, who will hesitate to avow that so specious an exterior is a mockery on true virtue, an imposition on the good sense of the world, and an insult on the life of Christ and the morality of His Gospel? Who will hesitate to admit that such a man may be aptly compared *to a mountain remarkable for sterility and elevation, which encumbers the earth with its pressure, while it chills all around with its shade?*

THE VANITY OF WEALTH.

"If they who lie there (pointing from the pulpit to the church yard), whose places you now occupy, and whose riches you possess (God only knows *how* possess); if they, I say, were at this moment to appear amongst you (don't tremble), it would not be to *reclaim* their wealth, but to bear testimony to *its vanity.*

PRIDE.

"How often have we seen the column of pride, erected upon the basis of infamy, and just when it hath begun to attract the gape and stare of the adulatory multitude, death, like a rocky fragment rolling from the mountain, crumbles into nothing the imaginary colossus.

LIBERALITY.

"Liberality is the most amiable feature of the human mind; a sacred tie which unites all jarring systems, promotes mutual affection and peace among men, inspires respect for the honest intentions and well-meaning opinions of all mankind, fervently wishes, but perhaps feels the impossibility, to unite all modes of religion upon one broad and rational basis. True liberality is more—it is expanded as the earth, stimulates the bosom to promiscuous benevolence, urges it to feel and to relieve the distresses of Turk or Jew as readily, and with as much warmth as those of the indigent who raise their hands within those walls; it wafts the mind over the waste of oceans into distant hemispheres, to let fall a tear at the couch of the *afflicted infidel*, as well as at the bed of a *sufferer of our communion;* these are the operations of this beautiful and angelic virtue, and are the pride and glory of every great soul. Thank God! that in the age and land we live, religion is at length becoming free and natural, and that all zealous contentions about particular systems are now clearly discovered to be unfriendly to the true interests of the community, as well as the peace and happiness of the world. Thank God! the day is rapidly advancing (and it is a day we should all look forward to with rapture and delight) when every citizen may think as he pleases upon subjects of religion, and freely offer sacrifice in whatever temple his inclination and opinions point to—the day, and I will call it the glorious day, when all religious societies, all ranks and degrees of men, will be collected together by one common and endearing tie of Christian benevolence and love; when the rancour of parties will cease, the altars of uncharitableness cease to smoke; the illiberal, narrow, and sophisticated reasonings of bigotry be drowned in the vast and public cry of an enlarged philanthropy; the hoary and venerable tyrant, superstition, plucked from his throne; when the frivolous and ridiculous contest about primogeniture will be no more; and the God of benevolence, of humanity, of mutual forbearance, and ardent charity, appear in the threshold of every sanctuary, and obtain an undisputed empire in every heart. Thank God! that day is advancing—I know it—I feel it, I can assert it; a period devoutly to be wished for; and, perhaps, the first opening since the Christian era of human happiness. If there is yet some prejudice, it is giving way; it must give way to liberal inquiry; it must retreat to the dark, uncultivated corners of the earth, and of course perish where it cannot grow. The tears of a few fanatics may accompany its fall; but I believe that every man who wishes to see the glorious restoration of reason, its dignity unfettered, and the dominion of real vital religion established; every man who has at heart the enlargement of human nature, and wishes to see the peace of society established upon a secure and permanent basis, will joyfully sing to its requiem, and manfully exert himself to oppose its second appearance in the world."

On the day when Dr. Kirwan preached every avenue used to be crowded long before he ascended the pulpit. Grattan finely said of this eloquent divine, that "In feeding the lamp of charity, he had exhausted the lamp of life."

The sure mark of a good preacher is his being much followed and much applauded. The Rev. Walter Blake Kirwan stands first in reputation for pulpit eloquence in this kingdom. His sermons are rather orations, resembling those of the Gregories and Chrysostoms in their most popular discourses. They touch on no controversial points, which most unchristianly inflame the minds of one sect against another, and prepare them for blood and slaughter, rather than the practice of the milder charities of the Gospel. They are not theological dissertations, on thorny, dark, and disputed points of divinity, which bewilder the best understandings, and fill the weaker with gloomy notions. Is it possible, with our present limited faculties, to fathom, or by language to explain, the mysteries of the Trinity, of election, and grace? Simple belief of these and other incomprehensible doctrines, is only necessary for salvation; their investigation is far beyond the powers of our reasoning faculties; whatever divines have written concerning them are mere phantasms; as ideal as the celestial illuminations of Baron Swedenborg, or his conversations with angelic spirits in the New Jerusalem. Mr. Kirwan administers no such unsolid food to his hearers, which may inflate but never can supply healthful nutriment. Neither does he waste his time in an useless display of subtle reasoning, nor metaphysical refinement, or in detailing curious erudition, the result of critical and extensive reading; these he relinquishes for matters of more general and higher importance. His preaching, *extempore*, frees him from all the inconveniences of written discourses; the latter are systematical and regular, and, of course, cold and lifeless. To preserve the reputation of a scholar and a man of sense and judgment, a logical connection must be preserved from the beginning to the end; such a composition may do very well in the closet, or for a select company; but in a mixed congregation it acts as an *opiate*, and its soporiferous effects are visible in the half-closed eye-lids of some, and the loud snoring of others.—*Anthologia Hibernica*, 1793.

The picturesque cottage of Fassaro, near the Dargle, is now in the possession of the talented, hospitable, and kind-hearted artist, Henry MacManus, Esq., R.H.A., who, for many years, was Head Master of the School of Design, Royal Dublin Society, Kildare-street.

POWERSCOURT HOUSE AND DEMESNE.

"It was with regret that I left the delightful and hospitable roof of Tinnahinch.* On my way to Dublin I paid my respects to Lord Powerscourt, and much regretted that time would not permit me to accept of the kind and cordial invitation of his lordship and his amiable lady to spend some days at the Castle, which stands in the proudest situation I ever beheld. The front of the house is of hewn stone, adorned with pilasters, which are very handsome and extensive; few mansions can boast of so noble and magnificent a banqueting-room as the Egyptian hall, which was designed and built by the architect of the Parliament House; it has a gallery on each side, supported by Corinthian pillars. The drawing-rooms are also very elegant; the avenues to the house beautiful; and the park, spread over the mountain, uncommonly fine."—"*The Stranger in Ireland*," 1805.

* See Appendix—Tinnahinch.

SECTION XI.

HOWTH, OR BEN-EDAR.

On the right of Dublin Bay is the rugged hill of Howth, with its caves and rocky indentations, wanting only a volcano to afford to the surrounding scenery the strongest resemblance to the beautiful Bay of Naples. On a summer day Ben-Edar appears in all its majesty. The softening hand of distance would seem as it were to cover its craggy sides with a russet robe. "Its natural wildness of scenery and sublimity of prospect, early attracted to it the attention of all who could feel interested in such associations. The cairn-crowned height of Sleivemartin is one of the landward summits of Howth first seen from the Irish Sea. The summit of Howth is elevated 578 feet above low water-mark. The north-eastern side of the hill presents somewhat the appearance of a miniature Gibraltar. Dalton says that it was anciently called *Ben-na-dair*, as it is supposed from the quantity of venerable oaks that then waved over its fertile declivities, and religiously shadowed one of those pagan altars or cromlechs, which yet remain attributable to a species of the Magian priesthood."*

* "Aid me to pierce the shade of ancient days:
The æras lost, assist me to regain ;
Those wrapt in song amidst the sylvan reign :
 *   *   *
Whose date the antique sage hath sought in vain ;
Which braves the wreck of time and swift decay,
That sweeps the labour'd domes of man away.

Corr Castle, a small square tower, is all that remains of the ancient castle of the Earls of Howth—Their modern residence is a long battlemented structure, flanked by square towers—the spacious hall of which is furnished with relics of antiquity, while in the saloon are several fine paintings and portraits, especially one of Dean Swift, by Bindon. It was painted in 1735, and represents him in his clerical costume, with *Wood* at his feet, to the right of the picture, writhing in agony.

Dean Swift had been a frequent visitor at Howth Castle. In one of his letters, in 1734, he writes: "The weather, yesterday, being very fine, I rode to Howth Castle, and as I was getting on horse-back to

> Time that from brass doth characters efface,
> And drops the cloud-hid turret to its base,
> Throws the symmetric temple to the ground,
> Its site forgot nor marble columns found:
>   *   *   *
> How vain!—to plan, to rear the immortal dome;
> While this rude pile hath countless ages stood
> The sap of time, and stemm'd oblivious flood;
> Mysterious circles, from your gloom'd recess,
> The priest, perchance, the implicit train might bless,
> For furious Odin might obtest the skies,
> And bless a hetacomb for sacrifice.
> While from this fane, just opening to the skies,
> Their mystic rites and hid oblations rise,
> Still by what powers raised,—remains unseen;
> Nature's august retreats are better known.
>   *   *   *
> Hark the burst anthem swells its notes around,
> And structur'd rocks grow vocal with the sound;
> For now the Druids seek their inmost place,
> Recess rever'd—forbid but to their race,
> To their high priest a reverent train succeed,
> With sacred mistletoe for rights decreed,
> The hallow'd parasites from oak they drew,
> Cut by the empyreal bill now borne to view.
> The Druid sisters rais'd the sacred mound,
> Their mantling coifs with holy fillets bound,
> Each in her dexter hand an oak-branch bears,
> Whose viscid leaves the etherial honey bears,
> Those mystic rights no Druid dare unfold,
> Enwrapt from sight, and never must be told."

return, I was seized with so cruel a fit of that giddinesss which at times had pursued me from my youth, that I was forced to lie down on a bed for two hours before I was in a condition to ride." The harbour of Howth cost £300,000, which did not admit vessels of large burthen or great draught. So injudicious was its location that, had it been constructed but one furlong to the eastward of its present situation, the navy of Great Britain might have been moored within it, sheltered from the prevailing winds, in a safe anchorage, and a depth of water uninfluenced by ebb or flow of tide. This harbour, so dearly purchased by the nation, has been superseded by the one at Kingstown, and another generation may traverse the mossy causeway, and vainly seek the spot where the first English Monarch landed in 1821 (George IV.), who came in peace to Ireland.

One of the few specimens of Gothic pointed architecture which the county of Dublin affords, is to be found in the venerable remains of the ancient Abbey of Howth, which is picturesquely situated on an eminence overlooking the sea. The orginal bells of this abbey are still preserved at the castle. The "Book of Howth," compiled in this abbey, which contains a romantic chronicle of Irish affairs from A. D. 432, is yet extant.

The plain of Moynalty, which can be seen from Howth, is that rich tract of tillage and pasture, extending from Clontarf over the northern part of the county of Dublin, and forming part of the more extensive plain of Bregia. It was called by the Irish "Plain of Flocks," from the flocks of birds resorting to it;

"When through the wintry air
The wide-winged wild geese to their pools by Liffey's side repair."

and received its name of "The Old Plain"—*Sean Mhagh Ealta*—from the traditionary tale that, of all the other plains in Ireland, this is the only one which never was covered with forest, but was always a "place of flocks and herds."

Howth is connected with the mainland by a dreary and uncultivated isthmus. On this isthmus, close to the sea, are the interesting ruins of the church of Kilbarrack.*

Dalton, in his admirable work on the Topography, &c., of the co. Dublin, offers the following remarks on the ancient graveyard of Killbarrack:—

".Unretarded by wall or ditch, or fence, the visitor, gliding among a few sodden and slippery graves, and forming his steps by the headstones and crosses that distinguish them, finds himself in the once votive chapel of the mariners who frequented the Bay of Dublin, and at whose altar, on their arrival, they had prayers offered up for the souls of those of their messmates who perished at sea ; a dutiful commemoration, which, however, some may deem superstitious, is the sublimest link in the religion of the Roman Catholic —the link that prolongs communication with the parent, the relative, and the friend, on whom this world is closed for ever. . . . The architectural appearance of Kilbarrack chapel is not imposing, only exhibiting some circular and pointed arches, without any visible remains of a steeple or belfry;

* The frequent recurrence of the names of places beginning with *Kill*, is not a little alarming to a stranger in Ireland, more especially if he be under the influence of those stupid prejudices which have been excited against this country. I have just enumerated in my memory no less than forty-nine of those *Kill* places. The name produced the following ridiculous mistake during the rebellion of '98 :—A soldier, a native of Devonshire, who was stationed at an outpost, stopped a countryman, and demanded who he was, whence he came from, and whither he was going. The fellow replied :

"And my name, my dear honey, is *Kilbride;* d'ye see, I've just been to *Killmany,* and am going to *Killmore,*" upon which the sentinel immediately seized him, expecting to receive a high reward for having apprehended a most sanguinary rebel, by confession, just come from murder, and going to a fresh banquet of blood."—*Carr's Tour in Ireland*, 1805.

the vista and sections of prospect, however, as framed by the arches and windows of the ruins, afford a series of views which cannot fail to gratify the commonest observer, and even well to recommend the artist. A broken tombstone in the graveyard has now ceased to record the once celebrated Higgins, well known by the soubriquet of the 'SHAM SQUIRE.'"

There is a peculiar freshness and purity in the atmosphere of Howth. So far back as the sixth century, this characteristic of its scenery was felt, and beatifully expressed in a poem, which is attributed to St. Columba :—

"Delightful to be on Ben-Edar,
Before going o'er the white sea ;
Delightful the dashing of the wave against its face,
The hareness of its shore and its border."

In old Irish topography, Bregh and Edar were brothers, who gave their names to the two headlands now known as Bray Head and Howth. Howth (Hoved) is a Norse word, signifying "head." The native Irish still know the hill as Ben Edar, and Ireland's Eye as Inis Meic Nessain, or "Island of the Sons of Nessan." This beautiful islet, in the day of Ossian, bore the name of Inis-Faithlenn, or Inisfallen. It was not till three centuries later that it became the abode of the sons of Nessan—three holy men, brothers, who here became eminent for piety and learning, and from whom it took its second name of Inis Meic Nessan. In the Felire Aengus, a calendar of Irish Saints, it is said of these holy men, "The sons of Nessan, of this island, loved the true knowledge of Christ." The remains of their stone oratory and round tower may still be traced near the beech on the side of the island towards Howth. Here was preserved, and probably executed, the remarkable manuscript copy of the Gospels, called the "Garland of Howth." The history of this wonderful book, with those of Kells, Durrow, Kildare and

Armagh, must prove interesting to every Irishman. It is from the pen of the late Dr. Petrie.

The love of ornament would seem to be an instinct in human nature; and some will even say that beauty in decorative art is a more healthy and desirable thing for a nation than beauty in the painting of pictures and the carving of statues; just as to use the illustration of a modern writer, "A nation blessed with lovely national melodies is better off, as a musical people, than one which, without these, might produce here and there a composer of lofty symphonies and oratorios." Whatever truth is to be found in this statement, we may, at all events, feel a just pride in the knowledge that the Irish nation was possessed of this gift, this instinctive power of expressing the beautiful, both in form and sound, of which we have so many proofs, as well in the specimens still preserved of their ancient illuminated manuscripts, sculptured stones, and jewellery, as in the stores of ancient melodies that have descended to us from the past.

It is acknowledged by the best writers on the subject that the Irish monks, from the fifth to the end of the eleventh century, brought the art of ornamenting manuscripts to marvellous perfection; and it would appear that the Scoto-Celtic form of this art spread from Ireland through Western Europe, carried by those men whose love and reverence for the sacred writing found expression in the beauty of line and splendour of colour wherewith they delighted to adorn their copies of them. The most remarkable specimen of this art now existing is the "Book of Kells," so called from having been preserved in the great Abbey Church of Kells, in the diocese of Meath. It was saved from destruction by James Usher, who was Bishop of Meath from the year 1621 to 1624, and was found in his library, which, having been confiscated during the Commonwealth, was granted by

Charles II., on the Restoration, to Trinity College, and thus the "Book of Kells" passed into the possession of that body, with whom it has since remained.

"The Garland of Howth," is preserved in the library of Trinity College, Dublin. It is an illuminated copy of the Gospels, spoken of by Archbishop Allen and by Usher as the "*Cethar Leabhar*"—the Four Books.

It belonged originally to the Church of Inis Meic Nessan, or the Island of the Sons of Nessan, a descendant of Cathair Mor, King of Ireland, by whose sons, in the seventh century, the Church of Inis Meic Nessain, now Ireland's Eye, was founded. Part of the tower belonging to this building was standing within the last few years, and some remains of the church may still be seen.

The ornamentation of "The Garland of Howth" bears all the marks of the highest antiquity. The frontispiece of the Gospel of St. Matthew, with that of St. Mark, still remains in tolerable preservation. On the first page, surrounded by interlaced ornamental work, two figures may be seen, both bearded; the first with upraised hands, the second holding a sword in one hand and a book in the other. In the frontispiece to St. Mark there is a figure standing at a desk, the face beardless, the hands folded in prayer. All three heads are without the nimbus.

The "Book of Dimma" is a copy of the Gospels, written about the seventh century, which contains representations of each of the Evangelists in a very rude style of art. At the end of the MS. the scribe has thus inscribed his name:

"*Finit. Amen.* ✠ *Dimma Macc Nath.* ✠"

This Dimma is believed to be the scribe mentioned in the life of St. Cronan, who lived A.D. 634, as employed by him to write a copy of the Gospels

This book was preserved at the Abbey of Roscrea, founded by Cronan.

The "Book of St. Moling" exhibits internal evidence of having been written in the seventh century, as it contains the name of the saint in autograph, who was Bishop of Ferns, A.D. 600.

The "Liber Hymnorum" is a beautiful manuscript, which cannot be assigned to a later date than the tenth or eleventh century, and was believed by Usher to have been, in his time, one thousand years old. It may safely be pronounced one of the most venerable monuments of Christian antiquity now remaining in Europe. It is ornamented in a very beautiful and elaborate manner, the illuminated letters exhibiting the same style of art as that found in the other MSS., and coloured with yellow, blue, and green.*

The "Book of Armagh" is most remarkable for the exquisite delicacy of execution and elegant forms of its initial letters; the whole writing in the book, indeed, is a wonderful specimen of penmanship. The date of this book has been determined by Dean Graves, who has proved it to have been written by Ferdomnach, described, in the "Annals of the Four Masters," as "a sage and choice scribe of the Church of Armagh," who copied out this manuscript, while Torbach, himself a scribe, was Abbot of Armagh, A.D. 808. There is reason to believe that this Ferdomnach retired to end his days at Clonmacnois, when Armagh was plundered by the Danes, in 831; and the late Dr. Petrie has found at Clonmacnois a tombstone bearing his name, which is most probably that of the Armagh Ferdomnach.

The "Book of Kells" and the "Book of Durrow" are copies of the Gospels, said to be in the hand-

* See "Liber Hymnorum," edited and translated by the late much-respected and eminent Irish antiquarian, the Rev. J. H. Todd, D.D., for the Irish Archæological and Celtic Society.

writing of St. Columba. Usher, in speaking of them, remarks: "It (Durrow, or Durrough, in the King's County,) had a monastery dedicated to St. Columba, among the records of which was preserved a very ancient manuscript of the Gospels, which the monks used to say had belonged to Columba himself; out of which, and another of no less antiquity, also ascribed to the same Columba (and held sacred by the inhabitants of Meath, in the town called Kelles, or Kenlis) I have collected for my own use two books of various readings, by a diligent collation of them with the Latin vulgate."

St. Columba is spoken of by his biographers as an indefatigable scribe, who from his early youth, devoted himself to the work of multiplying copies of the Psalms, Gospels, and other portions of the Scriptures; and there is an interesting passage in the "Annals of Ulster," A.D. 552, where St. Columba is mentioned as the possessor of a singular copy of the Gospels; and, again, in the same Annals, A.D. 1006, a book is mentioned as the "Book of St. Columba," which, if it were so, must have been upwards of 411 years old at the time the record was made. "The large Gospel of Columbkille was sacrilegiously stolen in the night out of the western erdomh (sacristy, or vestry-room) of the great church of Kennanus" (the old Irish name of Kells). "This was the chief relic of the west of the world, on account of its singular cover. This Gospel was found, after twenty nights and two months, with its gold stolen off, and a sod over it."

It is scarcely possible to doubt that the book now in the library of Trinity College, Dublin, is "the large Gospel of Columbkille," to which this record refers. That it belonged to the church of Kells in the eleventh century is evident, from the curious charters relating to the clergy of Kells which it contains; and it continued among the treasures of that church down to the time of Archbishop Usher; that is to say, down to the seventeenth century, for which fact we have the archbishop's own testimony. It may also be brought forward as evidence in favour of the antiquity of the book, that many manuscripts of the same style of art, and of equal beauty, seem to have existed in Ireland at this early time. Thus we cannot omit to mention another great copy of the Gospels, which was preserved in the Cathedral of Kildare up to the twelfth century. This has been described by Giraldus Cambrensis, who came into Ireland as secretary to Prince John, A.D. 1185, and his account of it might seem, indeed, to have been written as a description of the "Book of Kells" itself, so exactly does it apply to that book.

"Of all the wonders of Kildare," he says, "I have found nothing more wonderful than that marvellous book, written in the time of the Virgin (St. Bridgid), and, as they say, at the dictation of an angel. The book contains the concordance of the Evangelists, every page of which is filled with divers figures, most accurately marked out with various colours. Here you behold a majestic face, divinely drawn; there the mystical forms of the Evangelists, each having—sometimes six, sometimes four, and sometimes two wings—here an eagle, there a calf; there, again, a human face, or a lion, and other figures of infinite variety, so closely wrought together, that if you looked carelessly at them, they would seem rather like a uniform blot than an equisite interweaving of figures, exhibiting no skill or art, where all is skill and perfection of art. But if you look closely, with all the acuteness of sight that you can command, and examine the inmost secrets of that wondrous art, you will discover such delicate, such subtle, such fine and closely-wrought lines, twisted and interwoven in such intricate knots, and adorned with such fresh and brilliant colours, that you will readily acknowledge the whole to have been the result of angelic, rather than human skill. The more frequently I behold it, the more diligently I examine it, the more numerous are the beauties I discover in it, the more I am lost in renewed admiration of it."

It is especially worthy of notice, in considering the antiquity of Irish art, that its earliest specimens are unquestionably the most perfect, whereas the latest specimens indicate the decline of the art.

But whatever doubt may be felt as to the exact date of "The Book of Kells, no doubt whatever can be entertained as to the age of the "Book of Durrow," the writing of which is also ascribed to St. Columba, and in which there are illuminations of the same style of art, though inferior in beauty of execution; for, in this manuscript, we find the usual request of the Irish scribe for a prayer from the reader, expressed in the following words:—

" Rogo beatitudinem tuam sancte præsbiter Patrici, ut quicunque hunc libellum manu tenuerit meminerit Columbæ scriptores qui hoc scripsi ipsemet evangelium per xii. dierum spatium gratia Domini nostri."

" I pray thy blessedness, O holy presbyter, Patrick, that whosoever shall take this book into his hands, may remember the writer Columba, who have myself written this gospel in the space of twelve days, by the grace of our Lord."

An inscription in Irish was found upon the ancient Cumdach, or shrine, which was made for this work, by Flann, King of Ireland, who reigned A.D. 879–916. This shrine, or cover, has long been missing, but a copy of the inscription is preserved, and is thus translated:—

"THE PRAYER AND BENEDICTION OF ST. COLUMKILLE BE UPON FLANN, THE SON OF MALACHI, KING OF IRELAND, WHO CAUSED THIS COVER TO BE MADE."

This book, which was preserved at Durrow down to the Reformation, was given to the library of Trinity College, Dublin, by Dr. Jones, Bishop of Meath, A.D. 1584, in whose bishopric the church of Durrow was situated.

The "Psalter of Ricemarch" is a manuscript beautifully executed, with illuminations which exhibit the same style of art, but the ornamentation of which is less in design than the "Book of Armagh." The central spaces of the capitals are filled with plain colour, and bear a striking resemblance to those in the "Book of Leinster," a book of the twelfth century.

In the seventeenth century this Psalter passed into the possession of Bishop Bedell, Provost of Trinity College, A.D. 1627, and by whom the MS. was presented to the University. Interesting evidence of the literary reputation which Ireland enjoyed up to the end of the eleventh century, occurs in the "Life of Sulgen," who was Bishop of St. David's about the year 1070, in a poem, written by his son John, and in which we read that Sulgen came to Ireland to study there for ten or thirteen years, when that country was still termed sacred, and "a workshop of men famous for learning and sanctity."

"It would then appear that for a period of not less than six or seven centuries, Ireland possessed a school of art, which seems to have spread its influence over a large portion of Western Europe."[*]

The following are extracts from this highly descriptive poem:—

[*] *Extracted from the valuable Notes on Ornamentation, given in the* "Cromlech on Howth:" A Poem, by Samuel Ferguson, Q.C., M.R.I.A., with illustrations from the "Book of Kells and of Durrow," and drawings from nature, by Miss Mary Stokes, with Notes on Celtic Ornamental Art; revised by the late George Petrie, L.L.D., a work that should occupy a position in the library of every nobleman and gentleman in the British empire.

THE CROMLECH ON HOWTH.*

"They heaved the stone, they heaped the cairn;
  Said Ossian; in a queenly grave
We leave her, 'mong her fields of fern,
  Between the cliff and wave.
  * * * * * *

"A clear, pure air pervades the scene.
  In loneliness and awe secure;
Meet spot to sepulchre a queen
  Who in her life was pure.
  * * * * * *

"And oft at tranquil eve's decline,
  When full tides lip the old green plain,
The lowing of Moynalty's kine
  Shall round her breathe again.
  * * * * * *

"When mingling with the wreckful wail
  From low Clontarf's wave-trampled floor,
Comes booming up the burthened gale,
  The angry sand-bull's roar.
  * * * * * *

"And here hard-by her natal bower,
  On lone Ben-Edar's side we strive,
With lifted rock and sign of power,
  To keep her name alive.
  * * * * * *

---

* Aideen, daughter of Angus of Ben-Edar (now the Hill of Howth), died, according to an Irish legend, of grief for the loss of her husband, Oscar, son of Ossian, who was slain in the battle of Gavra;[1] Oscar was entombed in the Rath, an earthen fortress that occupied part of the field of battle. Aideen was interred at Howth, and bardic tradition represents Ossian and his renowned companions as present at her obsequies. The Cromlech at Howth is one of those rude stone monuments commonly called Druids' altars, but now recognized as the remains of sepulchral chambers, which in most cases were covered by earthen mounds. The "Cromlech on Howth," the funeral ode written by Samuel Ferguson, Esq., Q.C., M.R.I.A., is supposed to be pronounced by Ossian.

[1] The battle of Gavra has remained, as Henry Martin, the French historian observes, "as famous in the histories of Ireland as the struggles of Couravas and the Pandavas in the traditions of India."

> "Imperfect, in an alien speech,
>   When wand'ring here some child of chance,
> Through pangs of keen delight shall reach
>   The gift of utterance,
>
> To speak the air, the sky to speak,
>   The freshness of the tale to tell;
> Who roaming bare Ben Edar's peak,
>   And Aideen's briary dell,*
>
> And gazing on the Cromlech vast,
>   And on the mountain and the sea,
> Shall catch communion with the past,
>   And mix himself with me."

PUCK'S ROCK—A SINGULAR PRECIPICE.— ST. NESSAN—IRELAND'S EYE.

This wild rock seems to have been detached from Ireland's Eye by some convulsion, which also cleft it nearly in two by a deep perpendicular fissure. On one side, and near the summit, is the rude representation of a colossal human figure on the face of the rock, of which tradition preserves the following story.

St. Nessan, whose sanctity is still venerated by the people of Howth, was assailed, in his retreat on Ireland's eye, by an evil spirit, who, to terrify him the more, assumed a frightful gigantic form—the Saint, by good luck, was reading the holy book called the "Garland of Howth," which rendered him invincible by anything unearthly and unholy.

As his enemy approached, he struck him on the forehead with the book, and drove him with such force against the opposite coast, that he split the rock, and impaled the evil spirit in the fissure, where he remains to this hour struggling to extricate himself.

---

* "Aideen's briary dell." This rocky, "bosky" hollow lies between the cromlech and the cliff. The descent from above commands a fine prospect of the woods and towers of Howth Castle, and of the island of Ireland's Eye.

In the course of centuries he has nearly disengaged his body and arms, but one leg still remains firmly wedged in the rock. This imaginary figure is frequently viewed from boats, but few have courage to venture into the chasm of the rock within.
It was, however, a noted haunt of smugglers.

Howth—Its Historical Associations.

The Hill of Howth is celebrated in the most ancient annals of Ireland as the place of settlement of Partholanus and his colony.

The celebrated Fin Ma Coule and his band made Howth one of his great military stations, in the fourth century.

Howth was devastated by the Danes in the ninth century.

Sitric, the converted Dane, bestowed, in 1038, a considerable part of the lands of Howth, and the adjoining country, on his ecclesiastical foundations, and is also said to have built the church here.

Sir Armoricus Tristram, one of the most active adventurers during the English invasion, landed at Howth, with Sir John De Courcy, at the head of a chosen band. The place was then inhabited by Danes. They defeated them in a signal engagement at the bridge of Evora, the mountain stream that falls into the sea at the north side of Howth, opposite Inis Meic Nessain (Ireland's Eye). Sir Armoricus acquired the Lordship of Howth and the title of St. Laurence, in honour of the day of battle. The sword with which he fought is still exhibited amongst the relics at Howth Castle. St. Laurence and De Courcy made a compact in the Church of Ronen to unite their fortunes in arms, and abide its dangers and rewards. At one time a pattern was annually held on the Hill of Howth, on St. Laurence's day, to commemorate this victory. Some time ago, when sinking the foundation for the new church, a large quantity of bones, an antique anvil, bridle, bits, and portions of horse armour, were found.

In 1375, the King directed that proclamation should be made within the Lordship of Howth, that none should cross the sea from Ireland, merchants excepted, without license from the crown.

In 1449, Richard Plantagenet, Duke of York, father of Edward IV., landed at Howth, as Lord Lieutenant.

Sir Nicholas St. Laurence, the sixteenth Lord of Howth, was devoted to the interests of the House of Lancaster, and, during the frenzy that shook Ireland from its propriety and allegiance in the cause of Lambert Simnel, was one of those who most faithfully defended King Henry's title. He afterwards did homage before Sir Richard Edgecome, in the great chamber at St. Thomas's Court, Dublin. He died in 1526, and was buried with his ancestors in Howth Abbey.

In 1530, the celebrated "Silken Thomas," in the Geraldine

rebellion, had artillery placed on Howth, and from its commanding height cannonaded the English ships that were sent to reduce him.
In 1641, Howth was established a navy station by the Lords of the Pale for Leinster.
In 1690, King William is said to have slept in Howth Castle.
The Baily Light-house is situated on the most southerly point of Ben-Edar. The Bay of Dublin, from this point, is one of the most beautiful scenes the eye cau repose upon. Projecting far into the sea, at the end of a long white line, is the Poolbeg Light-house, which resembles a figure of white marble rising out of the ocean. According to tradition, the Baily Light-house is the spot where, on the memorable battle of Clontarf (fought on Good Friday, April 23, 1014), the most obstinate of the discomfited Danes retired, insulated the promontory of Howth, and defended themselves until they were carried off by the vessels of their countrymen.

"Night closed around the warriors's way,
And lightning showed the distant hill,
Where those who lost that dreadful day
Stood few and faint, but fearless still."

A LIST OF DISTINGUISHED MEN AND WOMEN WHO HAVE SHED LUSTRE UPON THEIR COUNTRY, BY THEIR CELEBRITY IN POETRY, HISTORY, PAINTING, MUSIC, THE DRAMA, &c.

Usher, chronologist, linguist, and biblical critic.
Boyle, philosopher.
Sir John Denham, poet.
Farquhar, dramatist.
Congreve, poet and dramatist.
Sir Richard Steele, poet and political writer.
Sir Hans Sloane, naturalist.
Berkeley, mathematician and metaphysician.
Orrery, belles-lettres.
The Two Parnels, poets.
Swift, politician and poet.
T. Sheridan, poet and translator.
De la Cour, poet.
Campbell, mathematician and historian.
Dr. Duncan, poet.
Sterrit, mathematician and engineer.

Lord Roscommon, poet.*
Sir James Ware, the Camden of Ireland.
Johnson, novel-writer.
The Three Hamiltons, mathematicians.
Young, mathematician.
Young, agricultural tourist.
Lord Charlemont, belles-lettres.
Kirwan, mineralogist.
Bickerstaff, dramatist.
Macklin, dramatist.
Malone, commentator.
Canning, poet.
F. Sheridan, political writer.
Griffiths, belles-lettres.
Courtenay, orator and poet.
Flood, orator and politician.
Barre, writer and orator.
Hussey, belles-lettres.
R. B. Sheridan, dramatist and orator.

* The muses' empire is restor'd again,
In Charles's reign, and by Roscommon's pen.—*Dryden*.

To him the wit of Greece and Rome were known,
And every Author's Merit, but his own.—*Pope*.

Dermody, poet (The Chatterton of Ireland).
Ball, poet.
Smith, naturalist and historian.
Harris, historian.
Murphy, dramatist and translator.
Archdall, antiquary.
Dr. Burke, historian.
Doase, surgeon.
Carolin, poet.
Fitzgerald, poet.
Helsham, mathematician and philosopher.
Bryan Robinson, physician.
Goldsmith, poet.
Sterne, sentimentalist.
J. Lynch (Cambrensis Eversus),
Atkinson, dramatist and poet.
Dr. MacDonnell, philanthropist and preserver of Ireland's National Melodies, founder of the Belfast General Hospital.
J. C. Walker, belles-lettres, and antiquary.
Boyd, poet.
Shee, poet.
Ledwich, antiquary.
Theophilus Swift, poet.
Edmund Swift, poet.
Dr. Browne, naturalist.
Dr. Barry, physician.
The two Sterlings, poets.
King, poet.
Wilson, biographer.
Drennan, physician and politician.
Patrick Lindon, poet.
O'Goran, poet.
Father O'Leary, polemical writer.
Tickel, poet.
Brooke, poet and dramatist.
Leland, historian.
Hales, philologist.
Stock, philologist.
Grattan, politician and orator.
Beaufort, mathematician and naturalist.
Lovell Edgeworth, belles-lettres.
Thomas Moore, poet.
Lord Viscount Straugford, poet and translator.
Tresham, poet.
Whitelaw, statist and philanthropist.
Sir Richard Musgrave, historian, politician, and belles-lettres.
Sir Laurence Parsons, historian.
Plunkett, politician and advocate.
Romney Robinson, poet.
Curran, orator and politician.
M'Nally, dramatist and advocate.
Lysaght, poet.*

---

* The following witty ANTI-UNION song, which has much of the spirit of Swift in it, is from the sprightly pen of Lysaght. Its poetical predictions have not been verified, and, the author feels confident, never will be:—

 How justly alarmed is each Dublin cit,
  That he'll soon be transformed to a clown, sir:
 By a magical touch of that conjuror, Pitt,
  The country is coming to town, sir.
  Chorus—Give Pitt and Dundas and Jenkin a glass,
   They'll ride on John Bull and make Paddy an ass.

 Through Capel-street, then, you may *rurally* range—
  You'll scarce recognize the same street;
 Choice turnips shall grow in the Royal Exchange,
  Fine cabbages down along Dame-street.
          Chorus.

The Gorgeous Eloquence of Burke. 347

O'Halloran, historian and physician.
Burgh, *belles-lettres.*
Edmund Burke, *belles-lettres,* politician, and orator.*
Bushe, politician and advocate.
Dr. Duigenan, *belles-lettres* and politician.
H. Kelly, politician and dramatist.

Lady Tuite, poetess.
Mrs. L. Pilkington, writer and poetess.
Mrs. H. Tighe, poetess (Psyche)
Mrs. O'Neill, poetess.
Lady Burrell, poetess.
Mrs. Grierson, translator.
Mrs. Griffith, *belles-lettres.*
Mrs. Brooke, novelist, and *belles-lettres.*

Wild oats in your College won't want to be till'd,
And *hemp* in your Four Courts (1) may thrive, sir ;
As of old shall your markets with muttons (2) be fill'd,
By St. Patrick, they'll graze there alive, sir.
        Chorus.
In the Parliament-house, (3) quite alive shall there be,
All the vermin your island o'er gathers ;
Full of rooks, as of old, Daly's club-house (4) shall be,
But the *pigeons* won't have any *feathers.*
        Chorus.
Your Custom-house quay full of woods, oh ! rare sport,
While the minister's minions, kind elves, sir ;
Will give you free leave, all your goods to export,
When they've left none at home for yourselves, sir.
        Chorus.
The alderman cries, corn will grow in your shops,
This Union must work our enslavement ;
That's true, says the sheriff, for *plenty of crops*
Already I've seen on your pavement.
        Chorus
We have loyal yeomen, dress'd gaily in red,
This minister's plan must elate us ;
And well may John Bull, when he's robb'd us of bread,
Call poor Ireland the land of potatoes.
        Chorus.

---

* Gorgeous eloquence was Burke's natural inheritance ; practical wisdom his chief accomplishment, while all the intellectual graces were his hourly companions. He was not the statesman of a period or of a place, but the enduring teacher of the universal family—the abiding light of the civilized world. The only charges ever brought against this great statesman were, that he pushed the principles of general justice and benevolence too far.

(1) The Courts of Law and Equity in Dublin.
(2) The word which the peasants, in the last century, understood sheep, probably taken from the French, *moutons.*
(3) The present Bank of Ireland.
(4) Once a celebrated gaming-house in Dublin.

Ecoli, commentator.
Thomas Molyneux, Physician, author of a work concerning the Danish Mounts, Forts, and Towers in Ireland.
Luke Aylmer Conolly, poet.
Hardy, *belles-lettres*.
Whyte, poet.
The Two Kearneys, philologists.

Mrs. Sheridan, novel-writer and *belles-lettres*.
Miss Brooke, poetess and translator of "Reliques of Ancient Irish poetry.
Miss Edgeworth, writer, and *belles-lettres*.
Mrs. Lefanue, *belles-lettres*.
Miss Owenson (Lady Morgan), novel-writer.

Artists.

Barry, historical painter.
Shee, R. A. (Sir), portrait painter.
Thresham, R. A., hist. painter.
Garvey, R. A.
Ashford, landscape painter.
Pope, portrait painter.
Hamilton, portrait painter.

De Grey.
Herbert, portrait painter.
Heweston, sculptor.
Williams, landscape and portrait painter.
Smith, modeller.
Hickey, sculptor.
Hand, glass stainer.

Composers.

Carolin.
Sir John Stevenson.

Moore.
Lady Steward.

Dramatic Performers.

Barry.
Sheridan.
Ryder.
Moody.
Betty.
Macklin.

Johnstone.
O'Reilly.
Pope.
Cherry.
Mrs. Woffington.
Mrs. Jordan.

Singers.

Sir John Stevenson.   Kelly.   Cooke.

Preachers.

Fleming.   Kirwan.

GASKIN'S IRISH VARIETIES,

ETC., ETC., ETC.

APPENDIX.

APPENDIX A.

DALKEY SOUND—COOLAMORE HARBOUR—CEREMONIAL
OF LAYING THE FOUNDATION STONE.

Page 5.

THE ceremonial of laying the foundation stone of the proposed new harbour at the Coolamore, Dalkey, took place on the 9th September, 1868.

James Milo Burke, Esq., J.P., on presenting himself for that purpose, was received with a warm and cordial greeting.

He expressed his deep sense of the honour, privilege, and duty devolving upon him as Chairman of the Commissioners.

He had been elected to that responsible office by his esteemed fellow Commissioners on the formation of the township, and he was extremely gratified that he had retained their confidence during the five years of their arduous and useful labours—but no circumstance more impressed him with the honour of that position than the present, enabling him to take a principal part in laying the foundation stone of a new pier—as the port of Dalkey had been at all times to him an object of the greatest interest.

The general management of the township was, he was justified in saying, carried out by the Commissioners with undeviating rectitude of purpose and solicitude, ever keeping prominently in view the improvement of Dalkey as the sole object of their exertions.

The work so auspiciously to be inaugurated to-day is but the prelude to many important improvements designed by the Commissioners. In due time, and having due regard to the limited finances at their disposal, these improvements will be accomplished.

Compare the *present* prosperous position of Dalkey with the *past*—not many years since it was a barren, rocky, yet picturesque waste, dotted over by squatters' huts, and inhabited solely by the poorest and humblest classes of society, including the workmen employed in the great and valuable granite quarries.

Now, magnificent terraces and beautiful villas—occupied by the wealthy and princely merchants, and *elite* of the medical profession of the city of Dublin, and the most refined and fashionable circles of society, legal and other professions—attest the wonderful magnitude of the change. But recently a poor and inconsiderable village, to-day we see an extensive town arise around us, with a large and increasing population, requiring the management and constant superintendence of a corporate body, selected by the people themselves.

When, in 1834, his father and himself made their first purchases of land in this district, they were considered as bereft of their senses. It was not believed that they would be allowed to retain their acquisitions—but that the people (termed Squatters) who were unjustly, and without good reason, stigmatised as "*lawless ruffians*," would forcibly resume occupation in the same manner as they had originally appropriated the land. The prophecy was not verified; the aspersion cast upon these poor but honest men was proved to be unjustifiable. These evil forebodings did not deter nor divert his father or himself from treating with the humble occupiers of the soil, on equitable terms; they resolved to confide in the squatters—to treat them liberally and fairly for what they had to dispose of. The squatters were perfectly satisfied with their terms, and they fulfilled their engagements honourably and faithfully.

Thus relying on the sacred principles of justice implanted by nature in the mind of man, and in no portion of the human race more deeply than in our own fellow-countrymen, and resolving to act upon the golden rule " to do unto others as we would wish that they would do unto us," we proceeded in our course fearlessly.

We were justified in our confidence by the result. The squatters on their side received the just reward of their fidelity—they had constant and good employment, with liberal wages. By them the barren waste was reclaimed; new roads and avenues laid out and constructed.

Some purchasers did not act in this spirit—dealing fairly and liberally.

His father denounced their sordid and illiberal selfishness, and declared that he would do all he could to make Dalkey the admiration of the kingdom, in despite of every obstacle. "You may thwart me," said his father, "but neither you nor those who act with you shall scare me from my purpose."

In opening and widening the roads—in some places barely eight feet wide—many difficulties were encountered, but happily all have been successfully overcome. Some who caused these difficulties have gone to their account—some remain, and see their former mistaken views and errors; and now all pull together harmoniously. I have refrained from stating names. I wish from my heart all bitterness and unpleasant recollections to be obliterated from our minds; all animosities and ill-feeling to be buried in the past—all our hopes, aspirations and united efforts to be directed to the welfare of Dalkey for the future.

On the rock overhead (said Mr. Burke pointing to the tablet cut thereon), I had the Irish name of "*Coolamore* inscribed, with a short history of some remarkable events which occurred at the place. I regret extremely that some mischievous and ill-disposed persons (no doubt enemies of Dalkey), have wantonly and maliciously defaced the tablet, and nearly erased the inscription. Mr. Burke concluded his address by reverting to the interesting ceremony of the day, and entered into some details about the port.

The port of Dalkey was at one time (he stated), designed as the site of an asylum harbour. Howth, and ultimately Kingstown, or rather Dunleary, was preferred, and the many natural advantages of Dalkey overlooked. A large grant has been expended in the construction of Kingstown harbour, which is, after all, insecure from the disastrous effects of storms from the N. E., and inadequate to the requirements of commerce ; so that an extension is under consideration. What a magnificent harbour, perfectly landlocked, and safe from every wind that blows, could have been raised at Dalkey at a comparatively small outlay ; and—strange caprice of fortune—the very stones of Dalkey, from her granite quarries, have been made to contribute to the greatness of her favoured rival. Thus exemplifying the lines of the Roman poet :—

"Sic vos non Vobis vellera fertis oves
Sic vos non Vobis mellificatis apes."

To which may be added, to complete the analogy :—

"Sic vos non Vobis ædificatis rupes."

The interesting proceedings terminated with a series of loud cheers from the workmen, and a salvo of blasts which did duty for artillery. The gentlemen invited to attend the ceremonial adjourned at its conclusion to the residence of Mr. Cunningham, the contractor, where a sumptuous *déjeûner* had been prepared; it was supplied in the best style possible, by Mr. Fleming, of South Great George's-street, Dublin. Mr. Cunningham presided, and Mr. Henry Parkinson acted as vice-chairman. Amongst those present were: James Milo Burke, Esq., J.P., Chairman, Dalkey Commissioners; Dr. Parkinson, T.C.; David Beggs, Esq., T.C.; Edward Harrison, Esq., T.C.; John Fleming, Esq., T.C.; William Murphy, Esq., T.C.; Gerard Tyrrell, Esq., T.C.; Henry Parkinson, Esq., T.C.; Henry Gonne, Esq., secretary; Alderman Manning, Esq., J.P.; John Crosthwaite, Esq., T.C.; Horatio N. Wallace, Esq., J.P., T.C.; P. Lagan, Esq., T.C.; Samuel M'Comas, Esq., J.P.; Eugene Quirk, Esq., C.E.; Anthony O'Toole, Esq.; J. W. Coffey, Esq., Solicitor; J. J. Connolly, Esq., Dalkey; Richard Kennan, Esq., solicitor; M. Short, Esq., Barrister; J. Simpson, Esq.; J. W. Perrin, Esq.; J. J. Conroy, Esq., Solicitor; W. A. Emerson, Esq., *Irish Times*; W. Robert Irvine, Esq.; F. Doyle, Esq., C.E.; C. Fleming, Esq., jun.; E. Gray, *Freeman's Journal*; G. Powell, Esq., *Daily Express*; W. R. Paine, Esq., Solicitor; A. G. Figges, Esq., Mr. James J. Gaskin; J. Burke, Esq., jun.; D. C. Bergin, Esq.; J. Quinn, Esq.; G. Alexander, Esq., &c., &c.

The cloth having been removed, Mr. Henry Parkinson, vice-chairman, rose, and said that he had been requested by their host, Mr. Cunningham, to accept that ancient and time-honoured office of toastmaster, and that his first official act would be to request all present to fill their glasses, and assist him to drink the health of her most gracious Majesty, Queen Victoria.

Mr. Parkinson proposed the health of their worthy host, Mr. Cunningham, and referred to the extensive works which, in the course of his career as a contractor, he had executed. He had built railway bridges and viaducts, including the splendid viaduct near Newry, and another on the Wicklow line. One of the latest works was the Stillorgan reservoir, which was one of the wonders of the age. The harbour commenced that day would be a work of which Mr. Cunningham would be proud. It would be of incalculable benefit to Dalkey, and was the forerunner of many other improvements (loud applause).

Mr. Cunningham,[*] who was most warmly received, returned thanks in appropriate terms, and gave the health of their universally esteemed and talented friend, Mr. Henry Parkinson,[†] who had already done so much good for the public institutions of the country (loud applause).

---

[*] Mr. Cunningham is a gentleman who has been reared in that school of self-reliance, progress, and enterprise, founded by Dargan, in which patience, untiring energy, and persevering industry were strictly inculcated. The origin of this school may be attributed to the Irish Industrial Exhibition of 1853, on which occasion, William Dargan, the man with his "hand in his pocket," refused a baronetcy, so graciously offered by Her Majesty the Queen. How applicable to such men are the following lines of the great poet, Pope :—

"Bid harbours open, public ways extend,
Bid temples worthier of the God ascend,
Bid the broad arch the dangerous flood contain,
The mole projected break the roaring main ;
Back to his bounds their subject sea command,
And roll obedient rivers through the land.
These honours peace to hopeful Ireland brings—
These are imperial works, and worthy kings."

[†] The author takes the opportunity of remarking that there are but few gentlemen who have rendered, during the past few years, so many and so distinguished public services to his fellow-citizens and the country at large, as Mr. Henry Parkinson, and that without any adequate recompense, or Government recognition, for the time he has lost, which otherwise might have been profitably employed in professional pursuits. It is, therefore, but common justice to briefly allude to one or two events in the history of this country with which Mr. Parkinson's name has been closely connected. In the year 1860, he was invited to take the post of Secretary to the Committee of the Royal Dublin Society's Fine Art Exhibition of 1861, and which, owing in a great measure to the exertions of Mr. Parkinson, in procuring works of art in England and elsewhere, and to his subsequent spirited management, was allowed to be not only one of the most interesting collections of

Mr. Parkinson and the Nine Apothecaries. 355

Mr. Parkinson responded, and, speaking of the healthy character of Dalkey, stated that he had known nine apothecaries obliged to leave the place from want of business (great laughter). He proposed the Municipal Corporations of Ireland, coupled with

Fine Arts, for its size, ever brought together in Ireland, but a pecuniary success. At the close of that Exhibition, it occurred to Mr. Parkinson that a permanent institution, analogous to that of the Crystal Palace in London, might be formed with advantage to the City of Dublin; and the Author can bear witness to the fact, that he was consulted on the subject by Mr. Parkinson, before he commenced to organize the Winter Garden Company. That to Mr. Parkinson's exertions, at least at the commencement, must be attributed the erection (no matter what may be its fate) of the noble building which now stands next Stephen's Green, at Earlsfort-terrace; and, further, that Mr. Parkinson was instrumental in causing the building to be opened with the International Exhibition of 1865, which was, undoubtedly, a great success, and brought thousands from all parts of the world into Ireland. Railway directors, in their reports, still allude to their receipts that year. The foregoing facts are verified by the following recorded words of the late lamented member for Dublin, Sir B. L. Guinness, Bart., when presiding at a public meeting, at which Mr. Parkinson was presented with an address by the citizens:—

"Mr. Parkinson, from my very long knowledge of you, and more especially from recent and continual observation of your zeal and efficient assistance in bringing to so successful a termination our great enterprise, the International Exhibition, I can bear my testimony to its success being greatly owing to your unwearied attention and exertion. I have also had an opportunity of knowing your courtesy and kindness to visitors that came there. I am sorry to say it was not followed up by others, to whom I shall not allude; but the fact only rendered your kindness and exertions the more conspicuous.

"The Exhibition could not have been held had not the previous undertaking been accomplished of building the Palace. Knowing something of the origin of that Palace, and the way in which it was got up, I can state that the citizens are indebted to you, and one or two others, for that magnificent building. I, therefore, feel not only a pleasure but a pride, in presenting to you this testimonial, as an expression of esteem and approbation for the manner in which you discharged your duties as Secretary of the Exhibition."

Mr. Parkinson, at the close of the Exhibition, published the magnificent book, at an outlay of £600, recording the principal features of the Exhibition, with descriptions of existing Irish manufactures, and the products of different countries. The undertaking, it is to be regretted, resulted in a considerable pecu-

the name of Alderman Manning, one of the most honoured members of the Corporation of Dublin (loud cheers).

Alderman Manning, J.P., on rising to acknowledge this toast, was received with loud and continued applause.

He alluded to the original formation of municipal institutions. "In the middle ages," he said, "when trade was in its infancy, they were designed to defend the Burghers from lawless aggression and rapine. By their means, the germs of freedom in the municipal towns, were nurtured to maturity, and a firm basis laid, on which great and thriving centres of commercial industry were raised to greatness, power and magnificence.

"In this enlightened age of reason and civilization, the arts of peace prevail—mutual defence is not now the essential object of municipal associations.

"The peace, progress, and prosperity of each and every community, now virtually and mainly depend on the due and faithful discharge of the important functions which devolve on the several municipal bodies in the different cities and towns through the kingdom.

"It is well," continued Alderman Manning, " to see municipal institutions extending under the provisions of the Towns' Improvement Act, in all directions— and a certain recognition of their general public utility, as well as a sure indication of commercial progress, and national civilization."

The worthy Alderman then dwelt upon the important and arduous business transacted by the Dublin Corporation. He said "he did not claim to be a frequent

niary loss to Mr. Parkinson. Not to dwell on Mr. Parkinson's efforts towards the formation of a co-operative society, the Author will only add, in conclusion, that the inhabitants of Dalkey may thank Mr. Parkinson for that locality being formed into a township, and the many advantages they now possess and enjoy.

His allusion to Municipal Institutions.

public speaker, but that he was a regular attendant on the Committees, *where the work was done*, and could, from personal knowledge, bear testimony to the large amount of work, and the useful and constant labours of the Committees, and he hoped he had there faithfully fulfilled his corporate duties to the satisfaction of his constituents.

"The several other corporate bodies had also arduous duties to perform—no less important to the welfare of the various municipalities in Ireland, and by their zealous attention to these duties, promoted general order and prosperity. On the part of all these corporate bodies, he had the honor to return grateful acknowledgments for the recognition of their services.

"As to Dalkey especially, he could truly say he had been attached to it for years, and every year he liked it better and better.

"In conclusion, he congratulated Mr. James Milo Burke, (whom he styled, *speciali gratia*, Lord Mayor of Dalkey,) the Commissioners, and the inhabitants, upon the useful work that day initiated, and trusted that the owners of property in Dalkey would generally and zealously co-operate, in order to promote the undertaking which would be not merely beneficial and pleasant to visitors and occupiers of villas, but would be the means of considerably enhancing the value of their own building ground and houses. An enterprise so material to local trade, to internal and international communication, to the ease and security of a seafaring community and the mercantile marine of a port of such ancient repute for the extent and importance of its foreign commerce, and the value of its imports, and which has been not inaptly said, from its position and natural advantages, to resemble the beautiful bay of Eleusis, between the Grecian mainland and the island of Salamis.*

* Here was achieved the great and celebrated naval victory of the Grecian fleet over the Persian Armada—Xerxes, the Persian

"He had no doubt that our equally useful and desirable improvements, such as a suitable bathing place —which would prove a great attraction and convenience—would be undertaken and completed by the excellent and enterprising Commissioners of the rising town of Dalkey."

On resuming his seat the worthy Alderman was again loudly cheered.

The remaining toasts, including the ladies and the press, having been duly honoured. The company soon after separated.

APPENDIX B.

DELVILLE, GLASNEVIN.—EXTRACTS FROM MRS. PILKINGTON'S WORKS.—DEAN SWIFT.

Page viii., "*Introduction.*"

On Tuesday last all day I stray'd,
In DELVILLE'S sweet inspiring shade,
There all was easy, gay, polite,
The weather and the guests were bright;
My loved *Constantia* there appear'd,
And SOUTHERN long for wit rever'd,
Who like the hoary *Pylian* sage,
Excels in wisdom, as in age."

* * * *

"I had a strong ambition to be introduced to Dean Swift, and as Dr. Delany had recommended and introduced my husband, Mr. Pilkington, to him, I thought it a little hard to be excluded from the delight and instruction I might possibly receive from his conversation ; * * * and as they were to meet the next day at the Deanery House, to keep the Anniversary of his Birth-day, I enclosed to Dr. Delany the following lines :—

TO THE REV. DR. SWIFT, ON HIS BIRTH-DAY.

"While I, the god-like men of old,
In admiration wrapt, behold !

---

monarch, sat in state on an eminence on an island, to view the engagement, in full assurance of victory, but his arrogance was signally reproved by the result, his hopes of conquest disappointed, and Grecian independence bravely, gallantly, and successfully maintained.

Rever'd antiquity explore,
And turn the long-liv'd volumes o'er,
Where *Cato*, *Plutarch*, Flaccus shine,
In ev'ry excellence divine ;
I grieve that our degen'rate days,
Produce no mighty souls like these ;
Patriot, philosopher, and bard,
Are names unknown, and seldom heard.
Spare your reflection, Phœbus cries,
'Tis as ungrateful as unwise ;
Can you complain this sacred day,
That virtues or that arts decay ?
Behold in SWIFT reviv'd appears,
The virtues of unnumbered years :
Behold in him with new delight,
The patriot, bard, and sage unite,
And know Ierne in that name,
Shall rival *Greece* and *Rome* in fame."

Doctor Delany presented these lines to the Dean ; he kindly accepted of my compliment, and said he would see me whenever I pleased. A most welcome message to me.

A few days after, the Dean sent the Doctor word, he would dine with him at *Delville*, and desired to meet Mr. and Mrs. P——n there. You may be assured I obeyed the welcome summons ; and a gentlewoman was so kind as to call on me to go with her ; when we arrived, Doctor Delany's servant told us his master, the Dean, and Mr. P——n were walking in the garden, we met there on a noble terrace, whose summit was crowned with a magnificent Portico, where painting and sculpture display'd their utmost charms. (Stella was dead before Mrs. Pilkington became acquainted with Swift).

The highly talented, but unfortunate Mrs. Pilkington, was personally acquainted with Swift, of whom she has written in her Memoirs an interesting account. She has also left on record a charming description of her "dear and faithful friend," the celebrated Colley Cibber, who inscribed the following verses to her :—

"Hail, charming fair, with low, but friendly lays,
' I'll tune my pipe, and vie to sing thy praise,
Ambitious always to defend thy fame,
And sing thy spotless, but much injur'd name :
Thy story oft with pitying soul I read,
         *   *   *   *   *

Ungrateful Man !* could neither wit nor art
Raise thy compassion or secure thy heart,

---

* Her husband.

When all the joys that please in human life,
Shone bright in her, and form'd a perfect wife ;
Respected and rever'd where'er she went,
Discreetly gay, yet strictly innocent ;
Her sprightly parts, her lively wit and sense,
To none but you e'er gave the least offence ;
But could the serpent with the lamb agree ?
No more could such a heaven born fair with thee.
Ambition, envy, acted each their part,
To 'sail what should be partner of thy heart :
Go, abject slave, you meanly spent your life
In low pursuits.
The Dean* first brought you from a low estate
On his account admitted to the great.'
　　 *　　 *　　 *　　 *　　 *
Yet be content while you in lustre shine,
And paint your wrongs in soft and well-tun'd line,
The world, tho' late, your merit shall befriend,
And all your sorrows in applause shall end."

Mrs. Pilkington and her father, John Van Lewin, M.D., are buried in St. Anne's Church, Dawson-street, Dublin.

APPENDIX C.

THE PROPOSED STATUE TO HENRY GRATTAN.—THE RT. HON. THOMAS O'HAGAN'S, LORD CHANCELLOR OF IRELAND, LETTER TO LORD CHARLEMONT.—SYDNEY SMITH'S OPINION OF GRATTAN.

Page xiii., "*Introduction.*"

The following letter was addressed by the Lord Chancellor to the Earl of Charlemont :—

"Rutland-square, West, Jan. 9, 1869.

" MY DEAR LORD CHARLEMONT—I inclose a cheque for £100, in aid of the fund for the erection of a statue to Henry Grattan, as I learn that you fitly take a leading part in the movement for that good purpose, which has been so generously and hopefully begun.

* Dean Swift.

"I tender to you my humble co-operation, because it is not the movement of a Party or a Sect, but of a Nation, offering its grateful reverence to one of its worthiest sons.

"I remember the feeling with which, long years ago, I stood in Westminster Abbey, beside a shattered slab, bearing the name of Henry Grattan; and thought it a symbol of the broken fortunes of the land for which he lived and died. It seemed to me a national reproach, that his dust should have been left in English earth, with no better monument, by the people to whom he had rendered such loving service. And now I rejoice that we are at last uniting, in a time of hope and progress, to put away that reproach for ever.

"We may hold various opinions with reference to Grattan's policy and conduct; but we can have no dissension as to his pure and earnest life; his public virtue; his indomitable courage; his true and unchanging devotion to his country; the achievements by which he lighted up the fairest page in our dismal story; the genius which made him matchless amongst the orators of the modern world.

"The Irish Protestant will not hold unworthy of his homage the chief of the great men, of his own faith, whose labours and sacrifices for Ireland have given lustre to their race.

"The Irish Catholic will be emulous to honour him who, in evil days—untainted by corruption and unawed by power—was the dauntless champion of Religious Liberty.

"The fame of Henry Grattan is the common and the proud inheritance of all good Irishmen. It is no longer obscured by the mists and heats of faction. It suffers no more from the insolence of authority or the fickleness of the crowd. It lifts him high on the roll of names which live through ages. And we are bound—one and all, of every class and creed—to

demonstrate, according to our power, how dear it is
to the memory and the heart of Ireland.
"Believe me, my dear Lord Charlemont,
"Ever faithfully yours,
"THOMAS O'HAGAN.
"The Earl of Charlemont."

In speaking of Grattan, the celebrated writer, the Rev. Sydney Smith, says:—

"Thank God, that all is not profligacy and corruption in the history of that devoted people; and that the name of Irishman does not always carry with it the idea of the oppressor or the oppressed; the plunderer or the plundered; the tyrant or the slave! Great men hallow a whole people, and lift up all who live in their time. What Irishman does not feel proud that he has lived in the days of GRATTAN? Who has not turned to him for comfort, from the false friends and open enemies of Ireland? Who did not remember him in the days of its burnings, and wastings, and murders? No government ever dismayed him; the world could not bribe him; he thought only of Ireland—lived for no other object—dedicated to her his beautiful fancy, his elegant wit, his manly courage, and all the splendour of his astonishing eloquence. He was so born and so gifted, that poetry, forensic skill, elegant literature, and all the highest attainments of human genius were within his reach; but he thought the noblest occupation of a man was to make other men happy and free; and in that straight line he went on for fifty years, without one side-look, without one yielding thought, without one motive in his heart, which he might not have laid to the view of God and man.

"He is gone! but there is not a single day of his honest life of which every good Irishman would not be more proud, than of the whole political existence of his countrymen—the annual deserters and betrayers of their native land."

APPENDIX D.

HEROIC CONDUCT OF EDMOND D. GRAY, ESQ., SON TO
SIR JOHN GRAY, M.P.

Page 7.

On Saturday afternoon, the 2nd January, 1869, the Committee of the "Tayleur Society" met in the Commercial Buildings, Dublin, for the purpose of presenting medals to Edmond W. Gray, Esq. (second son of Sir John Gray, M.P.), and to Patrick Freeny, for their heroic conduct in rescuing several persons from the schooner Bluevein, wrecked off Ballybrack, Killiney Bay, September 25, 1868.

On the motion of Mr. Bagot, hon. secretary to the Chamber of Commerce, Lord Talbot de Malahide, Chairman of the Tayleur Committee, was called on to preside.

Lord Talbot de Malahide, having taken the chair, said, "Gentlemen, it is usual on occasions of this kind to make a few remarks. I shall be very brief. The event which has caused us to meet is one that commends itself to the attention and sympathy of every right-minded—of every Christian man in the community. You are all aware that the society now ·assembled, the Tayleur Fund Committee, was established in 1854 on the occurrence of the lamentable disaster, when the Tayleur was lost off the coast at Lambay, and several hundred persons met with a watery grave. The circumstance at the time created great attention. It was melancholy in the extreme. A vessel starting for a distant land with a large number of individuals, who were hoping to better their condition by expatriation—persons of different classes in life—some of them, I may say, of the highest respectability—met this untimely fate. Amongst them was Mr. Codd, the brother of Mr. Francis Codd, who was known to you all, who was so highly esteemed, and who took so leading a part in the affairs of this city. The disaster created great sympathy, and a very considerable sum of money was contributed both in this country and in England. Her Majesty was pleased to give a donation of £25, evincing by that, that the same willingness prompts her on all occasions to assist good undertakings. After satisfying every demand on the Tayleur fund, there was a considerable surplus; and upon consideration it appeared to us that it could not be devoted to a better purpose than providing for the necessities of the shipwrecked, and rewarding the exertions of those who were foremost in rescuing victims from a watery grave. We have frequently given donations for this purpose, and, although they have not been made in the public manner of our proceeding this day, I think, without any feeling or any wish to show ostentation, it is a good course to do these things in a public manner. An example is contagious, whether for good or evil, and it is useful that there should be, on certain occasions, a display of the recognition which follows noble deeds. The facts connected with the event which has brought us together are patent to all. We are going now to present medals to two gentlemen who have distinguished themselves in the highest degree, who have rescued five individuals from a most dangerous position. It is no ordinary man who has the power both of body and mind to come forward on occasions of great peril. There are many noble deaths. It is a noble thing to die on the field of battle, fighting for the rights of one's country. There are other great deaths, if I may use the expression, but I must confess that if I was to choose a death, there is none I would sooner select than a death which would overtake me in the effort to save the life of a fellow-creature. This, indeed, would be euphanasia. Gentlemen, I will not detain you any longer, but conclude by reminding you that the ancient Romans were foremost in rewarding great acts done on behalf of the public. There were crowns of various kinds for military and naval prowess, but of all the crowns none ranked so high as the crown *cive salvato*."

Lord Talbot de Malahide then called on Mr. Edmond Gray, who, on coming forward, was received with loud applause. The noble lord said, "Mr. Edmond Gray, I have great pleasure in presenting to you, on behalf of the Tayleur Committee, this gold medal, for 'distinguished courage in saving life from the wreck of the Bluevein, at Ballybrack, on the 25th of September, 1868.' I have very great pleasure, I repeat, in presenting this medal to you. You have deserved anything we could bestow on you for your courage, energy, and Christian feeling on that occasion (loud applause). I would add, that you have shown in this act all the energy of your race" (applause).

Mr. Edmond Gray, who was loudly cheered, said— "My Lord Talbot de Malahide, I feel very thankful indeed for the beautiful and costly medal you have presented to me. To you, my Lord Talbot, my thanks are still more due for your kindness in presiding on this occasion, and for the very flattering terms in which you spoke of my exertions at the wreck of the Bluevein. I am quite certain there is not a gentleman in this room who, with the same ability, and placed in similar circumstances, would not have acted in the same way that I acted (hear, hear, and applause). From my youth I have been accustomed to swimming, and to do battle with the boisterous waves for my amusement. When I am near the sea, whether it be wet or dry, cold or warm, provided it be stormy, I nearly always have a swim. For that reason I was enabled to swim out to the wreck of the Bluevein with less danger to myself than might have happened to other people who were, perhaps, better swimmers, but not as accustomed as I was to struggle with the rough waves, I was, of course, conscious that there was some danger in doing so; but I considered it was my duty to run some risk to save people who appeared to be in imminent danger (hear, hear, and applause). I have received a medal before this, my lord, from the Royal Life-boat Institution. Of that medal I feel very justly proud, but I feel an immense number of times more proud of the medal presented to me this day by your lordship in this public manner, before some of the most eminent citizens of Dublin (applause). I feel very grateful also to the members of the Tayleur Committee, especially to my dear friend, Mr. Stokes, for their very great kindness on this occasion. I should also thank the Chamber of Commerce for their kindness in giving the use of the room to-day. I must add that I am glad to find that Patrick Freeny, whose courage was eminently displayed on the occasion of the wreck, has been rewarded in a suitable manner (hear, hear). I consider he well deserves what he has got. Again, my lord, I thank you and the gentlemen present most sincerely for the honour you have done me" (applause).

APPENDIX E.

"A Fragment of the History of Ireland, by Maurice Regan—Arrival of Strongbow—Dublin Besieged—Preface of Sir George Carew."

A.D., 1167.—It apperith that this history was written by one called Maurice Regan, who was servant and interpreter unto Dermott MacMurrogh, Kyng of Leinster, and put in French meetre by one of his familiar acquaintance. For thus he writeth in the begynnyng of the poem :—

"At his own desire the interpreter
To me related his history,

Which I here commit to memory;
Maurice Regan was the man,
Who, face to face, indited to me
These actions of the King;
And of himself showed me this history
This Maurice was interpreter
To the King, King Murcher;
These Kings this batchellor
Of King Dermod read to me;
This is his story."

It endith abruptly at the winning of Limerick, which was not full three yeres after Robert Fitz-Stephen, his first arrivall in Ireland.

Dermond* Kyng of Leinster, was a powerful prince; he invaded O'Neal and the Kyng of Meath, compelled them to gyve hostages, and constrained O'Kermll to send hym his son for a pledge into Leinster. At that tyme O'Rory, Kyng of Lethcoin,† whose country was woody and full of boggs, had to wyfe the daughter of Melaghlin MacColman, Kyng of Meath, a fair and lovely lady, entirely beloved of Dermond, Kyng of Leinster, who also hated O'Rory for an affront which his men had received at Lethmuth‡ in his country.

Dermond, by leters and messingers, pursued her love with such fervency, as, in the end, she sent him word that shee was ready to obey, and yeld to his will, appointed him a tyme and place where he should find her, and prayeing him to come soe strongly, as that he might by force take her away with him. Dermond presently assembled his forces, and marched into the county of Lethcoin; at Trimbruin§

* Dermond from the beginning of his government was a great oppressor of his people, and a cruel tyrant over his nobility, which made them ready to embrace the first opportunity of changing their master.—*Cambrensis*.

† This must certainly be an error in transcribing (Lethcoin being mistaken for Leitrim), for Regan could not be ignorant that O'Rory, more truly O'Roirke, was King of Breifni, a territory now comprehending the county of Leitrim, and not of Leithcoin, which was the half of Ireland, being all that lay north of the mouth of the river Boyne in a straight line to Galway.—*Antiquities of Ireland*.

‡ Lethnnth is not mentioned in any Irish history.

§ Trim-Bruin was the residence of O'Roirke. For Trimbruin Breifne, often called Hy-bruin Breifne, was a small district that lay in O'Roirke's County, in Leitrim.

he found this lady, tooke her awaye with him, spoiled the county, and returned with victory and content into Fernes.

O'Rory, full of grief and rage, addressed hymself unto the Kyng of Connaght, complaining of the wrong and scorne done unto hym by the Kyng of Leinster, and intreating his aid in the revenge of so grete an outrage.

O'Conner, Kyng of Connaght, moved with honour and compassion, promised him succour, and presently he dispatched messingers to the King of Ossory unto Melaghlin, King of Meath, to Hesculph, Mac Turkell* Lord of Dublin, and Morrough O'Birne, wyth whome he so muche prevailed, as they turned heads upon their Lord King Dermond.

The King of Leinster seeing hymself forsaken of his kinsmen, friends, servants, and principal followers, having sume more confidence in Murrough O'Birne than in the rest, took horse, and rode to speak with hym.

King Dermond being returned to Fernes, and lodged in the Abbey at Fernes, dedicated to the Blessed Virgin Mary, commanded the abbot to write a letre, which he subscribed, and to deliver it to one of his monks to carry it to the Morrough O'Birne, hoping thereby to perswade him to a meeting. The monke being dispatched, discharged the trust imposed upon him soe well as that he delivered the letre to O'Birne. The King followed the monke, and at a woodside saw Morrough O'Birne, who, beholdinge the King, menanced him presently to depart, or else he would repent it.

The distressed King, almost destracted with griefe and anger, returned to Fernes, and fearing to be betrayed there, and delivered by his people unto the King of Connaught, resolved to abandon his country, and instantly without delay he went to the Horkeran, where he imbarqued hymself for England, having in his company no other man of marke then Awliffe O'Kinade, and about sixty persons.

With a prosperous gale he arrived at Bristoll, and was lodged with all his companie in the house of Robert Hardinge, at St. Augustins, where, aftir some staie, he addressed his journey towards France, to speak with King Henry, who then had wars in that kingdom with the French King.

---

* Hesculph Mac Turkil was at this time the Danish petty King of Dublin and Fingall, whiqh he held of King Dermod by tribute; but now, he, as well as the King of Ossory, who was also subject to Dermod, took up arms against him to recover their liberties which he had invaded. The same thing did the O'Birnes in the now county of Wicklow.

When he came to the presence of King Henry, he related at large unto hym that he was forced to run into exile, and beseeching hym to gyve hym aid, whereby he might be restorid to his inheritance, which yf it should please him in his goodness to grant, he would acknowledge hym to be Lorde, and serve hym faithfully during his life.*

This pitifull relation of the distressed king so much movid King Henry to compassion as that he promised him aid, and willed him to return to Bristoll, there to remain until he herd furthir from hym; and with all he wrote to Robert Harding, requiring hym to receve King Dermond and his followers into his house, and to intreat them with all courtesie and humanitie he could; whereof Robert failed in nothing.

After King Dermond had remained more than a month in Bristol, and seeing no hope of aid from King Henry, weary of delaye, and comfortless, he went to the Erle Richard, intreating succours from hym, and promising, that if by his means he might be re-established in his kyngdome, that he would gyve hym his daughter to wife, and with her the whole Kingdom of Leinster for his inheritance.

The Erle, tickled with so fair an offer, made answeare, that if he could obtain leave of the King, his mastir, he would not fail to assiste hym in his person, and bring sufficient aid; but for the present he desired to be excused; for unless the King would give his assent therunto, he durst not entirtaine a business of that importance.

This faire and discreet answeare so well contented the exiled King, as he solemnly swore that whensoever the Erle did bring aide unto hym, he would give him his daughter in marriage, and after his death, the Kingdom of Leinster.

These conditions being agreed to on either party, Dermond departed, and went to St. David's, where he staid untill shipping was provided to transport hym into Ireland.

* * * * *

The King of Leinster finding it to be an impossibility for hym to recovir his kingdome, and to prevaile in his designs, without aide out of England, dispatched his trusty servant and interpreter, Maurice Regan, with letres in Wales, and with authority in his name to promise all such as would come to serve hym in his wars in Ireland, large recompence in landes of inheritance to souche as would staye in the

* Cambrensis asserts that King Dermond swore allegiance to King Henry, and to be his vassal and subject, whereupon King Henry took him into his protection, and gave him letters patent directed to all his subjects, to aid and help him.

country, and to those that would returne, he would gyve them good intertainment eyther in money or in cattle. As soone as these promises were divulged, men of all sortes, and from divers places, preparid themselves to goe into Ireland, first, especially Robert Fitz-Stephen, a man of good esteeme in Wales (who had lately been enlargid out of prison by the mediation of Dermond), unditrooke the imployment, and with hym some nine or ten knights of good account.

A.D. 1169.—This little army, transported in three ships, landed at a place called Bann, not far from the town of Wexford, from whence they immediately dispatched messingers unto King Dermond to give him notice of their arrivall, who without delay repaired unto them, and imbracing them with much joy, and rendering them thanks for their travile they had taken, that night they encamped by the sea-side. The next day Dermond and the Englishe marched directly to Wexford, and instantly gave an assault unto the towne, in the whiche eighteen Englishe were slain, and of the defendaunts only three. Nevertheless, the townsmen perceavinge themselves to be unable to make any long defence, demanded parle, which being graunted, they offered hostages to the King and to sware from thence forward to be evermore his loyall vassals. By the advice of the Englishe the conditions were accepted, and the town of Wexford rendered itself unto Dermond. Which done, he went to Fernes, as well to cure his hurt men as to feast the Englishe, where they rested three weeks.

* * * * *

Then Dermond called to hym Robert Fitz-Stephen and Maurice de Prindergast, tellinge them how much they and their nation were feared by the Irish; wherefore he had a purpose to invade the King of Ossory, his mortal enemy, and to chastise hym; but furst he required their advise and consent; who answered, that they came to that land to no othir end than to serve hym in his warrs, and that they would not forsake him in any interprize whatsoever he would undertake.

Dermond assemblid with grete expedition all his forces, to the number of thre thousande, besides the thre hundreth Englishe, and marched towards Ossory. When he was entred into the country, they found that Donald, King of Ossory* plashed a place, made large and deep trenches in the

---

* This Donald was surnamed Macgilla-phadruick, or Fitzpatrick, and was the head of a powerful sept in Ossory, from whence the Barons of Upper Ossory, a title now extinct, were descended, as also the Lord Gowan, now living (1745).

same, with hedges upon them, and manned with five thousaude men, through which place his enemies, of necessitie, must passe. Dermond's troops gave upon the trenches; the fight endured from morninge untill night; but at last, by the valour of 'the Englishe, the trenches were forced, the enemy discomfitted, but with much slaughter on either side. Then Dermond's light men harissed and burnt all the country, and returned with a huge prey.

* * * * * * *

1169.—After a number of engagements, Dermond, with his Englishe and Irish troopes, marched towards Glindelagh to chastise The O'Tohill* for refusing to come unto hym. When he came into the country he found no resistance.

* * * * * *

1170.—At this tyme, Richard, Erle of Pembrooke, sent Reymond Le Gros† into Irland with nine or ten knights, and some foot. They landed at Downdonnell, where Reymond remained, intrenchinge hymselfe with a slight fortification.

* * * * * *

While Reymond continued in his aboade there, the Erle Richard arrived at Waterford with fifteen or sixteen hundreth soldiers,‡ and, loosing no tyme, he presently attempted the winning of the city, which was governed by two chief magistrates, the one called Reginald, the other Smorth. The success was good; for upon St. Bartholemew's Eve the town was taken by force, with grete slaughter of the citizens; which done, they sent to King Dermond, praying hym with his Englishe to come unto hym, who without delay went to Waterford, and according to his promise made in England, he marryed his daughter unto the Erle,§ and with her he gave after his death the kingdome of

* O'Toole's Country was called Imayle. It lay in the heart of the County of Wicklow.

† Cambrensis places the arrival of Reymond Le Gros after Roderick O'Connor, King of Connaught had levied an army to oppose the invasion; and he is very particular as to the numbers brought over by Reymond: for he says that there came with him ten knights and three score and ten archers, well appointed.

‡ Cambrensis says two hundred knights and a thousand others. It is from Maurice Regan alone we learn that Waterford was under the joint administration of two petty princes of the Danes, Reginald and Smorth.

§ The celebrated Irish artist, Maclise, painted a grand historical picture of the marriage of Eva, daughter of King Dermond, with Strongbow. This work should be secured for the National Gallery in Dublin.

Leinster. From Downdonnell Reymond came to the Erle, and when the marriage was solemnized, by the general con sent of the King, the Erle, Reymond, Maurice de Prindergast, Meyler Fitz-Henry, and the rest, agreed to march to Dublin. Dermond with the Erle and the Englishe, went to Fernes, there to remaine untill their preparations were fully made. In the meanwhile the Erle was not unmindfull to leave a sufficient garrison for the defence of Waterford.

In this tyme the Englishe invasion had bred feare and terror in all the Irish throughout the land ; to prevent insueinge dangers, the King of Counaught amassed an army of thirty thousande horse and foote, to impede the intended enterprize against Dublin ; and the better to performe the same, he plashed and trenched all the places through whiche the Englishe and Dermond must have passed ; and the King of Connaught himself encamped at Clondalkin.* King Dermond, being advertised thereof, imparted the same unto the Erle, layeing before his judgement the difficulties whiche they should find in their passage to Dublin, and praying hym to advise upon the same. After consultation held, it was agreed by the chiefs of the army, that the enterprize should be attempted. The daye of their puttinge into the field beinge come, Miles de Cogan, a gentleman of grete worth and valour, was ordained to march in the vanguard, with a regiment of seven huudreth strong, and with Donell Kavanagh, with his Irish ; next unto hym, Raymond le Gros led the battle, with his regiment of eight hundreth English ; and with him, the King of Leinster, with a thousand of his followers. The rear, with three thousand English, was commanded by the Erle ; and in the rear of him, a regiment of Irishmen. When they came nere the enemy, their orderly march appalled them so much, as they gave way ; so as the army passed by the way of the mountaine, without any fight, till they came to Dublin ; and the King of Connaught, by the advice of his councill, dissolved his army, and returned to his own country.

Hesculph MacTurkill, to withstande his enemies, drew all the forces he could make or procure in the city of Dublin, whereof he was lord. The Erle and Dermond quartered a pretty distance from the towne ; but Miles de Cogan lodged close to the walls. From the Erle and Dermond, Maurice Regan was sent to summon the citty to yeld, and, for their better assurance, to demand thirty pledges. MacTurkill, fearinge the issue of the siege, pro-

* Clondalkin is a small village four miles from Dublin, at which there is a celebrated seminary.

mised to render both towne and pledges; but the citizens disagreeinge in the choice of their hostages, the tyme assigned was spent; whereof Myles de Cogan, taking advantage, without any direction from Dermond or the Erle, gave an assault, entred the towne, and, not without grete slaughter of the citizens, made hymselfe master thereof.* Hesculph MacTurkill, and most of the townesmen, saved themselves by the strand of the sea. The soldiers got good spoile, for the citizens were rich. The same daye, which was the daye of St. Matheu the Apostle, Dermond and the Erle made their entry, and found in the towne abundance of victuals.

After a few days' stay in Dublin, Dermond returned to Fernes; and immediately after Michellmas, the Erle Richard (leaving the citty of Dublin in the guard of Myles de Cogan) tooke his jornay for Waterford; and in the same winter, Dermond, King of Leinster, died at Fernes; after whose death, none of the Irish (except Donald Kavanagh, King Dermond's son, MacGely, of Tirbrun,† and Awliffe O'Carvy), came to the Erle; and Moriertagh, with the Kinsellagh, made warr upon the Englishe.

1170.—O'Connor, the Monarque of Ireland, levied a great army, with intent to besiege Dublin. At a daye assigned, all his forces (to the number of sixty thousande) assembled at Castle-Knock,‡ MacDunleve, King of Ulster, quartered at Clontarffe; O'Bryan, King of Munster, at Kilmainham; and Moriertagh O'Kinsellagh, with his troops, lodged at Dalkie.§ At that time the Erle was in the city of

---

* The motive for undertaking the siege of Dublin is imputed by Cambrensis to a mortal hatred which King Dermond bore to the citizens, besides their rebellion; for his father, being on a time at Dublin, and sitting at the door of an ancient man of the city, they not only murdered him, but in contempt buried him with a dog. He also imputes the treaty for submission to the mediation of Laurence O'Toole, then Archbishop of Dublin.

† Rather Tir-Bryn, or the lands and territories of the O'Byrnes, of which MacGely was the chieftain; their countries lying between the new conquests in Wexford and Dublin, in the possession of the English, which was a strong curb on the fidelity of that people.

‡ Castleknock is a village near the Phœnix Park.

§ This attempt upon Dublin is imputed by Cambrensis to the zeal and activity of Archbishop Laurence, who, out of love to his country, took infinite pains to cement an union among the other princes of Ireland. They also drew into the alliance Gothred, King of the Isle of Man, and other princes of the islands; so that the city was begirt, not only closely by land, but by sea, and

374 Dublin "Invironed with a Puissant Army."

Dublin, preparing all necessaries for his defence. From every place which was garrisoned, he sent for men ; and, among the rest, he sent for Robert Fitz-Stephens, who was then at Wexford, commanding him to send as manye men unto hym as he could possibly spare. The men of Wexford (who evermore hated Dermond and the Englishe), finding it to be now, as they conceaved, a fit opportunity to serve their turns, assailed Robert Fitz-Stephens, slew his men, and took him prisoner, whom they sent to Beckerin, which is a castle seated on the river of Slaine. Donal Kavenagh, with some of the O'Kinsellaghs, MacGely, and Awliffe O'Carvy, were the messengers that brought unto the Erle, Fitz-Stephens' disaster ; which, although it exceedingly troubled him, yet he seemed to make slight of it, willing them not to be dismayed or discouraged at the ill-fortune.

Dublin (as is say'd) being invironed with a puissant army, and the defendaunts within, neyther in number nor munition soe well provided as necessary, and, besides, being weakly stored with victuals, the Erle, out of these considerations, called unto hym his principall councellors, to advise upon the imminent dangers which threatened their ruin ; at which councill ther were present,

ROBERT DE QUINCY, MYLES FITZHENRY,
WALTER DE RIDDESFORD, MYLES FITZDAVID,
MAURICE DE PRENDERGAST, RICHARD DE MAROINE,
MYLES DE COGAN, WALTER BLUETT,

And divers others, to the number of twenty, unto whom the Erle addressed his speech to this effect :—

"You see," said he, "with what grete forces our enemies do beseege us. We have not victualls to suffice us longer than fifteen days ; wherfor, I think it best that we doe presently send to the King of Connaught to tell him, that if he will rise and depart from the seidge, I will submit my selfe unto hym, and be his man, and hold Leinster of hym ; and I am of opinion, that Laurence the Archbushope of Dublin, is the meetest man to negotiat this business."

strong parties were posted in several quarters near the city, as at Castleknock, three miles to the W. at Dalkie, about seven miles to the S.E. on the mouth of the harbour, to prevent supplies by water, which also was done by the shipping of the foreigners which lay there ; at Clontarffe, about three miles from the city on the N. side of the harbour, and at Kilmainham within less than a mile of the walls. Add to this, a scarcity of provisions within the town, and it is wonderful how it should escape falling into the hands of the besiegers.

The Erle's council was approved, and the Archbushope Laurence was sent unto the king; unto whom, when he had made relacione of his message, the proud king for answeare willed hym to tell the besieged, that unless the Erle would surrender up into his hands the citys of Dublin, and Waterford, and the town of Wexford, together with all his fortes and castles, and immediately, at a day assigned, abandone the land, and return into England with all his English forces, he would, without further delaye, give an assault upon the city, making no doubt but to carry it by force. The Archbushope being returned with this sad answear, they were amazed with the proud and exorbitant demands of the Irish Monarque, and grew to be pensive.

Then Miles de Cogan (rousing up his spirit) brake silence : "We are here," said he, "a good number of good men; our best remedie is to make a sallie which is least doubted by the enemy, and I hope in the goodness of God, that we shall have the victorie, or, at least, dye with honnor; and my desire is that I maye be the firste man appointed to give upon ther quarters."

With generall applause Cogan's coucell was approvid and the captains commanded to draw forth their companies; the vanguard was designed to Miles de Cogan, consisting of two hundreth; Reymond le Grosse with othir two hundreth, commanded the battle; and the Erle, with two hundreth, marched in the reare. In this enterprize, full of perill, they used not the aid of ther Irish soldiers; for in ther fidelity reposed they no confidence, saving only of the persons of Donald Kavanagh, and MacGely, and Auliffe O'Carvy, of whom they were assured, Unto Finglass they directed their march; when they approached the enemie's campe, who wer careless and secure, not mistrustinge any suche attempt, Myles de Cogan, to encourage his soldiers—"In the name of God," said he, "let us this day try our valour, and dye like men," and therewithall broke furiously into the campe, and made such slaughter as all fled before hym; Raimond, calling upon St. David, furiously rushed in amongst his enemies, and performed wonders—and so did the Erle Richard; but especially Myles FitzHenry's valour was admired by all men. In Boynhull, of the enemies were slain more than one hundreth and fifty. This overthrow so discouraged the Irish, as the siege was moerly abandoned; and in the enemie's campe, store of baggage was gotten, and such quantities of corn, meale, and pork, as was sufficient to victuall the citty for one whole year.

Dublin, being thus delyvered from ther danger it was in, the Erle leaving the command therof to Myles de Cogan, departed towards Wexford, with purpose to delyver Robert FitzStephen and his companions, who wer still detained prisoners in the castle of Beckerin.*

APPENDIX F.

A SHORT ACCOUNT OF THE LIFE OF CAPTAIN GLAS, AND EXECUTION OF THE FOUR PIRATES FOR HIS MURDER, AT ST. STEPHEN'S-GREEN, DUBLIN, ONE OF THE PIRATES AFTERWARDS HUNG IN CHAINS ON THE "MUGLINS," NEAR DALKEY ISLAND, 1765.

Page 55.

CAPTAIN GLAS was a native of Scotland, and bred a surgeon ; in that capacity he made some voyages to the coast of Guinea, and was at length master of a Guinea ship, in which station he continued till the late war began. Having saved a good sum of money in trade, he ventured part of it on board a privateer, and went himself as captain. He was not three days at sea before the ship's crew mutinied ; but at length, by fair speeches, were pacified ; and still more so by the capture of a French merchant-man of great value, which followed immediately.

This good fortune was soon dispelled by the appearance of an enemy's frigate about twice his strength, with which, however, he engaged. The contest was very warm for more than two hours ; but another French ship appearing, Captain Glas was obliged to strike, with the loss of more than half his crew, and himself shot through the shoulder. He remained some time in a French prison in the West Indies, and was treated with much severity ; but, being at last exchanged, he embarked the remainder of his fortune upon another adventure in the privateering way. He was again taken prisoner, and his whole fortune at once destroyed.

Upon being released a second time, he was employed by merchants in their service to and from the West Indies, and

---

* *Beckerin*, rather Beg-Eri, *i. e.*, little Ireland, an island lying off the port of Wexford, once famous for a school and monastery, erected there by St. Ibar, before the arrival of St. Patrick. See "Antiquities of Ireland," chap. vi., under the word *Edri* ; and chap. xxx. p. 198.—HARRIS.

was taken prisoner no less than seven times during the last war. However, he had, upon the conclusion of the late peace, amassed about two thousand pounds, and being an excellent seaman, he resolved to go upon a discovery in his own ship. He found out a new harbour on the coast of Africa, between the river Senegal and Cape de Verd, to which he supposed a very great trade might be driven.

He returned to England, and laid his discovery before the ministry ; and at length obtained an exclusive trade to his own harbour, for twenty years. Having prepared for his departure, with the assistance of one or two merchants, he left England, and arrived at the new-found harbour. He sent one of his men on shore with propositions of trade, but the natives murdered him the moment he landed. Captain Glas found means to inform the king of the country of the wrong done him, and the mutual advantage that might accrue from trading thither.

The king seemed to be pleased with his proposal, only to get him the more securely in his power ; but Glas, being on his guard, he failed in effecting his design. The king's next attempt was to poison the crew by provisions sent as presents to the captain ; this also failed of effect ; but Glas, for want of necessaries, was obliged to go to the Canaries in an open boat, in order to buy some from the Spaniards. In the meantime the savages fell upon his ship, but they were repulsed by the crew ; and the ship being obliged to quit the harbour, and not finding her captain return, sailed for England, where she arrived in safety.

In the meantime, the unfortunate captain landed upon one of the Canary Islands, and presented his petition to the Spanish Governor, but who, instead of treating him with the desired hospitality, threw him into prison as a spy, and there kept him for some months, without pen, ink, or paper.

He at length bethought himself of writing with a piece of charcoal on a biscuit, to a captain of an English man-of-war, then in the harbour, who, though with much difficulty, and after being previously sent to prison himself, at length effected the captain's release. Here he continued for some time, till his wife and daughter (a beautiful girl of eleven years old) came to him from home ; and from the Canaries they all joyfully embarked for England, on board the Sandwich, Captain Cochran, commander.

The ship sailed from London about the month of June or July, 1765, laden with bale-goods, hardware, hats, &c., for Santa Cruz ; at which place they arrived, discharged their cargo, and thence sailed to Orataira, one of the Canary Islands, and took in a cargo of Madeira wine, raw and manufactured silk, cochineal, and a large quantity of Spanish milled dollars, some ingots of gold, some jewels, and a small quantity of gold-dust ; and about the month of November, sailed from Orataira for London, and had then on board John Cochran, captain ; Charles Pinchent, mate ; Peter M'Kinlie, boatswain ; George Gidley, Cook ; Richard St. Quintin, Andrees, Zekerman, and James Pinchent, (brother to the mate) mariners ; and Benjamin Gallipsey, the cabin-boy ; and they took on board, as passengers, Captain Glas, his wife and daughter, with a servant boy belonging to them.

Before the ship left the Canaries, Gidley, St. Quintin, Zekerman, and M'Kinlie, entered into a conspiracy to murder all the other persons on board, and to possess themselves of the treasure. Accordingly, on Sunday, November 30th, at eleven at night, the four assassins, being stationed on the night-watch, and the captain coming to see everything properly settled, on his return to his cabin, M'Kinlie seized him, and held him fast, till Gidly killed him with an iron bar, and then threw him overboard.

The noise occasioned by this murder, and the captain's groans having alarmed the Pinchents and Captain Glas, they rose from their beds, and immediately came on deck ; and the Pinchents being foremost, they were attacked by the villains, knocked down, and thrown overboard ; Captain Glas instantly returned to the cabin for his sword, and his retreat being observed by M'Kinlie, who judged of his intent, secreted himself at the foot of the steps in the dark ; and as he was ascending the steps to get upon the deck, M'Kinlie seized him in his arms, and held him fast, and called out to his associates to assist him, who immediately rushed upon Mr. Glas, and with much difficulty wrested his sword out of his hand, in which scuffle Zekerman received a slight wound in his arm ; and in stabbing Mr. Glas, M'Kinlie received a wound through his left arm. When they had thus murdered Mr. Glas they threw him overboard. This soon brought Mrs. Glas and her child on deck ; and she having seen what the villains had perpetrated, implored for mercy ; but Zekerman and M'Kinlie came up to her, and she and her daughter being locked in one another's arms, they threw them both into the sea.

Having thus despatched all the persons on board, except the two boys, and being then in the British Channel, on their course to London, they immediately put the ship about, and steered for the coast of Ireland ; and on Tuesday, December 3rd, about two in the afternoon, they arrived within ten leagues of the harbour of Waterford and Ross, and then determined to sink the ship; and, in order to secure themselves and the treasure, they hoisted out their cock-boat, and loaded her with bags of dollars, to the quantity of about two tons, and then, knocking out the ballast port, quitted the ship, and got into the boat, and left the two boys in the sinking vessel to perish.

One of the boys having entreated to be taken on board, but refused, leaped into the sea, and by swimming laid hold of the gunnel of the boat, when one of the fellows gave him a stroke, and knocked him off, and he was immediately drowned.

Soon after they quitted the ship she filled with water and overset, and they saw the other boy washed overboard.

The boat having reached the harbour's mouth, about six in the evening, they rowed her about three miles up the river, and being afraid to proceed further with such a quantity of treasure, they landed within two miles of the fort of Duncannon; and having left out as much as they apprehended they could carry, they buried on the strand the rest of the dollars, amounting to 250 bags; they then proceeded up the river with the remainder, the ingots of gold, jewels, and gold dust, and landed at a place called Fisherstown, within four miles of Ross, and refreshed themselves at an alehouse, where a bag of 1,200 dollars was stolen from them.

On Wednesday, December 4, they proceeded to Ross, and put up at an alehouse, and there exchanged 1,200 dollars for their amount in current gold, and bought three cases of pistols, hired six horses, and two guides, and on Thursday, the 5th, set out for Dublin, where they arrived on the 6th, and stopped at the Black Bull Inn, in Thomas-street.

Having lavished a considerable sum in Ross, and an account having arrived there, that a vessel was driven on the coast, richly laden, without a living soul on board, it caused a suspicion that those persons had destroyed and plundered the ship; upon which the collector sent two gentlemen express to the chief magistrate of Ross, then in Dublin, to inform him of their suspicions, with intent that the said persons should be taken, and required to give an account of themselves.

Those gentlemen arrived on the 8th, and having informed the said magistrate of their errand, he, with proper assistance, apprehended St. Quintin and Zekerman, who, being examined separately, each confessed the murders, and other matters before related, and also, that since they arrived in Dublin, Gidley and M'Kinlie had sold to a goldsmith dollars to the amount of £300, by which means M'Kinlie was apprehended, and intelligence got that Gidley had set out in a post-chaise for Cork, in order to take shipping for England.

Having received an account of the dollars that were hid, the magistrate of Ross despatched back the two gentlemen with directions to the Collector of Ross and the commanding officer of the fort of Duncannon, to make search for the bags of dollars. In returning they apprehended Gidlie on his way to Cork, and had him committed to Carlow gaol, where they found upon him 53 guineas, a moidore, and some silver.

On the 13th they found 250 bags of dollars sealed up, and brought them to Ross under a guard, and lodged them in the custom-house.

There were found in the possession of M'Kinlie, Zekerman, and St. Quintin, some toys, a few guineas, an ingot of gold, and a small parcel of gold dust.

On Saturday, March 1, the four assassins were tried in Dublin, and found guilty; and on Monday, the 3rd, they were executed at Stephen's-green; their bodies were brought back to Newgate, and, on the Wednesday following, they were hung in chains, two of them near Macarrell's-wharf, on the South-wall; and the other two about the middle of the Piles, below the Pigeon-house. The bodies of Peter M'Kinlic and George Gidley, the two that were hung in chains on the South-wall, being found disagreeable to the citizens of Dublin, who walked there for amusement or health, were removed to the Muglins, near Dalkey Island.—*Gentleman's Magazine.*

The following is an extract of a letter written by the author to the *Irish Times*, on it being asserted that Dalkey Island was formerly a place of execution for pirates :—

"They were tried and found guilty, Tuesday, March 4th, 1766 (and *not* in 1776, as *all* historians state), and hung at Baggotrath Castle, the site of the present nunnery at Baggot-street, after having been brought past the "Quakers' Burial Ground," on which the present site of the College of Surgeons, York-street, is built, through the "Rapparee Fields," now Dycer's Repository, the "Beaux Walk," north side of the Green, past the "French Burial Ground," Merrion-row, to Baggotrath, the Golconda of Dublin executions at this period.

"The following note appears in all the Dublin papers of March 9th, 1766 :—

"'The bodies of the four murderers and pirates— M'Kinley, St. Quintin, Gidley, and Zekerman, were brought in the black cart from Newgate, and hung in chains, two of them near Mackarell's Wharf, on the South Wall near Ringsend (see Roque's Map of Dublin), and the other two about the Middle of the Piles, below the Pigeon House. The bodies of the four pirates remained suspended on the wharf and at the Pigeon House till the month of March following, On the 11th of March, however, a letter appeared in *Faulkner's Journal*, signed a " Freeholder," complaining of the hoops which bound the bodies as being very imperfect. On referring to the same journal for the 29th of March, I find the following :—" The two pirates, Peter M'Kinley and George Gidley, who hang in chains on the South Wall for the murder of Captain Coghlan, &c., being very disagreeable to the citizens who walk there for amusement and health, are immediately to be put on Dalkey Island, for which purpose new irons are being made, those they hang in being faulty. Richard St. Quintin and Andrea Zekerman, the other two concerned in this cruel affair, are to remain on the Piles at the Pigeon House. Accordingly, the same Journal, on the 1st and 12th of April, 1767, announces the removal of the bodies, in deference to public opinion, from the new wall, and that they were carried by sea to the rock on the Muglins, near Dalkey Island, where a gibbet was erected, and they were hung up in irons, said to be the completest ever made in the kingdom. It is *not a fact*, then, that Dalkey Island, a salubrious locality of singularly romantic beauty—a creation of Nature in her most sportive mood—one of the principal seats of Druidism in the West—where the *mariner's preserving deities* were supposed to reside, to whom sailors offered up their vows and their supplications for safety during their voyages—I say again it is not a fact, as most historians say, that this charming islet, the Istria of Dublin Bay, was ever used as a place of execution for public criminals."

APPENDIX G.

PULPIT ELOQUENCE.—AN ARTIST'S REMINISCENCE OF THE REVS. C. FLEMING AND W. B. KIRWAN.—THE ANTHOLOGIA HIBERNICA.—IN MEMORIAM.

Page 78.

There was a preacher of great eminence in Dublin, in my early days, of the name of Fleming ; he was a Roman Catholic clergyman of an enlarged mind, free from bigotry, and gifted with attributes of the highest quality to form a perfect orator. His taste for composition was pure and original; his language natural, yet poetically chosen to express his subject; his imagery grand, so that his sermons were pictures of human life, held up to view, and descanted upon with judgment, derived from a thorough knowledge of mankind, and prepared with a remedy for every vicious habit or reigning folly. In description, he was so clear that you could not mistake nor blink the question; then his voice was so harmonious, and his articulation so perfect, yet without apparent effort, that he delighted his hearers. I have attended, for sixty years, to every preacher of note in all places of Christian worship within my reach in Ireland, England, Scotland, and Wales, and I have never met any one equal to him. From the time I first heard him, when I was but nine years old, he never preached a sermon that I knew of previously without attending to his edifying discourse. Lest I should be considered partial, I can adduce some respectable names of members of the Protestant Church that were always to be found ranged round the foot of his pulpit, and often so numerous as to fill a gallery opposite. Nearly the whole of the Hutchinson family, the head of which family was the Provost of Trinity College, Grattan, Curran, Ponsonby, Yelverton, Michael Smith, L. Gardner, Isaac Corry, Brownlow, Hussey Burgh—I could add more, were these not sufficient to give some idea that excellence alone could have drawn such an assemblage of luminous characters, and to a place of worship not their own.

Dean Kirwan was the only preacher I have heard that could attempt to compete with Mr. Fleming; and the Dean having been exclusively employed in the cause of charity, prevents any fair comparison, although I think comparison by no means a fair test of superior abilities—for, unless the parties are similarly gifted in requisites, the comparison ends. Now, Fleming and Kirwan were differently supplied with natural attributes, and their modes, style of composition, delivery, action, &c., differed likewise; but each felt his power, and adapted the means of using it exactly to suit his purpose. The contrast might be discovered by referring to their respective manner of delivery.

Fleming was easy and familiar in his exordium, divided his subjects into parts, and proposed treating it in that order; he then gradually raised his voice, which was powerful and clear, so that he could be heard at the door of the chapel, without much effort. He painted in glaring colours the enormity or vice he wished to correct, and the attendant miseries brought on, perhaps, a whole family by a wretched husband or wife; the contrast drawn between the innocent children and their depraved parent formed so strong yet so true a picture of distress, that one might suppose, if he ceased speaking, and ended there, the horror and disgust were so felt, that a change would take place, if any power of reflection remained in the minds of those the painting might resemble. He generally sat down for five minutes, then rose and gave another picture, sweetly touched, of the pleasure to be enjoyed in our correcting any of our passions, but particularly of such destructive power as that one he had described; then of the value of religious application, and calling upon our Maker for His assistance; and, lastly, of the happiness hereafter promised to those who repent truly of their sins. He then made a feeling appeal, when his voice changed to a tone so truly fervent and pathetic, his auditors were moved, many to tears; and he closed with leaving an impressive interest in the hearts of all his hearers.

Dean Kirwan commenced with the Lord's Prayer; then looking at his paper, gave out the text, and proceeded to expose the helpless state of orphans left to casual supplies, obtained in the manner in which he was then engaged, pleading the cause of so many young, destitute creatures, preserved so far from starvation and ignorance, but entirely dependent from that day on the bounty of his auditors. He then drew pictures of luxury, and thundered his artillery against the great and opulent. His language was well chosen, and perfectly adapted to express his meaning; his figures transcendently beautiful, and following each other in rapid succession, delivered with great energy, and sometimes impassioned to a degree to the very extent of his powers, so that he was often obliged to pause for rest, from exhaustion. No man ever was more zealous in a cause that seemed to possess his heart and soul, and to have engaged his faculties of mind and speech to the utmost stretch; in fine, he appeared inspired on that part of his discourse; he used much action, and evinced talent for an excellent actor, statesman, or advocate. He was truly eloquent, and seemed to speak not from previous study, yet his deportment appeared studious and preconcerted. When he was nearly finished, in a subdued tone he lamented that his exertions were, he feared, likely to fail. He had not the art of touching their feelings. He then pointed to a number of the children, placed in a situation for public view; their claims were evident in their innocent looks and mild appearance; then, recommending them to the care of their Creator, he, in a fervent appeal, closed his discourse, always with some happy sentence. The effect of his eloquence was such upon his congregation, that many persons, after having emptied their purses, left their watches, until released by a further donation.

These two clergymen, it is said, studied in the same college, and were competitors for fame *in speaking ;* they were to the last friendly when they met in company, although of different religions. Mr. Kirwan became a Protestant, and was made a Dean, as the following paragraph will explain :—

Mr. Grattan, the great orator in the Irish Parliament, finding the Rev. W. B. Kirwan poorly provided for, although he had quitted the Roman Catholic religion and embraced the Protestant, and had been indefatigable in the cause of charity, so as to have severely injured his health, he (Mr. Grattan) rose one day and addressed the house thus :—" I rise," said he, "to speak in the neglected case of the Rev. Walter Blake Kirwan, a man of talent, of true Christian piety and virtue, a man who, in feeding the lamp of charity, has nearly extinguished the lamp of life ; and what has been his remuneration? *St. Nicholas-without or St. Nicholas-within.** Oh, shame! shame! shame! shame!" He sat down.

Not long after, Mr. Kirwan was made a Dean, and some comfortable emolument attached to it. I *believe,* however, he did not relax in his labours, but advocated still the cause of charity, until exhaustion placed him at rest in the grave.

It is but justice to the fame of those two eminent persons to say, that the sermons published in their names as their compositions, are vile impostures, and bear scarcely a sentence worthy of their admirable discourses. I, therefore, hope and trust my readers, should these garbled fragments meet their eye, will turn from them with merited disgust and aversion.

The following notice is taken from the *Anthologia Hibernica,* 1794 :—

The Rev. Christopher Fleming, the celebrated preacher and contemporary of Dean Kirwan, died in December, 1794. He was a Roman Catholic clergyman, connected with Adam and Eve Chapel, Dublin. The recollection of the man and his excellence will form his eulogy. As a preacher, his eloquence formed an era in pulpit oratory : unlike those who, possessing much speculative benevolence, permit it to eva-

---

* St. Nicholas-within and St. Nicholas-without are two livings of very limited means, and were even jointly a poor recompense to a man of such luminous talent, effectively employed in the cause of charity.

porate in theory and sentiment, his practice was a living comment on his doctrine. His splendid abilities excited general admiration and respect. His virtues prevented their brilliancy from being ostensive or oppressing. He was peculiarly distinguished by a sublime simplicity of manners. His versatile genius made him a pleasing, instructive companion to every age and description. In social life we have seen the man who, in the morning declaimed with more than oracular solemnity, in the evening become the soul of innocence and gaiety. He brought with him no unsocial gloom to damp the sprightly effusions of cheerfulness and wit. His attic festivity and good humour gave an animated glow to conversation, and communicated a high zest and elegant reasoning to the rational language of life. Dear to talent—dear to religion, he died universally regretted; and his memory will be universally respected as long as regard to departed merit remains among us.

APPENDIX H.

OBJECTS OF GEOLOGICAL INTEREST IN THE VICINITY OF DUBLIN.—THE GREAT GRANITE CHAIN FROM KINGSTOWN TO WATERFORD, READ AT THE BRITISH ASSOCIATION IN AUGUST, 1835.

Page 123.

THE vicinity of Dublin offers a great variety of interesting matter for the study of the geologist. Within a very limited distance from the capital, we are presented with an important series both of primary and secondary rocks. To the south of the bay of Dublin, primary rocks alone occur; which are remarkable not only from their variety, but from the indications of violence exhibited in the contortions of the strata, the intrusion of granitic veins into the micaceous schist, and the chemical changes which the schists have suffered when in contact with the granite. The primary rocks of the vicinity of Dublin consist of a central ridge of granite, on each side of which the micaceous and argillaceous schists, the quartz rock, and mountain limestone are arranged. This granite chain extends from Kingstown on the north into the county of Waterford on the south, a distance of nearly sixty miles. In the vicinity of Dublin the course of the granite chain is well ascertained: it extends from

Dalkey Island to Blackrock, and from thence passes southward to Dundrum and Rathfarnham; it then crosses the Military-road behind Montpellier-hill, and running across the northern extremity of Glenismaule, forms the basis of Seechon, and consequently supports the schist which constitutes the greater portion of that hill. On the east, that is, next the sea, the boundary of the granite is very apparent; from Dalkey it runs along the shore to Killiney, from thence it runs inland to Rochestown-hill, extending in nearly a right line to the Scalp, passing on to Glencree and Lough Dan, holding a southerly course.

This central granite ridge includes some of the loftiest hills in the vicinity; they are, however, rivalled by the adjoining quartz mountain, called the greater Sugar-Loaf, and the schistose mountains of Seechon and of Djouce. This granite ridge is destitute of the sharp and spiry outlines which so often characterize mountains composed of this rock; a circumstance apparently dependent on the inconsiderable elevation of the hills, and also on the very decomposible nature of some of the kinds of this rock, which disentegrate rapidly with exposure to the weather.

The mineral nature of the granite in general exhibits, nevertheless, but little variety, and is almost completely free from hornblende or other ingredients, not essential to its character. The felspar is for the most part of a pearly whiteness, and forms a striking contrast with the black mica. The stone is much employed for architectural purposes in Dublin and the vicinity, and considerable quantities of it are exported to Liverpool, and there employed for paving the streets. Near Killiney, at the junction of the granite with the schist, the quality of the former is rather different from that obtained in the quarries near Kingstown. It is harder; and the mica, instead of occurring in plates, has assumed the form of plumose mica. At Glencullen, Glenismaule, &c., the granite is more coarse-grained, and the mica is of light colour, forming large hexagonal plates, sometimes half an inch in breadth. This variety is less compact than the granite of Killiney, and contains more felspar and mica; hence, perhaps, its more decomposible nature. In the vicinity of Glenismaule the granite is often completely disintegrated for a depth of four feet or more; and the decay of the rock would proceed with great rapidity, if the covering of peat did not afford a protection against the destructive effects of the weather. This decomposed granite sand is brought to Dublin under the name of freestone, and is employed for scouring and other domestic purposes.

The mass of granite, whose limits have been defined, is

almost everywhere in contact with the micaceous schist, both on its western and eastern flanks, and the junction of the rocks may be studied at Killiney, the Scalp, and Rathfarnham. In the first of these situations, the schist is seen resting on its upturned edges, on a basis of granite, and traversed by numerous veins of that substance. As the granite veins run in two directions they often intersect, and one set runs parallel to the lamination of the schist, while a second set cuts across the strata. Many of those veins contain fragments of the schistose rock. Along the line of junction of the two rocks, the schist is much curved, and contains abundance of crystals of chiastolite, arranged in stelliform groups. The schist is not the only rock which is in contact with the granite ; for, from Blackrock to Dundrum, the limestone succeeds the granite, and consequently the whole series of primary strata are absent. The actual contact of the two rocks has not been observed, but at Blackrock they are within a few yards of each other ; and the limestone is extremely compact, consisting of angular fragments, as if it had been shivered into small pieces and subsequently re-united. The quartz rock of Shankhill, if not in actual contact with the granite, is only separated from it by the intervention of a thin film of micaceous schist ; and at Ballinascorney, the argillaceous schist is not far removed from the granite ; but, as the two schists graduate into each other, it is not easy to characterize them, in every instance, by precise mineralogical distinctions.

On the western side, the micaceous schist commences at Rathfarnham, and the junction of the two rocks may be seen, on the road side, near the commencement of the Military-road ; it then runs across Glenismaule, and forms the mountain of Seechon.

The micaceous schist exhibits the usual mineral characters of that rock, and consists of a mixture of quartz and mica, in valuable proportions. Sometimes alternating laminæ of the two ingredients are so fine that the mica appears to preponderate, and the quartz is not so apparent ; on the other hand, the quartz sometimes attains the thickness of an inch, and almost excludes the mica. Not unfrequently the quartz is replaced by argillaceous laminæ, and thus the rock passes into an argillaceous schist ; which, when in contact with the granite, is sometimes changed into hornblende schist. At Killiney the schist exhibits a peculiar mode of decomposition, which it is difficult to explain. At first little circular depressions may be observed in the schist, and as these enlarge, little cavities are formed, often the size of an orange, and giving the rock a remarkably corroded appearance, as if it had been an amygdaloid which had lost its mineral nodules. This, however, is not the case in the present instance, for the cavities are not caused by the falling out of nodules or portions of conglomerate, but appear to depend on some ill-understood concretionary structure.

The mica schist is followed by argillaceous schist and quartz rock; the former occurring on both sides of the granite chain, whilst the latter is only found on its eastern side; quartz rock also appears on the north side of the bay, constituting the peninsula of Howth. The schist occurs in continuous strata, which may be traced over a wide extent of country, but the quartz rock is found only in detached portions.

On the eastern side of the granite ridge, the argillaceous schist, being the outermost of the rocks on that side, is bounded by the sea. The other margin of the clay strata is bounded by the micaceous schist, and may be defined by a line drawn from Shankhill and passing to Enniskerry, and to the west of the great Sugar-Loaf, and continuing in the same direction beyond Loch Dan. It includes the country around Bray, the Dargle, and Glen of the Downs; and also includes several extensive masses of quartz rock, such as Shankhill, the two Sugar-Loafs, Bray Head, the Glen of the Downs, &c.

On the western side of the granite ridge, the commencement of the argillaceous schist may be seen, beyond Rathfarnham, where it is bounded by the river Dodder, which separates it from the micaceous schist; it then passes to the west of Seechon till it reaches the sources of the Liffey. There is often considerable difficulty in tracing the junction of the two schistose rocks, as they pass into each other by insensible gradations, and have both been greatly disturbed and contorted. The lower parts of the argillaceous schists often pass into greywacke schist, viz., into schist containing fragments of schistose rocks, which are fine in some cases, as near Bray, while they are coarse conglomerates near the Tallaght Hills.

Near the granite, these rocks undergo a very remarkable change; and as we trace them they gradually lose the stratified appearance, and even their schistose structure; they have become, in short, hard and compact, passing into a very close-grained green stone, consisting of hornblende and felspar, and where the crystals of felspar attain a larger size, a green stone porphyry is the result. In the ravines, portions of schorl in acicular crystals are very common, but they have not been traced to their source.

Lambay Island, to the north of Dublin, may be included

under the head of argillaceous schist. The island consists of strata of schist and beds of green stone and porphyry. The schistose strata are much indurated, and are contorted in a most intricate manner, and these contortions occur both on the minute and the great scale. These strata often lose their stratified appearance, and pass into green stone and porphyry. The porphyry is sometimes amygdaloidal, containing nodules of calcareous spar. The crystals of felspar often exhibit a very peculiar laminar structure.

The quartz rock exists in two states, either alternating with schist, and in that case decidedly stratified, or destitute of all foreign intermixture, and in these examples the stratification is very indistinct. The hills composed of quartz rock are easily recognized by their conical outline, a circumstance which has served to give names to some of them. The chief masses of quartz are Bray Head and Howth, in which it alternates with schistose strata; Shankhill, and the greater and lesser Sugar-Loaf, in which no schistose strata occur.

The quartz of the peninsula of Howth exhibits the phenomenon of contorted strata in a very beautiful manner. The stratification is very obvious, and the schistose beds exhibit a great diversity of hues, from purple to red, thus rendering the contortions more apparent. Some of the strata rest on their edges, others are undulated, and sometimes curved upon themselves, so as to resemble the concentric crusts of some spheroidal concretion. The same phenomenon is observable at Bray.

The only secondary rock that occurs in the vicinity of Dublin is the Mountain Limestone, which constitutes all the country beyond the primary strata, occupying the counties of Meath and Kildare, and greater part of the county of Dublin. No limestone is found in the county of Wicklow, and the farmers of that county, on the eastern or sea-side, obtain their supplies from Howth, or from the beds of stratified calcareous alluvium, the only condition under which limestone occurs in that county. On the opposite side of the county the supplies of lime for building and agricultural purposes are chiefly drawn from the county of Carlow.

The limestone exists in two very distinct states in the vicinity of Dublin; in the one it has the character of the ordinary carboniferous limestone, containing the usual organic remains; but near the primary strata it is very impure, has a schistose structure, contains but few organic remains, and is the calp of Kirwan. The calp is distinctly stratified, the strata seldom exceeding two feet in thickness, and being separated by thin beds of slate clay. This limestone, which is much used for architectural purposes, occurs in many localities around Dublin, and everywhere exhibits marks of contortion and violence, which may be observed in almost every quarry around Dublin. At Lucan there is a beautiful example of contorted limestone strata; and equally interesting instances may be seen at Portrane, where the sea-coast has exposed numerous sections, in which the nature of the calp is fully displayed.

Besides the calp, magnesian limestone occurs in a few localities, as at Howth, near the junction of the primary and secondary strata, and on the Dodder, between Milltown and Classon Bridge. This limestone contains no organic remains, but occasionally, as at Howth, we find it contains imbedded fragments of the mountain limestone.

APPENDIX I.

AN IRISH PRIEST, FATHER EDGEWORTH.—SHORT SKETCHES OF THE LAST MOMENTS OF LOUIS XVI. AND MARIE ANTOINETTE.

Page 224.

When she heard her sentence read, she did not show the smallest alteration in her countenance, and left the hall without saying a single word to her judges or to the people. It was then half-past four o'clock in the morning, October 16th, 1793. The Queen was conducted to the condemned hold in the prison of the Conciergerie.

At five o'clock the general was beat. At seven o'clock the whole armed force was on foot; cannon were planted in the squares, and at the extremities of the bridges, from the palace to the Square de la Révolution.

At ten o'clock, numerous patrols passed through the streets. At half-past eleven in the morning Marie Antoinette was brought out of the prison, dressed in a white dishabille. Like other malefactors, she was conducted upon a common cart to the place of execution. Her beautiful hair from behind was entirely cut off, and her hands were tied behind her back. Besides her dishabille, she wore a very small white cap. Her back was turned to the horse's tail. During her trial she wore a dress of white and black mixture. On her right was seated, upon the cart, the executioner; upon her left a constitutional priest, belonging to the Metropolitan Church of Notre Dame, dressed in a grey coat, and wearing what is commonly called a bob-wig. The cart was escorted by numerous detachments of horse and foot. Henriot, Rousin, and Boulanger, generals of the revolutionary army, preceded by the rest of the staff-officers, rode before the cart.

An immense mob, especially women, crowded the streets, insulted the Queen, and vociferated, "Long live the Republic!" She seldom cast her eyes upon the populace, and beheld with cold indifference the great armed force of 30,000 men, which lined the streets in double ranks. The sufferings she sustained during her captivity had much altered her appearance, and the hair on her forehead appeared as white as snow.

The Queen, without anguish or bigotry, was speaking to the priest seated by her side. Her spirits were neither elevated nor depressed: she seemed quite insensible to the shouts of "Vive la Republique!" She showed even a kind of satisfaction to look forward for the moment which might rid her of her miserable existence. When she passed through the Rue St. Honoré, she sometimes attentively looked at the inscriptions of the words liberty and equality affixed to the outside of the houses. She ascended the scaffold with seeming haste and impatience; and then turned her eyes with great emotion towards the garden of the Tuilleries, the former abode of her greatness.

At half-past twelve o'clock the guillotine severed her head from her body. She died in the thirty-eighth year of her age. The executioner lifted, and showed the blood-streaming head from the four direct corners of the scaffold, which is shown only from one side in all other common executions. The mob instantly vociferated, "Long live the Republic!"

A young man who dipped his pocket handkerchief in the Queen's blood, and pressed it with veneration to his breast, was instantly apprehended. Upon him were found the portraits of Louis XVI. and of Marie Antoinette.

The corpse of the ill-fated Queen was immediately after buried in a grave filled with quicklime, in the churchyard of the Madelaine, where Louis XVI. was buried in the same manner.

LAST MOMENTS OF LOUIS XVI.

Paris, Jan. 22, 1793.

Conformably to the arrangements made by the Executive Council, Louis was yesterday put to death, at the Place de la Revolution, heretofore Place de Louis XV.

Twenty-five citizens of known principles, well armed, acquainted with the manual exercise, and having each sixteen rounds of shot, were chosen from each section, to form a guard of twelve hundred men, who accompanied the unfortunate monarch to the place of execution. Strong detachments from the different legions were posted in the streets through which the royal prisoner was to pass, and also in the avenues leading to the Place de la Revolution; to prevent any confusion, and each section had a body in reserve, ready to move at a moment's notice to maintain public order.

Cannon were also distributed in every quarter where it was thought they could be any way serviceable, had even events made it necessary to employ them; for, even to the last moment, the sanguinary faction who pronounced the death of the unfortunate monarch, manifested symptoms of fear that some attempts might be made to rescue him.

Between eight and nine o'clock in the morning, Louis proceeded from his apartments in the Temple, and got into the mayor's carriage, who accompanied him, as did also M. Edgeworth, an Irish priest, who he specially requested might attend him.

Louis was dressed in a brown great-coat, white waistcoat, black breeches and stockings—his hair was dressed.

The procession, commanded by Mareschal Santerre, proceeded along the Boulevards to the place of execution. One hundred gendarmes, on horseback, formed an advanced guard to the procession. The rearguard was composed of one hundred national guards from the military school, also mounted. Various reserves of calvary lined the procession, and patrolled all the outskirts of the city.

The unfortunate monarch arrived at the foot of the scaffold at twenty minutes past ten. He mounted the scaffold with firmness and dignity; he appeared desirous to address the people; but even this last wish was denied him; drums and trumpets gave the signal, and, at twenty-two minutes past ten,

HIS HEAD WAS SEVERED FROM HIS BODY.

The Place de la Revolution was so strongly guarded by troops that no person was suffered to pass after the King had entered it. Some, however, who had previously taken their stand near the scaffold, notwithstanding the indecent noise of drums and trumpets, heard him plainly pronounce these words:—

"Citizens, I forgive my enemies, and I die innocent!"

After his death the nearest spectators divided among them what of his hair had been cut off by the stroke of the guillotine, and several persons were so inhuman as to dip their handkerchiefs in his blood, which they afterwards carried about, crying, "Behold the blood of a tyrant!"

When the executioners showed his head to the people, cries of "Vive la Nation! Vive la République!" was heard on all sides; and several groups made use of the following expressions: "We always wished well to him, but he never wished well to us!"

Many, however, showed emotions of a different nature, but which they were obliged to conceal as much as possible for their own personal safety.

His body was taken to the Church of the Madeline, where it was interred between the persons who lost their lives during the illuminations on account of his marriage, and the Swiss who fell on the 10th of August.

Louis, before his departure from the Temple, delivered to the Commissioners of the Council General, who were upon guard, his latter will, two copies of which he had written on the 25th December, 1792.

The city remained quiet, in gloomy silence through the day; in the morning the shops were shut, and no woman was allowed to be in the streets till the procession had returned with the body of Louis.

APPENDIX K.

IRISH ELOQUENCE—GRATTAN, CURRAN, FLOOD.
Page 322.
Specimens of their Eloquence.

GRATTAN.

During the latter part of the ninteenth century, many persons asserted that Grattan was the author of Junius's Letters. The very soul of that immortal writer seemed to vivify all his speeches and writings: the same sagacity, the same richness of language, the same irony, the same impassioned energy of expression, combining conciseness with ornament, strength with beauty, and elegance with sublimity.

Extracts from his Speeches.

PROVIDENCE.

"So it frequently happens; men are but instruments of providence, and without knowing it, fulfil her way. The zealot is *but an inflamed organ* bursting forth with unpremeditated truths."

TOLERATION.

"The source of your reason tells you that you should embrace every sect of religion; how, then, can you hope to receive sovereign mercy if you are deaf to the cries of your fellow-creatures? The doctrine of the *dark conclave* of *bigotry*, which, bursting, overwhelmed the nations of the earth, may be urged in favour of such criminal apathy; but the pangs of him who suffered a cruel crucifixion, will rush from the sepulchre to upbraid you with ingratitude, and involve your future tranquility."

ILLIBERALITY.

"When a bill for the improvement of barren lands, and the encouragement of industry among the lower orders of the people, was, in the last session, resisted by the spiritual peers, a right reverend prelate was said to have declared as a principle, that the poor should not be relieved, if the clergy were to be at the expense. Such a sentiment coming from a Christian and a Protestant bishop —Grattan was a Protestant—must have smitten every breast with deep and sincere affliction; but, if we are cast down by so great and grave an authority on the one side, we are consoled again by a still higher interposition, the express commands and practice of the Scriptures on the other. The Saviour of man suffered on a principle different from that which the right reverend prelate has introduced. The apostles, the martyrs, and *that flaming constellation of men*, that in the early age of Christianity *shot to their station in the heavens, and fell, and falling, illumined the nations of the earth with the blaze of the Gospel*, they rose and they fell with inspirations of a different kind. Had Christ been of the prelate's opinion, he never had been born, and we never had been saved. Had he said to his apostles, 'The poor are not to be fed, the valley is not to laugh and to sing at the expense of our church;' or, had the apostles said to the nations of the earth, 'Ye are not to be benefited at the expense of Christian pastors;' or, had the martyrs expostulated with themselves, 'we will not suffer for mankind,' what had become of the Christian religion? Let the pagan priest of Jove, or the sensual priest of Mahomet, deliver such doctrine, but don't you part with the palm of Christianity, nor relinquish the lofty self-surrendering precepts of your Gospel, to poach in politics for little and wicked tenets, in order to brand your prayerbook with the image of sorry selfishness, which would disgrace the frontispiece of Machiavel."

DESCRIPTION OF A GREAT CHARACTER.

"I speak of some, not all. There are among them men whom I revere. Such is one whom I don't name, because he is present; mild, pious, and benevolent; a friend to the meekness of the gospel, and a friend to man. Such is another whom I may venture to name, because he is not present. He has the first episcopal dignity in this realm – it is his right—he takes it by virtue of the commanding benevolence of his mind, in right of a superior and exalted nature. There are men possessed of certain created powers, and who distinguish the place of their nativity, instead of being distinguished by it; they don't receive, they give birth to the place of their residence, and vivify the region which is about them. The man I allude to I know him not, or know him as we know superior beings, only by his works.

WEAKNESS OF HUMAN NATURE.

"Our contemplation, the most profound, on Divine nature can only lead us to one great conclusion—our own immeasurable inanity; from whence we should learn that we can never serve God but in serving his creature; and to think we serve God by a profusion of prayer, when we degrade and proscribe his creature and our fellow-creature, was to suppose Heaven, like the court of princes, a region of flattery, and that man can there procure a holy connivance at his inhumanity, on the personal application of luxurious and complimentary devotion."

THE FRENCH REVOLUTION.

"A gigantic form walked the earth at this moment, who smote crowns with a hundred hands, and opened for the seduction of their subjects a hundred arms."

EXTENDED EMPIRE.

"When England had conquered France, possessed America, guided the councils of Prussia, directed Holland, and intimidated Spain; when she was *the great western temple* to which the nations of the earth repaired, from whence to draw eternal oracles of policy and freedom; when *her root extended from continent to continent, and the dew of the two hemispheres watered her branches* —then, indeed, we allowed with less danger, but never with justice that she might have made sacrifices of the claims of the Irish."

BOROUGH INFLUENCE.

"The king had another instrument more subtle and more pliable than the sword, and against the liberty of the subject more cold and deadly, a court instrument that murders freedom without the mark of blood—palls itself in the covering of the constitution, and in her own colours, and in her name, plants the dagger—a borough of parliament."

REFORM.

"In that American contest we saw that reform which had been born in England, and banished to America, advance like the shepherd lad in Holy Writ, and overthrow Goliah. He returned, riding on the wave of the Atlantic, and his spirit moved on the waters of Europe."

SELF LEGISLATION.

"Self legislation is life, and has been fought for as for being. It was that principle that called forth resistance to the House of Stuart, and baptized with royalty the House of Hanover, when the people stood sponsors for their allegiance to the liberty of the subjects; for kings are but satellites, and your freedom is the luminary that has called them to the skies; but your fatal compliances (speaking of the then parliament) have caused a succession of measures which have collected upon us such an accumulation of calamity, and which have finally, at an immense expense and through a sea of blood, stranded those kingdoms on a solitary shore—naked of empire, naked of liberty, and bereft of innocence, to ponder on an abyss which has swallowed up one part of their fortunes, and yawns for the remainder."

Grattan thus finally portrays some of the great political characters of Ireland, during the latter part of the 18th century—Mr. Malone, Lord Percy (Lord Shannon), Duke of Leinster, Mr. Ponsonby, Mr. Brownlow, Sir William Osborne, Mr. Burgh, Mr. Daly, Mr. Yelverton, Mr. Ogle, Mr. Flood, Mr. Forbes, Lord Charlemont, and Gerrard Hamilton.

THE EARL OF CHARLEMONT.

"In the list of injured characters I beg leave to say a few words for the good and gracious Earl of Charlemont. An attack, not only on his measures, but on his representative, makes his vindication seasonable—formed to unite aristocracy and the people, with the manners of a court and the principles of a patriot; with the flame of liberty and the love of order; unassailable by the approaches of power, of profit, or of titles, he annexed to the love of freedom a veneration for order, and cast on the crowd that followed him the *gracious shade of his own accomplishments, so that the very rabble grew civilized as it approached his person;* for years did he preside over a great army* without pay or reward, and he helped to accomplish a great revolution without a drop of blood. Let slaves utter their slander, and bark at glory which is conferred by the people; his name will stand; and when his clay shall be gathered in the dirt to which it belongs, his monument, whether in marble or in the hearts of his countrymen, shall be consulted as a *subject of sorrow and a source of virtue.*"

FLOOD.

"Mr. Flood, my rival, as the pamphlet calls him—and I should be unworthy the character of his rival if in his grave I did not do him justice—he had his faults, but he had great powers, great public effect; he persuaded the old, he inspired the young; the castle vanished before him; on a small subject he was miserable;

---

* "The Irish Volunteers."

put into his hand a distaff, and, like Hercules, he made sad work of it; but give him the thunderbolt, and he had the arm of a Jupiter; he misjudged when he transferred himself to the English Parliament; he forgot that he was a *tree of the forest, too old and too great to be transplanted* at fifty; and his seat in the British Parliament is a caution to the *friends of Union to stay at home*, and make *the country of their birth the seat of their action.*"

MR. BURGH.

Afterwards Lord Chief Baron of the Exchequer.

"Mr. Burgh, another great person in those scenes, which it is not in the little quill of this author to depreciate. He was a man singularly gifted—with great talent, great variety, wit, oratory, and logic; he, too, had his weakness—but he had the pride of genius also; he strove to raise his country along with himself, and never sought to build his elevation on the degradation of Ireland. "I moved an amendment for a free export; he moved a better amendment, and he lost his place; I moved a declaration of right. 'With my last breath will I support the right of the Irish Parliament,' was his note to me when I applied to him for his support; he lost the chance of recovering his place, and his way to the seals, for which he might have bartered. *The gates of promotion were shut on him, as those of glory opened.*"

MR. DALY.

"Mr. Daly, my beloved friend—he, in a great measure, drew the address of '79, in favour of our trade, that 'ungracious measure;' and he saw, read, and approved of the address of '82, in favour of constitution, that address of 'separation;' he visited me in my illness, at that moment, and I had communication on those subjects with that man, whose powers of oratory were next to perfection, and whose powers of understanding, I might say, from what has lately happened, bordered on the spirit of prophecy."

MR. FORBES.

"Mr. Forbes, a name I shall ever regard, and a death I shall ever deplore—enlightened, sensible, laborious, and useful—proud in poverty, and patriotic, he preferred exile to apostacy, and met his death. I speak of the dead, I say nothing of the living, but that I attribute to this constellation of men, in a great measure, the privileges of your country; and I attribute such a generation of men to the residence of your parliament."

Grattan had the highest veneration for the talents of Flood; but the latter was jealous of his fame, and more jealous of the splendid reward bestowed upon him by the nation; in a stormy debate, *Flood bitterly* reflected upon the conduct of Grattan, and even stooped to personalities, which drew one of the finest philippics ever heard from the latter, who observed, turning to Flood, whose nose was disfigured :—

"He resembles an ill-omened bird of night, that with sepulchral notes, a cadaverous aspect, and broken beak, hovers over the dome of this assembly, shedding baneful influence, and ready to stoop and pounce upon his prey ; he can be trusted by no man ; the people cannot trust him, the minister cannot trust him ; he deals out the most impartial treachery to both ; he tells the nation it is ruined by other men, while it is sold by himself ; he fled from the Embargo-bill, he fled from the Mutiny-bill, he fled from the Sugar-bill ; I therefore tell him in the face of his country, before all the world, and to his very beard, he is not an honest man."

IRISH GENTRY.

"I think," said he, "I know my country ; I think I have a right to know her. She has her weaknesses ; were she perfect, one would admire her more, but love her less. *The gentlemen of Ireland act on sudden impulse, but that impulse is the result of a warm heart, a strong head, and great personal determination.* The errors incident to such a principle of action must be their errors, but then the virtues belonging to that principle must be their virtues also ; such errors may give a pretence to their enemies, but such virtues afford salvation to their country."

CURRAN.

Extracts from his Speeches, &c.

UNIVERSAL EMANCIPATION.

"*Universal Emancipation !* No matter in what language his doom may have been pronounced ;—no matter what complexion, incompatible with freedom, an Indian or an African sun may have burnt upon him ;—no matter in what disastrous battle his liberty may have been cloven down ;—no matter with what solemnities he may have been devoted upon the altar of slavery ; the first moment he touches the sacred soil of Britain, the altar and the God sink together in the dust ; his soul walks abroad in her majesty ; his body swells beyond the measure of his chains that burst from around him ; and he stands redeemed, regenerated, and disinthralled, by the irresistible genius of universal emancipation !"

GUILT.

"You find him coiling himself in the scaly circles of his cautious perjury ; making anticipated battle against anyone who should appear against him ; but you see him sink before the proof."

DESCRIPTION OF AN INFORMER.

"This cannibal informer, this demon, O'Brien, greedy after human gore, has fifteen other victims in reserve, if, from your verdict, he receives the unhappy man at this bar. Fifteen more of your fellow-citizens are to be tried on his evidence. Be you, then, their saviours; let your verdict snatch them from his ravening maw, and interpose between yourselves and endless remorse."

FREEDOM OF THE PRESS.

"I do not pretend to be a mighty grammarian, or a formidable critic; but I would beg leave to suggest to you in serious humility, that a free press can be supported only by the ardour of men who feel the prompting sting of real or supposed capacity; who write from the enthusiasm of virtue or the ambition of praise, and over whom if you exercise the rigour of a grammatical censorship, you will inspire them with as mean an opinion of your integrity as your wisdom, and inevitably drive them from their post; and if you do, rely upon it, you will reduce the spirit of publication, and with it the press of this country, to what it for a long interval has been, the register of births, and fairs, and funerals, and the general abuse of the people and their friends."

AN INNOCENT VICTIM.

"That after that period of lingering deliberation passed, a third respite is transmitted; that the unhappy captive himself feels the cheering hope of being restored to a family that he adored, to a character that he had never stained, and to a country that he had ever loved; that you had seen his wife and children upon their knees, giving those tears to gratitude which their locked and frozen hearts could not give to anguish and despair, and imploring the blessings of eternal Providence upon his head who had graciously spared the father, and restored him to his children; that you had seen the olive-branch sent into *his little ark*, but no sign that the *waters had subsided*. 'Alas! nor wife, nor children, more shall he behold; nor friends, nor sacred home.' No seraph mercy unbars his dungeon, and leads him forth to life and light; but the minister of death hurries him to the scene of suffering and of shame, where, unmoved by the hostile array of artillery and armed men, collected together to secure, or to insult, or to disturb him, he dies with a solemn declaration of his innocence, and utters his last breath in a prayer for the liberty of his country."

VIRTUE OPPOSED TO HEREDITARY RANK.

"A similar application was made in the beginning of this, in the lords of Great Britain, by our illustrious countryman, of whom I do not wonder that my learned friend should have observed, how *much virtue can fling pedigree into the shade*; or how much the transient honour of a body inherited from man, is obscured by the *lustre of an intellect derived from God!*

OPPRESSION.

"Merciful God! what is the state of Ireland, and where shall you find the wretched inhabitant of this land? You may find him perhaps in a gaol, the only place of security, I had almost said of ordinary habitation;—you may see him flying from the conflagration of his own dwelling; or you may *find his bones bleaching* on the green fields of his *country*; or he may be found tossing upon the surface of the ocean, and mingling his groans with those tempests less savage than his persecutors, that drift him to a *returnless* distance from his family and his home."

MODERATION IN GRIEF.

"My miserable client, when his *brain was on fire*, and every fiend of hell was let loose upon his heart, he should then, it seems, have placed himself before his mirror; he should have taught the stream of agony to flow decorously down his forehead; he should have composed his features to harmony, he should have writhed with grace, and groaned with melody."

LOVE.

"Love is a noble and generous passion, it can be founded only on a pure and ardent friendship, on an exalted respect, on an implicit confidence in its object."

DESCRIPTION OF SILENCE.

"The weakest voice is heard—the shepherd's whistle shoots across the listening darkness of the interminable heath, and gives notice that the wolf is upon his walk, and the same gloom and stillness that tempt the monster to come abroad, facilitate the communication of the warning to beware. Yes, through that silence the voice shall be heard; through that silence the shepherd shall be put upon his guard."

LIBEL.

"Perhaps, gentlemen, he may know you better than I do: if he does, he has spoken to you as he ought; he has been right in telling you, that if the reprobation of this writer is weak, it is because his genius could not make it stronger; he has been right in telling you that his language has not been *braided and festooned as elegantly as it might; that he has not finished the miserable plaits of his phraseology*, nor placed his *patches and feathers with that correctness of millinery* which became so exalted a person. If you agree with him, gentlemen of the jury; if you think that the man who ventures, at the hazard of his own life, to rescue from the deep the drowned honour of his country, must not presume upon the *guilty familiarity of plucking it up by the locks*, I have no more to say; do a courteous thing. Upright and honest jurors! find a civil and obliging verdict against the printer! and when you have done so, march through the ranks of your fellow-citizens to your own homes, and bear their looks as they pass along; retire to the bosom of your families and children, and when you are presiding over the morality of the parental board, tell those infants, who are to be the future men of Ireland, the history of this day. Form their young minds by your precepts, and confirm those precepts by your own example; teach them how discreetly allegiance may be perjured on the table, or loyalty be foresworn in the jury-box; and when you have done so, tell them the story of Orr; tell them of his captivity, of his children, of his crime, of his hopes, of his disappointments, of his courage, and of his death; and when you find your little hearers hanging from your lips, when you see their tears overflow with sympathy and sorrow, and their young hearts bursting with the pangs of anticipated orphanage, tell them that you had the boldness and the justice to stigmatize the monster who has dared to publish the transaction!"

CHARACTER OF THE IRISH PEASANTRY.

"The people of our island are by nature *penetrating, sagacious, artful, and comic.*"*

---

* In battle, on shore and at sea, the Irish soldier and sailor have been remarkable for their valour, steadiness, and subordination. As far back as SPENSER's time, the bravery of the Irish soldier was honourably mentioned. That happy genius says:—

"'I have heard some great warriors say, that in all the services which they had seen abroad in foreign countries, they never saw a more comely man than an *Irishman*, nor that he cometh on more bravely to his charge.'

"BARON FINGLAS, in the days of Henry the Eighth, thus speaks of the Irish in his *Breviate of Ireland*:—

"'The laws and statutes made by the Irish on their hills they keep firm and staple, without breaking them for any favour or reward.'

"SIR JOHN DAVIES (Attorney-General in the reign of James the First) acknowledges—

"'That there is no nation under the sun that love equal and indifferent justice better than the Irish; or will rest better satisfied with the execution thereof, although it be against themselves.'

"COKE also says:—

"'For I have been informed by many of them that have had judicial places there (Ireland), and *partly of mine own knowledge*, that there is no nation of the Christian world that are greater lovers of justice than they are; which virtue must of necessity be accompanied by many others.'—Coke's *Institutes*, chap. lxxvi."

FLOOD.

Extracts from his Speeches, Letters, &c.

"TO LORD TOWNSHEND ON HIS PUBLIC CONDUCT IN IRELAND, ENGLAND AND AMERICA.

"We, my lord, who have beheld your predecessors, thought nothing at this time could be new in a Lord Lieutenant, except virtue. Rashness could not astonish a people who had seen the Duke of Bedford; weakness could not astonish a people who had seen the Duke of Northumberland; and a despicable character ceased to be a novelty, for we had not forgotten Lord Hertford: but there remained one innovation in politics, which we had no conception of; a man who had all the defects of these great personages without the allay of their virtues; who was rash, weak, and contemptible, but was not intrepid, splendid, or decent; a man who had not spirit to assert government, and yet was audacious enough to violate the constitution; whose manners were ludicrous, whose person was despised, whose disposition was vehemence without firmness, and whose conduct was not steady oppression, but rather the tremor of tyranny; such a man could not have been foreseen; but at length the miracle was produced, and this phenomenon at the Castle appeared in your lordship.

THE DEATH OF WOLFF.

"From the impartial observer let me become a monitor, my lord; and, above all things, let me warn you against the avarice of fame. Nothing is so dangerous. I will make an error of your own my example. In your mind, I am told, it is your glory to have served at QUEBEC. Take care that it may not be your shame. You were *third* in command under the Great Wolfe. You saw the military hope of the British nation expire. A great man might have envied him his death. A *fiend* only could have envied him his glory. I appeal to your lordship, for in this you must be my testimony, as well as my theme. You saw him struggling, according to his own expression, with a choice of difficulties. You saw him bending under a complicated and increasing infirmity. He had a noble heart, a wise head, and a performing hand. In such circumstances, and by such qualifications, when you saw him become the idol of a fond nation, and of an applauding army; when you saw him smiling in death, because it was accompanied by his country's victory; with what passion were you inspired? Did the nobleness of emulation seize you? Like Themistocles, did the triumphs of Miltiades deprive you of repose? Or, like Cæsar, did you weep over the tomb of Alexander? No. If you went to his grave, you went not to offer the applause of surviving heroism to the illustrious dead; but to supplant his monument, and defraud him of his fame.* How did the people of England feel, the untutored people? His death filled his country with lamentation. After a considerable interval, the remains of that great man landed in Great Britain. No honour which the living can pay to the deceased was omitted. As if victory still followed him, the news of fresh conquests soon succeeded. Every part of the kingdom resounded with congratulation, except one. The region adjacent to the residence of the venerable matron who had given him birth was silent. An universal sentiment of heroic compassion struck the people. They stifled even public joy, and would not suffer a sound of triumph to invade the solemnity of her just grief. Thus did that undistinguishing multitude, whom you affect to despise, mark their veneration for their departed hero; whilst you, my lord, a brother soldier, and connected with him in command, had the justice and generosity to endeavour to defame him."†

FLOOD'S ANSWER TO 'BROGHILL'S' DEFENCE OF LORD TOWNSHEND.

* * * * * *

"To whatever degradation his Lordship may in other things have submitted, you maintain that he scorned the degradation of stipulation with individuals. Where he or his advocates have found this idea, I know not. It has not been the system of his predecessors. It is as little founded in the facts of his administration, as in the precedents I have mentioned. Not to speak of his excellency's first winter, no sooner was his present secretary invested with his office than he began the traffic. Lord Loftus, then a commoner, went to London, his door was besieged night and morning by the secretary. Those terms (with something more) which have since overcome Mr. Beresford, were pressed on Lord Loftus if he would forsake the Speaker. That nobleman had not

---

* I thought it unnecessary to mention that you usurped the province of your brother commander who survived, as well as the fame of the departed; and with an ignorant, or arrogating hand, signed the capitulation, which ought to have been subscribed and ratified by the signature of the second in command. If it were absurdity, we are used to overlook it in your lordship; and if it were intentional, an injury to the living is more easily to be forgiven, than inhumanity to the dead.

† The only part of his administration which we should call his own, is his peculiar ingratitude to this nation; a nation which received him with such partiality, that they seemed to have drank oblivion to every former action of his life, from the time when he pilfered the fame of his general, before the wounds of the conqueror, or the tears of his soldiers, had ceased to flow, to the day when he offered to cram the Stamp Act down the throats of the Americans.

then learned the immortality he would acquire, by deserting at once his country and his friends.*
"Consider Lord Townshend's character, and that of those by whom he is governed. The servile abettor of every unconstitutional measure, the tool of Bute and of everything which wears the livery of Bute; the *practiser* of corruption in every period of his life, and at length the *missionary*, is nominally governor. A Weymouth, a Sandwich, a Rigby, a Northington, a Hertford, and a Holland, are his directors. Are these the men who have forbidden him to stipulate with individuals? Are these men averse to corruption? or are they the most conspicuous examples of venality in a venal age? How have the fraternity of the present administration, how have the gang of Bloomsbury obtained their offices? We will readily believe that they seldom have refused, but we cannot believe that they never stipulated for places. We cannot so utterly discredit every profession of our sovereign, as to attribute their elevation merely to his choice. Or have the public been perpetually mistaken? And is it the mildness of Weymouth, the purity of Sandwich, the diffidence of Rigby, the disinterested and elegant spirit of Northington, the munificence of Hertford, and the popularity of Holland, that have recommended them to each other, as well as to a pious and a discerning prince? A pretence to principle, in such a viceroy, governed by such an

---

* "The eyes of the public are upon you. Gratitude, family affection, private faith, and public consistency call aloud to you. You have still an option between honour and infamy; but the first day of the session will close the alternative. In the dream of affluence, and amidst the soothing of deceivers, you may, perhaps, have forgot your condition; I wish to awaken, not to wound; to prevent, and not to punish. *   *   *
And if, in defiance of every principle of honour and prudence, you were to betray the public and your friends on this great occasion, consider how fatally you would betray yourself; if Government were defeated in the contest, ruin and infamy would seize you together.
*   *   *   *   *

"The present Viceroy, Lord Townshend, must infallibly, in a few months, be removed; and upon the first change you will find your folly; despised by friends, renounced by relations, cast off by Government, and hooted at by a nation. But if, in spite of everything, you are determined to be infamous, at least have the reward of infamy. Go to the Castle, and if you are resolved on rapine (to use the simile you politely applied to the Lord Lieutenant) act like a highwayman, rather than like a pickpocket. Apply the blunderbuss of your gang to Lord Townshend's breast, and bid him *deliver*. You will find your error; and if you cannot go forward to profit, endeavour to return to honour."—*Letter to Lord Loftus.*

administration, instead of being imputable to virtue, or even to the hypocrisy of clumsy vice, can be nothing but the insolent irony of a profligate and audacious venality. And, to speak of this kingdom, was it the austerity of Andrews, the patriotism of Hutchinson, or the consistency and wisdom of the Earl of Tyrone, that has marked them out to his Excellency's favour? The world will not easily believe that motives, such as these, induced his Excellency to promise a bishopric to the recommendation of a man who is fitter to preside over a brothel than an university; or to be conducted by another, whose flippery prostitution has rendered even his infamy ridiculous. Nor will they believe, that the Earl of Tyrone, after having violated every engagement, private and public, into which he ever entered, has been selected for his consistency and honour; or that his abilities have recommended him, when they reflect, that the elder Brutus must have been a less dissembler than the Earl of Tyrone has been from his earliest years, if his lordship's incapacity be counterfeit. His lordship will pardon this trait of his character in a piece where he is not the principal. He deserves, and may receive a full delineation.

APPENDIX L.

TINNAHINCH HOUSE, COUNTY WICKLOW.

Page 322.

"Upon quitting St. Valori Cottage, near the Dargle, I paid a visit to that great man, Grattan, whom I have with so much gratification mentioned, at his beautiful seat called Tinnahinch, or the Little Peninsula, the approach to which is very fine. Tinnahinch, or Teine Inch; the latter applies to some great altar of the pagan Irish, in or about the place so called. Teine signifies water; it also means stagnated water, and the water-marks of a river. *Inch*, or inis, or enis, signifies an island; the Irish give this name even to lands not quite surrounded by water, as Inche-core, near Dublin, which has the Liffey in front, and a small stream parallel to it at the back, running to Kilmainham Gaol. Tinnahinch House stands at the base of a vast mountain, finely clothed with wood and verdure; a little from the summit is Powerscourt, the princely residence of Viscount Powerscourt.

"Soon after my arrival, the distinguished owner of Tinnahinch conducted me through his beautiful grounds. The surrounding objects corresponded with the mind of my guide. Before us a winding river, here fertilizing meadows, there foaming over rocks, the rich romantic foliage of the woods, and the lofty mountains that half enclose the Dargle, represented his eloquence, lucid, rich, copious, and sublime; whilst behind the cloud-capp'd Scalp, serrated with broken rock, resembled the terrible force of his

Grattan's Electioneering Eloquence.

roused philippic. I had the peculiar happiness of seeing this great man in the bosom of his amiable, elegant, and accomplished family; and in one of the greatest orators and politicians of the age, I saw the affectionate husband, the fond father, the luminous and profound scholar, the playful wit, and polite, well-bred, hospitable gentleman. Such is the man who, in his speeches upon the question of the paramount right of England to change the constitutional government of Ireland, displayed an eloquence before unknown to that, and never surpassed in any country. This question underwent several discussions in 1780, 1781, and 1782; the speech which he delivered on the 19th of April, 1780, was, as I was informed by a gentleman who had the good fortune to be present when it was delivered, most brilliant, energetic, and impressive; it effected the repeal of the 6th of George I., and for a period gave independence to his country; for THIS SPEECH ALONE the Irish Parliament, by an almost unanimous vote, granted him the sum of FIFTY THOUSAND POUNDS! His speech also on the propositions, in 1785, is said to have teemed with the highest eloquence.*—*The Stranger in Ireland,* 1805.

---

* On the election in question, I* was proposed by Mr. George Ponsonby, and upon Mr. Grattan rising next to vote upon my tally, he was immediately objected to as having been expelled on the report of Lord Clare's committee. A burst of indignation on the one side, and of boisterous declamation on the other, forthwith succeeded. It was of an alarming nature; Grattan meanwhile standing silent, and regarding, with a smile of the most ineffable contempt ever expressed, his shameless accusers. The objection was made by Mr. John Giffard, of whom hereafter. On the first intermission of the tumult, with a calm and dignified air, but in that energetic style and tone so peculiar to himself, Mr. Grattan delivered the following memorable words—memorable, because conveying, in a few short sentences, the most overwhelming philippic—the most irresistible assemblage of terms, imputing public depravity, that the English, or, I believe, any other language is capable of affording :—" Mr. Sheriff, when I observe the quarter from whence the objection comes, I am not surprised at its being made ! It proceeds from the hired traducer of his country—the excommunicated of his fellow-citizens—the regal rebel—the unpunished ruffian—the bigoted agitator! In the city a firebrand—in the court a liar—in the streets a bully—in the field a coward ! And so obnoxious is he to the very party he wishes to espouse, that he is only supportable by doing those dirty acts the less vile refuse to execute." Giffard, thunderstruck, lost his usual assurance, and replied in one single sentence :—" I would spit upon him in a desert !"—which vapid and unmeaning exclamation was his sole retort! I called for the roll, and, on inspection, Mr. Grattan's name appeared never to have been erased. Of course, the objection was overruled ; my friend voted, and his triumph was complete.

* Sir Jonah Barrington.

APPENDIX M.
THE CASTLE OF DUBLIN.
OF MODERN DAYS.

[From *All the Year Round*. Published by the kind permission of Charles Dickens, at the request of his friend, George Hodder, Esq., *Morning Post*.]

THE cheerful city which stands on the banks of the Liffey has special features and attractions of its own, and which almost take it out of that uniform pattern which belongs to most cities in the United Kingdom. It has architectural pretensions of no mean order, all its public buildings being in the same style, and almost of the same era; being disposed, too, with an eye to picturesque position and effect, under the direction of a parliament which, though corrupt, had the redeeming merit of being sumptuous in all matters relating to the public. Of a fine summer's day, these broad streets, with what looks like a Grecian temple at a corner far away in the haze, with the bridges, and the ships lying at the quays, and the columns and statues, and the general air of vivacity, the crowded pathways and the light cars, which spring along cheerfully with the Celtic drivers standing up carelessly on one side looking out for fares, and, like "jolly young watermen," never in want of one, give a curiously festive and almost foreign air to this Irish city.

How then does a city, without trade, or manufactures, or law, look as gay and busy as if it were fattening on trade, and manufactures, and wealthy citizens? We may set all this down to the presence of a Court—a Court which has been called "Brummagem," "a sham," and a hundred such contemptuous names (who does not remember Mr. Thackeray's epigram about a Court Calendar being bad enough, but a *sham Court Calendar*), but which has still an extraordinary and unsuspected influence on the social prosperity of this city. A Court, after all—"Brummagem" or otherwise—is a Court; that is to say, if it can boast a fine income, a handsome palace, has its guards, officers of state, and everything in keeping.

At the proper time in the "season" the show begins, the grand rooms are thrown open, the Viceroy and the Vicereine are ready to see their subjects, to feast them in their halls. Then Irish paterfamilias, delighting in his beeves and his fields, with a sigh gives way. Mamma and the three daughters (they are like mothers and daughters everywhere else) have joined to persuade and intimidate. And paterfamilias, like his kind elsewhere, is not strong enough to withstand such pressure. He is reminded of what his duty is to his "girls," under the just penalty of being stigmatised as a "brute." And thus, when the season sets in, the country families come flocking up, and take houses in "Fitzwilliam-street" and "Fitzwilliam-square," in "Pembroke-place," and other "genteel and genteely-named localities.

We may suppose it to be the beginning of the season, and the night of the first drawing-room—for levees and drawing-rooms have been going on here for centuries—and, with a sensible eye to picturesque effect, the drawing-rooms are always held at night. Towards ten o'clock carriages are converging to the little hill from half-a-dozen different points, and form into one line ; inside of which, fluttering young girls, all trains and lapets, are folded up somehow. A crowd is at the gates, laughing, jesting, criticising, half satirically, but mostly with respect, the charms that pass them by. Inside, in the court-yard, all the tall windows are lit up in long files, and the soldiers and police are drawn up ; and afar off under the arcade, where there is a blaze of light, the carriages are "setting down," and driving away. Inside, there are great halls lined with soldiers, and a grand staircase, and long galleries lined with servants and soldiers, and the long, long room where the company wait their turn, and crush on—as genteel crowds always will crush, even at places of yet better quality—to the barrier of the Pen. Under the brilliant light is seen a curious crowd, like the chorus at the opening of an opera, a variety of uniform that would delight an Aulic councillor. For, to say nothing of the dreadful "court suit," still from necessity in universal favour, there are soldiers of every "arm," sailors, privy councillors, in the rude rasping high collars, with coats of the "robin redbreast" cut, and a host of other varieties that would "intrigue" the Queen's chamberlain ; for Ireland, like France and Germany, is a uniform-ridden country. The police uniform is a uniform infinitely more showy than that of the Queen's rifles. The inspectors of this and that government office have their special dress. Even the Clerks of the Crown, legal officers, are resplendent in blue and silver, and "run" French senators very closely. Mixed up with all these are the stately matrons and the fresh young girls from the country, the special "Irish" faces, the "violet eyes," placed beside the established reigning belles of the city itself. There is an endless chatter going on. Beyond, is a second room and another barrier; and beyond that is the Throne-room, where what we may hear a country gentleman call "the sermony" takes place. Here we are at the barrier, kept sternly but not unkindly by a gigantic dragoon serjeant; and now, fluttering, blushing, round-cheeked Miss Glorvina, you may get ready.

For a "sham," and a thing that we are taught is Brummagem, the matériel for a "sermony" is very complete. Peeping into this Throne-room, which is all a-blaze with gold, with a coved ceiling, which has rich amber hangings and furniture to match, and which recals a state-room in the palace of St. Cloud, we can see a throne with a handsome canopy, and for a matter of spectacle, a very glittering pageant indeed. In front of the throne the Viceroy himself, who may be assumed to be that genial, gracious, pastimeloving, and Irish-loving nobleman, the late Earl of Carlisle, whose strangely heavy white hair, rosy full face, and gartered knee, make a picture that will be long recollected. On each side, in a semicircle, are his "staff," the dozen or so of "aides," the "master of the horse," "comptroller," "chamberlain," "gentlemen at large," "state stewards," "private secretaries," "physicians to the household," "surgeons to the household," make up a respectable and showy gathering. But opposite them, thus making a sort of semicircular lane, is a yet more effective crowd, the dignitaries and persons of quality of "the Court," who have been privileged with what is called the "private entrée." Here we have archbishops and primates, and lord chancellors and lord justices, chief justices, lord mayor, deans, chaplains, heralds in gorgeous tabards, knights of St. Patrick, commanders of forces, privy councillors in profusion, earls, marquises, barons, and all the "ladies" of these illustrious persons. When we think that everyone looks their best and wears their best, and that every family diamond is put on to the best advantage, the whole must be a rather dazzling sight. But for them the whole spectacle must be a show of great interest and amusement. For here, now, the pages are letting down the agitated little Glorvina's train, and the dreadful moment is at hand. Her stately mamma, well accustomed to such a process, has stalked on majestically, undismayed if a whole regiment were drawn up there. Already the officials have got the little girl's card, and are passing it on from hand to hand, and the last has chanted it aloud: "MISS GLORVINA SARSFIELD!" with the addition "TO BE PRESENTED!" which, translated into English, means a viceregal privilege consecrated by immemorial usage. The deputy king has his tenths, as it were, strictly levied on every first presentation. The charming little Glorvina—a Connemara rosebud—now making her curtsey (practised again and again in Merrion-square for many nights, and last night with papa standing up as viceroy on the rug, and the brothers doing the "staff"), is drawn over, and the osculatory tribute exacted in a half paternal fashion. Sometimes the confusion and maiden modesty are so intense, that Cæsar can only obtain his tribute by a sort of game of hide-and-seek. But when a new viceroy arrives, everybody is presented, and the saluting of some six hundred Irish ladies, however agreeable an occupation for a preux chevalier, is not without its alloy, for the process becomes wholesale and indiscriminating, and in the long female procession the most courageous might be occasionally appalled.

This ordeal passed through, Miss Glorvina's train is carefully gathered up and restored to her, and she emerges into the long room, or gallery, where there is the crowd who have successfully passed through. One of the most entertaining things in the world is to stand at this door and study the play of human female expression as each emerge —the satisfaction, shyness, and complacency, which all struggle in the one face. This room is a fine picture, and has its own interest besides its architectural merits, for it is hung around with the lords-lieutenant of nearly two hundred years back—the Buckinghams, Westmorelands, Dorsets, Townshends, and nearly every noble family in England. The series has been carefully and almost religiously kept up; and people fond of prophecy discovered an omen in the fact, that after Lord Carlisle's picture there would be room for no more. But both prophecy and judgment failed together—another lord-lieutenant came, and another more observing eye found room for a new picture.

A study of these portraits is full of profit, and in these facts we might almost read the story of the government of the country. For here are clever, and weak, and cunning faces; open, jovial, and unsuspicious countenances; the reckless Townshend, the free debauched Rutland, the diplomatic Clarendon, the good-natured Eglinton, and the genial Carlisle.

Next we troop into ST. PATRICK'S HALL—the grand ballroom—with the painted ceiling and the galleries, where the musicians play, and the mirrors and the scarlet tiers of seats. Here, too, is a daïs, and another throne. And down this room, when the drawing-room is done, and the thousand or so of ladies, gentle and simple, have passed by, there is

"THE PROCESSION," and vice-King and vice-Queen march solemnly and stately down, to the drumming and trumpeting of music in the gallery. By one o'clock all have departed ; and in the next morning's papers we have the "correct list" in due order of precedence, and, more pleasant reading still, a minute account of the jewels, dresses, laces, lappets, "bouillons," "buffons," and the rest.

Almost next day, set in the dinners and balls. Country paterfamilias with his wife and daughters—a staunch supporter of government—is bidden. The late Lord Carlisle dispensed an almost sumptuous hospitality. Those weekly "banquets," as they were called, where a hundred guests were entertained in the large St. Patrick's Hall, as elegantly and as perfectly as if it were a dinner of twelve, will not be soon forgotten. This amiable nobleman delighted in having "his friends about him." He loved everything that the Irish would call "sport," and was never wanting where "sport" called for him. It was worth seeing this Viceroy at the curious ceremony on St. Patrick's Day, when the guards were relieved at the Castle, and the bands played Irish airs, and the Viceroy appeared on his balcony literally loaded with shamrocks. A mass of the great unwashed below, crowded densely, listening to their national airs ; and when some stirring jig struck up, the charm became irresistible, a number of rings were instinctively formed, and then was Pat and Andy "footing it," regardless of all proprieties. Police rushed up to avert the profanation ; but the good-natured Viceroy was seen protesting as furiously from his balcony, and the odd morning entertainment proceeded. As the fun waxed furious the contagion spread, more circles broke out, and presently the great yard was a mass of human beings dancing like dervishes.

Of this St. Patrick's night was always, too, a special feature—a great ball in court dresses. The routine was always strictly the same. It was a sight to see. As the clock struck ten, the two lines of dancers formed, the court suits and swords making it look like a ball of the last century, and then at the signal the music in the gallery struck up "ST. PATRICK'S DAY IN THE MORNING !" and a fierce country dance set in. The king's heart was in that measure, and it was delightful to see with what unwearied vigour he pursued the fatiguing course, "turning" every one conscientiously until he reached the end. A "Castle ball" is always "voted" capital, and, indeed, about one floats a memory of a floor vast and smooth as ice, good dancing, brilliant lights, and the charming music of a Vienna valse. But there are other delights of which this festive hall is the scene. Periodically a knight of St. Patrick is made, and the result is a "show" of no mean brilliancy—collars, mantles, heralds gorgeous in the knave of diamonds tabard, with that best and most efficient of all heralds, "Ulster"—better known to us as Sir Bernard—uniforms again, chancellors and prelates of the order, flitting to and fro, and crossing each other like the strands of a parti-coloured cord. This, too, is succeeded by the "banquet," than which, in Ireland as in England, nothing can so worthily "crown the work." Here, too, when the late earl was "king," were pleasant concerts, choruses of pretty ladies, and solos, for our late sovereign was an amateur, and loved a charming and brilliant voice just as much as he admired a charming and pretty face. Nothing was more delicate than the half-gallant half-fatherly encouragement he had for all the belles of his court, and they were many ; so, too, with the interest and pride he felt in their success, and their marriages were nearly always celebrated with a handsome present, and honoured with his own presence. But among other shows and festivities. bound up in a manner with "Castle life," is one which has a special charm. Long before the feeble halting society called the "London Royal Academy of Music" had come into wheezy life, there existed in Dublin, fully a hundred and twenty years ago, a society of the same class—the Irish Academy of Music, which has always a kind of fashionable patronage. Roman visitors will recollect the charming "Societa Filarmonica" and their delightful concerts, the feature of which was the rows of the fairest Roman ladies of the first quality and beauty, a princess or two even, sitting charmingly dressed, and giving an opera of Donizetti's. These refined and tuneful "ladies" will not soon be forgotten. It was truly an amateur performance, and was as pretty to look at as to listen to. Now in the Irish capital—and this may be quoted as an instance of kindred in Celtic nations—precisely the same thing may be seen, and at two concerts of this Irish Academy are there tiers and rows of rank and beauty—ladies who have been dancing the night before at Lady Mary Kilshandra's, in Merrion-square—are to be seen seated side by side, and with a strange indifference to the purposes of social meetings, consent to a sort of enforced and cloistered segregation. But, to produce due musical effect, tenors must sit with tenors, and soprani with soprani. On one side the wreaths and ribbons are one colour, on the other side they are different. Here the "amateur" may see violet eyes and oval faces in plenty.

Then for the performance. In this way have been "recited" nearly every opera of note—Martha, Don Giovanni, Il Trovatore, Ernani, La Sonnambula, Norma, &c., with no lack of prima donnas or tenors. These are the most pleasing entertainments that can be conceived.

Indeed, the rage for music is quite a Dublin feature. The excitement is great, and at private houses the "concert" is going on all the year. Sometimes we see, about five o'clock, a street blocked with carriages, and from open windows have the music of the Italian quartette borne to us, and know that this is a musical "tea" going on. But the gala-time for the lower classes, for the shilling gallery and pit, is when the opera sets in (and we have nearly two months' opera every year), and then Titiens and Santly reign, and are borne on the wings of a tumultuous but discriminating applause. Not often do we find, as the writer has seen, the great finale in the third act of Ernani encored by an "unwashed" audience ; nor is it only in Italy that singers have "ovations." Who will forget the Piccolomini furor, and the birds and wreaths lowered down to the stage, the speeching of that piquant little lady at one o'clock in the morning from her hotel window to a crowd of a thousand persons, the dragging home of her carriage every night? Or, as was the case with Grisi on her farewell, the torchlight procession? These things take us a little out of the world of prose and conventional buckram.

The theatre, too, like music, is a special Irish taste. Amateur acting is in great favour. The "soldiers" have their season of five nights every year, taking the theatre, which is barely smaller than Drury-lane. It is built on the principle that the audience are to be "shown off" to the best advantage as well as the actors, the whole " dress circle " being a sort of balcony ; and when the company are crowded close, and the house full from floor to ceiling, the effect is very gay indeed. And on these "command nights" the viceregal box blazed with mirrors, and chandeliers, and hangings, and was filled with a staff, and soldiers mounted guard on the stairs and lobbies, and the manager, according to old custom, was seen in a court suit, and with a pair of wax-lights, walking backwards and showing the Viceroy to his box. So important an officer is he looked upon that the Theatre Royal manager may present himself "at Court." As we look back through that old reign, very many of those pleasant theatrical nights present themselves, that white head—always conspicuous—that genial heart, ready to welcome and encourage all these pastimes. Now there was a tragedy, now a comedy ; now there was a comedy of French manners skilfully adapted from the French, as skilfully acted and set off with new music, new dresses, and new scenery. The result was a gradual training of a corps of amateur actors, who were fast becoming a pleasant feature in the place, when there came that strange and gradual sinking, and the final break-down. These were the nightly joys.

But when the summer evenings set in, there were other entertainments of an *al fresco* sort to amuse this pleasure-loving society, and files of carriages were seen trailing through the pleasant avenues of the Park, making for the charming gardens of "The Lodge"--the Viceroy's country house—where were the dairymaids, and the cows, and the syllabub, fresh as new milk could make it, and the music playing, and the quadrilles of little children on the bowling-green--perhaps the most amusing feature of the whole. More pleasant still were the cricket meetings, there being a viceregal club, for he delighted, not in the play itself, but in looking on and following it, and marking. Hither came every English club of note, specially I Zingari, with their gipsy colours, who were made welcome and "put up " vice-royally in the cheerful apartments of "The Lodge" while the days of play lasted. In honour of these guests, the ball and the concert were set on foot, and many of I Zingari remember pleasantly those cheerful old cricket festivals.

Yet with all this junketing, and fiddling, and high jinks night and day, this feasting and making merry, the city is not in a morally healthy condition. The strangest feature is the utter absence of the influence or presence of a middle class—a broad, loud-voiced, strong trading class. For all purposes of power or tone, this body, which should be the bones and muscles of every sound community, is a mere cypher. They make no sign. They are weak and retiring. For them is no round of honest middle-class amusement, the monster halls with the huge oratorios, an honest school of politics, an independent sterling school of politics, which should be sufficient for them. There is nothing of this kind. They fluctuate between those above them and below them. They pant for the cheap glories, the Brummagem "fashion" that is over their heads. They spend their lives sighing to be admitted into those choice enclosures, and are at last happy in their old age if they are allowed to look in over the rails, or sit on the wall. Nowhere, it must be confessed, does this upas of false "gentility," this aping at selectness and "fashion," spread its branches so wide and do such mischief as in the pleasant community. In no city are there such sacrifices made to the Juggernaut Fashion, or is that pelican in a frock coat —the Dublin father--so handsomely drained of his blood by his "fashionable" family. And he opens his veins, it must be said, cheerfully. On every side we can see the "slaving" barrister and the "slaving" doctor, sitting up of nights, rising by candlelight, and with infinite pain scrapes together, out of fees ill paid and faithlessly promised, his thousand a-year or so, while mamma and the lovely Eliza are prancing it down the square, or plunging up to Madam Mantalini's, or mapping out their fifth or sixth "steet dinner," or writing "kerds" for the third ball. Madame Mantalini already holds bills of papa's for a very large amount, and presently will be pressing. By-and-bye the poor pelican dies a little suddenly, and very akwardly, too, perhaps only the day before the festival to which the commander of the forces had been got to come; and then we have whispers and shrugs, and a wail of sympathy— "Very bad that of poor Dawson Dowdall! I hear not a sixpence for the creditors. Mantalini has his bill for eight hundred."

Pleasant as are the "high jinks" of the modern Dublin Court, they pale before its older glories. Ireland, a hundred and twenty years ago was like a separate kingdom, and was always spoken of as "this kingdom." Dublin was some four days' journey from where there were no accidents; but accidents were the rule, and delays at sea and on the road made a leisurely journey reach to a week. The fact of there being a parliament, a House of Lords and Commons, with a prime minister, a handsome revenue, a Chancellor of the Exchequer to regulate it, a set of brilliant debaters, the fame of whose eloquence became almost European, and, besides this, an "Irish establishment," that is, a regular Irish army, raised and paid in that kingdom—these were elements enough to render the nation of an importance which it is pardonable its sons should look back to with regret and pride. There was yet another feature not quite so admirable, another sense for what was called the "Irish Establishment," which bore lightly and cheerfully a load of English pensions for German princes and German mistresses, a "pension on Ireland" being the favourite "job." It was only when this degrading burden reached to between sixty and seventy thousand a-year that the Irish Parliament modestly but gently began to remonstrate.

To the readers of the old memoirs of those days, what

brilliant flashes come back! There was plenty of money in the country, though the peasantry was a miserable unenfranchised horde of serfs; but the gentry and the nobility were in their turn the unenfranchised serfs of pleasure, building palaces worthy of Venice (and which are now to be seen standing), dancing, fiddling, gambling, drinking, and fighting, as a gallant gentleman of those days should.

The grand cynosure of the Dublin Court was the stage. Those were the happy days for both theatres and actors, and with what happy effects their patronage was attended may be conceived from the splendid list of dramatic artists that Ireland has produced. The names of Barry, Macklin, Sheridan, Mossop, Ryan, Delane, among the men, and of Woffington, Kitty Clive, Mrs. Fitzhenry, Mrs. Bellamy, can scarcely be matched in any country. One hundred and thirty years ago there were four theatres in that city, all handsome and elegant, one of which now actually exists, and a portion of the wall of another where Garrick played, but helps to support a chapel, still stands.

We look back very far to the days of Lord Chesterfield, the hollow, polished nobleman—yet not so false in Ireland—winning favour in that country, making epigrams on the Irish beauties, and "cultivating" Alderman Falkener. It was in his reign that the great Mr. Garrick paid his second visit to Dublin, and appeared at the "Smock-alley" Theatre. The Viceroy and his court were there every night, and his Excellency, the Dublin papers said, was pleased to compliment Mr. Garrick rather extravagantly as the greatest actor that had ever appeared on *any* stage. Then was the Garrick fever brought on by overcrowding in the boxes and galleries, and the Dublin barrister, walking down to court by a short-cut, may thread his way through the "Blind Quay," and the old, mean, and wretched houses, then houses of persons of quality, who must have been disturbed by the block of carriages, and the flashing of torches, and the shouts of footmen attendant on the ovation to the great actor.

There was a pleasant gaiety, even an elegance, in the relations of the noblemen and gentlemen of this court. Amateur theatricals were all the rage—a taste that has always prevailed in Ireland. Each play was sure to be ushered in by some elegantly turned verses from "an eminent hand." Indeed, every gentleman was trained to versify, and every compliment to a beauty assumed the unsubstantial shape of rhyme.

The professional poet, Churchill, took a savage view of the

Amateur Actors before the Union—St. Cecilia. 417

most seductive place in the world; as some cynic did in the following halting lines:—

> Massbouses, churches, mixed together,
> Streets unpleasant in all weather,
> The church, the Four Courts, and hell* contiguous,
> Castle, College-green, and Custom-house gibbous;
> Few things here are to tempt ye,
> Tawdry outsides, pockets empty.
> Five theatres, little trade, and jobbing arts,
> Brandy and Snuff-shops, post-chaises and carts;
> Warrants, bailiffs, bills unpaid,
> Masters of their servants afraid;
> Rogues that daily rob and cut men,
> Patriots, gamesters, and footmen;
> Women lazy, drunken, loose,
> Men in labour slow, of wit profuse,
> Many a scheme that the public must rue it,
> This is Dublin, if ye knew it.

A pleasant subject, of a gossiping sort, would be the history of private theatricals, into which the annals of the Irish private stage would enter very largely. Everyone has heard of the Kilkenny theatricals, whose records are already set out in a book of their own; but it is impossible to peep into any social corner of Irish life without getting a glimpse of the amateur stage with lamps lit, and the noble ladies and noble gentlemen in rich dresses, playing their parts. Every old faded newspaper is full of complimentary notices. One short specimen will show in what "style" these things were done before the Union. In 1793, a number of noblemen and gentlemen took Malachy's Theatre, set Italian artists to work, to paint and decorate. The ceiling was gorgeous with Apollo, and Tragedy and Comedy; mirrors were let in to the pilasters of the boxes; the seats were all upholstered in scarlet and fringe; the decorations were all white and gold figures, with festoonings of gold and crimson tassels; servants in gorgeous liveries attended on everyone in the boxes. The orchestra was filled with amateurs, and the players were Lord Westmeath, Captain Aske, Lord Thurles, Lord Cunningham, Buck Whaley, and many more. They played the Beggar's Opera, the Poor Soldier, the Rivals, School for Scandal, and such pieces. These were not mere stray performances; but there was a regular season, and the theatre was rented for a number of years, until the Rebellion and the Union scattered both audience and company.

Nor must we pass by a picturesque tribute to music, which is not so honoured in our time. St. Cecilia, the patroness of music, had her day kept with all honour. At the Castle

---

* A narrow, dark lane at the rere of Christ Church.

was maintained a full state band, generally under the command of some musician of eminence, and Dubourgh, who played with Handel, filled this office for a long time. On St. Cecilia's Day, all the court and persons of quality repaired in great pomp to St. Patrick's Cathedral, where the Reverend Doctor Swift, the Dean, no doubt, objected to such "tweedle dum and tweedle-dee." A fine orchestra was erected, and Mr. Dubourg and his men fiddled away at Corelli, and Dr. Blow, and Purcell. The performance lasted from ten till three o'clock, and there was not standing room. Another custom obtained, which was that of keeping the king's birthday with great state and solemnity. There was a court in the morning, with a ball at night, and Sheridan, or Mr. Brooke, or Captain Jephson, or some Irish laureate, wrote an ode, which Mr. Dubourg "set," and which was sung and fiddled by a large choir and orchestra. A "Castle" festival, a hundred and forty years ago, took place in the "old Beefeaters' Hall," and with seven hundred people all seated in tiers, the topmost row of the ladies' heads touching the ceiling. By eleven at night all the minuets were over, and the Viceroy and his lady adjourned to the basset table in another room.

After an hour's play, the Duke and Duchess and their nobility adjourned to the supper-room, where there was a holly tree lit up with a hundred wax tapers, which made a prodigious impression; but an English lady, who was present, and saw the spectacle of the noble company bursting into the supper-room, says the scene was not to be described, "squalling, shrieking, all sorts of noises;" ladies were stripped of their lappels, hustled, squeezed in the scuffle; and poor Lady Santry was left more dead than alive.

A glimpse, too, of the old coffee-houses, where the gentlemen of Ireland drank wonderful claret at "Lucas's," deservedly considered the most "convenient," as there was a charming garden, or enclosure, at the back, where "difficulties" were settled with delightful promptitude. The gentlemen had only to move their chairs near to the windows, and were thus able to see the whole "fun" with comfort and ease. Lucas's was a haunt for certain persons of quality, and where anyone who wished to see what were called "The Bucks" was sure to be gratified. The Bucks were the fine gentlemen of the time, if finery consisted in ostentatiously savage manners and barbarous behaviour. Some belonged to the "Hell Fire Club," and one of this society's feats is recorded—namely, setting their club-room on fire, and enduring the flames until they were all but suffocated and burnt to death. This was by way of bravado, and to show their contempt for the torments which were held up to them from pulpits. Some were called Pink Diudies, whose pastime was cutting off an inch or so of the scabbard of their swords, and prodding the victims of the jests with the blades, which thus could not penetrate much below the surface. The odious race of duelling bullies swarmed over the town— the "Tiger Roches" and others. One Buck would walk up and down Lucas's with a train to his cloak, and if any one trod on it, would instantly draw his sword. An old gentleman, who was alive not long since, recollected a scene of this sort at Lucas's, produced by this literal challenge to tread on the tail of one's coat, and where the unconscious offender was lucky enough to anticipate the bully's attack by running him through the body. In short, the fashionable *mode* for the Bucks was to range the city and seek for excitement by maiming or annoying the canaille, which was carried out by "pinking," or "sweating." We know what "pinking" was; "sweating" was bursting into a house and carrying off guns and swords as trophies, just as knockers used to be wrenched by the "bloods" of yesterday's generation.

Another set of gentlemen went about as "Chalkers." Their pastime consisted of marking or maiming a person about the face. And the quality of these ruffians is at once characteristically determined by the Acts of Parliament passed against the practice, in which, though visiting it with the severest penalties, it is stipulated there shall be nothing to corrupt the offender, or prejudice his family.

Even now, next to the old Parliament House stands a stately building, cut up into half-a-dozen houses of business. This was once "Daly's Club-house," where all the noblemen and gentlemen of both Houses would adjourn to dine and drink; where were seen Mr. Grattan, and Mr. Flood with "his broken beak," and Mr. Curran, and those brilliant but guerilla debaters, whose encounters both of wit and logic make our modern parliamentary contests sound tame and languid. There was seen that surprising Sir Boyle Roche, whose name and whose surprising "Bird" had done such good service, both in books and speeches. And there, too, we see honourable members emerging from under the classical portico, hot with rage and fury, and driving away to "the Phœnix" to arrange their differences. As we pass by and see that picturesque temple given over to the money-changers, and transformed into the Bank of Ireland, it is impossible for one who is thoroughly Irish not to regret those brilliant days, and the abrupt change from nationality to pure provincialism.*

The year before the Union, as "old inhabitants" have told the writer, Sackville-street, long and broad as it is, was literally crowded with coaches and six, waiting, drawn up, to take down noble lords and noble gentlemen to "the House." Only the year after the Union, as an ancient and fossilised coach-builder has also told us, the auction-marts and carriage-yards were encumbered with coaches and carriages and horses; noblemen and gentlemen, now "out of work," with their calling gone, literally flying from the unhappy capital.

About the old Music Hall, now Fishamble-street Theatre, where Handel sat at his harpsichord, float the ghosts, and clouds of a hundred fairy scenes and glories. Here it was that Lord Mornington—of "ye spotted snakes" memory—founded this musical academy, which, by the rules, was to be strictly independent of all "mercenary professors." A hundred years ago it was flourishing. The president was the facetious Kane O'Hara, who wrote "Midas;" the leader of the band was Lord Mornington; first violins, Count M'Carthy, Right Hon. Sackville Hamilton, Rev. Dean Bayley, and others; bassoon, Colonel Lee; violoncellos, Earl of Bellaunt, Sir John Dillon, two Hon. and Rev. Deans; flutes, Lord Lucan, Captain Reid, Rev. J. Johnson; harpsichord, Right Hon. W. Brownlow, Lady Freke, Miss Cavendish; singers, Right Hon. Lady Caroline Russell, Mrs. Monck, Miss O'Hara, and a host of other notabilities. This place still stands; and every night Malachy, enterprising manager as he is, gives the illegitimate drama, where the noble earl led the band, and my Lady Freke sat at the harpsichord. Masquerades, too. Mr. Gardiner, of the Blessington family, flits by as an old woman carrying her father in a basket; considered the best and most ludicrous mask in the place, and Mr. Hamilton as a French gouvernante. There passes by Mr. Yelverton as a Methodist preacher, Counshillor Doyle as a friar; and, strangest spectacle of all, Lord Glerawly as "a sideboard of plate." This was certainly the most mysterious of all characters, and did honour to his lordship's ingenuity. Captain French as Diana Frapes. But the character that we should have wished to see, and which has an interest for us beyond the gentleman who walked as Sterne's Slaukenbergias, fresh from the promontory of Noses, was "Mr. Boswell," who

* Only last year died the last surviving member of the Irish House, one of Nature's gentlemen—no mere remnant of an old generation, but fresh, buoyant, keeping pace with the younger world, the delight and admiration of his friends.

had, by this time, emptied his head of Corsica, and who was content with the character of Douglas.

The chapter of Irish beauties at the Irish Court has always been a large one. Looking back, we can catch glimpses, at every era, of a train of belles of reputation. When all London was running wild after the lovely Gunnings, and when a Secretary of State actually sent a guard of soldiers to walk after them in Hyde Park to keep the mob off, and when these brilliant but bold young ladies were rather courting such admiration, it was surprising that no one thought of hunting up the old stories of their Irish triumphs; for they, too, had been at "the Castle," yet under circumstances a little humiliating. Their father, John Gunning, Esquire, had ruined himself, like many a fine Irish gentleman; but his daughters, like many fine Irish ladies, must still go to the "shows" and keep up appearances; yet both money and credit were unhappily gone, in which difficulty their mamma called in Mr. Thomas Sheridan, the manager of the Theatre Royal, Smock Alley, who kindly allowed the handsome girls to choose from the rich wardrobes of his green-room, and in this way they were enabled to go to "the drawing-room." On another occasion, a charitable actress, passing through Great Britain-street, heard women crying in a second floor, and going in, found the two beauties and their mamma in the deepest distress, bailiffs having put in an execution. John Gunning, Esquire, was happily out of the way, as he always contrived to be. She befriended and rescued them. Long after, when the Irish girls made their wonderful matches, and became Lady Coventry and Duchess of Hamilton, it is said that the Irish manager had humbly asked to be invited to one of their parties, and was refused; and Mrs. Bellamy, the actress who had saved them from the bailiffs, is also said to have met with the same neglect. Still, theirs were awkward secrets to bring to your host's party.

In later times lively and not too strait-laced saturnalia prevailed. Jovial vice-kings enjoyed their reigns. The Dublin caricaturists were never idle a moment. Looking over their works, we find open allusions to three very well-known ladies, who are always put down as Lady C——r, Lady C——e, and Lady Denny. The pranks of these dames amused the whole city; their rivalries, their battles in the box lobbies of the theatre, and their doings at Court. All the world knew Lady Cahir, Lady Denny, and Lady Clare, but they did not heed what the world knew. One of the caricatures gave each a motto, more witty than complimentary. For Lady Clare, "I declare for all men;" for

422 The Game of "Cutchacutchoo" at Dublin Castle.

Lady Cahir, "I care for all men ;" and for the last, "I deny no man." But the greater scandal was occasioned when it was known that one of these ladies had introduced an extraordinary game, in high favour at the Castle, and which went by the name of "Cutchacutchoo."

Two recesses were fitted up at the end of the grand saloons; and here, behind a curtain, the ladies prepared their toilet for the exciting sport. In a moment the floor was covered with a crowd of belles, and dowagers, and beaux, hopping about in the sitting attitude required by the game. Great was the laughter when a gentle dame of high degree was overthrown by the heavier assault of a stouter rival. Presently, as the fun waxed more furious, dresses were torn, hair disordered, paint on the fair faces began to rub off, and the whole became a romp. We are told, by an amusing satire, which dealt very severely with these high jinks, that a vice-queen tried to stop them—

> Fair Hardwicke, thou whose social schemes
> Steer justly 'twixt the nice extremes ;

but she was quite powerless.

The theatre, after Mr. Garrick's departure, was in a lawless state; "bloods" ranged the stage and green-rooms as they pleased; the manager was helpless. The pretty but overbearing Miss Bellamy—whose pettish quarrels with Garrick are amusing theatrical reading—was passing off the stage. One gala-night, when the viceroy and court were present, and the house crammed, one of the "bloods," a Captain St. Leger, who was standing at the wings, had the freedom to put his lips to her shoulder as she went by. The offended actress at once turned on him, and gave him a slap on the face that rang through the house. The act took place in full view of the audience, who applauded loudly; and Lord Chesterfield was seen to rise in his box, and clap his hands in approbation. He presently sent Major Macartney, his aide-de-camp, to require that Captain St. Leger should make a public apology, which was accordingly made in due form.

APPENDIX N.
Page 32.
THE MEETING OF GRA-NA UILE AND QUEEN ELIZABETH.
The meeting of Gran-na Uile and Elizabeth is a circumstance as singular as it is well authenticated. Dressed in the simple costume of her country, with her crimson mantle flung across her shoulder, the Irish chieftainess approached the stately Tudor, seated on her throne, and surrounded by her glittering court, and undazzled by the splendour of the scene, addressed the Queen of England, less as a mistress, than a Sister Sovereign.

FROM THE IRISH.

I.

There stands a tower by the Atlantic side—
  A grey old tower, by storms and sea-waves beat—
Perch'd on a cliff beneath it, yawneth wide
  A lofty cavern—of yore, a fit retreat
    For pirates' galleys; altho' now, you'll meet
Nought but the seal and wild gull; from that cave
  A hundred steps doth upwards lead your feet
Unto a lonely chamber!—bold and brave
Is he who climbs that stair, all slippery from the wave!

II.

I sat there on an evening. In the west,
  Amid the waters, sank the setting sun;
While clouds, like parting friends, about him prest,
  Clad in their fleecy garbs, of gold and dun;
    And silence was around me—save the hum
Of the lone wild bee, or the curlew's cry.
  And lo! upon me did a vision come,
Of her who built that tower, in days gone by;
And in that dream, behold! I saw a building high.

III.

A stately hall—lofty and carved the roof—
  Was deck'd with silken banners fair to see.
The hangings velvet, from Genoa's woof,
  And wrought with Tudor roses curiously;
    At its far end did stand a canopy,
Shading a chair of state, on which was seen
  A ladye fair, whose look of majesty,
Amid a throng, 'yclad in costly sheen—
Nobles and gallant knights proclaimed her, England's Queen!

IV.

The sage Elizabeth! and by her side
  Were group'd her counsellors, with calm, grave air,
Burleigh and Walsingham, with others, tried
  In wisdom and in war, and sparkling there,
Like Summer butterflies, were damsels fair,
Beautiful and young : behind a trusty band
  Of stalwart yeomanry, with watchful care,
The portal guard, while nigher to it stand
Usher and page, ready to ope with willing hand.

V.

A Tucket sounds, and lo! there enters now
  A stranger group, in saffron tunics drest :
A female at their head, whose step and brow
  Herald her rank, and, calm and self-possest,
Onward she came, alone, through England's best,
With careless look, and bearing free, yet high,
  Tho' gentle dames their titterings scarce represt,
Noting her garments as she past them bye ;
None laughed again who met that stern and flashing eye.

VI.

Restless and dark, its sharp and rapid look
  Shew'd a fierce spirit, prone a wrong to feel,
And quicker to revenge it. As a look,
  That sun-burnt brow, did fearless thoughts reveal ;
  And in her girdle was a skeyne of steel ;
Her crimson mantle, a gold brooch did bind ;
  Her flowing garments reached unto her heel ;
Her hair—part fell in tresses unconfined,
And part, a silver bodkin did fasten up behind.*

VII.

'Twas not her garb that caught the gazer's eye—
  Tho' strange, 'twas rich, and, after its fashion, good—
But the wild grandeur of her mien—erect and high.
  Before the English Queen she dauntless stood,
And none her bearing there could scorn as rude ;
She seemed as one well used to power—one that hath
  Dominion over man of savage mood,
And dared the tempest in its midnight wrath,
And thro' opposing billows cleft her fearless path.

---

* A yellow boddice and petticoat. Her hair gathered to the crown and fastened with a bodkin, with a crimson mantle thrown over her shoulders, constituted the court-dress of the Irish heroine.

VIII.

And courteous greeting Elizabeth then pays,*
 And bids her welcome to her English land
And humble hall. Each looked with curious gaze
 Upon the other's face, and felt they stand
 Before a spirit like their own. Her hand
The stranger raised—and pointing where all pale,
 Thro' the high casement, came the sunlight bland.
Guilding the scene and group with rich avail ;
 Thus, to the English Sov'reign, spoke proud Gran-na Uile :

IX.

"Queen of the Saxons ! from the distant west †
 "I come ; from Achill steep and Island Clare ;
"Where the wild eagle builds, 'mid clouds, his nest,
 " And ocean flings its billows in the air.
 "I come to greet you in your dwelling fair.
 " Led by your fame—lone sitting in my cave,
  " In sea-bent Doona—it hath reached me there,
 " Theme of the minstrel's song ; and then I gave
 " My galley to the wind, and crost the dark green wave.

X.

" Health to thee, ladye !—let your answer be
 " Health to our Irish land ; for evil men
 " Do vex her sorely, and have bucklar'd thee
 " Abettor of their deeds ; a lyeing train,
 "That cheat their mistress for the love of gain,

---

* The reception of Gran-na Uile by Elizabeth was most gracious ; she even offered, at parting, to make her a countess, which the proud Irishwoman refused, but accepted the title of earl for her infant son. It is a remarkable fact, that during the voyage from Clare Island to Chester, where she landed, she was delivered of a son—thence named in Irish—"*Toberduagh na Luig,*" or Toby of the Ships, from whom descend the Viscounts Mayo.—*Irish Annals.*

† The Islands of Achill and Clare—the neighbouring coasts of Mayo and Connemara, were the favourite haunts of Gran-na Uile. Clare Island is still in the possession of Sir Samuel O'Malley, who claims descent from the "Dark Lady of Doona ;" and at Carrighooly, "the castle in the nook or secret place," they show an aperture made in the sea-wall of her chamber, through which a cable was passed, fastening her galley at one end, and coiled round her bed-post at the other. It was on her return from her visit to the English Queen, that the remarkable abduction of the young St. Lawrence, of Howth Castle, took place.

"And wrong their trust—aught else I little reck,
 "Alike to me, the mountain and the glen—
"The castle's rampart or the galley's deck;
"But thou my country spare—your foot is on her neck!"

XI.

Thus brief and bold, outspake that ladye stern,
 And all stood silent thro' that crowded hall;
While proudly glared each wild and savage kern
 Attendant on their mistress. Then courtly all
 Elizabeth replies, and soothing fall
Her words, and pleasing to the Irish ear—
 Fair promises—that she would soon recall
Her evil servants. Were these words sincere?—
That promise kept? Let Erin answer with a tear.

INDEX.

A.

Abbey of Howth, 332
——— Holy Cross (Tipperary), 95
——— Kill, co. Dublin, 201
——— B.V.M. (Dublin), 95*n*
——— St. Thomas, the Martyr, 26, 27, 77*n*
Absenteeism prohibited, 61
——— injurious to Ireland, 62
——— increased by the Union, 116
Absentees of Ireland, 62
——— statute against, 62
——— Verses on (from *Anth. Hib.*, 1793), 62
Academy, Royal Hibernian, 168
——— Royal Irish, 152, 177
Adrian's Bull, 22*n*
Aideen, of Ben Edar, now Howth, 342
Aileen aroon, 174
Alexander the Great, Greek medal of, found at Ferns, 151
Allen, John, Abp. of Dublin, 155*n*
——— the Mark, Inn, 37
Alma, Edward L., ascertains locality of "The Churls," 143
All the Year Round, 407
Anacreon, Moore's version of, 105
ANECDOTES OF :
——— Armitage, Stephen (King of Dalkey), 219, 256

ANECDOTES OF—*continued.*
——— Battier, Mrs., 221, 257
——— Byrne, John, 7
——— ——— Patrick. 8*n*
——— ——— Courtney, Philip de 9, 10
——— Creed, Capt., 310
——— Cunningham, Mr., 354
——— Curran, xi *n*, xv, 224
——— Delany, Dr. P., vii, 202
——— Essex, Earl of, 16*n*
——— Flood, Sir H., 419
——— Glas, Capt. 376
——— Grattan, xiii *n*. 419
——— Gunning, The Misses, 421
——— Harwood, B. 8
——— Incledon, C., the singer, x, 257
——— Kingdom of Dalkey, ix, 218 to 268
——— Macnamara, 310
——— Maclean, the dentist, 8
——— Magee, of the *DublinEvening Post*, 139
——— Mara (Mdmo), x*n*
——— Matthew, T. Thomastown House, 296
——— Moore, 98, 101
——— O'Connell, 108, 110

ANECDOTES OF—*continued.*
— O'Meara, T., ix, 254
— Pack, Major, 310
— Parkinson, H. 354
— Perrot, Sir J., 15
— Petrie, Geo., xii, 164
— Petrie, Jas., 165
— Pilkington, Mrs. L., viii, 359, 360
— Scott, Etty, 84
— Sheridan, Dr. Thos., 307n
— Sheridan, the actor, vi n
— Stanley, Sir John, 9
— Stevenson, Sir J., xiii, n
— Swift, vii, 35, 42, 202, 209, 295, 306, 308
Annals of the Four Masters, 68, 95, 337
Annals of Henry VII., Henry VIII., Edward VI., and Queen Mary,* 25
Annals of Ulster, 338
Annular Inscriptions, 181, 195
Anthologia Hibernica, 60, 62, 69, 98, 203, 265, 297, 329, 384
— Ledwich and Moore, contributors to, 98
Antiquities near Dublin, 153n

Antiquities at Rathmichael, 197
— of Tullagh, 194
Arbutus unedo, grows at Dalkey, 48
Archdall's *Monasticon Hibernicum*, 94, 95
Archibold's Castle, Dalkey, 37
Archiboll, Richard, 29
Architecture of Ancient Irish Churches, 94, 105
Ardfinan Castle, picture of, by Petrie, 168
Armagh, Book of, 337
— its date ascertained by Reverend Dr. Graves, 337
Armitage, Stephen, ix., 219, 256
Arran Islands, Petrie's visit to, 173
Ars Pun-ica, by Dr. Sheridan, 307
Artists, Irish, 38, 317
Aspin's (J.), Analysis of Universal History, 150
— Geo-Chronology of Antiquity, 150
Asyk, Sir John, Lord of Doulek, now Bullock, 269
Avatar, The Irish, 111
Audain family, 302n
Audoen's Church, Dublin, 301n
Aumarle, Duke of, 10
Author's Concert of Ancient Irish Music, 161
Author's Geography & History, made Interesting, 156

* *Annals of the highest estimation relating to Ireland, viz., Henry VII., Henry VIII., Edward VI., and Queen Mary.*—"There is no perfect chain of records existing through all the several periods of the English government, occasioned partly by the decays of time, partly by the negligence of officers, and the bad condition of repositories in ancient days, and partly from the casualties from fire. Of accidents of this last kind, there is to be seen an ancient memorandum enrolled in the Chancery Office, Anno, 2 Edward II., to this effect: 'Memorandum, that all the rolls of the Chancery, were, in the time of Master Thomas Cantock, Chancellor of Ireland, to the twenty-eighth year of King Edward, son to King Henry III., *destroyed* by an accidental fire, in the Abbey of the Blessed Virgin Mary, near Dublin, at the time when that abbey was burned down, except two rolls of the same year which were delivered to *Master Walter de Thornbury* by the king's writ This loss is partly supplied by Maurice Regan, partly by Giraldus Cambrensis, and the Abbot Benedict, Alan's Registry, and the Black Book of Christ's Church Dublin.'"—*Dublin*, 1747.

Index. 429

Author's Lecture on Dalkey, v
—— work on the late Earl of Carlisle, 116n
—— Search for the body of Captain Boyd, and account of the storm in which he perished, 124

B.

Baggotrath Castle, 380
Baldwin, tenant of church-lands in Dalkey, 30
Ball, Mrs., foundress of Loretto Abbey, Dalkey, 91
Ballads, satirical, on Lord Townshend's administration—A List of the Pack—Advice from the Liberty, 287-289
Ballinclay, Killiney, 199
Ballybeggan, Co. Kerry, 296
Ballyboter, now Booterstown, 29
Ballybough River, 3
Ballybrack, 7
Ballybrittas, defeat of the Earl of Essex by O'More, 129
Ballymurphy, Dalkey, 91
Banks, sand, 8
—— Bennet's, 8
—— Bulls, North and South, 3, 269
—— Burford, 8
—— Kish, 8
—— Rosbeg, 8
Barataviana, 279, 281
Barber, Mrs., 206
Barrett, Dr. John, 202
Barrington, Sir Jonah, 34
Barrington, Manliffe, 188, 191
Barry, the actor, 207n
Barry, Robert, 52
Barton, Wm., do 215
Battier, Mrs., of Fade-st., Laureate of Dalkey, 221n
Battle of Gabhra, 342
Bayview House, Dalkey, 37

Bedell, Bp., 341
Beefstake Club, xv, n
Beg-Erin, 376n
Beggs, D., T.C. of Dalkey, 38
Begneta, St., of Dalkey, 21
Bellamy, Georgiana, 421, 422
Bellingham, Sir Edward, 14
Ben Edar, now Howth, 342
Bennet's Bank, 8
Beranger's Views of Irish Antiquities, 50
Bermingham, Justice, 29
Billiards at Dalkey, 36, 49, 52
Bindon's Portrait of Swift, 331
Black Book of Abps. of Dublin, 51, 155n
Black Castle, Dalkey, 36
Black Rock, 155
Bladderchops, Judge, 143
Blakeney, Sir Edward, 9, 46
Bloody Bank, Bray, 321
Bloyke, *see* Bullock.
Books, Irish MSS., 335
Book of Armagh, 337
—— Black, of Abps. of Dublin, 51
—— of Dimna, 336
—— of Durrow, 337, 340
    Translation of the inscription on its cumdach, 340
—— of Howth, 334, 336
—— of Hymns, 337
—— of Kells, 335
—— of Leinster, 341
—— of Ricemarch, 341
—— of St. Moling, 337
Borlase's *Irish Rebellion*, 188
Boswell, James, 420
Botanic Garden, Glasnevin, 202
Boucher, Mr., 160
Boulek, now Bullock, 269
Boyd, Captain, 6, 123
Brabazon family, 77n
Bradley, Tom, 130
Bray, 195n, 313, 320, 321
Bray Head, finest of Irish promontories, 153, 314
Bregia, plain of, 332
Brenuan, Mr., of Bray, 130, 316

	PAGE		PAGE
Brennanstown House,	190, 191	Byron's, Lord, *The Irish Avatar*,	111
Breslin, Mr. Edward,	130, 316		
Brett, Geoffrey le,	215	Byron's Lines on the death of the Duke of Dorset,	179
Brewer's *Beauties of Ireland*,	182		
Brien, Michael,	91	C	
Broghill's Defence of Lord Townshend, answered by Flood,	403	Caah Hill, Dungiven,	170
		Cabinteely,	190
		Callanan's Lines on Gougane Barra,	169
Brooke's, Miss Charlotte, *Reliques of Irish Poetry*,	82, 83	Calp,	389
Bryan, P. W.,	130	*Cambrensis Eversus*,*	21n
Buckhurst's *Gorboduc*,	180n	Camden's *History of Queen Elizabeth*,	14
Bucks, The,	418		
Budgell, Eustace,	82	Caoine, ancient Irish, sung at concert in memory of Dr. Petrie,	161
Bull, property in Dalkey,	35, 36, 37		
Bulls, the North, and the South,	269n	*Capel's Letters*,	19n
		Carew, Sir Geo. transl. from the French *the History of K. Richard II. in Ireland*,	10n, 14n
Bullock,	55, 83n, 268, 279n		
—— Castle of,	8n, 55, 83n, 269		
Bulkely, Patrick,	30n		
Bunting's *Ancient Music of Ireland*,	161	Caricature of Ladies Cahir, Clare, and Denny,	421
Burford Bank,	8n	Carlisle, Earl of, 120; His hospitality and urbanity, 411; observance of Saint Patrick's Day, 411; Saint Patrick's Ball, 411; His Reception at theViceregal Lodge, 414; his departure from Kingstown,	121
Burgh, Hussey	xv, n		
Burk, Sir Bernard, *Ulster*,	412		
	397		
Burke, J. M., *Dedication*, 5, 349			
—— Martin,	iii. 91		
—— Ulick,	vii		
Butler, originally Le Boteller,	213		
Burns', Robert, Poem on Capt. Grose,	97n	Carolan's *Monody on death of Mary Maguire*,	82
		Caroline of Brunswick, Geo. IV.'s queen,	111
Byrne, Miss Hannah,	99		
Byrne, Pat,	87, 91	Carr's, Sir J., *Stranger in Ireland*,	323
Byrne, Robert, of Cabinteely,	201		
		Carrickmines,	188
Byrne, Walter, of Cabinteely,	199	Carysfort, Earl of, a proprietor in Dalkey,	37

---

* "CAMBRENSIS EVERSUS.—This work was written by John Lynch, a secular priest, and titular archdeacon of Tuam, was a native of Galway. He published his *Cambrensis Eversus* An. 1662, under the feigned name of *Gratianus Lucius*. It was written in Defence of his country against the fabulous and malicious Reports made of it by *Gerald Barry*, commonly called *Cambrensis*, wherein with a judicious and sharp Pen he exposeth the numberless Mistakes, Falshoods, and Calumnies of that Writer; shewing, in confuting him, that he was well qualified to undertake the subject by a great compass of knowledge in the History of his country, and in other polite learning."—WARE.

Index. 431

Castlereagh, Lord, 114
Castle of Bullock, 55, 71
—— Carrickmines, 188
—— Dublin, vi, n 407
Castle House, Dalkey, vi, 36, 81
Castles of Dalkey, 2, 36, 64, 70
—— Howth, 331
Castle Lyons, formerly Castle Lehane, 106
Castle Street, Dalkey, 36, 38, 89
Cecilia's Day, St., observance of, in St. Patrick's Cathedral, Dublin, 417
Centenarians of Dalkey, 9n, 44n
Chabot, Viscount de, 296
Chalkers, The, 419
Chapelizod, 190, 297
Chapels at Bray Head and Old Connaught, 188n
Charlemont, Earl of, 396
Chenevix, Mrs., 208n
Cherrywood, 187
Chesterfield, Philip, Earl of, 208n, 416
Chateaubriand, 69
Churches, ancient Irish, 94, 105
Churl Rocks, 144
Churls, the Three, 143
Clarinda Park, Kingstown, 130n
Clare's, Lord, Visitation of Trinity College, Dublin, 103
Clibborn, Edward, on Saxon coins found at Dalkey, 65
Clifford, Sir Conyers, defeated by O'Rourke, 17n
Clogh-hobber-gillinestone, on Dalkey Hill, 55
Cloncurry, Lord, Fitzpatrick's Life of, 187
Clonmacnoise, described by Petrie, 171
Clonmel, Earl of, 139
Club, Royal Irish Yacht, 131
—— Royal St. George Yacht, 131
Coal, Whitehaven, price at Dunleary in 1768, 59

Cogan, Milo de, 21n
Coins, Saxon, found at Dalkey, vi, 65, 151
Comet, The, Newspaper, 1n
Commons of Dalkey, 35, 36, 38, 45, 53, 77, 91, 277
Conchology of Dublin Bay, by M. J. O'Kelly, 198n
Connolly, J. J., 36
Conolly, Mr., 37
Coolamore Harbour, 2, 5, 7, 349
Cooney's* Morning Post, 220, 222, 260
Coronation of Lambert Simnel, 25
Coronation of Stephen, king of Dalkey, 222
Coronation Ode by Mrs. Battier, 237
—————— by Moore, 264
Corr Castle, 331
Corrigan, Sir Dominic, 44n, 91n
See Inniscorrig.
Corruic-na-Greina, seat of C. Leslie, Esq., 59n
Courtney, Ph. de, Lord Deputy, A.D. 1386, lands at Dalkey, 9
Cowley, Walter, 30
Cox's Irish Magazine, 143
Crawford's History of Ireland, 22n, 68
Creswick, praise of the sunrise in Dublin Bay, 38
Crimean army embarks at Kingstown, 119
—— returns, 119
—— banquet given to, 120
Crithmum maritimum at Howth and Killiney, 156
Croceæ, or cross lauds, 216n
Cromlech on Howth, poem, 341n
Cromlechs near Killiney and Shanganagh, 191
Cromwell, Oliver, 33, 34, 42
S. Cronan of Roscrea, 336
Cross, ancient, at Tullagh, 196

* Cooney's *Dublin Morning Post and Courant* for 1790, and following years to 1798, inclusive. In the library of Dublin Castle.

Index.

Cross, ancient, at St. Valori, 324
Crowley, Robert, 217
Cruelty of Colonel Gibson after taking Carrickmines Castle, 188
Cunningham, contractor, 353, 354
Curran, John Ph. xi, xv, 224, 419
—— Extracts from his Speeches, 398
—— His Song, The Deserter's Meditation, xii, n
Curran, Miss, 166; Moore's poem, "She is far from the Land," 166n
Curwen (Curwen's Sketches of Natural History, 1785) xii, 81
Cutchacutchoo 422

D.

Dalcassians returning wounded from the battle of Clontarf, are obstructed by the Ossorians, 15
DALKEY, 1, 20
—— granted by Hugh de Lacy to see of Dublin, 20
—— survey of, in 1725, 35
—— in 1763, 36
—— Castles of, 2, 36, 64, 66
—— Church of, 9n, 37, 51, 94
—— Coolamore Harbour, 5, 7, 349
—— Commissioners of, 36
—— Commons of, 35, 36, 38, 45, 53, 77, 91, 277
—— Cromlech, 277
—— Druidical circle, 277
—— Fairs and Markets of, 22, 25
—— Geology of, 386
—— Hill, 55
—— lead ore found at, 53
—— Port of, 2, 3, 9
—— historic notices of, 9, 10
—— The Archbishop of

DALKEY—continued.
—— Dublin's Port, 7, 13, 24
—— admiralty jurisdiction of, 24
—— Regatta,
—— Salubrity of, 1, 31, 44
—— Saxon coins found at, 65
—— Sound, 3, 4
—— Proposed Harbour, 3
—— Town Hall, 36
—— tolls and customs, 23
—— Town, Provost and Bailiffs of, 2
—— Wells at, 59n
Dalkey Gazette, ix
Dalkey House, 37, 52, 59, 83
—— Lodge, 37, 52, 59
—— Island, 4, 5, 6, 54, 155
—— Church of St. Begneta on, 54
—— Kingdom of, ix, 218, 268
—— Coronation ode, 237
—— Coronation Sermons, 224, 240
The Dalkey Gazette, ix, 219, 220
—— Stephen, King, 219-253
—— Birthday ode to, 246
—— John, the last king, 254
Dalkey, Modern, 45
—— Proprietors of, 35, 36
—— Purchasers of the commons, 91
—— Tenants in 1763, 36
Daly, D. B., 397
Daly, Club-House, 347, 419
Daly's Coffee-House, 82
D'Alton's History of Co. Dublin, 12n, 187, 194, 202, 216n, 333
Dangan Castle, 209
Dargan, William, 130, 315
Dargle, 313, 321
Darley, Alderman, 118n
Delany, Dr. Patrick, vii, 201
Delany, Mrs. Autobiography 204
Delville, Glasnevin, vii, viii, 358
—— Swift's description of, 203
Denis, 91

Index.   433

Dermody, Thos., lines to   Dublin Bay, 38, 40, 42, 107, 155
  J. C. Walker,   324   ——— Lines on, 40, 107
Desmond, Earls of,   270n   —— Blackfriars' Monas-
Destruction of cromlech and   tery (where now
  Druidical stone circle at   the Four Courts)   25n
  Dalkey,   277   —— Castle,   viz. 407
Devereux, Robert,   201   —— Christ Church, 26, 95n
Devitte, James, of Old Dal-   —— Church of St. Mary
  key, House,   37   les Dames, 25n, 28, 29
Diamonds, valley of,   vii, 315   —— Guildhall, of   28
Dickens, Charles,   407   —— St. Mary's Abbey,   32
Dillon, J. B.,   192   —— St. Patrick's Cathe-
Dimna, Book of,   336   dral, 75, 95n, 123, 207n
Dodder, river,   3   —— St. Thomas' Court,   26
Dorset, Lionel, Duke of, Ld.   —— Siege of Dublin by
  Lieut.,   32n   King of Ireland,   21n
Dorset, Duke of, accidentally   Dubourgh, Master of the
  killed at Killiney,   80, 178   State Band, Dublin Cas-
St. Doulough's Church,   153n   tle,   418
Doyle, Wesley,   102   Duels between Macnamara
Drake, John, Mayor of Dub-   and Creed,   311
  lin,   215   ——— Matthew and
Druidical circle on Dalkey   Pack,   311
  Common,   277   Dufferin's (Lady) lines on
Druidical customs,   157-192   Dublin Bay,   40
Druidical monuments in   Dungan's Castle, Dalkey, 37
  Bretagne,   192n   DUNLEARY, 106—See Kings-
Druidical remains at Killi-   town.
  ney,   181, 192   —— harbour,   5, 77, 129
Druid's Head in S. Great   Durrow, Book of,   337, 340
  George's-street, Dublin,   222n   ——— Inscription on
Druid Lodge, Killiney,   181   its Cumdach,
Druids, order of, founded by   translation of. 340
  King of Dalkey,   222n
Drumcondra,   E.
——— Burial place of   Earlsfort, Lord (afterwards
  Grose the An-   Earl of Clonmel),   139
  tiquarian,   97   Eastmount, Dalkey,   48
——— Florists' club in   Edgecombe, Sir Richard, 25
  Drumcondra-   ——— his Voyage into
  lane,   298n   Ireland in 1488, 25
——— Forteck's gar-   Edgeworth, Father, an Irish
  den at,   299n   priest attends Louis XVL,
Dublin Examiner,   181, 196   223, 392
——— Penny Journal,   134, 160   Elsinore,   86, 91
——— University Magazine,   Elizabeth, Q., visited by
                        16, 93, 184   Grana Uile,   423
Dublin, Sir John de Stanley,   Einmot, Robert, said to be
  Marquis of,   10   interred in Glasnevin
Dublin in 1399,   13   Churchyard,   202n

                                                      3 H

Emmet, Robert, Posthumous Portrait of, 166
——— Recollections of, by Moore, 258
——— Verses by Moore, "She is Far from the Land," 166n
English defeated by O'Byrne, 16n
——— ——— by O'More, 129n
——— ——— by O'Rourke, 17n
Environs of Dublin, 153n
Erris, A. Young's character of, 322
Espinasse, Richard, 201
Essex Bridge, 3
Essex (Arthur Capel), Earl of, lands at Dunleary, in 1672, and in Dalkey, in 1675, 18
——— (Robert Devereux), Earl of, lands at Dalkey, in 1599, 16, 41
——— defeated by the Irish at Ballybrittas, 129n
Evergreen Oaks at Delville, Glasnevin, 205n
——— ——— at Rochestown, 200

F.

Fade Street, Dublin, 221n
Fagans, of Feltrim, 276, 301n
Fairies, 189n
——— la Roche aux Fées in Bretagne, 192n
"Faithless Emma," harmonized by M'Grath, xiv
Farransheball, a house in Dalkey, 37
Fassaro Castle, 324
——— Cottage, 323, 325
Ferdomnach, scribe of the Book of Armagh, 337
Ferguson (Sam), 273; his Poem—*The Cromlech on Howth*, 341, n 342
Fern Hill, Dalkey, 92
Fiat Hill, seat of Magee, of the *Evening Post*, 139

Fiat Hill, Olympic Pig Hunt at, 140
Fitzgeralds, Florentines in their origin, 182
Fitzgerald, Lord Edward, 166, 182
Fitzgerald, Maurice, 21n
Fitzgerald, Thomas, Earl of Kildare, 31
Fitzpatrick, Mrs., 175n
Fitzpatrick's, W. J., "Ireland before the Union," and other Historical works, 139, 143n
Fitzwilliam, Thomas, of Merrion, 15
Flann, King of Ireland [9th cen.], 340
Fleming, Rev. Father, 78
——— Rev. Father Christopher, 384
Florists' Club at Drumcondra, 298n
Flood, Henry, xvn, 396, 419
——— Extracts from his Speeches and Letters, 402
Forbes, Mr., 397
Fortune, Mr., of Bray, 316
Four Masters, Annals, 68
French privateer captures a Spanish trading vessel in Dublin Bay (contrary to law of nations), and tortures one of the crew, 19
Frescati, Blackrock, residence of Lord E. Fitzgerald, 182
Froelich, 151
Furnival, Lord, 14

G.

Gabhra, Battle of, 342
Gardening in Ireland, J. C. Walker on, 203n
——— Botanic, at Glasnevin, 202
——— at Thomastown, 296
Garland of Howth, 334, 336

Garrick, D., 416, 422
Gaskin's *Geography and History, made interesting,* 156
Gaskin's Memoirs, speeches, &c., of the earl of Carlisle, 116
Gentleman's Magazine, 37, 55, 380
George, IV.,
——— Pig races to honour his birthday, 140
——— visit to Ireland, described by Moore, 108; and by the anonymous writer of 'Ancient and Modern Times,' 145
——— arrival at Howth, 147
——— departure from Dunleary, 9, 108, 110
——— Judy's lament for, 117
——— Poem on, by Lord Byron, "The Irish Avatar," 111
Geology of Co. Dublin, 385
Geraldine, Dalkey, 86, 91
Geraldines, i.e., Fitzgerald's, 182
Gibbetting of Pirates in Dublin Bay, 380
Gibson, Colonel, slaughters the garrison and other inmates of Carrickmines Castle, 188
Gidley, George, one of the murderers of Captn. Glas, gibbetted at the Muglins, 381
Gilbert's (J. T.) History of Dublin, 17n
——— Viceroys of Ireland, 116n
Gillespie, chief Druid of kingdom of Dalkey, 222
Giraldus Cambrensis,* 339

Glas, Captain, murdered by Pirates, his murderers hanged in Dublin, and their bodies gibbetted in the bay, 376, 380, 381
Glasnevin, 198n, 201
Glenagery, 80
Glen, Bride's, 130, 188
——— Druid, 130, 188, 191
Glendalough, 217
Glengariff, 185
Gloucester, Earl of, 12
Goat's Castle, Dalkey, 36
Goat Whey, 59
Golden Ball, 192
Golden Spears, The, 91n, 185n
Gonne, Henry, 92
Goshawks, 276
——— Mrs., Landscapes by, 92
Gougane Barra, 169
Grace O'Malley.—*See* Grana Uile, 31, 41, 423
Granite, 314, 385
Granuweal, Old Song, 32
Grattan, Henry, xiiin, xv, 112, 393, 419
——— Extracts from his Speeches, 393
——— Political characters, sketched by, 396
——— Mrs. H, 321
Gravell, M. le, Commander of a Brest privateer, acts piratically in Dublin Bay, 19
Graves, Dr. Charles, Bishop of Limerick, ascertains age of Book of Armagh, 337
Gray Edmund D., heroic conduct of, 7, 363
——— Sir John, M.P., 7
——— Robert, of Temple Hill, 140
Greek Medal found at Ferns, 151

* *Giraldus Cambrensis.*—He was born in Pembrokeshire. He was sent into Ireland in 1185, by King Henry II., in quality, as secretary to his son John, who made him an offer of the Bishopricks of *Ferns* and *Leighlin;* but he refused them, and made it his whole study to collect materials for writing his *Topography of Ireland,* and his vaticinal history of the conquest of that nation.—*The Writers of Ireland, by Ware.*

Gresham Terrace, Kingstown, 130, 144
Gresham, Thomas M., 130
Grose, Captain Francis, 97n, 99n,
—— Antiquities of Ireland, 97, 263
—— Burns' Poem on Grose, 97n
Guinness, Sir B. L., 75
Gunning, John, 421
Gunning, The Misses, 421

H.

Hamerton, E., 8n
Handel, 418, 420
Handel's *Messiah*, first performance of, 209n
Hanmer's, Dr., *Chronicle of Ireland*, 41, 95
Hanna Mount, Dalkey, 92
Harbour, Dalkey, *see* Coolamore,
—— Dunleary, *see* Kingstown,
—— Howth, 5, 332,
—— Kingstown, 5, 123
Harcourt, Sir Simon, 188
Harrington, Sir H. defeated by the O'Byrnes of Wicklow, 16n
Harris, Walter, *Hibernica*, 22n
—— *History of Dublin*, 95
Harrison, Edward, vi, 36
Hasculph, Prince of Dublin, 21n, 41, 368n
Hasler family, vi n
Hasler, Sir John, vi, 36, 37, 247
Hayes, Edwin, sketches in Dublin Bay, 38
Hasler, Sir John, 81
Hell-fire Club, 418
Henry V., knighted in Ireland by K. Richard II., 11, 12, 39
Henry, Thos. E., of Dalkey Lodge, 52n
Herbert's account of Moore's early years, 101

Herbert's Recollections of kingdom of Dalkey, 252
Higgins, F., the Sham Squire, 139, 334
—— favoured by the L. Chief Justice Scott, E. of Clonmel, 139
Hilton, John, 66
Hodder, George, 407
Hollinshed's *Chronicles*, 2
Holly and Ivy, 158
Holyhead Mail Packets, 135
Hospitality, Irish, in 18th century, vii, 295
—— characterized by Curran, 312
Hotel, International, (Breslin's) Bray, 316
Hotel, The Queen's, at Dalkey, 65
Hotel, Royal Marine, at Kingstown, 130
House, Castle, Dalkey, 36, 81
Howth, 31, 39, 330, 344, 389, 390
—— *See* Ben Edar, 342
—— Abbey, 332
—— Book of, 332, 334, 336,
—— Castle, 331
—— Garland of, 334, 336
—— Harbour of, 5, 6n
—— Poem by S. Ferguson, "The Cromlech on Howth," 341, 342
Howth-View House, Dalkey, 37
Huguenots improve gardening in Ireland, 298n
Hymns, ancient Irish Book of, 337

I.

Incledon, Charles, x, 257
Inis-Faithlen, now Ireland's Eye, 334
Inis Meic-Nessain, 334

Index. 437

Inniscorrig, residence of Sir
 D. Corrigan at Dalkey, 44*n*, 86, 91*n*
Innishowen, Knight of, 1, 5, 45, 75, 91*n*
Inscriptions, Annular, 181, 195
Ireland, Ancient Music of, collections by Bunting, and by Petrie, 161
Ireland's Eye, 137, 155*n*, 334, 343
Irish Authors, &c., of last two centuries, 345
Irish Eloquence, 393
Irish Hospitality in 18th century, 295
Irish MSS. and their peculiar ornamentation, 334 to 341
The Book of Armagh, 337
——— Dimna, 336
——— Durrow, 337, 340
——— its Cumdach now lost, 340
——— Howth, 334, 336
——— Hymns, 337
——— Kells, 335
——— Leinster, 341
——— St. Moling, 337
——— Ricemarch, 341
Irish besiege English invaders in Dublin, 373
Irish Gentlemen, 398
Irish Peasantry, 401
Irish Taste for Music, 412; and for Theatricals, 413
Irish victorious at Belleek, 17*n* and in Wicklow, 16*n*

J.
James II., 190, 191
Jerome, St., 95
John, King of Dalkey, 254
Juggy's Well, Monkstown, 8, 131

K.
Kavanagh, Mr. P., of Castle-street, Dalkey, 36
———— Pat, *Ali Baba*, 90
Keenan, P. J., 202
Kells, Book of, 335, 340

Kelly, Rev. Matthew, 164
Kendrick's Picture of the Queen's Departure in 1849, 39*n*
Kent Terrace, Dalkey, 37
Kilbarrack, 333
Kildare MSS., Gospels, 339
Kilgobbin Castle, 74
Kill Abbey, seat of R. Espinasse, 201
Kill-of-the-Grange, 200
Kilkenny, Statute of against the Irish, 30
KILLINEY, 57, 150, 155
——— Ancient Church of, 94, 95
——— Obelisk at, 57, 150
——— Stone coffin found at, in 1831, 150
Killiney Bay, 155
Kilmainham, Prior of, 28, 29
Kilronan, 173
Kilrothery, *see* Kilruddery.
Kilruddery, lands of, granted to Brabazons, 77*n*
Kilternan, 79, 192
——— Cromlech at, 192
King, Sir Abr. B., 117*n*
Kingdom of Dalkey and the Muglins, 218 to 268
Kings of Dalkey:
 Stephen, 219, 256
 John, 254
Kings of England:
 Edward III., 62
 Henry IV., 11
 ——— V., 11*n*, 39
 Richard II., 10
KINGSTOWN.—(*see also* Dunleary), 107
——— Carlisle Pier, 121
——— Harbour of, 5, 123
——— Earl of Carlisle's departure from, 121
——— Victoria Pier, 119, 130
Kirwan, Rev. W. B., 324, 382
Kish Bank, 8
Knight of Innishówen, 1, 45, 75, 91*n*

Index.

L.

Lambay, 8, 388
Lambe's house built on site of the ancient inn, the Mark Allen, 37
Lancaster, Henry, Duke of, (afterwards King Henry IV.) 11, 12, 39
Landlords of Wicklow, resident, 318n
Langrishe, Sir Hercules, 116
Laurel, Henrietta, Countess of, poet-laureate of the mock kingdom of Dalkey, 221
St. Laurence O'Toole, 20n, 374
Lawless, Sir Hugh de, 186
Lawless, Stephen, Bishop of Limerick, 167
Lea Castle surrenders to O'More, 129n
Lead ore found at Dalkey, 2, 53
Leary, Patrick, 92
Ledwich, Rev. Edward, 69, 98
Lees, Sir Harcourt, vi n
Leinster, Book of, 341
Leinster, Emily, Duchess Dowager of, 183
Leinster, Duke of, 63
Leixlip, 209
Leslie's "Killarney," a poem, 298
Leslie, Charles, of Corruicna-Greina, Dalkey, 59, 91
LETTERS:
——— Alma, E. L., 143
——— Clibborn, Edwd., 65
——— Gaskin, J. J., 124, 127
——— Meyler, W. T., 67
——— Smith, Geo., 66
Liber Niger MS. 155n
Lifeboat at Kingstown, 124, 126
Liffey, river, 3
Limestone, 389
——— argillaceous, 389
——— carboniferous, 389
——— magnesian, 390
Loftus, Henry, Lord Viscount, 56, 150
Loftus Hill—See Killiney.

Lombard's, Archbishop, De Regno Hibernicæ, 182
Longevity, instances of, 9n, 44n
Longford Terrace, Monkstown, 130
Long Rock at Dalkey, 86, 87, 88
St. Lorcan O'Tuathail—See St. Laurence O'Toole.
Loretto Abbey, Dalkey, 91
Lota, 86
Lover's Leap at the Dargle, 322
Loughlinstown, 79
——— Camp at, 190
Lucas' Coffee-house, 416
Lysaght's, counsellor, song against the Union, 345n

M.

Macartney, William, 59
MacCarthy's, D. F., lines on the Bay of Dublin, 42—on the Vale of Shanganagh, 93, 184—on home to be preferred, 319
MacConnell, 30n
M'Cormick's tile works at Kill-of-the-Grange, 200
Macklin, Mrs., a Dalkey centenarian, 45n
MacManus, Henry, 329
MacMorongh, 12, 13
MacMorough of Leinster, his conference with Earl of Gloucester and Henry of Lancaster (afterwards King Henry V.) 13
Magee, of the Dublin Evening Post, 139
Maguire, Mary, Carolan's monody on, 82
M'Grath, Terence, vicar-choral, Dublin, xiv n
M'Guire, Patrick, 92
M'Kinley, pirate, gibbeted at the Muglins, 55
Maiden Rocks, 6, 7
Mails between Dublin and London in 1793, 136
Malony, Crosdaile, 52

Index.

439

	PAGE.
Malpas, Christopher,	199
Malpas' estate brought by marriage to the Talbots of Malahide,	199
Malpas, John,	57, 80
Map of Dublin, and the surrounding country. At end of volume.	
Marquess' picture, "The Home of the Sea Gull,"	39
Maryborough Castle,	120n
Martello Towers,	277
Masquerades,	420
Massey, Sir George,	ix
Mathews, Thomas,	vii
Maunsel, captain, of Dalkey Lodge,	37
Mayne, Sir William,	36
Maynooth,	26, 64
Meath, Earls of,	77n
Melody, Sir Charles, of the Kingdom of Dalkey,	x, 257
Mercer family, tombstone of, at Tullagh,	195
Merchant's-quay, Dublin,	17
Mergillina, the seat of Sannazarius,	91n
Merrion,	188, 210
———— Fitzwilliam's house at,	15, 188
Mervyn's *Letters on Ireland*,	83, 197
Messiah, sacred oratorio by G. F. Handel,	209n
Meyler, W. T., on Saxon coins found at Dalkey,	67
St. Moling of Ferns,	337
———— Book of,	337
Molloy, J.,	91
Monks of the Screw,	xvn
MONKSTOWN,	130
———— Castle,	71, 74
———— Church,	131
———— Victoria Gardens,	131
Monument of Capt. Boyd,	123
———— of Duke of Dorset,	80, 178
Moore, Mrs. J., poetess and dyer,	222n

	PAGE.
Moore, Thomas,	ix, 47, 98
———— earliest poetry in the *Anthologia Hibernica*,	99
———— Herbert's account of his youth,	101
———— refusal to betray his fellow-students in T.C.D.,	104
———— journal of his life, edited by E. Russell,	108
———— song, "The Prince's Day,"	108
———— verses on the wounded Dalcassians,	15
———— verses to Sir John Stevenson,	xiv
———— *History of Ireland*,	197
———— anecdotes of kingdom of Dalkey,	221n
Moran, chimney sweeper, occupies one of the Dalkey castles,	70
Mornington, Garrett, Earl of,	xv, 209n, 420
Mountains of Dublin,	39
Mount Druid House, Killiney,	192
Moynalty,	332
Muglins,	6, 7, 55
Murtough, prince of Hy-Kinsellagh, encamps at Dalkey in 1171,	20
Music, ancient Irish,	161-173
Music Hall, Fishamble-st.,	420
Myatt, Esq.,	117

N.

Neil, Edward,	91
Nessan, St.,	336, 343
———— ruined Church of, on Ireland's Eye,	336
New Ross, Co. Wexford,	270 to 276
Nicknames, Judge Bladderchops,	143

Nick Names, Sham Squire, 139
Norbury, Lord, nicknamed "Bladderchops," 143
Northington, Earl of, 129
Notices, Historic, of Bray, 213, 320
—— of Dublin Bay, 41
—— of Dalkey, 2, 9, 20, 44, 48
—— of Dublin Castle, 407
—— of Dunleary, 106, 129
—— of Howth, 344
—— of Killiney, 178
—— of the O'Byrnes and the O'Tooles, 213
—— Puck's Castle, 190, 217
—— Shanganagh, 186
—— Trim Castle, 270n

O.

Oaks, evergreen, at Delville, Glasnevin, 205
—— at Rochestown, 200
Obelisk, George IV.'s, at Dunleary,
—— at Killiney, 57, 150, 160, 199
—— at Stillorgan, 57, 150
O'Brien, the Informer, 399
O'Byrnes, Princes of Glenmalure, 213
O'Byrnes of Wicklow defeat the English under Sir H. Harrington, 16n
O'Connell, Dan., 108—presents a laurel crown to George IV., 110
—— his procession to Kingstown, on his way to England, after the Clare election, 145
—— Sepulture of, 277
O'Curry, Eugene, 173
O'Donohoe, John, editor of *Freeman's Journal*, 162
O'Flaherty, Patrick, the prototype of Terry Driscoll, 265

Ogle, Geo., xvn.
O'Hagan's, Lord Chancellor of Ireland, letter to Lord Charlemont on proposed statue of Grattan, xiii, 115, 360
O'Hara, Kane, 82, 253
O'Kelly, Matthias J., 198—his collection of Irish conchology, 199
Old Connaught, 188n
O'Leary, Father A., xv n
O'Mally, Grace (*Grana Uile*) 31
O'Malley, Sir Samuel, 425n
O'Meara, T., ix
O'More defeats the English at Ballybrittas, 129n
O'Neill, Hugh, Earl of Tyrone, 16n
—— Shane, 17
O'Rourke defeats the English under Clifford, 17n
O'Rourke, Mr. Hugh, of Dalkey, 37, 83n
Ossian, 342
Ossorians hostile to Dalcassians returning from the battle of Clontarf, 14n
O'Toole, Anthony, of Raheny, 217
O'Toole, St. Laurence, Archbishop of Dublin, 20, 94, 194
O'Tooles, the, Princes of Imail, 213, 217
O'Tooles, the, in 1537, 190n

P.

Pack, major, 310
Page's, Sir Thomas, plan for Dalkey harbour, 5
Paine, J. W., of Sandycove Avenue, 151
Pale, the English, 29, 30
Parkinson, J. (Mus. Doc.) vicar-choral of Christ Church and St. Patrick's, xv n
Parkinson, Dr., 37, 91
Parkinson, Mr. Henry, 195, 196
Parkmore, Dalkey, 36

Parliamentarian Fleet in Dublin Bay, 33, 41,
Parliament of Pimlico, 266
Pass of the Plumes, 129n
Payne, 83
Patrick's Hall, St., Dublin Castle, 410
Perrot, Sir John, Lord Deputy of Ireland in 1584, 15, 51
—— Lines on, by N. White, 15n
Petrie, George, xii, 66, 73, 94n, 95, 160, 161, 168, 195, 334, 335
—— collects the ancient music of Ireland, 161
—— His researches on the round towers, 164
—— Mrs., 67
PICTURES:
—— Biudon's of Swift, 331
—— Kendrick's departure of Q. Victoria, 39n
—— Marques' Home of the Seagull, 39n
—— Petrie's (Geo.) Ardfinan Castle, and Puck's Castle, 168
—— Puck's Castle, 168
—— Petrie's (James) Portraits, 166
—— Reilly's departure of King George IV., 144
—— Watkins' of Gougane Barra, &c., 169n
Piers, Sir Pigot, builds obelisk at Stillorgan, 150
Pig Races in honour of the Prince of Wales' (George IV.) Birth day, 140
Pilkington, Mrs., 358, 359
Pimlico, Parliament of, 266
Pink Dindies, The, 419
Pims, The, 191
Pinkerton on coins, 151
Pirates gibbeted at the Muglins, 55
Plague in Dublin, 31, 44
Plunket, Justice, 28

Poem on Grana Uile's visit to Q. Elizabeth, 423
Poets laureate of the Kingdom of Dalkey—Mrs. Battier, 221n; Moore, Th., 264; O'Hara, Kane, 253
Poolbeg Light-house, 39, 53
Porter, William, 36
Powerscourt, Lord, his reception of George IV., 108
Prendergast, James, Bailiff of Dalkey, in 1451, 25
Prince Patrick Terrace, Dalkey, 91
Prophecy of Hermes, 60
Proprietors of lands in Dalkey, 35, 36, 37
Puck's Castle, 74, 168, 184, 190, 195n, 217
Puck's Rock, Ireland's Eye, 343
Puckstown, 174n
Punch's offering to O'Connell, 277
Pun-Sibi's, Tom, *Ars Punica*, 307n

Q.

Quartz at Bray Head, 389
—— at Howth, 389
—— at Shankhill, 387, 389
—— at the Sugar Loaves, 389
Queen's Hotel, Dalkey, 65
Queen Victoria's departure from Kingstown, 39n
Quercus virens, at Delville, Glasnevin, 205
—— at Rochestown, 200
Quin, J. of Bray, 130, 316
Quintin, Richd. S., hanged for murder and piracy, gibbeted in Dublin Bay, 391

R.

Railway, Dublin and Kingstown, 132, 134
—— the Terminus at Kingstown, about the site of the Churl Rocks, 144

3 I

Rapparee Fields, on west of St. Stephen's Green, 380
Rathfarnham, 215
Rathmichael, 195, 197
———— Antiquities at, 197
———— Rath, 197
———— Round Tower, 197
———— Skull Hole, 197
Raymond le Gros, 21n
Regan's (Maur.), History of Ireland, 22n, 320n, 366
Regatta, Dalkey.
———— Kingstown, 131
Reilly, John Lushington, 144
Revolutionary atrocities, 223n
Ricemarch's Book MS. 341
Riugsend, 34
Robin Adair, 174
Rochestown, 57
———— Avenue, 198
———— House, 198
Roche, Sir Boyle, vi, 81, 82, 419
Roche, Tiger, 419
Rocking stone at Bullock, 276
Rolls, Chancery, of Ireland, MSS. 215n
Rosbeg Bank, 8
Round Towers, Dr. Petrie's work on, 164
Ross, Co. Wexford — *See* New Ross.
Rutland, Earl of, with ships of war, arrives in Dalkey A.D. 1399, 10
Rutty's,* Dr. John, *Natural History of the Co. Dublin.* 2n, 184n

S.

Sackville, Lord, 180n
Sackville-street, Dublin, 420
Saint Begneta, 21, 23
———— Columba, 337, 338
———— Cronan, 336
———— Laurence O'Toole, 20, 94 194

Saint Moling, 337
———— Nessan, 343
Saint Patrick's Cathedral restored by Sir Benjamin L. Guinness, 75
Salisbury, Earl of, 11, 13
Salthill, 132
Sandycove, 6
Sannazarius, 91n
Satirical verses on Dublin, 417
Scalp, the 193
Schist, argillaceous, 388
———— micaceous, 387
Scotchman's Bay, 6
Scott, Etty, 84
Seals (Phocæ) captured at Howth, 39n
Seven Castles of Dalkey, 2, 36, 49, 50
Seven Churches of Glendalough, 217
Shakspeare's "Young Harry with his beaver on," 11, 12, 39
Sham Squire, 139, 334
SHANGANAGH, 93, 184
Shanganagh Castle, 74, 186
Shanganagh, Vale of, Poem by D. F. MacCarthy, 184
Shankhill, 187
Sheehan, J., editor of *Comet*, 1n
Sheepbells, a novelty in 1768, 58
Sheppard, 36
Sheridan, Thomas, 207n, 421
Shrewsbury, Dukedom of, extinct in 1718, 14
Shrewsbury, Earls of, 14
Siege of Dublin, by King of Ireland, 373
Simnel, Lambert, crowned in Dublin, 25
Sirr, Major, 222n
Skeffington, Sir William, 14
Sletty (*Slacht-ga*), the royal seat in the heathen times before St. Patrick, 192
Smith's, Dr. Chas., *History of Kerry,* 206n

* "John Rutty, M.D., was an ingenious and learned Quaker. He practised physic in Dublin for many years, with great reputation. His *Natural History of the County Dublin*, in two volumes [8vo, Dublin, 1772], is considered a valuable performance."—*Anthologia Hibernica.*

Smith, George, ou Saxon coins found at Dalkey, 66
Smith, James, 92
Smith, John, architect of Poolbeg Lighthouse, 53n
Smith's, Sydney, opinion of Grattan, 362
Smock Alley Theatre, 416, 421
Societies, convivial of 18th century, xv n
——— Beefsteak Club, xv n
——— Kingdom of Dalkey, 218-268
——— Monks of the Screw, xv, n

SONGS:
——— Ancient and Modern times, 145
——— Beautiful Bay, 40
——— Granuweal, 31
——— How justly alarmed is each Dublin Cit, 345n
——— Judy's Lament on George IV.'s departure, 117
——— Kilruddery Hunt, 78
——— Oh! you're welcome to Puckstown, 175
——— Oh! Wirs Sthru, 117
——— Tho' dark are our sorrows, 108
——— 'Tis when the cup is smiling, 47

Sorrento, residence of Surgeon Tuffnell at Dalkey, 44n

SPEECHES:
——————— Extracts from, 393
——————— Curran's, 398
——————— Flood's, 402
——————— Grattan's, 393

Stanley, Sir John, Lord Deputy of Ireland, A.D., 1387, 9
Steam Packets between Kingstown and Holyhead, 135
Stella, Portrait of, by Mrs. Delany, 202
Stephen, King of Dalkey, ix, x, 219, 253

St. Leger, Sir Anthony, 15, 129
Stevenson, Sir John, xiii
——— Moore's lines to, xivn
Stillorgan Obelisk, 150
Stokes, Miss Mary, Drawings from Books of Kells and Durrow, 341
Stokes, Dr. Wm., Life of George Petrie, xiin, 162
Storm of February 9, 1861, 123; noticed in *Freeman's Journal*, 163; and in *Belfast Northern Star*, 164
Strongbow, 21n, 213
Sugar Loaves, the greater and less, mountains, 156, 185n
Sullivan, A. M., his magnificent donation for a statue of Grattan, 112n
Surrey's Verses to the Fair Geraldine, 183
Sussex, Earl of, 30, 41
Sweeny, John, keeper of the Druid's Head, South Gt. George's-street, Dublin, 222n
Swift's Portrait by Bindon, 331
——— return to Ireland in 1726, 35, 42
——— verses to Dr. Delany, 106n
Swinburne's Travels,
Sydney, Sir Henry, L. Deputy, lands at Dalkey in 1565, 15
Sutton, Sir John, 215

T.

Tacitus, notice of Ireland unreached by the Roman arms, 76
Talbot, Sir John, 14
——— Reginald, feudatory of Dalkey, 23, 24
——— Richard, of Malahide, 215
——— Richard, Hon. Cap., 199
Talbots of Malahide acquire Malpas estate by marriage, 199

444   Index.

Tanner, James, surveyor of
  Port of Dublin in 1675,   19
Tempe Terrace, Dalkey,   91
Temple Bar Magazine,   22
Temple Hill, seat of Lord
  Clonmel,   139
Theatre in Smock Alley,   416, 421
Theatre Royal in Dublin,   415
Theatricals in Kilkenny,   417
Thomastown, County Tip-
  perary,   295
Thomastown Castle, the seat
  of Major Gen. the Visct.
  Chabot,   296
Three Rock Mountain,   11
Throne Room, Dublin
  Castle,   409
Tickell, the poet,   202
Tiger, Roche,   419
Tinnahinch,   xiii, n, 405
Todd, Rev. Dr. J. H.,   337
Tolka River,   3
Tomb of Byrnes of Cabin-
  teely,   201
——— Mercer family,   195
——— O'Connell, de-
  signed by Petrie,   277
Tower, round, at Rath-
  michael,   197
Townshend's, Lord Visct.,
  embarkation at Bullock in
  December, 1771,   279
——— political writers
  for and against
  his administra-
  tion,   279n
——— satirical ballads on   286
Townshend, Marquis of,   vi n
Trench, R. C., Abp. of
  Dublin,   75, 208n
Trim Castle,   270n
Trinity College, Dublin,
                         3, 103 109
——— Historical Society,
                          130, 258
——— United Irishmen in,
                          103, 256
——— Visitation by Lord
  Clare,   103

Tudor Hall, Dalkey,   91
Tudor House, Dalkey,   xv, 37
Tuffnell's, Jolliffe, Surgeon,
  seat at Sorrento,   194
Tullagh, near Cabinteely,
                           184, 194
Tyrone, Hugh, Earl of, un-
  successfully attacked by
  an English army under
  Essex,   16, 17n
Tyrrell, Gerard,   92
——— Hugh,   270n

U.

Ulvertou Road,   36
Union :
——— injurious effects of, 116
                               420
——— Lysaght's song agst., 345n
United Irishmen,   222n
Usher, Arland, mayor of
  Dublin in 1557,   31n
Usher, James, Bp. of Meath
  (in the late Established
  Church),   335, 337
Usher, John, Capt.,   30n

V.

Vale of Shanganagh,   184
Valley of the Diamonds, vii, 315
Valori, St.,   323
Vanessa, death of, at Cel-
  bridge,   209
Vavasour property in Dal-
  key,   37
Verses, Swift's, to Sheridan, 308
Vico Road, Dalkey,   92
Victoria Gardens, Monks-
  town,   131
Victoria Pier, Kingstown,
                          119, 130
Victoria, Queen, arrives in
  Dublin Bay, August, 1849,   42
Victoria Square, Kingstown, 130
Viceregal Court in Dublin,   407
VIEWS COLOURED :
——— *Bray Head and
  Esplanade*,   313

Index.   445

	PAGE		PAGE
VIEWS COLOURED—*continued.*		*Ware, Sir James, *Antiquities of Ireland*,	77, 320
—— *Dalkey Island and Sorrento.*	1	Ware, Robert, MSS. of,	31
—— *Killiney Bay, with Hill and Obelisk.*	150	Warner's History of Ireland,	68
—— *Kingstown.*	106	Watkins, B. Colles, 169n,	202n
Visitation of Trinity College, Dublin, by Lord Clare,	103	Watson, John, of Bullock Castle,	37, 55
		Wellington, Arthur Duke of,	209n
W.		Wells—St. Begneta's at Dalkey, 59—St. Bridget's Co. Clare, 168—Juggy's at Monkstown, 8, 131—Our Lady's at Dalkey,	59
Wakeman, John, grantee of St. Mary's Abbey,	32		
Wakeman, W. F., on the Castles of Dalkey and Bullock, 70—his *Archæologia Hibernica*,	96	White's, Nic., lines on Sir J. Perrott,	15n
Walker, J. C.,	323	White, Sam., his school in Grafton Street, Dublin, 102—attended by Thomas Moore, 102—by George Petrie,	165
—— Essay on gardening in Ireland, 203n, 298n, 299n			
—— Essay on the Irish stage.	31	Whitworth, Earl,	77, 123
—— Memoir of Italian Tragedy	323	Wilde, Sir William,	315
—— Memoirs of the Irish Bards,	82	Williamstown, first railway train to,	132
Walpole's Anecdotes of painting in England,	296n	Willis', Dr. Thomas, formerly of Ormond-quay, now of 18, Rathminesroad, recollections of the Druids and United Irishmen,	222n
Walsh, Edmund,	187		
Walshes, the, of old Connaught,	188		
Ward, Hill of, near Athboy,	192	Wilson,	36, 37
		Wilson, John,	52

---

* *Sir James Ware's Antiquities of Ireland.*—Sir James was born in Castlestreet, Dublin, on the 26th of November, 1594. He was educated in Trinity College, which he afterwards ably represented in the Irish Parliament in 1639. His friend and patron was Dr. Usher, afterwards Lord Primate of Ireland. This learned prelate concludes the first edition of one of his immortal works in these words:—

"Interim dum nos, &c. In the meantime, having finished that task, which I looked upon as a Debt due by me to my Country and Fellow Citizens, while I am entering into the consideration of digesting into Method the antient Chronology of the *Hebrews, Greeks, Romans,* and other Nations, the courteous Reader may, from the Labours of *Sir James Ware,* of *Dublin,* knight, our most worthy Auditor-General, expect the *Annals of Ireland,* together with a catalogue of the Writers of our Country, out of which may be drawn a considerable Supplement to those particulars in which I have been defective."

"And it was in that very year, 1639, in which the Archbishop's Book *de Primordiis* came out, that Sir James Ware published his Treatise *de Scriptoribus Hiberniæ.* He was called the "Camden of Ireland."

Wilson's, Peter, account of
  Dalkey in 1768, 48
Wirra sthru, 116
Wolverton's Castle, Dalkey, 36
Worthies, the Six, played
  in Dublin in 1557, 31n
Wren hunting on St. Stephen's day, 156, 157
Wright's *Guide to the Co. Wicklow*, 190

Y.

Yacht club-houses at Kingstown, 131
Yelverton, Lord Avonmore, xv
Young, Arthur, xii, 322

Z.

Zekerman, pirate, executed for murder of Captain Glas, 380 -- gibbeted at the Muglins, 381

THE END.

Printed by J. M. O'Toole & Son, 6 and 7, Gt. Brunswick-st.

GASKIN'S
VARIETIES OF IRISH HISTORY,
ETC., ETC., ETC.,

MADE INTERESTING.

Illustrated with Chromo Lithographs, and a beautiful Coloured Map. Strictly limited to 250 copies, Large Paper.

PUBLISHED UNDER THE PATRONAGE OF THE NOBILITY AND GENTRY OF GREAT BRITAIN & IRELAND.

FIRST LIST OF SUBSCRIBERS TO THE GUINEA EDITION.

His Excellency, EARL SPENCER, K.G., Lord Lieutenant of Ireland, Viceregal Lodge, Phœnix Park.
His Grace The DUKE OF DEVONSHIRE, K.G., F.R.S., Chatsworth.
The Most Noble The MARQUIS OF DONEGAL, K.P., P.C., F.R.S., 22, Grosvenor Square, London.
The Right Hon. THOMAS O'HAGAN, P.C., Lord Chancellor of Ireland, 27, Rutland Square, Dublin.
The Most Noble The MARQUIS OF KILDARE, Kilkea Castle.
The Most Hon. The EARL of DUNRAVEN, Adare Manor.
The Most Hon. The EARL OF ST. GERMANS, 37, Dover-street, London.
The Hon. Vice-Admiral EDWARD GRANVILLE HOWARD, Woolbedding, Midhurst, Sussex.
The Hon. CHARLES WENTWORTH HOWARD, M.P., Naworth Castle.
The Right Hon. RICHARD MONTESQUE BELLEW, P.C.
The Right Hon. CHICHESTER P. S. FORTESCUE, P.C., M.P., Chief Secretary for Ireland.
T. H. BURKE, Esq., Under Secretary for Ireland, Dublin Castle.
General HALL, C.B., Merville, Donnybrook.
The Right Hon. Major-General SIR THOMAS A. LARCOM, K.C.B., P.C.
The Rev. P. S. HENRY, D.D., President Queen's College, Belfast.
Colonel J. W. P. AUDAIN, 13, Fitzroy Avenue, Belfast.
The Right Rev. David Moriarty, D.D., Lord Bishop of Kerry.

Lady Elizabeth Grey, The Rectory, Morpeth.
Lady Taunton, 27, Belgrave Square, London.
Lady Caroline Lascelles, 62, Eaton Square, London.
Mrs. General Wardlaw, Crebilly, Ballymena, Co. Antrim.
Sir John Bernard Burke, LL.D., Ulster King of Arms, Dublin Castle.
Jonathan Pim, Esq. M.P., Greenbank, Monkstown.
Thomas M'Clure, Esq., M.P., Belmont, Belfast.
Sir Edward Coey, D.L., Merville, Belfast.
J. R. Corballis, Esq., Q.C., LL.D., Rosemount, Roebuck, Co. Dublin.
J. Haughton, Esq., J.P., 35, Eccles-street, Dublin.
Wm. Stokes, Esq., M.D., Physician in Ordinary to the Queen in Ireland, 5, Merrion Square, N., Dublin; and Carrickbrack, Howth.

J. M'Donnell, Esq., M.D., Poor Law Commissioner, Poor Law Office, and 4, Gardiner's-row, Dublin.
The Library, Queen's College, Belfast.
P. J. Keenan, Esq., Delville, Glasnevin.
The Library, Office of Education, Marlboro'-street, Dublin.
A. H. Taylor, Esq., Library, M'Birney and Co., Aston's-quay, Dublin.
Dr. J. Tufnell (Surg.), F.R.C.S.I., Mount-st., Dublin.
Dr. J. R. Parkinson, T.C., Tudor House, Dalkey.
J. H. Foley, Esq., R.A., Sculptor, Studio, 10, Osnaburgh-street, London.
Henry MacManus, Esq., R.H.A., Fassaroe Cottage, the Dargle, Co. Wicklow.
J. Richard Marquis, Esq., R.H.A., Studio, 18, Upper Gloucester-street, Dublin.

J. Wren, Esq., B.A., Science Master, &c., Belfast Model School.
James Milo Burke, Esq., J.P., T.C., Queenstown Lodge, Dalkey.
Manliff Barrington, Esq., J.P., Glen-Druid, Cabinteely, Kingstown.
William Smith, Esq. ("Wm. Scribble," author of the celebrated satire "Old Carlisle Bridge"), 10, Herbert-place, Dublin.
Thomas Gresham, Esq., J.P., Raheny Park, Raheny, Co. Dublin.
Frederick Hasler, Esq., M.D., M.R.C.S., Bellair, Killiney (Two copies).
J. Haslor, Esq., Mount Pleasant, Kingstown.
Edward Breslin, Esq., J.P., Royal Marine and International Hotels, Bray.
Sandrehim Bell, Esq., M.D., Medical Hall, 54, Lower Sackville-street, Dublin.
Willett Mortimer Audain, Esq., Solicitor, 1, Arthur-place, Belfast.
John Coulter, Esq., B.A., Solicitor, 1, Arthur-place, Belfast.
J. L. Drury, Esq., J.P., Abbeyview, Dalkey.
Wm. R. O'Byrne, Esq., J.P., Cabinteely House, Co. Dublin. (Two copies.)
Samuel M'Comas, Esq., J.P., Dalkey.
Joshua Magee, Esq., Solicitor, Newry.
John Burke, Esq., Queen's Royal Hotel, Dalkey.
Alderman James Wm. Mackey, Esq., J.P., Clonsilla House, Clonsilla.
James Vokes Mackey, Esq., J.P., T.C., Scripplestown House, Cabra.
Alderman J. Manning, J.P., Harcourt-st., Dublin.
John S. Sloan, Esq., M.R.I.A., Engineer of Irish Lights' Department, Woodlands, Fairview, Dublin. (Two copies.)
Alderman Tarpey, Nassau-street, Dublin.
E. Fox, Esq., J.P., Glen-na-Geragh Hall, Dalkey.
Michael Crooke, Esq., Valuator and Auctioneer, 10, Lower Ormond-quay, Dublin, and Dalkey.
Henry Parkinson, Esq., T.C., Barrister, Tudor House, Dalkey.
Anthony O'Toole, Esq., Raheney.
Frederick Flint, Esq., Auctioneer, 89, Leinster-road, and 9, Ormond-quay, Upper, Dublin.
Captain H. Bellew, Clarinda Park, Kingstown.
Charles Edward Hawker, Esq., Inverary, Sydenham, Co. Down.
John Dolan, Esq., the Firm of Sir John Arnott and Co., Henry-street, Dublin.
J. C. Taylor, Esq., Education Office, Marlborough-street, Dublin.
J. J. Conroy, Esq., 9, Brighton Terrace, Sandycove.
P. J. Graham, Esq., M.A., LL.B., 18, College-green, and Haddington-road, Dublin.
Thomas Perrier Davies, Esq., Montpellier, Dalkey.

E. Love Alma, Esq., Peafield Terrace, Blackrock.
Gregory Kane, Esq., T.C., Shamrock Lodge, Glenageary, Kingstown.
James Joseph Cunningham, Esq., 29, Summer-hill, and Sidmonton-terrace, Bray.
Marcus Moses, Esq., 5, Leeson Park, Wenton-road, Dublin.
J. W. Foley, Esq., River View, Drumcondra, Dublin.
George Glenny, Esq., M.D., 36, Manchester Road, Southport, England.
Wm. M'Dermott, Esq., Sunnyside, Blackrock.
F. O'Rourke Owen, Esq., General Post Office, Dublin.
James Cosgrave, Esq., Dalkey.
John Cunningham, Esq., John Ville, Dalkey.
James Finlayson, Esq., Johnstone, Glasgow.
John Emmerson, Esq., 7, Donegal-square, North, Agent of the Singer Manufacturing Co.
Wm. L. Burgess, Esq., 81, High-street, Belfast.
John Browne, Esq., Waringstown, Lurgan.
Hugh Stewart Wallace, Esq., Linen and Muslin Manufacturer, Franklin-place, Belfast.
Hugh Ferguson, Esq., H.M.V.S.1., Dublin Castle.
Henry Gonne, Esq., Hanna Mount, Dalkey.
Thomas Fortune, Esq., Bray.
J. Wilson, Esq., Alexandra Hotel, Dublin.
N. Bailey, Esq., 3, Duke-street, Dublin.
J. I. Connolly, Esq., Castle-street, Dalkey.
Patrick Byrne, Esq., Castle-street, Dalkey.
John Burke, Esq., 13, Upper Sackville-street, Dublin
John Chancellor, Esq., Sackville-street, Dublin.
John O'Duffy, Esq., Surgeon-Dentist, Westland-row, Dublin.
John Crosthwaite, Esq., T.C., The Hall, Kingstown.
W. Davidson, Esq., Gt. Brunswick-street, Dublin.
John Murphy, Esq., Builder, 79, Gt. George's-street, and Holywood.
T. H. Hevey, Esq., Architect, 12, Linen Hall Street, Belfast.
Thomas Kane, Esq., Crown Entry, Belfast, and Cave Hall, Co. Antrim.
John Scully, Esq., Ulster Club, Belfast.
Edward Kelly, Esq., 54, Antrim-road, Belfast.
Messrs. Hart and Churchill, Pianoforte and Music Warehouse, Castle-place, Belfast.
Thomas F. Brady, Esq., Inspector of Fisheries, Ireland, 6, Percy-place, Dublin.
Francis Robinson, Esq., Mus. Doc., 28, Lr. Fitzwilliam-street, Dublin.
Æneas O'Malley, Esq., Riddell and Co., Donegal Place, Belfast.
D. Purdon, Esq., 64. Donegal-street, Belfast.
Bernard Keely, Esq., 1, Wesley Terrace, Dublin.
P. Madden, Esq., 6, Flinder's-street, Stanley road, Liverpool.
William M'Coyd, Esq., Public Accountant, 5, Donegal-place Buildings, Belfast.

www.ingramcontent.com/pod-product-compliance
Lightning Source LLC
Chambersburg PA
CBHW022058300426
44117CB00007B/505